Forced

Choices

SUNY series in
the Sociology of Work and Organizations

Richard Hall, editor

Forced
Choices

Class, Community, and Worker Ownership

Charles S. Varano

STATE UNIVERSITY OF NEW YORK PRESS

Production by Ruth Fisher
Marketing by Anne M. Valentine

Published by
State University of New York Press, Albany

For information, address the State University of New York Press,
State University Plaza, Albany, NY 12246

Library of Congress Cataloging-in-Publication Data
Varano, Charles S., 1957–
    Forced choices : class, community, and worker ownership / Charles
S. Varano.
        p.   cm. — (SUNY series in the sociology of work)
    Includes bibliographical references and index.
    ISBN 0–7914–4181–4 (hc. : alk. paper). — ISBN 0–7914–4182–2 (pbk.
: alk. paper)
    1. Weirton Steel Corporation. 2. Employee ownership—West
Virginia—Weirton. 3. Steel industry and trade—West Virginia—
Weirton. 4. Weirton (W. Va.) I. Title. II. Series.
HD5658.I52W48 1999
338.7´669142´0975412—dc21   98-31713
                                                              CIP

10 9 8 7 6 5 4 3 2 1

For my parents and grandparents.
In memory of Dolores Tice, Virginia Bettino,
and Lisa Grossi.

Contents

Illustrations   ix
Acknowledgments   xi

PART I. INTRODUCTION

Introduction   3
    Weirton: The Place and Its People
    An Ethnography of Class, Community,
      and Worker Ownership

1. Worker Ownership and Class in America   15
    Worker Ownership
    Employee Participation
    Paternalism and Class
    Class and Class Consciousness
    Outline of Chapters

PART II. HISTORICAL ANTECEDENTS

2. Forced Choices I: Company Town   39
    The Antecedents of Paternalism: 1909–1933
    The Challenge: 1933–1951
    Quiescence: 1951–1982

3. Forced Choices II: "Buy It or Lose It"   79
    One Side of Paternalism's Legacy
    Divided Loyalties
    "Business is Business, Morals is Morals"

The Limits of Dissent
The Final Deal

PART III. WORKERS BY DAY

4. Forced Choices III: Employee Participation   143
    Participation by Decree
    The Structure of Employee Participation
    Ideology and Employee Participation
    Summary

5. A Fragile Trust: The Normative Order of
    Employee Participation   179
    Facilitators as Industrial Therapists
    Workers and Employee Participation
    Internal Communications: Public Relations at Work

PART IV. OWNERS BY NIGHT

6. Class and Worker Ownership   227
    Worker Ownership and the "Equity Solution"
    Owners by Night . . .
    . . . Workers at Heart

7. The Moral Economy of Worker Ownership   243
    The Value of Labor
    Property Rights
    Community, Nepotism, and Local Control
    Summary

8. The Struggle for Control   293
    A Changing of the Guard
    Confrontation
    Two Years Later: The Struggle Continues

9. Conclusion   321
    The Lessons of Worker Ownership and Participation
    at Weirton Steel
    Class, Community, and Worker Ownership

Notes   337
Bibliography   377
Index   387

Illustrations

Map 1.1.   Weirton and Surrounding Areas   6
Figure 4.1. EPG Projects by Type of Activity   156
Figure 7.1. Labor Force Levels 1910–1980   250

Acknowledgments

Many people helped me begin and complete this research, but none were as important as my parents, Marshall and Christine Varano. Their encouragement and financial help was exceeded only by their enduring love and faith. I am also deeply grateful to Jean Davenport and Constance Bettino for introducing me to my second family in Weirton. Tom and Lisa Grossi, their children Tommy and Katie, and the late Virgina Bettino welcomed me into their lives and their home. I am deeply saddened, however, that Lisa passed away just as this book was in its final stages of publication. Both she and her mother Virginia became dear friends and confidants to me during and after my research. Without my two families, this book would not have been possible.

I would also like to express my deepest thanks to Sam Kusic and the late Mary Kmetz. Mr. Kusic introduced me to many people in town and he also kept me informed of local developments after I left the field. His interest in my work and ongoing support are greatly appreciated. Mary rented me the most comfortable apartment connected to her basement, but I will always remember the strength of her character and the comfort of her friendship.

A special thanks is extended to the members of the Tri-State Conference on Manufacturing in Pittsburgh, Pennsylvania, and the Ohio Valley Industrial Retention and Renewal Project in Wheeling, West Virginia. They welcomed me to their meetings, considered me a fellow member, and taught me about the politics and passion of grassroots organizing. I am also grateful to Fathers Jim O'Brian and Brian O'Donnell of the Wheeling coalition, and Jim Benn of Sustainable America. Their dedication to a more humane and just economy still inspires me.

A number of people helped inform, critique, and encourage this research at one point or another. I am especially grateful to the editors at the State University of New York Press and the reviewers who critically commented on the original manuscript. I would also like to thank Kozy Amemiya, Ellis Boury, Ken Cornwell, Cynthia Deitch, Robert Erickson, Chester and Rose Grossi, Monica Grossi, Joseph Gusfield, Dan Hallin, Robert Horwitz, Yakov Keremetsky, John Lichtenstein, John Machover, Irwin Marcus, Avi Munroe, John "Bud" Rajcic, Alberto Restrepo, Linda Robinson, Ruben Rumbaut, Raymond "Rusty" Russell, and Judy Ruszkowski. The staff at the Weirton public library were very helpful directing me to regional census data and old local newspapers. I would like to thank Associated Interstate Mortgage Company, Inc. for the use of their copy machine. My friends and the Royals softball team were also a bedrock of support throughout my research and writing.

Bennett Berger, the chairman of my dissertation committee, patiently stood by me as I matured through this project, and his thoughtful critiques led me to reformulate and clarify my arguments. He also taught me that to study culture one must "loosen up" but keep both feet firmly on the ground. Richard Madsen helped me think about my work in a larger theoretical context without ever ignoring the human context of sociology. And Michael Schudson was a steady voice of insight and support who brought clarity (and a title) to my work at times when all I could see was confusion. I would like to extend a special thanks to Christena Turner, who graciously joined my committee at the last minute, carefully read my work, and offered invaluable suggestions for publication revisions. I also want to thank Harley Shaiken for the many interesting and insightful discussions we had on labor, the labor process, and labor unions.

Three people were especially important to my finishing this research. Jacqueline Wiseman believed in me during a difficult period of my graduate studies, and she always reassured my growing sociological imagination. Mary Frefield was one of the finest teachers I have ever had. Her passionate and unyielding interest in labor and class first inspired me to begin this project. And this book would not be what it is without Dana Farnham. A dear friend and model scholar, Dana spent countless hours carefully editing each chapter, for which I will always be grateful.

Finally, I want to express my deepest love and appreciation to Sande Varano, who suffered my torturous rough drafts alongside her own arduous illness and recovery. Sande helped me find my voice in this project, yet I trust that her intellect, heart, and personal strength have also found a place in these pages.

P^{*art I*}

Introduction

Introduction

"If this mill goes, so does the town." In 1982, such was the view of most people in Weirton, West Virginia, as National Steel (now National Intergroup) announced it would stop investing in its local plant. For millworkers, their families and friends, and residents in this small town of 25,000, a plant shutdown was the furthest thing from anyone's mind. "Weirton Steel has always been here and always will." Then, suddenly, it might not be.

A way a life was under siege and, like other communities across America facing a plant shutdown, people here had few options and they saw even fewer. National's divestment would eventually whittle a fully integrated steel mill employing almost 12,000 workers into a finishing mill with some 3,000–4,000 workers at best. Workers and their families in Weirton were in trouble, but so too were those living nearby in Ohio and Pennsylvania. The upper Ohio Valley area, perhaps the most prosperous of the Appalachian region, was facing a crisis.

How did millworkers and area residents get to this point and, subsequently, how did dire economic conditions and worker ownership both reinforce and challenge their most basic assumptions about their mill and community? The statement "if this mill goes, so does the town" brings together two spheres of human life that

3

we often wish to keep separate: our lives at work and our lives at home. For the people of Weirton, life in the mill was never so easily separated from living in the town. Work and home, mill and community had been institutionally and culturally inseparable for over seventy years in this paternalistic company town.

"Generations of people living here have gone into the mill" was the refrain heard over and over again. "Is it over now?" The same day of National's announcement one choice overshadowed all others—the employees could buy the mill and make steel as a worker-owned company. Employee Stock Ownership Plans (ESOPs) had gained renewed popularity throughout American political and business circles, and in 1982 Weirton Steel was poised to become the largest worker-owned industrial firm in the country. For the next eighteen months National Steel negotiated with local mill and union officials and their ESOP consultants over the terms of sale and the structure of the new company. Finally, on January 22, 1984, workers voted to approve the buy-out. Weirton and the Ohio Valley had gained a reprieve—at least for the moment.

When National Steel offered to sell the mill, workers acted not only in their economic self-interest, but also from an institutional context rooted in a history of paternalism; a locally situated normative order that emphasized a strong bond between the mill and family and community life. Paternalism filtered the basic class relations of life in the mill and town, blunting the sharp edges of class antagonisms but never fully replacing them. As they pondered their situation—and what lay ahead—people here reluctantly conceded that the mill would never provide for the town like it once had. The roles of mill and community had suddenly reversed, and so too had the normative order of obligations and expectations. Mill elites had once taken care of the community. Now the community had to care for the mill.

This cultural legacy, where economic issues are framed alongside notions and sentiments about family and community, still mediates fundamental class divisions in Weirton. This has contributed to solidarity and motivation among workers and townspeople over the years, but it has also fostered a potent, though contradictory, challenge to worker ownership that is evident in public controversies and labor-management conflict in the mill. By the third and fourth years of worker ownership (1986–87), company policies and unforeseen events raised these local customs and values to the surface of public awareness and scrutiny. The controversy, dissension, and solidarity of these years center on a changing relationship between mill and community where control, once securely held by paternal elites, was now "up for grabs."

As the 1990s arrived the town and the worker-owned steel company that bears its name were surviving. But the controversies and struggles I observed in 1986–87 continued to wax and wane, punctuated by a company public stock offering that was blocked in 1994 under union pressure and employee shareholders' concern that they would lose local control of the mill they bought ten years earlier. In one sense it is remarkable that Weirton Steel has survived given uncertain market conditions and competition from mini-mills and foreign steel. And in the context of labor-management-executive conflicts that have festered from 1990 to the summer of 1996 when I last visited, it is especially noteworthy that the company is still profitable, continues to modernize its facilities, and just recently began re-issuing profit-sharing checks—thirteen years after it became worker-owned. Still, the questions of what worker ownership means, and where control lies, have remained unanswered since I first drove into town in 1985.

Weirton: The Place and Its People

I first arrived in Weirton via the single-lane State Highway 2 that winds north along the Ohio River from Wheeling, West Virginia, up through Weirton to the Ohio border at East Liverpool, Ohio (Map 1.1). Nestled along the river valley, the town stretches east up the low hills of West Virginia's northern panhandle and comprises the entire three-mile portion of state territory tucked between Ohio and Pennsylvania. Unlike the mill towns of the Monongahela Valley south of Pittsburgh where U.S. Steel and plant closings left blackened mills, vacant streets, and boarded-up buildings, Weirton appeared alive and relatively clean. "Years ago," I was told, "you'd wade through the carbon on the streets and couldn't even see the sun at noon. We used to call it 'Weirton Red' and you were always washing your car and house down." Resembling the tone of people in growing cities who talk of how clean the air "used to be," people here and in other declining

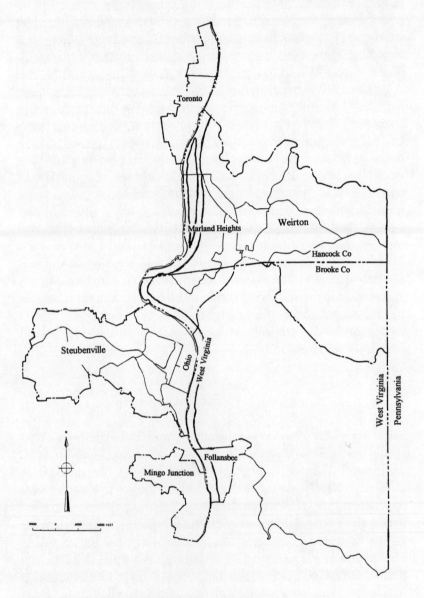

Map 1.1.   Weirton and Surrounding Areas

Source: U.S. Department of Commerce, Bureau of the Census

industrial towns throughout this region speak nostalgically of the dense choking haze of steel's halcyon past.

Today, people say, things are a lot cleaner, yet Main Street is still busy with cars and belching, rumbling, long-bed semi-trailer trucks hauling away large steel coils. During a shift change in the mill downtown traffic is often congested, especially if one must wait for one of the slow-moving mill freight trains that routinely block two of the main routes in and out of town. During the 1940s the company built a bridge that elevated downtown traffic over the mill, effectively connecting the northern and southern ends of Hancock and Brooke Counties, respectively. This not only helped ease growing traffic problems, but it also precipitated a move south of the town's business district. Main Street was literally rebuilt from its original location at the far northern end of town, which today is practically vacant.

Weirton's population first began declining during the 1960s. After climbing to a high of 28,201 in 1960, local population steadily dropped to 25,371 by 1980.[1] This trend marked the first population decline in the town's history as area youth slowly began moving away for college and jobs, a trend that has only been hastened by mill downsizing following the 1984 buy-out and stubbornly hard economic times in this part of America's industrial belt. By 1990 local population had dipped even further to 22,124.

Ironically, by 1970 barely half of Weirton's residents had completed high school, but as the 1980s approached the mill offered fewer highly paid entry levels jobs and more young people began attending college and technical schools. Still, most people in town either worked in the mill, had once worked there, or had a family member working there—on the shop floor, in administration, or in management. A much smaller, but quite visible, business and professional class may have garnered some prestige from their "higher" education, but high steelworker incomes often matched or exceeded those with more formal schooling. Weirton is still a fairly prosperous town relative to the state of West Virginia and the Ohio Valley region in general, virtually an economic oasis within the historically impoverished hills and valleys of Appalachia. At the time of my research the mill was the largest employer and taxpayer in West Virginia, and its steelworkers the most highly paid in the country, if not the world.

Weirton is also quite ethnically heterogeneous for such a small and isolated town. Heavily southern European, just over one fourth of the resident population is comprised of either first or second generation immigrants. While those of English, Irish, and German heritage make up the largest northern European ethnic groups, they are closely followed by descendants of Italian, Polish, Hungarian, Russian, Greek, Czechoslovakian, Croatian, and Serbian ancestry.[2] Other notable ethnic groups include more recent immigrants from India and Southeast Asia (most of whom work in the local hospital or own small businesses). Ethnicity is still a standard reference and a readily used mark of distinction (and behavior according to everyone I spoke with) in town. As one longtime mill employee explained, mill jobs are also distributed along ethnic lines: "Arabs and Middle Eastern groups had the tough jobs, and the Italians, Greeks, and Poles had it better. The blacks got the worst jobs and still do."

Like neighboring Steubenville, racism is a persistent and troubling aspect of community life in Weirton. Yet race relations in Weirton are relatively peaceful by contrast as antagonisms have been historically muted through paternalism. As one resident put it coarsely, "We don't have any problems with our niggers here like they do over in Steubenville or in Pittsburgh." Blacks make up about 5 percent of the population (compared to just under 13 percent in Steubenville) and most live alongside the eastern flank of the mill in the original, yet abandoned and decaying, downtown section. As a neighbor explained,

I'm not a bigot, and I try not to be. But it's here. Just look around, do you see any blacks on this street, the next one over, the one next to that? No, you don't. I don't know how it happened but blacks live in their own areas. It's not right, but people on this street would go nuts if a black family moved in. I know a lot of people on this street breathed a sigh of relief when we moved in because they were afraid a black family would move in. Why do you think that house across the street isn't sold? It wasn't put up for public sale because a black family would probably move in. He wants to control who gets in there. Now that's not right. Now don't get me wrong. I have good neighbors, real good neighbors. But they're worried that a black family would move in and let the place get run down. Now, I don't want that, either, from any neighbor, but I'm sure a black family would keep up the house just like everyone on this street. They probably feel they're moving up and would want to look it.

"Moving up" in Weirton had always meant literally moving up the hills away from the mill to either Marland Heights overlooking the Ohio River or Weirton Heights to the east. And this often resulted in ethnic as well as racial segregation. "Hunkytown," an area just up the eastern slope from the mill and Weirton's black residents, refers as much to the ethnic makeup of its southern European residents as their lack of formal education and low-skilled positions in the mill.

Recently, townspeople are trying to hold on to what they have and most have been "staying put."[3] According to the owner of a local tool and lumber business, lumber sales have declined especially since the economic downturn of the 1980s, as people have been improving the home they have by "expanding rooms or converting their basements." During the 1970s there had been some new home development along the eastern edge of town that borders Pennsylvania, but few of the original units sold so construction was halted. During my research these homes dotted a barren landscape, connected only by empty streets winding through a neighborhood of empty lots.

In the meantime, townspeople were awaiting the completion of a new (and architecturally modern) bridge to replace the one currently linking Weirton with Steubenville, Ohio. Standing half complete at the time of my field research in 1986–87, construction of this bridge had been prolonged due to labor conflicts and funding problems arising from the states of West Virginia and Ohio joint collaboration in the project. Besides easing the traffic congestion that plagues the old and narrow "Freedom Way" bridge (that, along with downtown Weirton, must be traversed when traveling through town to either Pittsburgh or Ohio), many people hoped that improved transportation through the area would attract business and support local economic development.

This bridge was finally completed when I returned in 1992, but now people wondered if it was diverting potential customers from downtown and its small and struggling business sector. Not only were local people being drawn to malls and discount stores in

Steubenville and western Pennsylvania, but local shops and restaurants were slowly losing ground to large corporate chains and fast-food outlets. "That crap they call food is about as bland as the people that own those chains," said a close friend in town. "I don't want my kids eating there." And he went on,

> We have some of the best ethnic food around here, and people go and eat there. Besides, the money they spend there don't stay here. It goes to these big companies that could care less about Weirton. We need to support our local businesses. At least I try to.

Weirton was losing hold of more than its local economy and young people. It was also losing hold of its customs and a sense of provincial autonomy that people I met from outside of town found disturbingly impenetrable. Often while in Pittsburgh and Wheeling I described my research to questioning people who would inevitably ask how I managed to "get in there." Business people grumbled of how hard it was to market there, labor unionists bemoaned their failure to organize there, and those who knew someone from Weirton still spoke of its people as "closed and tight" and harboring a peculiar arrogance that "put off" rather than invited outsiders.

My experience was quite different, but I too was aware of the local exclusiveness that outsiders found so daunting. Certainly my fortuitous connections in town helped me to meet people. As my key informant explained after I met some of his friends at a local bar, "They don't know you yet, but they'll warm up. You're my friend, so they can trust you." Likewise, my family roots in a coal mining town in central Pennsylvania seemed reassuring to people when I told them I was from southern California. But I also think that my being a graduate student doing his dissertation research for an entire year without any institutional funding helped me establish rapport with townspeople. Unlike "those journalists" who sweep in quickly, grab a few quotes, and then leave to write critical articles "without knowing us," people might have felt less threatened and more comfortable helping an aspiring student. Though I could not explain how my research might benefit them (nor did I try), everyone I met went out of their way to assist me.

Contrary to the outsider perception of local "arrogance," millworkers and residents wondered why I came to Weirton of all places—"there's nothing here." When I explained my interest in worker ownership and its relationship to community life, people would sigh and nod. "Hopefully," I was told, "you'll get it right." If I do, it is because of their goodwill. For what those outside Weirton found arrogant and standoffish about townspeople was less a matter of smug superiority and shunning outsiders than a desire to protect themselves and their ambivalent sense of community from forces they had little control over.

An Ethnography of Class, Community, and Worker Ownership

My research grew from a passionate interest in labor and community resistance to industrial plant closings, and the tristate area of Ohio, West Virginia, and Pennsylvania had for some time witnessed widespread organizing among union locals, and community and religious activists. In the late 1970s, about 100 miles north of Weirton in Youngstown, Ohio, such an alliance had failed to stop the closing of Youngstown Sheet and Tube. Then during the early 1980s, layoffs and plant closings wreaked havoc among steelworkers and other industrial workers in the Ohio Valley, particularly throughout the Monongahela Valley just south of Pittsburgh. From this emerged grassroots coalitions of religious, labor, academic, and community activists who opposed what they saw as "reckless and socially irresponsible" corporate behavior.[4]

For these groups the closing of industrial plants meant more than the elimination of well-paying jobs; it was destroying communities and human lives. From their view, corporations were breaching more than contractual obligations or legal codes. They were ignoring and making a sham of the normative order upon which a "social contract" with labor rested, at least since the 1940s. Corporate behavior, they argued, not only threatened the *interests* of America and its communities, it was also *immoral*. I was interested in the details and historical roots of these moral claims, and what social and cultural support for them existed in the areas being organized.

In the fall of 1986, I began a year of field research in Weirton and the surrounding tristate area as my dissertation project. As a student of the workplace and social class, I was drawn to this area by the prospect of workplace democracy where community involvement played a decisive role in forming and supporting such firms. In the larger context of deindustrialization, plant closings, and a growing gap between rich and poor during the 1970s and 1980s, I was also interested in the nature and form of working-class consciousness and how this might support or hinder such a democratic transformation of industry.

Field researchers often "find" rather than plan their way into the field and, once there, spontaneously follow wherever their contacts and chance take them. In my case, I knew nobody in Weirton or the Ohio Valley region including Pittsburgh, though I did have relatives living in eastern Pennsylvania. Good fortune came by way of one of my students (who was from Wheeling, West Virginia), and a friend of a friend (who was originally from Weirton and still had family living there). Through my friend I was able to find affordable housing (and a dear landlady) just up the street from her family, and they included me as a member of their extended family and friends. Through my student I met a former city official who introduced me to his circle of friends and to this day continues sending me newspaper clippings on local developments.

Through these initial contacts, I met and talked with hundreds of people, most of whom lived in Weirton, but also many who were from the surrounding towns in West Virginia, eastern Ohio, and western Pennsylvania. During the ten months I lived in Weirton, and again the following summers of 1988, 1992, and 1996, I interviewed residents, millworkers, managers, executives, local politicians, civic administrators, city workers, local merchants, and religious leaders. Over time I became very close to people working in- and outside the mill, their families, children, and friends. Whether visiting or sharing meals, mowing lawns, or helping shovel snow, I was able to talk with many people, of all ages informally and at length during my stay. Throughout this book I have altered the names of people I interviewed personally or in groups to ensure their anonymity, but I have used the correct names of people who were quoted from public sources such as newspapers, journal articles, and historical documents.

The following ethnography is based upon these many and varied discussions as well as my participant-observations of mill and community life. But I have also drawn upon other materials that complement and enhance the field researcher's analysis, such as demographic data, local documents and records, historical materials, and secondary sources pertaining to the Weirton case. Throughout my research I was interested in how the Weirton case fit into the larger context of regional deindustrialization and labor/community activism in nearby Pittsburgh and Wheeling. While I do not undertake that question here, I did consult other case studies on plant closings and community-labor responses that shed light on the Weirton case.

Scholars of work and organizations have noted that more participant-observation case studies are necessary to flesh out the dynamics of the relationship between labor relations reform and worker ownership, and this study is an effort to fill that gap. In addition, I seek to complement research on work and organizations with an ethnography of the complex relationship between class and community in America. Because my approach straddles and blends a diverse literature, which I discuss in the following chapter, I risk frustrating some readers who might wish a more focused (and comparative) effort on either work and organizations or class and community. Likewise, there may be those who would insist on more (or less) history, ethnography, or theory in what follows. My hope is that the balance I do achieve brings more clarity and understanding to the relationship between industry and community and the Weirton case of worker ownership than a more specialized approach might render.

Finally, this case study speaks to fundamental currents in American culture and political thought, especially the struggle of American liberalism to navigate effectively and justly a global economy. As public debate rages over the "breakdown of morality and values" (most often directed at the family, politicians, media, and the poor), capitalism and its "free-market" morality have not only been spared but celebrated.[5] Given the impact of global economic changes in reversing historical trends of social mobility and equality in America, I wanted to look at people's moral reasoning about economic issues at a micro, *local* level. Weirton and its steel mill stand as an important empirical case of worker ownership, but the people here also tell us a great deal about the intersection of class and community and their struggle to make moral sense of the forced choices of economic transformation in late-twentieth-century America.

_C_hapter _O_ ne

Worker Ownership and Class in America

Immediately following the 1992 Democratic National Convention, then presidential and vice-presidential candidates Bill Clinton and Al Gore traveled to Weirton, stopping there first on a nationwide bus caravan campaign. Worker ownership and employee participation at Weirton Steel, they claimed, were examples of "what was right in America," of what worked, the future of American industry. As Clinton and Gore spoke they were framed by a familiar sign in town: mill employees (one black, one white, a woman, and an executive) pulling a rope connected to a Weirton Steel logo with the words "working together works." Ironically, it was a sign that captured the beleaguered spirit of liberalism that Clinton and Gore carried across America, and it belied the conflict over worker ownership that was soon to erupt in the company.

A few days later I spoke with some friends in town. "So you all made the national news again. What did you think?" Well, they did not think much of it actually. "No big deal," most said. "Just a bunch of Secret Service," and for a while "the streets were jammed." But a few were offended by the jeans and work shirts worn by the candidates, a tired populist portrayal of a hardworking president praising a hardworking town for something that worked. "What are we, a town of working stiffs," grumbled one resident. "They could have at least worn a suit and tie—shown some respect." People still fondly recalled when John Kennedy, and later Robert Kennedy, visited Weirton—they both wore a suit and tie. The offense had touched a nerve deep within the class structure of local life, a nerve that worker ownership had also strained.

Liberalism was indeed being tested in Weirton. Whether at a shareholders' meeting in the community center gym or on the shop floor of the tin mill, at an employee participation training session in the executive dining room, or on the expansive lawns of the general offices for an annual food festival, the subordinate role of "worker" still contradicted their celebrated status of "owner." By itself, this is neither surprising nor unexpected in most cases of worker ownership in America that have been imposed by capital and its consultants on both labor and management. Indeed, what is most interesting about worker ownership here is that despite structural and cultural barriers to a democratic Employee Stock Ownership Plan (ESOP), as well as determined efforts during and after ESOP negotiations to avoid one, *workers gradually became more activist in demanding a more democratically structured company*. Contrary to what many observers speculated when Weirton Steel first drew national attention in 1982–84, over the past ten years it has been the site of protracted struggles over *control* in the company. How did this come to pass? What were the sources of this unexpected challenge and what factors have shaped its evolution and form?

Worker Ownership

The significance of the Weirton saga is best understood in the context of debates over worker ownership and participation, and class in America. For most of American history worker ownership has encompassed everything from counterculture cooperatives, to corporate-initiated profit-sharing plans, to radical calls for economic democracy. Since the mid-nineteenth century political elites have tried to claim worker ownership as a "solution" to problems of productivity and the growing antagonism and conflict between capital and labor. In wresting the issue away from labor, political elites (occasionally joined by business and academia) upheld a version of worker ownership that focused on *equity* rather than *control*.[1] Simply put, this version of worker ownership sees workers as consumers and bases its appeal on financial incentives (primarily, stock ownership or some form of profit sharing) to bring labor and management together under one roof to improve productivity, quality, and overall company performance.

Most recently, this "consumerist version" of worker ownership has been elaborated by Louis Kelso and Mortimer Adler in *The Capitalist Manifesto* (1958) and carried into Congress by Senator Russell Long who initiated legislation in 1974 enticing business leaders to form Employee Stock Ownership Plans (ESOPs).[2] Legislation has focused primarily on tax incentives, credits, and deductions for firms setting up such plans. In the last decade ESOP legislation has slowly expanded into regulatory policy over banks, retirement funds, and labor law reform.[3]

The most rapid growth of ESOPs came between 1983 and 1986 following tax credit legislation that benefited high salaried employees but excluded rank-and-file (often unionized) workers.[4] With the repeal of this tax credit in 1986, ESOPs have become less a federal grant to corporations and more a legal mechanism for corporations to set up trusts and then either use their own funds to create a stock bonus plan with immediate tax deduction benefits (nonleveraged ESOP) or borrow funds from commercial lenders with the advantage of deducting both the principal and interest (leveraged ESOP) from corporate taxes. The tax credit ESOP accounted for most of the ESOP participants (some 90 percent), leaving just 310 leveraged or nonleveraged ESOPs in the publicly traded corporate sector by 1986, the period of my field study.[5]

But the growth of ESOPs has slowed in recent years. From 1983 to 1988 the number of employees in ESOPs grew 66 percent to 9 million, but by 1995 that number climbed only 11 percent with some 9,500 ESOPs covering approximately 10 million employees.[6] According to Corey Rosen of the National Center for Employee Ownership, roughly half of the 9,500 ESOPs today in America are,

used to provide a market for the shares of a departing owner of a profitable, closely held company. Most of the remainder are used either as a supplemental employee benefit plan or as a means to borrow money in a tax-favored manner.[7]

Likewise, Raymond Russell notes that ESOPs should be distinguished from employee stock purchase plans that have existed much longer and involve far more people and firms. In stock purchase plans employees buy shares of company stock and take immediate title to them, whereas ESOPs are structured as retirement plans where stock is held in a trust and shares are not issued until employees either retire or leave the firm. Russell cites a 1986 U.S. GAO study that found about 5% of ESOPs actually paid dividends directly to individual employees, even though legally entitled to since 1976.[8] And Rosen notes that by 1996 less than 5% of ESOPs were used to defend a hostile takeover or save a failing company, only 3% of all ESOP participants gave up pension plans for their ESOPs, and only 4% of the ESOP companies required wage concessions.[9] While close to 85% of all ESOPs are privately held companies, Rosen finds that public company ESOPs are becoming more popular. Some of the most well-known ESOP companies where a majority of company stock is owned by employees include Melville Corporation, Avis car rental, and most recently, United Airlines, while some lesser known majority-owned ESOP companies include Publix Supermarkets and Science Applications International, Inc.[10]

Once again, worker ownership is being summoned by political and business leaders to solve a myriad of contemporary problems, from deindustrialization and declining productivity, to the decline of organized labor and growing inequality in America. With the resurgent popularity of ESOPs proponents also expanded their claims, arguing that worker ownership not only improved productivity and company performance but it also reduced labor-management conflict, created an "identity of interests" between employees and their company, and led to improved worker satisfaction in the workplace.

Support from American intellectuals for this dominant consumerist version of worker ownership has been mixed. Tacit support has come from research on American workers that has (a) stressed their interests as consumers[11] and (b) shown that employee-owners do not want control over those issues not directly related to their job or immediate work area.[12] Still other scholars have argued that workers *do* want more control in the workplace, but they are either blocked by management, undermined by organizational and cultural factors, or deterred by the state or their institutionalized unions.[13] I share this latter view and argue that the "consumerist" version of worker ownership ignores workers as producers and minimizes or excludes any inclinations they have toward control. Indirectly, it seeks to manage such inclinations by structuring another financial stake for workers beyond their wages in exchange for obedience and discipline.

The United Airlines case noted above, like the Weirton Steel case discussed in this book, raises the issue of control once again. Both are rare examples of ESOPs insofar as they are troubled industries where deep concessions were accepted in exchange for worker representation on the company's board of directors, both seating three employee representatives on a twelve-member board.[14] In 1994 United Airlines became an ESOP company when its pilots and mechanics agreed to wage concessions in exchange for a 55 percent interest in the airline. However, they only represent 8,172 and 26,633 employees respectively, whereas 17,376 flight attendants though the Association of Flight Attendants chose not to participate in the deal. Should they choose to join the ESOP, flight attendants would also be given a seat on the board. Some 27,942 non-union employees, including managers and reservation agents, had no choice about whether to participate in the deal because United's executive management unilaterally decided they would.[15]

Despite the publicity given such cases, companies with worker directors make up a tiny minority of all ESOPs in America. Research on employee representation on the board of directors and decision-making in employee owned companies has tended to show that workers do not desire influence beyond their immediate jobs and working environment. As Rosen notes, "while control and participation are very important to some workers in some companies, they are not so important to others. Instead, it is the financial part of employee ownership that matters most."[16] Likewise, Raymond Russell found that by 1988 "in only 4% of all firms with ESOPs had union representation or other representatives of non-managerial employees been elected to serve on company boards."[17] And Robert N. Stern finds that worker/union directors "change very little about decision making unless they are chosen by the workers they represent and enter a board environment in which they are accepted as legitimate participants."[18] Both of these conditions are rare indeed.

Reviewing the research on workers' control in worker-owned companies, Joseph Blasi once put forth the notion that workers "tend to have a dual culture conflict."

> On the one hand, they believe they should not have influence over top policy and managerial decisions and desire to leave a lot to management. On the other hand, when they perceive a substantial gap between their desire for some changes and transformations in the company and the fact that there has been almost no change, they express considerable frustration and often increase their attachment to the union as a mechanism to dominate the resolution of such issues.[19]

The observation that worker consciousness is conflicted over issues of workplace control is not new, and researchers from John Commons to David Halle have documented the complex and often contradictory identities and outlooks of America's working class.[20] This should not be considered unusual insofar as they (and other classes) live complex and contradictory lives which are understood and expressed as such culturally. But is this evidence of a "dual culture conflict" or are their attitudes about worker ownership in general, and control in particular, evidence of a more complex and dynamic working-class culture, the roots of which extend beyond the factory gates and into the communities where people live? In my view, workers' ambivalent attitudes about control in the workplace have as much to do with their experiences as a *class*, as with worker ownership per se; ambivalence that is magnified by their subordinate position in the working class and their ambiguous status as "worker-owners."

While the United Airlines case will be interesting to watch, the Weirton case suggests that how workers interpret worker ownership and what they claim as their legitimate sphere of control is shaped by more than economic rationality or their position in the workplace. Looking at how workers reason over issues of control I show how their "desires," and the "gap" between these and their perception of change, are shaped in the community as well as at work. What is now considered a "dual culture conflict" might once have been more complementary *and less* conflicted under conditions where work and home, industry and community were more integrated. Before exploring this further I wish to consider employee participation reforms, which are far more common than board representation in worker-owned firms in America.

Employee Participation

Employee participation reforms are hardly a recent innovation in American labor-management relations. Such "cooperation" programs date back at least to the Employee Representation Plans that were common during the 1920s. Since that time, industrial sociologists, psychologists, and engineers have diligently researched the workplace and helped design programs to raise productivity, improve labor-management relations, and impose labor discipline.[21]

In the past twenty years labor relations reform has included various forms of employee participation and "quality circle" programs initiated solely by business and outside consulting agencies.[22] Yet results have been mixed at best, and scholars of work and industrial relations are divided in their evaluations of this most recent wave of reform. The current debate over the "new industrial relations" has been dominated by two opposing perspectives. At issue is whether these programs have deskilled workers and eroded what control they have over work or whether they have enhanced workers' skills and their influence in industrial production.

On the one hand, theorists of the "post-Fordist/flexible specialization" school argue that recent changes in labor relations herald a significant movement away from previous strategies deployed by capital to control and organize the labor process and workers.[23] From their perspective, the reorganization of industrial production and labor relations results from changing market conditions that increasingly require new technologies and organizational structures to meet a growing demand for specialized goods and services. Mass production technology and organizational forms that dominated industry along the lines of Taylorist principles no longer effectively meet these demands and have been (or must soon be) abandoned. Employee participation represents a potentially empowering opportunity for workers to improve their knowledge and skills and contribute to the firm's success.

Challenging this view are those who argue that employee participation reforms are little more than managerial attempts to extend their control over the labor process and placate American labor under conditions of increasing foreign competition and a growing global division of labor and capital. For theorists of the "labor process/deskilling" perspective recent innovations in technology and industrial organization not only undermine the skills workers have but, in the case of participation programs, have induced workers into collaborating in their own exploitation. It is no surprise, they point out, that such reforms have historically coincided with attacks on organized labor and currently follow upon a thirty-year decline in union membership and strength.[24]

Just how effective has employee participation been in reducing labor-management conflict, promoting cooperation, and improving productivity and company performance? Given the variety of employee participation programs and the difficulty showing direct causality between such reforms and these results, research is still inconclusive. Several studies have shown a positive correlation between many forms of participation, and productivity and company performance.[25] Yet Raymond Russell cautions that recent studies have cast doubt on "many of these comfortable conclusions about the effects of participation on satisfaction and performance."[26] Likewise, he notes that employee ownership (through some form of profit-sharing or "gainsharing" formula) by itself is also unlikely to significantly improve employee performance or satisfaction.

On the other hand, Corey Rosen argues that *combining* employee participation and ownership does lead to significant improvements in productivity and company performance.

> Researchers now agree that "the case is closed" on employee ownership and corporate performance. Findings this consistent are very unusual. We can say with certainty that when ownership and participative management are combined, substantial gains result. Ownership alone and participation alone, however, have, at best, spotty or short-lived results.[27]

Other research supports Rosen's optimism,[28] yet the case may still be open. Russell suggests that although "the social scientific evidence regarding the effects of various kinds of participation may still be weak or inconclusive, the quality of this evidence may in actuality be less important than the question of what corporate managers perceive the impact of participation to be."[29] Several studies have shown that American managers believe participation improves employee and company performance. But an interesting finding is that management remains ambivalent about participation reforms and frequently terminates successful experiments rather than expand them throughout the firm.[30] Why? According to Russell, a number of factors are at play, including;

> resistance by supervisors whose authority is threatened . . . ; a lack of support for or commitment to the experiments from middle or top levels of management; a perceived lack of compatibility between a democratic experiment and the managerial practices and organizational traditions dominant in other parts of the firm; and a tendency for employees involved in successful experiments to begin insisting that their increased effort or productivity ought to be rewarded with some sort of increased pay.[31]

So even though employee participation has often shown its "bottom line" value, especially when combined with employee ownership, it has yet to be completely embraced by corporate America. This suggests that the "productivity" dimension of worker participation and ownership is important *only if, and to the extent that, it is combined with the dimension of control.* In this context, the current participatory impulse is more of an ideological construct useful in struggles for control over the labor process than simply an issue of efficiency or productivity.

Likewise, studies on the impact of participation on worker attitudes and satisfaction, and labor-management cooperation remains inconclusive at best. Reviewing data from opinion surveys, statistical analysis, and case studies, Barry and Irving Bluestone find that although survey data (on management/executives, rank-and-file employees, and union leaders) generally indicate widespread approval of employee participation, statistical and case study research shows little impact on satisfaction and labor-management cooperation one way or the other.[32] They do note research showing that such reforms *do* have a positive impact in these areas to the degree that unions are involved in their design

and implementation.[33] This, however, is quite rare as most participation programs have been designed and initiated by management.

In his review of ESOPs during the period of my fieldwork in
Weirton (1986–87), Joseph Blasi cautioned against assuming any
inevitable improvement in labor-management relations under
worker ownership.

> [The] fundamental conclusion from recent experience demon-
> strates that labor-management cooperation does not emerge
> automatically when publicly traded companies move into
> employee ownership. [And] it is clear to see that the cor-
> porate uses of employee ownership tend to ignore industrial
> relations.[34]

While Rosen and Russell would urge employee owned companies
not to ignore industrial relations, it remains an open question just
how employee participation and ownership will be combined and
with what consequences. As Blasi notes, even when workers buy
a public company "there is no evidence that employee ownership
leads to efforts toward greater labor-management cooperation,"
but he went on to say,

> companies such as Weirton Steel [a privately held company
> during my research] that have bucked this trend have be-
> gun to redesign the system of industrial relations in their
> companies.[35]

Weirton Steel has indeed spent a great deal of time, money, and
effort in implementing wide-ranging employee participation reforms, but my research suggests that instead of "bucking" the
system they have reinforced it. After three years of worker
ownership, the rhetoric and deployment of employee participation
reforms were significant precisely because questions of control in
the mill were far from settled following the ESOP negotiations.
Workers were unsure of their new role as worker-owners and they
held vague expectations about "our" mill, but they also held
doubts about company leadership and where it was taking them.
Whatever these expectations, the main impact of employee participation was to further *bureaucratize* the workplace, reinforcing
the role of "worker" and the distinctions—and divisions—between
labor and management. Even though millworkers accepted an or-

ganizational hierarchy, they still desired more say in who management was and what they did.

More, workers' conceptions of control were both supported and contradicted outside the mill, where community and familial relations shaped their ideas about workplace relations and authority. Since 1987, workers have become frustrated with, and critical of, employee participation. I argue this is due as much to the demise of a paternalistic order that once governed labor relations as it is to the failure of employee participation to provide an adequate alternative normative order under worker ownership. To further explore worker ownership in this larger context, we first need to consider the historical intersection of paternalism and class in Weirton.

Paternalism and Class

In 1909 E. T. Weir stood high atop a hill overlooking the Ohio River, gazed confidently at a farming valley of "indifferent crops of wheat and apples" and declared Hollidays Cove the site of his new steel mill. The "story" of Weirton's beginnings is told in town histories and depicted in a film produced by the Weirton Steel Company.[36] How accurate it is matters little compared to its cultural significance. The incident has become almost mythical and serves as a symbolic signpost, a cultural marker of Weirton's past as a company town. The image of Weir standing in a long black coat and hat, the camera panning the lush valley and rumbling, smoking steel mill below, resembles as much a benevolent patriarch contemplating his traditional duties and obligations as it does an eager entrepreneur surveying his prospective financial fortunes. This image of strong-willed, determined independence with its normative overtones is part of Weirton's cultural heritage as a company town; a paternalistic order integrating a steel mill, its workforce, and a community, although one not without its contradictions and ambiguities.

The concept of paternalism has often been used to describe relations of domination and subordination under rural or early industrial conditions,[37] or in the case of slavery in the American antebellum South.[38] With the notable (and debated) exception of Japanese industry, paternalism has been viewed as a form of traditional authority that would inevitably be transformed by encroaching market forces and bureaucratic modes of organization.[39]

But despite its common usage, paternalism remains a loosely defined concept that raises important questions about authority relations and the dynamics of class struggle.

Nicholas Abercrombie and Stephen Hill argue that paternalism "is primarily an economic institution concerned with the
manner of organizing a productive unit and regulating relationships between subordinates and the owners of the means of
production or their agents."[40] Paternalism is constituted by differential access to power and resources and an unequal exchange of
goods and services. It is typically a diffuse social relationship covering all aspects of a subordinate's life—the whole person. The
ideological dimension of paternalism, which Abercrombie and Hill
argue is overemphasized and often misapplied, legitimates elite
control and privilege on the basis of personal care and benevolence toward subordinates dependent on elites for their well-
being. Finally, paternalism is also a collective form of social
organization where, despite the rhetoric of individual obligation,

> subordinates' obligations and duties, and the reciprocal pa-
> ternalistic benefits, become common to the whole group
> rather than varying from person to person, and the custom-
> ary regulation of relationships develops for all. . . . This ex-
> plains how paternalism can flourish without face-to-face
> interaction between an owner and employees: it becomes
> part of the organizational rule system and the normative
> structure of management.[41]

In contrast to the contract exchange of rational free-market
individualism, paternalism is an attempt to mitigate the worst
aspects of industrial capitalism—class conflict—by blending traditional family and community norms within industrial organization. As Howard Newby writes, nineteenth century industrialists
felt that,

> the sedative effects of paternalism were of a kind that would
> bring about stability and order and an identification of the
> workers with their "betters" [and] therefore enabled power
> relations to become moral ones, so that not only would work-
> ers believe that their employers *did* rule over them, but they
> felt they *ought* to do so [original emphasis].[42]

This moral dimension, however, ultimately masked the primary interests of industrialists which rested on regulating a labor force at higher levels of productivity. And as Richard Sennett notes, unlike the factory experiments of Robert Owen in Scotland, paternalism in nineteenth-century America placed far less emphasis on the *moral* betterment of workers than on removing "the sting" of industrialism through elite oversight and community welfare. Employers of the company towns built throughout the American east and Midwest, writes Sennett,

> claimed that they were acting for their employees in the employees' own best interest; but, in contrast to the older Benthamite or Owenite schools, they claimed that mutual economic advantage to the employer and employee resulted, as well as a moral environment. Like the Walthamite industrialists, they worried about community services for their employees, but unlike the Walthamites, they argued openly that these services were morally valuable because happy workers were more productive and less strike-prone than unhappy ones.[43]

Likewise, Michael Burawoy and Newby argue that factors associated with labor force needs and production technologies spurred the development of "factory regimes" or paternal institutional and normative structures.[44] In any case, most observers view the ideological and moral claims of paternalism as secondary to its exploitative institutional arrangements.

This raises a fundamental question that scholars have grappled with and is central to the Weirton case: What of the contradictions between the benevolent and coercive sides of paternalism and the forms of opposition and challenge they engender? As Newby notes, paternalism may combine simultaneously "autocracy and obligation, cruelty and kindness, oppression and benevolence, exploitation and protection."[45] Much of the confusion over paternalism, argues Mary Jackman, lies in the difficulty researchers have reconciling its friendly and coercive dimensions: "warm feelings seem incongruous with a discriminatory intent."[46] Jackman resists the assumption that paternalistic ideology is any more insincere or intrinsically flawed than other forms of social control, claiming that paternalism is a negotiated order, albeit reached under unequal conditions, that is fundamentally exploitative but *is not* therefore any less affective. Or, as Reinhard Bendix has written, "a personalized exploitation can be every bit as cruel as an impersonal one."[47] Indeed, "it is precisely this ambiguity and subtle deception," notes Jackman, "that makes paternalism such an insidious form of social control. . . . [T]he coercive potency of paternalism draws vitally on the 'inconsistent' attitude structure that lies at its core."[48]

But then so too does the potential for opposition. On the whole, most scholars generally acknowledge that paternalistic authority leaves elites vulnerable to challenges by subordinates based on its own normative and moral codes. As Newby puts it,

> [Paternalism] thus tends to disguise, however imperfectly, fundamental conflicts of interest and to mediate, however unjustly, between one class and another. In doing so, however, it grants to subordinate individuals certain prerogatives which, while technically in the gift of those in power, tend over time to be appropriated as "rights." Custom therefore sanctions claims upon those exercising a paternalist mode of control which frequently leads to paternalism being redefined from below in a way which may form the basis for the overthrow of paternalism itself.[49]

Further, Newby points out, the economic interests or conditions of employers "that demand that workers be treated as impersonal commodities subject to the vagaries of the labour market" may collide with the ideology of paternal obligation that demands "they be personally protected and cared for as far as possible."[50]

Jackman argues that because analysts assume that exploitation necessarily involves conflict and open hostility between dominant and subordinate groups, periods of calm and stability are taken as evidence of "false consciousness" or complete acceptance. Again, she questions this assumption and suggests that exploitative intergroup relationships under paternalism should not be defined purely in terms of conflict and open hostility but also involve periods of genuine goodwill, peace, and stability. Paternalism elicits loyalty and submission (though incomplete), but it is also subject to challenge and opposition (partial as it may be). To assume subordinates' total submission during periods of calm, hence caught in an ideological spell, makes it difficult to explain the nature and form of opposition when it arises, except in terms of "hidden resistance," or what Eugene Genovese refers to as "simultaneous accommodation and resistance."[51] The question then becomes *what* is to be considered accommodation and resistance?

Although my study is primarily ethnographic, I needed to look more closely at Weirton's history to better understand a moral economy that derives from paternalism and is still evident today in the practices and outlooks of residents and mill employees alike. The concept of moral economy was first developed in the work of social historians, particularly E. P. Thompson in his studies of capitalism and an emergent working class in eighteenth-century England.[52] Briefly stated, Thompson analyzed resistance among the English poor to market transformations that undermined traditions and customs of an earlier period of economic production and exchange. Grievances among the poor, Thompson notes, "operated within a popular consensus as to what were legitimate and what were illegitimate practices in marketing, milling, baking, etc."[53] These popular sentiments of "right and wrong" regarding the production, distribution, and exchange of economic goods were,

> grounded upon a consistent traditional view of social norms and obligations, of the proper economic functions of several parties within the community, which taken together, can be said to constitute the moral economy of the poor. An outrage to these moral assumptions, quite as much as actual deprivation, was the usual occasion for direct action.[54]

Thompson argues that the moral economy of the English poor was not an articulate political ideology, but neither was it *un*political for it "supposed definite, and passionately held, notions of the common weal," many of which found support in the paternalistic traditions of authorities.[55] Indeed, the poor validated their grievances and direct action by a "selective reconstruction" of a receding paternalistic code governing economic behavior.

Thompson's analysis has been criticized primarily on the grounds that it is (*a*) too cultural and (*b*) too political. On the one hand, critics argue that Thompson places cultural traditions, customs, and moral norms ahead of economic and political structures in shaping working-class struggle and opposition.[56] Similarly, many scholars have argued that the idea of "moral economy" mistakenly emphasizes notions of cultural identity and collective action over rationally calculated self-interest in explaining people's economic behavior.[57] On the other hand, Thompson attributes political significance to the vaguely articulated, partially conceived, but strongly felt moral codes that inform and direct working-class protest, while many scholars question just how "political" and effective such opposition is and can be. Richard Sennett, for example, has argued that resistance to paternalism is circumscribed by the very symbolic framework it deploys.

> The negation of authority does not transcend the ethos of capitalism: "possession" is the ruling term. The vision of a better social order, or a truly responsive and nurturing authority, of *better* authority, is not germinated by this resistance. . . . The potency of paternalism is more, however, than a matter of deflecting protest. One consequence of this highly charged conflict is that the worker can reject anyone who reaches out to him in the name of helping him. . . . Learning to disbelieve, *per se*, is what the worker took away from the original experience [original emphasis].[58]

While I see Weirton's moral economy as a product of the historical evolution of paternalism, I am also arguing that such normative and moral codes still persist today and shape how people perceive and act toward worker ownership. But what were the lessons of this history for workers and residents of Weirton? Was periodic resistance insignificant in shaping paternalism and later struggles, or did it nurture a "vision of a better social order"?

Class and Class Consciousness

The debates over paternalism and opposition speak to the same problem facing theorists of class. Research on class and class consciousness has tended to portray the American working class as rather docile; one that may be a *class in itself*, organized under exploitative capitalist relations of production, but not *for itself*, that is neither conscious of a class identity nor politically mobilized as such. The working class in America has been considered apolitical, disorganized, and rarely militant as a class, though ethnic, racial, and sexual divisions often become aggravated, thus complicating and compromising fundamentally shared class interests. But as Rick Fantasia has noted, exceptional periods of labor unrest in America have thus been seen by many scholars as the model for "true class consciousness," for these outbursts of political opposition conform more closely to the assumptions of theorists who see the working class as, in the Marxist sense, "a historical force" for radical social change.

This view derives in part from survey research methods that define and measure class in discrete statistical terms, what Eric Olin Wright calls a "gradational" view of class,[59] and in part from theoretical assumptions concerning the "historic role" of the working class. In gradational terms, class is viewed as a group of people who have differential access to some set of resources in a vertical system of stratification defined by quantitative measurements. Here, class becomes a set quantity, either of people or resources, rather than a qualitative process of relationships between people. Survey research has tended to identify those who fit these set quantities and define class consciousness, then, in terms of the views and attitudes they expressed at a given point and time.

But this provides a rather fixed, or static view of people's outlooks, a picture of class consciousness that may, as Fantasia notes,

> capture some important attitudinal trends, but crucial dynamics of collective interaction are lost, and thus what is being measured may not represent the *collective* class consciousness that studies purport to show [original emphasis].[60]

Surveys that find a passive American working class or "satisfied" workers have often failed to explain or predict sudden explosions of opposition as well as the high degree of worker militancy throughout American history to the present. More, survey techniques separate cultural expression from lived experience and behavioral routines of people; forms of association that also exhibit cultural forms often at variance from those documented in surveys. For example, Fantasia notes the 1959 Lubell Poll of American steelworkers that showed overwhelming opposition to a possible strike only to be followed by workers enthusiastically supporting a 116-day strike—the longest in the history of the industry. Or John Goldthorpe's surveys of English automobile workers in the *Affluent Worker and the Class Structure* (1969), which showed them firmly integrated into the class system and holding no serious grievances, only to erupt into "wild rioting" at their factory before the book had been published.[61]

Instead, Fantasia adopts a more "relational" view of class that focuses on the relationships between groups and the exploitative context of those relations.[62] In this sense, class and class consciousness are more dynamic, unfolding, and always subject to the conflictual conditions and situations given by market forces, economic organization, and family and community life. For Fantasia, the expression of class consciousness is fundamentally rooted in collective action and as such may become manifest in various forms of acceptance *and* opposition, neither of which alone accounts for the "true" nature of class struggle but together constitute a lived experience combining both objective social relations and their subjective ideational forms.

Here, Fantasia's approach to class analysis helps clarify the confusion in debates over opposition to paternalism and the form such resistance might take. Rather than either assuming, or imposing, a specific political orientation for working-class struggle, Fantasia suggests looking at class consciousness through "class action as it is expressed in specific industrial conflicts and framed by institutional trade unionism and the industrial relations system in which it operates."[63] He adopts the concept "cultures of solidarity" to refer to the "cultural expression that arises within the wider culture, yet is emergent in its embodiment of oppositional practices and meanings."[64] Following the lead of E. P. Thompson and Raymond Williams, Fantasia views class and the political dimension of class struggle as both an objective condition of exploitation and subjective cultural outlook that are constantly evolving through what Marx termed "praxis,"

[a] purposive activity that changes the world and is changed by it at the same moment. From this perspective, human labor in capitalist society takes place within an exploitative context that generates opposition. The activities of workers against capital contain in themselves transformative potential, for in the course of struggling to liberate their "social being," they are simultaneously liberating their "subjectivity."[65]

Ethnographic analysis provides the best method for studying these emergent forms of class association and opposition because "a victory" or "politically correct" outlook in these struggles is less important than understanding how cultural forms are acted out in collective action under exploitative conditions and against employer strategies that seek to repress or contain them. My research seeks to analyze how such choices are structured and acted out.

Adopting this approach, in my view, helps to explain the complex intersection of paternalism and class, and the evolution of worker ownership in Weirton. Like other company towns, Weirton was dominated by the mill and its powerful elites. But the social order these elites envisioned was challenged by workers, not only in 1919, but again from 1934 to 1951. Paternalism in Weirton was never successfully opposed, nor was it completely embraced. Instead, the lives of people living there are better understood in the context of a complex history that included elements of elite dominance and local resistance, worker quiescence and opposition. And if Weir and fellow elites exercised considerable power, paternalism repeatedly intersected with national and international developments—two world wars, economic booms and busts, New Deal policies and politics, national union organizing—and was a product of these forces as much as of elite design or desire. What developed was a series of "forced choices," leading to what two scholars of a company town in England noted as "exaggerated deference" alongside "dull resentment."[66] Weirtonians "got what they could get" but they always knew whom they were getting it from—the mill and town elites.

Outline of Chapters

In chapter 2 I examine the social and cultural order of Weirton until National's announcement in 1982 to divest its Weirton Steel division. Paternalism organized mill and community life from controlling employment, labor force size, compensation levels, promotions and thus social mobility, to regulating personal lives, enforcing civic obligation, and even influencing marital choice. Paternalism sought profit and labor discipline but it also entailed the obligations of a benevolent, though autocratic, version of community. At the same time, federal opposition and significant agitation

within the mill workforce for an independent union shaped paternalism and the moral codes that are still evoked today.

In chapter 3 I look closely at the ESOP negotiations that
evolved over a two-year period from 1982 to 1984. Ironically, both
critics and supporters agreed that in the Weirton case strong community sentiments and close-knit local and family relationships
would help secure the eventual mill buy out and later become an
integral component of a successful ESOP. But this view fails to account for the town's conflicted history, the divisions that characterize Weirton today, or the animosity and ambivalence many
people expressed toward the town and the mill. While sensitive to
how "community" designated geographical boundaries as well as
social relationships, I was also interested in "community" as an
ideological construct that carries normative and moral prescrip-
tions for those who consider themselves members.[67]

From the start the idea of worker ownership became the only
option for workers and residents alike. It was vigorously pursued
by local management and union officials, but a small group of
workers challenged the secretive and nondemocratic negotiations.
Eventually other groups emerged in protest, though an alliance
among dissenters never formed. At this point, a consistent history
of losing the battles of confrontation became manifest in traditions
of compliance, of avoiding conflict, and of pessimism regarding
how much, if anything, labor militancy in the name of economic
democracy could do. With dissent fragmented, calls for more
worker involvement and a democratic ESOP were steadily discredited in a symbolic struggle over "community" that threatened
the buy-out and the very community people were trying to save.

Part III focuses on labor relations reform at Weirton Steel. In
chapter 4 I discuss the structure and operation of employee participation where its primary impact is the *bureaucratization* of labor. Employee participation (EPG) reinforces the role of worker
and the distinction between workers and management through
its "problem-solving" orientation. This bureaucratization is further supported through the employee participation training program and the ideology of "participative management."

How workers, management, and employee participation staff
evaluate these reforms is the subject of chapter 5. Employees generally find the *idea* of participation appealing while remaining
skeptical of how well it works. Management is skeptical of em-

ployee participation and resistant. And EPG staff adopt a therapeutic perspective that illustrates both the popularity and lingering obstacles facing employee participation reforms. The ideology of employee participation serves as an important symbolic weapon in the struggle over control in the mill, but it does not provide an adequate normative order that reconciles class divisions and antagonisms. My discussion of Weirton Steel's internal communications system illustrates this problem.

This leads, in part IV, to an analysis of worker ownership at two levels: how it is structured, and what it means to people. In chapter 6 I consider the argument that extending ownership status to workers through profit-sharing and stock ownership plans motivates them to work harder and more efficiently while integrating them into the company they own and into corporate capitalism in general. This has not been the case in Weirton where workers were already integrated into the company but do not feel like capitalists, nor do they sense much control over the company as 'owners." Instead, they respond to, and challenge, company officials and policies *as a class;* as workers who have ties to their community as well as their jobs.

For townspeople who either work outside the mill or own their own businesses it is a more complex story. This leads to a detailed analysis of mill and community life and how the moral economy of Weirton mediates people's views about worker ownership. In chapter 7 I identify the main elements of this normative order by exploring the feelings and attitudes people have about the town and mill. A number of events seemed to crystallize people's frustrations and hopes and served to highlight the moral ambivalence of people who think of themselves as a "community," but whose lives are structured in class ways.

Mine is not a cultural explanation of events and controversies as solely the result of locally specific values and outlooks. On the contrary, I have considered the influence of paternalistic customs and moral sensibilities in the context of company policy and changing social conditions. My position is that local debate over Weirton's ESOP and the social antagonisms I observed were informed by such customs and sensibilities, though not exclusively determined by them. Normative and moral claims designate what people should "pay attention" to, where the source of responsibility rests (on the individual, a group, or a larger collective), and on what side of the debate participants stand. When workers opposed how the company was organized and run, and when residents denounced workers for their irresponsibility and complaining, they frequently did so from a symbolic context of community and family, but always from within a class structure that compromised and contradicted these norms. Norms of economic obligation and responsibility were being redefined as worker ownership appeared to be less humane, less concerned with the plight of workers and their families, and less involved and accountable to the "common weal."

Chapter 8 shows how worker frustration grew into collective action against company executives and their policies, culminating in a blocked stock offering in 1994 that workers felt threatened local control. I examine how traditions of local control, loyalty, and accountability reinforced class-based opposition to company executives and policies that undermined this heritage. I conclude in chapter 9 by exploring the future of worker ownership in Weirton and how this case illustrates and refutes aspects of the larger debates over worker ownership and participation, and class in America.

$P^{art\ II}$

Historical Antecedents

C*hapter* T*wo*

Forced Choices I: Company Town

There is never peace in West Virginia because there is never justice.

—Mother Jones

On September 21, 1919, the charismatic and militant labor organizer Mother Jones rallied a crowd at the Rex Theater in Steubenville, Ohio. A few days earlier she aroused the passions of steelworkers in Mingo Junction, ten miles up the Ohio River.

Did not the 13 colonies in the Revolution form a union to accomplish their ends? Men who say you can't form a union are not Americans. They had better go to George the Third or Go to Hell. We stand today with the iron heel of dollars on our back also. Every insidious institution is against us, but we will organize to break the chains.[1]

Into her 90s, Mother Jones agitated vigorously and eloquently for what became known as the "Big Steel Strike of 1919." America's

giant steel trusts were being challenged as returning war veterans
joined iron and steel workers to press for higher wages, better
working conditions, and union representation. Steel mills throughout the country were being organized and the Ohio Valley bristled
feverishly as the strike and autumn unfolded. The words Mother
Jones spoke undoubtedly carried farther than her voice. Workers
from the giant mills etched throughout Pittsburgh were within
earshot and chances are her message found its way a few miles
east of Steubenville, across the Ohio River into the northern West
Virginia panhandle.

There, company officials of a steel mill only ten years old prepared for a proposed march on what was then not much more
than a camp. "If [the] Weirton mill is not shut down tight by Monday afternoon," warned strike organizer Frank Wilson, "between
6,000 and 8,000 steel strikers will march on Weirton. I cannot
stop them and neither can anyone else. They are determined to go
and there will be trouble when they do."[2] They never went.

The fever of the Big Steel Strike of 1919 is exemplified by
Mother Jones and strike organizer Frank Wilson. That it reached
Weirton is evidenced by the proposed strike there involving 6,000
to 8,000 workers. What is significant here is *not* that Weirton
workers were moved by the appeal and momentum of the strikes
in nearby areas, but that even so moved, they did *not* strike.

I see three periods in Weirton's history that overlap but are
distinct in terms of the structure of paternalistic control and the
dynamics of class struggle under changing economic and political conditions. The first period begins in 1909 when Weir starts
building his steel mill and lasts until 1933. These years mark
the earliest stages of paternalism and perhaps the most unim-
peded control by Weir in creating his vision. At the same time,
class relations that would threaten this vision were gradually
taking form.

The second period, beginning in 1934 and lasting until 1951,
marked a more serious challenge when Weirton became a battle-
ground over union organizing under the National Industrial Recovery Act of Franklin D. Roosevelt's New Deal. During this
period Weir negotiated—and fought—to preserve his vision of paternalistic order on three fronts: through the courts, in the mill,
and in the community of Weirton. He challenged the paternalism
of an emerging welfare state with his own brand of local welfare,

supported a series of company unions, and resisted all outside intervention into the affairs of his town.

Eventually, Weir lost the legal battle. But in the face of court defeats, he was able to secure the town's allegiance by setting in motion the institutional foundations of a prosperous community life, albeit one extremely dependent on the mill he controlled. This second period is best characterized by the contested nature of paternalism where challenges to Weir by workers, national unions, and the federal government met with an intimidating yet benevolent face of paternalism. It was during these years that the moral economy of paternalism became institutionalized in mill and community life.

The final period—from the early 1950s until National Steel's announcement to divest the Weirton mill in 1982—I consider years of reinforcement and stability. The town grew, prospered, and eventually reorganized in 1947 when Weir Cove and Hollidays Cove incorporated into the present city of Weirton. In 1951 a company union finally prevailed over the CIO–United Steelworkers in an election supervised by the National Labor Relations Board. The Independent Steelworkers Union presided over what became the highest paid workforce in the steel industry by negotiating contracts that slightly bettered those between the United Steelworkers of America and other steel companies. During these postwar years Weirton workers never went on strike, a decision that provoked outsiders to label Weirton "scab town." Prosperity helped workers and their families endure such notoriety (still common among people living outside Weirton today) but National Steel's hardline policies during the 1970s foreshadowed paternalism's demise and set the stage for worker ownership and another struggle for control that continues as of this writing.

The Antecedents of Paternalism: 1909–1933

Ernest T. Weir Builds His Mill

Making the mill was the easy part. E.T. Weir was born in Pittsburgh, August 1, 1875, the son of newly married immigrants from northern Ireland.[3] After grade school, Weir took a job as an office boy with the Braddock Wire Company, then left for Pittsburgh's

South Side and the Oliver Wire Company, where he worked for a number of years. It was here that he first cut his teeth in the business world as a traveling salesman of barbed wire.

After becoming chief clerk with Oliver Tin Plate Company, Weir joined the American Sheet and Tin Plate Company. In 1903 he was promoted to general manager of its Monongahela plant where he befriended James R. Phillips, who managed the sheet and tin plate sales for U.S. Steel.[4] Their friendship and aspirations grew, leading them to the financially troubled Jackson Sheet and Tin Plate Company at Clarksburg, West Virginia. With loans of $15,000 and $10,000 respectively (and additional funding from a group of ten Pittsburgh men) Phillips and Weir bought shares and formed a new company that would have Weir as senior manager with Phillips securing a customer base. Two months later in May 1905 Phillips died in a train crash and Weir assumed presidency of the company. With John C. Williams, a Welshman who was general superintendent of tin plate operations, Weir began building the steel complex that would soon bear his name.

Weir's immediate goal was to build a fully integrated plant, one that was independent of other steel firms and industries that might disrupt its operations, either through high prices for supplies, lack of supplies, or what was for Weir the major evil, labor unrest. In 1908 the search began for a location with an abundant water supply in the mainstream of steel production and distribution. Weir found it in a valley on the Ohio River near Hollidays Cove, a farming village he described as "producing indifferent crops of wheat and apples." This idyllic site offered many advantages over the Clarksburg location, the key one being its relative isolation among small towns and its seclusion from a growing and militant labor movement. It was an opportunity where steel mill and community could be forged unhindered.

In 1909 construction began and by year's end a ten-mill plant was operating. The Hollidays Cove plant grew to twenty mills by 1910 and soon an additional six mills replaced what had once been apple groves. After acquiring the twelve-mill Pope Sheet and Tin Plate Company across the river in neighboring Steubenville, Ohio, Weir owned plants in three locations. By 1915 he operated fifty hot mills with an annual tin plate production surpassed only by U.S. Steel. By his forty-third birthday E. T. Weir had created a steel empire and on August 1, 1918, the company was reorganized as the Weirton Steel Company. In less than ten years, Weir, his brother David, and J. C. Williams had transformed a farming valley into a bastion of industrial might. Weirton Steel was competitive in a most prosperous industry during the heyday of monopoly capitalism and with profits from the original Clarksburg plant, it was becoming the industrial giant Weir had envisioned a decade earlier. With a larger mill, however, came a larger labor force. And for Weir, making steel also meant building a community.

Building the Community

Making a community proved to be much more difficult than making steel, but Weir sought a workforce that needed him as much as he needed them. Weir recruited immigrants from southern Europe and the Middle East, blacks from Georgia, Virginia, and the Carolinas, and West Virginia mountain people to work in his mill.[5] The Clarksburg plant sent hundreds of men north to construct and work in the mill, and former Clarksburg residents numbered highly in Weirton's early population. According to one estimate about 500 original residents of Hollidays Cove remained when the mill was built and by 1919 Weirton's population had grown to almost 10,000. The *Steubenville Herald-Star* reported the following residential profile of pre-1920 Weirton: "500 Blacks, 250 Polish families, 400 Findlanders [sic], 3,500 Greeks, 400 Italians, 300 Slavish [sic], 400 Hungarian and 1,500 construction workers of all nationalities."[6] This leaves somewhere close to a thousand second- and third-generation Americans, most of whom were of northern European heritage as was Weir and his early management team. How many of these people came from the surrounding farming villages is not clear, but it is likely they made up a large proportion of Weirton's early settlement.

These early demographics suggest that ethnic, racial, and regional divisions prevailed and were manifest in group segregation and isolation—both inside and outside the mill. The southern European composition of Weirton's population was a largely unskilled, formally uneducated labor force with little exposure to the rhythms and discipline of industrial life.[7] Anglo-Americans made up most of the skilled labor force, and despite some vague improvement over their lives in the South, black workers toiled in the hardest and most disagreeable jobs. As in other steel towns during this period, blacks bore the brunt of immigrant animosity.[8]

Language differences also accentuated ethnic isolation and fostered intergroup suspicion, and ethnic lodges were soon established that sustained group identity and solidarity. Weirton's early population was also largely rural in origin, and the Appalachian culture of this period, notes Kai Erikson, included a mixture of Protestant faiths but also a common "distrust of Rome" that strained relations with newly arriving Catholic immigrants from southern Europe.[9] These social divisions within the labor force were likely to have been magnified vis-à-vis a managerial class that was predominantly white, Anglo-Saxon Protestant. The immigrant's place was clear. They were working class, but their local status would evolve in the context of mill and community life.

By 1919, Weirton was more or less a collection of bungalows for an assortment of working men and their families from the hills of West Virginia and southern Europe. Housing problems soon reached critical proportions and the ensuing overcrowding replicated the harsh conditions workers suffered in the mills. According to the *Steubenville Herald-Star*,

> In some quarters of the town as many as ten families reside in one house. The Negro colony has grown up in the past nine months. To take care of the men engaged on construction work a large number of shacks or shanties have been erected as billets for the men and each has from fifty to a hundred workmen. . . . Schools are overcrowded, churches all have larger congregations. Lodges are attaining record memberships. Houses are scarce, although more than 100 have been built here the past summer and a dozen more are nearing completion at present.[10]

By 1919 houses were being built by millworkers, with mill supplies and mill financing. Company influence in this matter, as with other aspects of Weir's paternalism, suggests a more insidious, subtle form of control than that exercised in the mold of, say, a George Pullman. Weir encouraged home ownership and the sense of independence this promoted. But home ownership was predicated on the favor of elite controlled banks and an endless stream of mill supplies. In addition to his duties as vice-president of Weirton Steel, Weir's brother David served as president of the People's Bank of Hollidays Cove and he was director of the Bank of Weirton and the National Exchange Bank of Steubenville.[11]

Legal jurisdiction was carried out through Hancock County court houses, jails, and police, though Weirton Steel officials employed their own "security" forces who routinely worked hand-in-hand with county sheriffs. Practically the entire Weirton police force held similar positions in Clarksburg and any allegiance to locality stopped south of Wheeling. With few ties to the northern panhandle, the police force was made up of mountain people already skeptical of foreigners. Intimidation was a constant means of social control, and police were regularly imported from southern West Virginia to oversee a budding young community and a labor force that surely found life extremely arduous. Social control was also enhanced by the relative isolation of the Weirton mill. News about Weirton was carried in a small column on the back pages of the *Steubenville Herald-Star* or the *Wheeling Register*. It rarely exceeded more than a few paragraphs about some new mill construction, housing project, or personal profile.

If there was a legacy common to the first laborers of Weir's mill it lay in the patriarchal order of the "old country," and this fit the paternalism he sought to invoke. Weir extended a benevolent hand in a manner that appeared respectful of the traditions of independence that many of his ethnic and Appalachian workers either brought with them from their native country, or sought in this country. But his goodwill rested, ultimately, on control over major financial institutions, mill resources, and mill employment. If his benevolent hand failed to secure the loyalty of his workers, it could swiftly become a fist.

The Big Steel Strike of 1919 clearly showed that if Weir wanted a company town, he would have to deal with the class relations endemic to the shop floor of his mills. A push by the American Federation of Labor (AFL) to organize the steel industry came to Weirton just when Weir and Williams had begun to expand their operations and were importing workmen daily. A closed shop was a prerequisite of a closed town and Weir was not inclined to open either.

Weirton and the Big Steel Strike of 1919

The strike began on September 22 with only one plant in the Ohio Valley fully operating and that was Weirton. There, conflicting reports were issued daily as the district strike committee and plant management publicly exchanged membership counts in an effort to rally support for their respective causes. Rather than negotiate, Weir immediately closed his Steubenville plant, thus sending a clear message to his Weirton workers of their fate should they heed the strike call.

Workmen from the Weirton mills reported that forty-five men were working in the stripped steel department where five hundred men were regularly employed, but the tin mill was working in full. To organizers and strikers this signaled that Weirton would need to be "induced" to join the movement. On September 23, the *Steubenville Herald-Star* reported that a march was being planned to organize the Weirton workforce. Railroaders were called out on strike after Weirton was put on an "unfair list" and company officials hired five hundred deputies to patrol the tin mill. Hancock County Sheriff Armour S. Cooper posted notices prohibiting public gatherings and Weirton officials warned they would bar the demonstration in "upholding law and order."[12] The following day the district strike committee postponed the proposed march and instead scheduled a mass meeting in Steubenville for Weirton workers. Should this fail to rally the men, warned lead organizer Frank Wilson, a mass march on Weirton would take place the following Monday.

Alarmed state officials soon began speaking of an "invasion" that threatened West Virginia state sovereignty. Telegrams between Governors Cox of Ohio and Cornwell of West Virginia were rife with paranoia and anti-immigrant sentiment. The proposed march, stated Governor Cox, was more than a dispute between capital and labor and that "the laws of the state must and will be respected and enforced. The spectacle of aliens establishing a code of their own is something that will not be tolerated upon Ohio soil." He continued,

America has maintained a liberal attitude toward foreigners who come here, but it must be presupposed at all times that while they are here, they must recognize what American ideals and experience of society suggests in the manner of individual conduct.[13]

As in other steel towns, the conflict was quickly becoming an issue severed from the harsh realities of the workplace and workers' demand for fair and democratic union representation. It was, instead, becoming a pretense for harsh company measures to crush the strike in the name of protecting American values and rooting out the "Red" menace.[14]

At this point support for the strike among Weirton workers appeared lukewarm at best. Weirton was not unlike other mills in the country that continued operating throughout the strike, but the movement was strongest in the Midwest and Weirton (along with the Pittsburgh mills) stood in the way of a fairly extensive shutdown in the steel industry. As historian David Brody notes, Weirton was one of a few steel towns that strike organizers "hardly dared to enter."[15] More than a few workers claimed that most millhands were satisfied and unsympathetic to the strike and this reinforced public statements by company officials denying that the Weirton mills were about to fall. At the strike meeting in Steubenville on September 26, only a few workers attended and many who had stayed out since the strike began returned to work earlier in the day.[16] It was becoming clear to union officials and strikers that support from Weirton would not come easily.

How much of the reluctance of Weirton workers to join the strike can be attributed to their sincere wishes and how much to company pressure? Undoubtedly there were divisions between the American skilled craft workers and the unskilled immigrants, most of whom had only recently arrived in the mills. Immigrant participation carried the strike for the most part, notes David Brody, but immigrants were also those most unsure of their status in America and thus were more likely to feel the tension between the values of industrial democracy and being labeled Bolshevik radicals in their new home.[17] This was exacerbated by a red scare campaign waged through company propaganda and searing newspaper headlines that marginalized strikers as it reframed union organizing that had consistently stressed patriotic and democratic themes.

The proposed march itself is perhaps the strongest evidence that Weirton workers were reluctant to join the ranks of strikers. It would be a mistake, however, to assume that the march was engineered solely by overly ambitious strike organizers. It was, rather, a spontaneous outgrowth of a determined rank-and-file that more often moved of its own accord than in line with strike leadership. It is also possible that many of the marchers had been locked out of the Steubenville plant. In any case, strikers heeded the call by union officials that Weirton would soon close on its own and the march was scrapped.

By now, however, company officials and state authorities had collaborated in a covert agenda that would stifle any union organizing in Weirton for some time to come. The proposed march set the context for what amounted to martial law in Weirton: a ban on public gatherings, strictly enforced curfews, and the presence of increasing numbers of mounted state troopers and secret police. Immigrant workers were being watched closely for any subversive activity while intimidation inside and outside the mill gates became routine. A few days into the strike notices were posted throughout the town warning against disorder and violence.

As the second week of the strike approached, the streets of Weirton were quiet. People had likely not forgotten of Frank Karlowski, a twenty-nine-year-old Pole who was arrested in July on charges of "spreading Bolshevik doctrine and teachings and creating discontent among the workmen and citizens at Weirton . . . especially the foreigners."[18] A "quiet investigation" leading to Karlowski's arrest had created "considerable excitement" in town. Upon his release Justice James Bradley of the Hancock County grand jury reprimanded the accused subversive saying, "Weirton was not a healthy place for a man of his sort and that the authorities were on the lookout for others of his kind who would be brought to justice if more evidence is gathered."[19] To underscore this warning, a vigilance committee consisting of World War I American soldiers had formed under Weir's direction to ensure that Weirton remained a "healthy" place to live.

All seemed calm on October 6 as general manager John C. Williams reported that "at least 98 percent of the company's American workers reported this morning as well as a number of foreigners."[20] The Weirton plant was the first in the district to attempt resuming full operations, but the Steubenville plant remained closed. It appeared the strike had been short-lived. The next day Weir made certain that any spirit of resistance remaining among his workers was crushed.

Extracting Homage

"As far as the Weirton Steel Company is concerned," declared J. C. Williams on October 7, "the steel strike is broken."[21] This public statement came after 186 alleged Wobblies (members of the Industrial Workers of the World or IWW) were rounded up at noon, marched to the town square, and forced to kneel and kiss the American flag. As fights broke out the accused were given ten minutes to leave town or join their leaders who had been jailed in nearby New Cumberland. The undercover operation of the previous few weeks had led Hancock County deputies to a Finnish hall where they seized "half a ton of literature of the most lurid 'red'."[22] County officials claimed the suspected "undesirables" were identified by name cards found during the raid, though local police and state authorities had been observing the meeting hall for several days.

The event had subdued any opposition to Weir's power and humbled the largely immigrant workforce laboring in his mills. The spectacle of the town square affair had a powerful impact despite the gross infringement on civil liberties and the fact that no charges had been filed. Perhaps the most glaring injustice was done the Finnish workers who were singled out as troublemakers and made up the majority of those forcibly evicted from town. Afterwards, Weir ordered that his personnel department hire no more Finns, a clear signal to other ethnic groups that their well-being depended upon their continued subservience.[23] Indeed, immediately following the flag-kissing demonstration Greek and Polish residents gathered at police headquarters to display their loyalty to the flag and announce their return to work the following morning. Later that afternoon an American flag was carried at the head of a Greek funeral procession "to avoid any possibility of a misunderstanding."[24]

The following days were fraught with charges and counter-charges, none of which were confirmed, but all of which served to create an atmosphere of fear and suspicion. Sworn affidavits by Finnish, Greek, and Polish workers attested that they had been beaten up, fined, and evicted from company housing for refusing to go to work. Company officials denied these allegations. Axel Graham, a naturalized Finnish resident, denied any of the workers were radicals but admitted that about one third did belong to the Finnish Socialist Party, affiliated with the Socialist Party of America.[25]

The AFL stood in support of the deported workers but refused to protect any workers affiliated with the IWW or similar organizations. AFL officials who arrived in Weirton to investigate the charges disassociated the union from "any radical organization" and were "anxious to expel from its ranks any such agitators."[26] They began a formal inquiry into the substance of the seized literature, but there was no public disposition of the case and findings of the investigation were never reported publicly. This did not seem to matter in light of a crackdown that demonstrated just how far the power of the company extended beyond the plant gates.

In the days that followed, local police began to redefine the conflict as "ethnic unrest" claiming that "trouble had been brewing between a certain faction of Finnlanders [sic], known in Weirton as the Red Guard Bolsheviks and Americans of the town since the war due to the attitude of the former regarding liberty bonds."[27] Police also claimed that the Black Hand (the early Italian Mafia) had sent death letters to the wives of Finnish workers who did not quit their jobs. These allegations were denied by union officials and Finnish spokespersons and none were ever confirmed. Still, the conflict was neatly portrayed as a case of un-American behavior amid ethnic hostilities.

Finally, most of the deported workers were said to have been "floaters," unmarried men from outside the town who had arrived only for the purpose of "spreading the rankest kind of propaganda."[28] This stigmatized the accused workers by attacking their status as family and community members (an accusation that does, however, seem to contradict police reports about Black Hand threats). Statements by company officials and county police polarized the town and neatly framed the dissension in terms of outside forces threatening the tranquility of Weirton.

With ethnic anxiety and suspicion magnified, these public statements also justified elite imposition of strict, and often violent measures in *protecting* townspeople from evil subversives. Company and county authorities were elevated to the stature of benign guardians and thus absolved of their role in perpetuating the turmoil. At the very least, elite interpretations created a confusing set of accounts that placated public sentiment over the issues of the strike and highlighted the events—and lessons—of the IWW roundup.

The strike of 1919 withered slowly as winter approached and the struggle of steelworkers to unionize would lay dormant until the Great Depression. In Weirton, the strike's aftermath was littered with reminders that opposing the company meant more than grievances over shopfloor issues, wages, and hours; *it meant opposing a way of life.* Rumors surfaced in October that the company would dismantle its Clarksburg plant and remove it to Weirton. These rumors were neither officially confirmed nor denied, but on October 30 a committee representing business and labor from Clarksburg met with company officials. People may have considered having another plant operating in town promising news, but it also reinforced in their minds the arbitrary power of the company; they too could face the prospect of a plant closing if Weir so deemed it.

They could also rely on little assistance from a sputtering union movement. On November 12, Vice President David M. Weir issued a statement on the reopening of the Steubenville plant.

I want to state most emphatically that the Steubenville works of the Weirton Steel Company will resume operations only as an "open shop," the policy prevailing when the plant was closed Oct. 22, and since the company has operated [it].[29]

The lockout had ended, and though members of the Amalgamated Association of Iron, Steel, and Tin Workers retained their standing, their influence was clearly negligible and support from the National Steel Strike Committee was not forthcoming.

Finally, on November 24, the remaining Finns in Weirton were rounded up by the chief of police to testify against a thirty-five-year-old Finlander who was arrested after "acting suspicious." He was alleged to have kept men from going to work, threatening to kill them if they did not leave Weirton, and circulating IWW literature throughout the town. None of the charges were formally filed and the accused was turned over to state and federal authorities.[30] But his arrest and public disposition showed that local authorities were ever watchful of subversion and on guard against any signs of ethnic agitation and disloyalty.

Solidifying Control: The Seeds of Paternalism

The symbolic impact of the strike and its aftermath clearly meshed with efforts by Weir and local authorities to extend their control over workers and their families. But symbolism disengaged from the routines of everyday life is a risky, hollow gesture that can be later used to discredit and challenge those who invoke it. Weir's project was twofold: to build a prosperous company and to create a community that was as fully integrated as were his mills. His power was formidable, but in the future this would increasingly depend upon his ability to lure the sensibilities of workers over to his vision of what life could, and, more importantly, *should* be. The strike had threatened Weir and town elites, and they were well aware that coercion alone would not secure their control. To this end Weir joined other supporters of Progressive reform and began efforts to acculturate his largely immigrant workforce.

A brief article in the "Weirton Notes" section of the *Steubenville Herald-Star* is quite telling in a number of respects, but especially in how it conveys the normative and moral dimensions of the paternalism that Weir sought to evoke. After some comments about the building of a new community center came the following opinion of Weirton and the challenges facing company officials there, which I reprint in full:

> Another issue that is worthy of mention at this time is the fact that for some time past the officials of the company have been working out a plan to [join] in the great Americanization movement that is now afoot throughout the country, and they have been fortunate in procuring a man who has been doing work of this nature and who is familiar with the policies that are now in practice in other mill towns where they have a great Cosmopolitan element to contend with. They are encouraging with the assistance of the local school officials, the promotion of the movement of teaching the children of foreigners to influence their parents to learn to read and write the English language and to take more of an interest in the welfare and progression of the community in which they are living. *The men at the head of the steel company and the town are to be commended for the unselfish motives that are prompting them in these movements, and the*

*people of this district should feel very thankful and grateful
to those men who are not only making it possible for them
and theirs to enjoy the very best of working conditions but are
also trying to make their social and private lives more pleasant* [emphasis added].[31]

That this "cosmopolitan element" had to be "contended with" is
rather ironic given the fact that the ethnic makeup of Weirton
was often a point of pride for town elites who boasted of how so
many different groups could live and work so peacefully together.
But cultural diversity was not endearing to company officials who
once sought and exploited it if this hindered the development of a
disciplined and faithful labor force.

What is perhaps most revealing in this quotation, though, is
how company and town elites are portrayed.[32] The "unselfishness"
of their motives evokes the essence of paternalism; civic intervention guided by benevolent and altruistic overseers. That townspeople "should feel very thankful," even "grateful," for these
efforts brings an emotional and moral prescription to what was
clearly a call for devotion and homage. People had to be convinced
that elites knew, and could provide, what was best for them. They
also needed to be reassured that elites were decent, caring and,
above all, men of integrity. In 1921, the Weirton Social Service
was organized by Weir's brother David to help the needy, indi-
gent, and troubled of the community.[33] Weir was deftly reaching
for the hearts and minds of his workers as the 1920s unfolded.

During this period Weir remained a Pittsburgher and commuted
to Weirton by train, then later by automobile as roads improved.
This made him somewhat of an absentee landlord whose public image could more easily assume mythical proportions. He spoke at
public gatherings and before local assemblies on the virtues of hard
work, independence, and the glory of free market economies. He referred constantly to his background as a "self-made man" while
conveniently omitting his political connections and influential social networks. And though Weir held the reigns, he exercised power
through local elites that distanced him personally from any un-
pleasant features of life in the mill and community.[34]

Weir projected these traits sincerely to an audience that found
solitude and credibility in what Reinhard Bendix calls "affectionate
tutelage," a relationship between master and servant characterized

by strict enforcement of discipline and efficient organization of production that was authoritative as well as amiable, moral, and sentimental.[35] As I noted earlier, the majority of Weirton's early population consisted of rural and immigrant groups that found the patriarchal system of authority at least somewhat familiar to that of the "old country." There were, certainly, some clear differences, but the dominant role of the father continued and the obligations associated with that role remained intact. In Weirton, the authority relations subsumed within paternalism meshed with more personal relations experienced daily between men and women and within the ethnic working-class family. One need not strain much to *feel* the connection.

Echoing other scholars, Richard Sennett notes that paternalism also intended to soften the impact of industrialism by blending elements of community and family with more market-based motivations: individualism, discipline, impersonal hierarchy. As with other attempts to forge utopian communities, the paternalistic company town sought to recreate the normative order of rural societies and retain "the wholesomeness of family values."[36] In this Weir firmly believed, and if his strict and stubborn outlook reinforced a wrathful fatherly image, he also insisted that the more disruptive aspects of a market society be tempered by his own brand of benign intervention.

This was played out through perhaps the most extensive effort to integrate workplace with community since Robert Owen in eighteenth-century Scotland.[37] Weir wanted workers and management to live near each other, belong to the same churches and fraternal organizations, and in many cases belong to the same family.[38] He encouraged mobility in the company and provided the positions by which people could achieve this (which, in part, led to the present-day top-heavy management structure). He maintained an informal management structure where workers and management "rubbed elbows," but also so he could exercise personal control over mill operations.

J. C. Williams continued as president of Weirton Steel and he was quite a visible presence in town. Then, in 1928, a fighter pilot and former stunt flyer by the name of Thomas Millsop joined Weirton Steel as a sales representative. His local background (a native of nearby Sharon, Pennsylvania), mill experience, and public exploits made him a bit of a celebrity to townspeople, and his integration into the community served him well when he assumed presidency of the company following Williams' death in 1936. Unlike Weir, Millsop would eventually settle here and become an ever-present representative of paternalism in Weirton. In the meantime, Weir concentrated his efforts on building an industrial empire.

Weirton Steel: The Seed of an Empire

With the union movement silenced and his workforce subject to unfettered managerial control, Weir entered the 1920s fully charged to exploit a lethargic steel market. The automobile industry provided the impetus for a period of amazing growth in the company. U.S. Steel and other steel giants controlled the market for heavier steel such as rails, plates, and structural shapes, but Weirton led the way in light sheet and strip steel. Structurally flexible and innovative firms like Weirton Steel (known as "Little Steel" firms) exploited the market niche of an expanding automobile industry and reaped the benefits.[39]

The innovation of continuous hot-rolling at Weirton Steel led to a meeting of Weir and George R. Fink, founder of Michigan Steel Company near Detroit. Weir and Fink had a mutual friend and supplier in George M. Humphrey, chief executive of the M.A. Hanna Company in Cleveland. Under a Delaware charter, these men merged operations and formed the National Steel Corporation in October 1929.[40] National grew to become the fifth largest steel producer in America, second only to U.S. Steel in ore resource holdings in Minnesota and Michigan.

National Steel established headquarters in Pittsburgh although their only operation in Pennsylvania was the Isabella Coal Mine. This location was the center of top administrative and financial functions, and board meetings were normally held there. Weir wanted to be near his competitors, especially U.S. Steel. His was a "one-man show" and he directed all operations at Weirton and, for the most part, at National Steel. Weir's ability to dictate the company's direction was complemented by a loose administrative structure and small staff of loyal followers.

Interestingly, when the stock market crashed in 1929 National Steel continued to soar, posting more profit than all other steel companies combined. In 1932 National was the only profitable steel firm and it never posted a loss during the Depression. Weir made enemies among steel producers who saw his good fortune resulting from price cutting that undermined them.[41] Early in 1933 Weir declared that the worst of the Depression had abated and he began making public statements against wage cuts. He held business leaders responsible for their dismal ledgers, advising them to become more politically involved in government. And as if to spite his competitors, Weir raised wages in his Weirton plant 15 percent in July 1933 as U.S. Steel and other steelmakers continued slashing wages.

This posture was convenient given his comfortable niche in the automobile market (and a recent major contract with Henry Ford). It was also characteristic of Weir, who evoked populist themes and portrayed himself as an independent entrepreneur who was not afraid to shake his fist at anyone, or any power, that blocked his path. Weir ridiculed financiers as merely "shrewd and successful gamblers—what did they build?" He financed his expansion during the 1920s by selling $40 million in stock directly to the public. "I got it," he often said in his most populist rhetoric, "not from Wall Street but from Main Street."[42]

A lifelong Republican, Weir would soon challenge the Roosevelt administration and growing federal power that threatened to undermine his vision and his control. In June 1933, Weir initiated an employee representation plan at his Weirton, Steubenville, and Clarksburg plants and found himself in a political, legal, and social struggle that continued for almost seventeen years. During this period, local and national agendas intersected to form the context out of which paternalism finally emerged as an institutional and cultural way of life.

The Challenge: 1933–1951

On September 27, 1933 Weirton Steel issued the following statement in the local press:

> Some of the departments of the Weirton Steel Company operations at Weirton, West Virginia are shut down due to a walkout on the part of the men, while other departments are continuing full operations. The Weirton Steel Company has

in operation the Employee Representative plan, by which system the various plants have committees of employees. . . . The management of the various plants are at all times prepared and willing to discuss with these committees matters in which employees may be interested. . . . No demands or requests were presented to the management through any of these committees and the company is therefore unable to state the cause of the present conditions.[43]

A strike had begun that more or less fell upon the lap of an aging union with youthful and inexperienced leaders. The Amalgamated Association of Iron, Steel and Tin Workers (AAISTW) represented an astonishing example of durability and dedication at the grassroots level of labor organizing. Having seen its glory days during the Homestead Strike of 1892, the AAISTW survived the defeat of the 1919 Big Steel strike and endured the silent 1920s by working closely with rank-and-file workers at the local level. Their adherence to democratic values and opposition to corporate power endeared them to younger workers whose idealism and militancy had not yet been tested. The leaders of the Weirton strike were primarily in their twenties, had never called a strike much less participated in one, and their subsequent meetings in Washington, D.C., with Roosevelt officials proved to be a "heady" experience for them all.[44]

The spontaneous walkout took the senior Amalgamated leadership by surprise. William Long, president of Weirton local 66 of the AAISTW declared the work stoppage a "holiday" while Edward W. Miller, international vice-president of the Amalgamated in Pittsburgh referred to it as a wildcat strike. "You've violated all the rules and laws of your union in calling this strike," Miller told workers, "but we are going to do our best to get you out of this difficulty."[45] Seizing the opportunity, Long declared,

The crisis has arrived prematurely, but since we're in it, let's stick like men. We'll hold the picket line but at all costs avoid violence. We will stay out until the company recognizes the Amalgamated association as our representative.[46]

Early support for the strike call suggests that Weir's authority was far from complete, even though his power soon became very evident. Close to 5,000 workers walked out on September 27, and after six days more than 11,000 joined the ranks of the strikers— practically the entire workforce at Weir's three plants. Labor was challenging the control Weir and town elites had over their lives in the mill and in the community.

Local Resistance to Paternalism

How many workers supported the walkout and how many were forced out by the work stoppage is uncertain, but there is evidence of widespread support. A day after the strike began 400 Steubenville workers voted to declare "a holiday in sympathy with the workers at Weirton." The Clarksburg plant emptied after one fourth of its workforce voted to go on the picket lines, and ninety percent of the elected representatives of the company-sponsored union resigned their positions and joined the AAISTW. This general response even caught Amalgamated leaders by surprise as they repeatedly called for "restrained enthusiasm" and cautioned against violence and damage to mill property.[47]

Picketing was also heavy and effective. The Steubenville plant was shut down after strikers successfully blocked the main entrance. A day after the walkout state troopers estimated that 3,000 of the strikers were on picket duty and at the Weirton mills pickets worked four-hour shifts over a twenty-four-hour period. Strike leader William Long urged pickets to "hold our ground as law-abiding citizens, [and] at all times avoid violence."[48] For the most part this plea was heeded by strikers, though both pickets and workers sporadically clashed in front of the mill gates.

Public support for the strike also appears to have been substantive. Daily crowds estimated at three to four thousand joined pickets and congregated in the streets either to show support or as onlookers (which fostered an image of public support). Often, crowds would jeer workers they thought were strikebreakers attempting to enter plant gates. Local businesses also showed sympathy with the strike action. After the first week of the strike seventy-two Weirton grocers met and decided to extend credit to the striking workers as long as possible. Even the *Weirton Daily Times* appeared to cover the conflict fairly. It routinely noted union meeting times and places, and at times seemingly catered to pro-union sentiment. Front page reports noted how "peaceful" strikers were and referred to the strike as the "holiday" that local union leaders labeled it.

As the strike entered its second week, pickets and spectators gathered in front of plant gates to discourage those who began returning to work. Only a few hundred workers had remained in the mill, doing necessary maintenance work and keeping electricity and power running to the town (the company provided both, as well as water). But clashes between returning workers and pickets at the Steubenville plant left many workers wary of what the company might do and more of them began to question the strike. Up to now, violence had been limited to a few incidents, but on October 6, the coercive nature of Weir's paternalism reemerged as tear gas and police clubs dispersed a large crowd of men, women, and children who had formed a barricade to stop workers from entering the mill. Company guards hurled tear gas and hand grenades at the fleeing crowd while bystanders were overcome by the windswept fumes. Four days later three to four thousand people were silenced as state troopers again used tear gas to open a mill entrance that had been blocked by pickets. Weirton's first— and only—strike lasted for just two weeks.

The strike had been broken and Amalgamated leaders looked to the federal government to ensure fairly elected worker representation. They put their faith in the newly formed National Labor Board (NLB), which was established under the provisions of Roosevelt's National Industrial Recovery Act (NIRA). Section 7a guaranteed workers the right to elect and form unions without company interference. AAISTW leaders charged that the employee representation plan was a company union, that it did not represent the majority of workers, and that it was not an elected body. After futile attempts to speak with Weir and local management, strike leaders appealed to the NLB and became the first union in the United States to challenge company representation plans under the fragile New Deal political structure. An agreement was reached between Senator Richard Wagner, chairman of the NLB, Weir, and the union to accept an NLB-supervised election in December 1933.

Workers were sorely disappointed, however, as Weir rebuked federal officials who had arrived to oversee the December 15 elections. Insisting that the election follow rules established by officials of the Employee Representation Plan rather than what federal officials and the Amalgamated leaders had agreed upon, Weir steadfastly refused to bargain with AAISTW leaders. Weir also rejected what he called "interference" by the federal government and refused to comply with the NRA code. The election took place and the Employee Representation Plan was initiated amid charges of intimidation and coercion by both Weir and the AAISTW.

A Class Struggle for Worker Independence

Why did workers decide to challenge Weir now? They were isolated from other major centers of steel production and thus distant from urban union organizing. By 1933 the town had been spared the worst of the Great Depression. Mill layoffs were few and infrequent and local unemployment was low relative to the nation as a whole. Weir had, for the most part, held the line against wage reductions and the mill continued to provide a reasonable standard of living for its workers. Over the years a secondary commercial sector had also developed that supported residents in Weirton and the surrounding region. By now, employment in the plant had reached the level (approximately 12,000) that it would remain, more or less, until 1982. An internal occupational structure held out the promise of advancement—mobility that Weir encouraged and not a few workers experienced. Indeed, if there was anywhere in America that could hold confidently that recovery was just around the corner, it was Weirton. The irony is that steelworkers here should be the first to challenge the open shop and therefore predate the organizing drives by the Steel Workers Organizing Committee (SWOC) and the Congress of Industrial Organization (CIO) by almost three years.[49]

On the other hand it is not surprising that workers here were willing to challenge the company when they did; they had little to recover from and much to gain. The company was doing remarkably well and workers were not clinging to their jobs with the same ferocity as those at other steel firms. The youthful leadership of the strike had not experienced the humiliation of the 1919 crackdown and, two decades later, were likely less susceptible to paternalism than their parents. Weirton's working class acted in behalf of their independence from Weir and their desire to maintain some representation in the face of overbearing and arbitrary elite control. They did not want higher wages, rather they demanded a union independent of Weir and local company officials. To borrow Rick Fantasia's term, Weirton's working class had formed a "culture of solidarity" in defiance of Weir's paternal order of subservience and loyalty.[50]

Their challenge met with a comprehensive response by Weir and town elites. In the early months of 1934 Weir continued to defy federal officials sent to investigate charges of company coercion, and on January 31 Roosevelt issued an executive order for polling workers on whether they wanted another election. During one meeting with an AAISTW delegation Roosevelt laughed at reports that workers were compelled to wear Hoover buttons by foremen during the recently contested union vote. But Weir was not laughing, nor were the workers in his mills.

Finally, on March 21, the Roosevelt administration asked for a restraining injunction against the company in a federal district court in Wilmington, Delaware, where the company was incorporated. For frustrated AAISTW leaders, however, this was "not enough" and in a letter to Roosevelt they stated:

> Even if this proceeding wins it does not force Weir to deal with our union. We wish to point out secondly that this court proceeding may last a year until the NRA is over. You are not helping starving men a bit by this. We wish to point out thirdly that all your rulings and orders have been disregarded completely and that the government has allowed months of stalling by the Weirton Steel Company. Finally, therefore, we call upon you to get Weir to comply with the NRA within 48 hours or get the Wagner bill passed this week or else stop pretending that any immediate and effective action by the government is possible. In that case, in view of your earlier statements, we ask you to call upon the steel workers of this country to strike to get the rights you can't get otherwise.[51]

On February 28, 1935, the court ruled in favor of Weir and his representation plan when section 7a of the NIRA was held unconstitutional and void when applied to companies not engaged in interstate commerce. The court also held that company interference had not been proved and that the company union was "free of intimidation, domination, and control by management."[52]

Over the next sixteen years Weirton Steel was engaged in almost continuous litigation with the NLRB (representing first SWOC, then later the CIO) over the status of union representation in its mills. During this period company power was manifested in specific ways that ultimately ensured elite control over the mill and town but that also institutionalized Weir's "affectionate tutelage." The two faces of paternalism—the company's use of force and intimidation combined with timely and generous public welfare—crystallized both the lengths to which Weir would go to contain labor unrest and the costs that townspeople would have to endure resisting.

Through court testimony and thousands of pages of affidavits filed by the company and workers, charges of coercion and intimidation became public events that had a significant impact on workers and residents.[53] Even if these "private" acts of control were difficult to prove (as the lengthy sixteen-year court appeals suggest), their public disclosure created an atmosphere of fear and distrust among people in town. Though only a small minority of workers made such charges, their public stand in court showed others that opposing the company was futile. Their courage may have been admired, but concern for one's life and livelihood was prudent.

The Coercive Face of Paternalism

In 1936 William Green, then head of the AFL, charged that during the 1933 strike Weir had posted machine guns at various locations along the mill parameters making Weirton an "armed camp."[54] Workers charged that the company paid workers (what union organizers referred to as a "hatchet gang") to get rid of union organizers and beatings were routinely reported to aloof local police. When SWOC, and then later the CIO, renewed organizing efforts, additional police were hired by the company under the pretense of combating local "crime waves." Weir admitted that the company hired its own police, but that he knew nothing about their operations. Mill foremen were said to have intimidated workers by threatening to fire them unless they voted for the company union. An espionage system in the mill (the Weirton Steel Employees Security League) made workers suspicious of any talk supporting the CIO. Outside the mill, the Weir Cove Community Security League was formed to patrol the community. Funded by the company to denounce and harass CIO organizers and sympathetic workers, the Security League also organized counter-demonstrations in the form of parades and community events.

More subtle means of coercion were also charged by workers. Many claimed that the company union held parties prior to union elections where alcohol was liberally distributed to those attending. Temporary layoffs and intermill transfers to undesirable jobs were commonplace for those accused of union agitation. And the first systematic effort by the company to exact its ideological control came in the form of the *Weirton Steel Bulletin*, established in 1934 just after the AAISTW strike. According to testimony by NLRB representatives in 1940, the company spent $70,000 between 1933 and 1937 to publish an "endless stream of propaganda replete with epithets" denouncing the CIO and endorsing the Employee Representation Plan.[55] Over the next 30 years, the *Bulletin* celebrated the company's role in caring for practically every facet of workers' lives while emphasizing themes of patriotism, free enterprise, and community solidarity.

National publications also followed the local saga, but their framing of events also seemed to bend toward Weir and company propaganda. A 1937 issue of *Life* magazine featured a pictorial of the NLRB court hearings. In the "case of the CIO vs. Weirton," pictures of accusing workers and CIO T-shirts suggest that Weirton was a hotbed of conflict and suspicion. But only a few issues later, *Life* ran a follow-up cover story on "Weir of Weirton" that spoke glowingly of "a West Virginia steel town with a difference." With Weir's grandfatherly smile on the cover, this was a far more flattering pictorial of successful, home-owning steelworkers who rose through the ranks, earned almost as much as company president Thomas Millsop, and played golf at the town's private country club.[56] The marked difference in framing and tone of the *Life* coverage suggests that Weir's influence extended much further than Weirton.

In my interviews with employees many of these accusations against the company were confirmed, as was the general sense of unease and distrust over my inquiries into outside union representation. During one group interview I asked workers if they thought that the USWA would have represented them better during the ESOP negotiations. As they nervously shuffled in their chairs and exchanged anxious glances, one worker asked if I was "trying to start a fight" and suggested that I move on to another question. When I referred to this sensitive moment during an interview with another worker, he cautioned me to be careful. "They're going to get the wrong impression about you. Some of them will. Some won't." He then recalled how those who supported the CIO during the late 1940s and early 1950s were quietly dealt with by the company:

> Years back when they tried to get the CIO in, they were standing in front of the gate getting their papers out, and a couple of guys in the mill, this one guy got involved real good. He was a representative, one of the CIO people, but he worked for Weirton Steel. Him and his buddies, they worked together for years. His buddies were punching him out [on the time clock]. They used to do that for each other. Well, then they got him to punch them out. And they turned his ass in and he got fired. These other two guys got fired, too, but they came back, he never did. They all got fired, but the other two guys came back. One of the guys, he was a real hatchet man from way back, he came back. They set it up to get his ass *out*! That's a fact, I seen that happen.

Others I spoke with murmured about how "things happened" to people they knew and that they never saw them again. One worker's father "never talked about [CIO organizing] much" with him, although his image of his father was of a "worker with a baseball bat in the streets." From what he had heard, "it was a bad time." A company official, whose family had participated in forming a company union during this period, also confirmed these accounts.

> Yeah, the CIO. I've heard my mother warn us, those terrible stories about my dad receiving threats, he and my mother. The CIO was importing people from Detroit, gunslingers, thugs. We went out and got ours from Chicago. (*Laughs*) Oh my. [Workers] wanted a union and the company probably

started out by saying the union is probably not a bad idea if we have some voice in and control of it. I think ultimately that the company took the position that, well, "I'd rather have a union, a local independent union, then I wouldn't have to deal with the international action." I can't prove that, but that's my feeling. Tom Millsop, the [company] president of the time, E. T. Weir who was the founder, my dad knew those people very well. I would think they probably did have some say, but I don't think they ever—I'd like to believe that they didn't interfere.

Throughout this period, Weir, Millsop, and company and union officials held the Roosevelt administration and the NLRB guilty of interfering with the rights of workers to choose their own representatives. In their view, Roosevelt, the NLRB, and the CIO acted in collusion to frustrate the uncoerced desires of Weirton workers. In court hearings, they entered countless appeals claiming that the NLRB was actively persecuting the "freely elected" independent unions and that the courts were ignoring the "smear tactics" of the CIO. Counsel for the company and the Weirton Independent Union (formed in 1941) charged that the CIO issued bribes to lure workers in 1943 and that NLRB attorneys were present at the time.

But for Weir, Millsop, and company officials, the battle over union representation was more than a legal contest, and it was more than a struggle over the legitimate use of federal powers. It was also a struggle over which version of public welfare would prevail in the lives of workers and residents of Weirton.[57] At the national level, Weir joined the newly formed American Liberty League in 1935 as a member of its advisory council to challenge New Deal policies. He later became treasurer of the Republican Party and donated heavily to its candidates up through the 1950s. At the local level, and with local elites, Weir turned his efforts to building community institutions that would outlive them all.

The Benevolent Face of Paternalism

Only a few weeks following the disputed vote between the AAISTW and the Employee Representation Plan, the first of a series of public welfare measures was announced. Though much of this philanthropy was consistent with the traditional noblesse oblige of company and town elites, these projects could not have been more timely given the turbulence of the early 1930s. On January 24, 1934, J. C. Williams, then company president, announced plans for the construction of two public swimming pools to be funded by a D. M. Weir trust fund and himself. A month later the company advanced $54,000 to the local school board to pay its teachers and employees. The company also donated land for a golf course to be named after J. C. Williams, and its clubhouse and fairways hosted various community events, including high school proms and July 4th fireworks displays. The adjoining Weir Memorial Park was also commemorated on July 4, 1934, and its recreational facilities were operated by the company's Industrial Relations Department. In 1939 Weirton Steel closed its mills for two days and sponsored trips to the World's Fair in New York, bringing 3,500 workers and their families to the event.

Company and elite philanthropy embraced all religious and ethnic groups. The company donated the services of engineers who supervised the planning and construction of the Greek Orthodox Church, and the mill produced the stainless steel that covers the church's dome and tower. A plaque bearing the likeness of the church's benefactor, Thomas Millsop, sits among church icons inside. Practically every home I entered during my research was either reinforced by mill-produced steel beams or constructed with mill supplies. And with schools segregated until 1955 in West Virginia, the first black school was built on land that Weir donated.[58] With the dispute over union representation still unresolved as the 1930s ended, the company continued its dominance both inside and outside the mill.

There were two notable sources of disruption in the 1940s: public setbacks and indiscretions, both of which might have reinforced any oppositional sentiment that remained among the millworkers and residents. On May 5, 1943, the 3rd Circuit Court of Appeals in Philadelphia upheld an NLRB suit to disestablish two company unions and reinstate seventeen workers who were allegedly dismissed because of CIO union activity during the mid-1930s. (By this point, workers were organized in two unions: production workers under the Weirton Independent Union and the mill security force under a separate Independent Guards

Union.) Then, on November 15, 1945, the company was fined $148,125 for violating a War Productions Board order when it obtained an air-conditioning system presumably for the mill hospital but instead installed it at the company-owned J. C. Williams golf clubhouse.

But these potentially humiliating events occurred in the larger, and perhaps more personally felt, context of a continuous rise in the standard of living for most residents. Millworkers received systematic wage increases from 1942 to 1948 that were on the average slightly higher (by about 5 cents) than what the CIO gained for its members in other mills. The company also granted additional benefits and vacation time while raising its base pay for employees a fraction higher than other firms. In late 1945, when steelworkers nationwide voted overwhelmingly to strike in demanding a $2 daily wage increase, Weirton Steel was the only steel firm not participating in the vote.

Then, in 1948 plans for two major public works were announced: the Weirton General Hospital and the Thomas Millsop Community Center. Both were liberally funded by the company and town elites, but the company also enforced community voluntarism by setting up a payroll deduction plan "for employees who wanted to contribute" to the Community Center. According to one account, "pledges from Weirton employees averaged a full week's pay."[59] This practice of initiating payroll deductions for employee donations to public welfare (for example, community chest drives) reinforced the structural link between the mill and community. If steel could be engineered, so too could public morality.

It is likely, then, that rather than damaging the company's image, federal sanctions served to ennoble it by highlighting the persistence of local welfare in the face of meddlesome outside forces. The struggle over the last decade had become a "local dispute" and it would ultimately be dealt with by "our own people." By the time the CIO had begun its most aggressive organizing drive in 1950, the campaign of public welfare amid intimidation and corruption had taken its toll. With the apparent impotence of the federal government to prosecute the company effectively, gnawing ethnic and racial divisions, and growing suspicion among workers and residents, any opposition to the status quo faced institutional barriers as well as general resentment.

Quiescence: 1951–1982

The CIO could never match what Weir and the company could deliver, and even if it did, it could not protect workers in their community. As Charles Murray launched the CIO's campaign in 1950, he only partially spoke to the concerns of a group of workers when he said, "The first objective in our campaign is to destroy fear, fear that Weirton employees will lose their jobs if they select a union of their choice."[60] But workers also had to *live* in Weirton, and their mill experiences had become intimately part of family and community life. By now, local businesses favored a company union, and divisions among relatives working outside (and inside) the mill made social gatherings at least awkward, and potentially volatile, during talk of the CIO.

Two other factors should be noted in this connection that, in my view, reinforced paternalism or at least hindered opposition to it leading up to the period of quiescence: the role of women and the incorporation of Weirton in 1947. With the institutionalization of local welfare during the 1940s women entered the community sphere in a more public and active way. Women's associations and community groups formed, and though routinely headed by the wives of company elites, these social networks served as a status link for the wives of millworkers who sought membership or personal acquaintance. Even if this social network of women's groups remained elitist (a view not a few local women's expressed during interviews), their public image reinforced the community morality of paternalism and sanctioned the "proper" role of women in public affairs. As one sixty-six-year-old widow recalled of the 1940s, "I guess I was considered a 'bad girl' because I snuck smokes and liked to dance. I wasn't, but you had to keep low if you wanted to step out of line or have fun." Indeed, those women who were "stepping out of line" in support of SWOC and CIO organizing drives faced more than a "bad girl" stigma.

Then during World War II, women entered the mill to replace the primarily male workforce that left to fight in the war. Many women proudly recalled to me how they operated heavy cranes and worked in the dirt and danger of the mill during this period. As they spoke of "keeping the mill going until the men returned," it is not unreasonable to presume that many women influenced husbands and mates into rejecting the CIO. They had worked in the mill and saw what was happening to those who objected. They persevered, and so too should the men. And if women were concerned about protecting their children from reprisals, they were also likely to find that unpopular positions taken by the men in their lives tarnished their image in the community and strained social relationships among neighbors, friends, and their extended family.

A second institutional support for paternalism came in 1947 with the incorporation of Hollidays Cove and Weir Heights into the city of Weirton. In 1940 only 2,976 of 7,353 eligible voters rejected a similar proposal by a 2 to 1 margin. But seven years later, company president Thomas Millsop (a lifelong Republican) became Weirton's (a Democratic city) first mayor. In 1951 he returned for a second term, capturing 87.6 percent of the vote. In a most civic and paternal gesture, he announced that he would serve this term with no pay.[61]

The company had now become formally charged with running essential civic services (gas, water, and electricity) while providing manpower and expertise for city maintenance and special projects. It began organizing the July 4th celebrations and it provided the Christmas decorations. Local politics became an institutional niche where company officials easily moved from the mill to town council and then back to the mill; everyone knew who held the purse strings and who "called the shots" in city politics. City officials could boast of their efficient, "strictly business" approach to local government they brought with them from the mill, but they also relied on significant company subsidies. The Municipal Building cost the city $1 a year rental, and by 1952 Weirton Steel paid almost 80 percent of the local property taxes.[62]

Under the circumstances, a company union looked like the best workers could get. On August 1, 1950, the 3rd Circuit Court of Appeals in Philadelphia found Weirton Steel guilty of interfering with union organization and it ordered the company to dissolve the Independent Union and Guards Union. Seven executives and five WIU officials were found in contempt of court and the company was ordered to pay court costs and fines, as well as reinstate eighteen employees who were discharged or disciplined in relation to CIO organizing during the 1940s.

But the struggle against elite control had taken its toll. Two months later, workers voted for the Independent Steelworkers Union (ISU) over the CIO in an NLRB certified election. The

Weirton Steel Bulletin saw the preelection campaign as coming down to a "few fundamentals":

(1) Can Weirton employees manage their own affairs or do they need outside union leadership?; (2) An Independent Union means continued labor peace; an outside Union means a possibility of strikes; (3) The issue of Communism.[63]

The "fundamentals" of the twenty years prior to this election, however, read somewhat differently. The "red scare" had been a constant theme in Weirton's history and the *Weirton Steel Bulletin* regularly denounced socialized steel in its pages. In the current climate of anticommunist hysteria, any alliance with CIO organizers was symbolically tainted, if not demonized. And the previous seventeen years had been a constant struggle and were far from peaceful, but were employees actually managing their own affairs? Out of 11,520 eligible voters, 11,213 went to the polls and 7,291 chose the ISU with 3,454 voting for the CIO. The outcome was never in doubt, but close to *one third of the workforce still favored* the CIO; evidence of the lingering doubt and resentment many workers held toward the company and local elites.

How much of this oppositional vote came from workers living in Steubenville and surrounding towns is unclear. This may account for most of the dissent, as might the age and skills of workers (with younger unskilled and semiskilled workers favoring the CIO). It is also likely that a significant number of those voting for the ISU shared these sentiments but voted to end the struggle rather than for the company union. As one worker recalled, "We got a union, not the CIO, but we got a union and I guess it's better than nothing." They actually got two unions with the ISU representing production workers and the company's security forces organized under the Independent Guards Union. There was peace in Weirton, but was there justice?

A Bittersweet Compromise

Over the next thirty years the United Steelworkers of America made several efforts to organize in Weirton, but it was unable to mobilize the support and sentiments of workers that Weir and local elites had so forcefully secured. At the same time, what more could the AFL-CIO and USWA do for workers than the ISU? By this time, the CIO had surrendered its claim to worker control on the shopfloor in exchange for steady improvements in wages and benefits. Then, a 1973 USWA agreement to a no strike clause contractually enforced among other steelworkers what Weir had informally induced among his workers. And with the growth of "human relations" departments throughout American industry, the situation facing Weirton steelworkers was not much different than what other steelworkers faced.

On the other hand, Weirton workers certainly enjoyed better wages and benefits. Regular agreements between the ISU and company followed collective bargaining contracts between the USWA and steel firms, and the company continued its policy of slightly bettering the compensation packages negotiated industrywide. In 1951 an elaborate job classification and wage rate survey resulted in 1,200 jobs being classified under thirty-one wage rates. This created wage standards comparable to the industry and an internal "pecking order" of minor pay differentials that helped to isolate employees who were individually motivated toward higher pay.

Weirton workers also received low-cost health and hospitalization insurance, and had deductions waved when surplus funds allowed.[64] Vacation time was generous and because vacation pay was computed on the basis of a forty-eight-hour week rather than the average hours per week worked, vacation pay rates were substantially higher than other steel firms.[65] Overtime pay became a staple in many workweeks when the company and union agreed to what amounted to double time for most overtime hours, and even more for some holidays.[66] Meanwhile, union dues were minimal as the company paid the salaries of all union officials and ISU operating costs.

Gradually, workers here became the highest compensated steelworkers in the United States, perhaps even the world. Not only the CIO, but other businesses in town could not—or would not—compete with Weir and the company. Compared to "mill money" minimum wage jobs dominated Main Street (still the rule today) and other jobs were commonly considered temporary until an opening came in the mill. People worked on the side during layoffs, but they always came back—to "where the money was."

Typical of how people entered the mill and why they stayed there is reflected in my neighbor's experience:

> I got a job through my wife's dad, and he's still working as an hourly. When I saw my first paycheck I couldn't believe it. That's the reason I went to work in the mill. The money was so good. I mean it was three times anything I'd ever made before. I couldn't go anywhere else and make that.

Hiring practices followed family and friendship networks, and the company encouraged workers' children to apply when they were eligible for work. A summer job program was set up for college students whose families worked in the mill. As "temporary helpers" young people not only earned good money, they also got their first taste of mill work. During the 1960s and 1970s more young people began attending college, but many came back to the mill before, and after, they graduated—"for the money."

The company also recruited for promotions internally and it routinely celebrated the skills and performance of its workforce, in the company bulletin as well as on the shop floor. In 1955 a precursor to employee participation was established in the "Ideas for Improvement" program in which individual employees were eligible for cash awards for ideas "on which cost savings can be reasonably calculated."[67] In 1960 a similar program (Cost Improvement Program) was implemented for nonunion salaried employees. Weirton Steel produced a quality product, and its workers took pride in their sense of craftsmanship. It was expected that jobs and skills would be passed on to sons (and, more recently, daughters).

Weir paid a heavy price for the loyalty of his workforce and during Christmas 1955, he announced a $200 million investment program that would make the Weirton division of National Steel one of the most modern steel facilities in the country for years to come. In the community he continued to shower civic welfare. In 1951 Weir donated $144,500 to construct and furnish the infant section of the new hospital, and in 1958 Mary Weir funded construction of the current public library. During these boom years Weirton Steel employees boasted a prosperity and security that bettered the steadily rising living standards of most other industrial workers.

Workers too paid a cost, although one that most were willing to bear. Work was hard, and workers were driven. Management controlled the mill, and the company controlled the community. Other steelworkers considered Weirton a "scab town" because workers here prospered from contract standards they negotiated. More, Weirton Steel would continue working during USWA-CIO strikes, filling orders that would otherwise be left standing. By 1974 the cost began to rise as aging company elites, increasing global competition, and corporate reorganization undermined the social contract that company elites and workers had forged under paternalism.

The Legacy of Paternalism

Ironically, much of the demise of Weir's paternalistic order sprang from earlier decisions he made in creating it. Foremost was the creation of National Steel in 1929. When Weir was president and CEO of National Steel, and later from 1954 to 1964 when Thomas Millsop assumed those responsibilities, the Weirton steel division held a most "favorable status" position in the National Steel conglomerate. But with Weir's death in 1957 and Millsop's retirement in 1964 Weirton became just another steel mill, just another source of profit for an impersonal and distant corporate entity. After National Steel reorganized in 1964 it soon abandoned Weir and Millsop's approach to management and internal promotion by recruiting people who had no social or cultural links to the community or millworkers. Recent college graduates from outside town took up supervisory positions putting large numbers of experienced local people on layoff.

For many, it no longer seemed that the company valued their skills and experience; it appeared that their muscle and endurance were all the company wanted. During the 1970s workers complained of work speedups and deteriorating mill safety as National management pushed them to their limits. Jack Redline, who had once served as division president during the 1960s, was brought back and, as one worker recalled,

> started pushing like hell to break records. . . . I mean, we were putting out production records like you wouldn't believe. I

mean, every other day you'd see a new record broken. They
had hundreds and hundreds of extra bosses around, pushing
and pushing. And if you stepped out of line one little bit,
boom, they'd give you time off or fire you.[68]

Unlike production speedups that had punctuated the mill's history, this renewed pressure occurred in the context of a more competitive global economy. It also came at the direction of National
Steel officials who did not command the respect—the authority—
that Weir and Millsop had.

Further, with the gradual substitution of plastics and aluminum for tin-plated steel in many markets, National decided to
cut investments on capital improvements in the Weirton division
and began diversifying into what appeared to be more lucrative
markets, something nobody could have imagined Weir or Millsop
doing. But far worse in the eyes of residents and workers was how
National pillaged profits from the Weirton division to pay for their
escape from town and its people. National invested heavily in
Savings and Loan institutions during the 1970s and moved from
the fourth largest steel company to the fourth largest owner of
Savings and Loans. Then, as if to add insult to injury, National
moved into the aluminum market, more than tripling its interest
in the metal that was threatening Weirton's niche in the tin plate
market.[69] Even the company-backed ISU found reason to begin
accumulating a strike fund. As a reporter for the *Washington
Monthly* put it, "Both workers and townspeople of Weirton were
beginning to feel like unwanted stepchildren of the National Steel
conglomerate."[70]

This reference to the paternalistic history of Weirton speaks to
its legacy, but it may obscure the contradictions of that legacy.
When Thomas Millsop died in 1967, Weirton lost the most visible
and reassuring symbol of elite benevolence and authority. Everyone I spoke to during my research held fond memories of Millsop
and his wife, often recalling chance meetings in town or in the
mill that were always marked by warm greetings and pleasant
exchanges. On the other hand, when people could remember,
Weir was not viewed in this light. People thought of him more as
the stern, rugged businessman that started everything and presided over the most disturbing period of Weirton's history. His
memory was a history lesson for most post–World War II Weir-

tonians, not a personal remembrance. The almost mythical picture of Weir drawn in local historical accounts probably conflicted with the silent nods of family members that had lived through Weir's domain. His memory, at any rate, paled next to that held of the Millsops.

At one level, then, people may have been dependent on the company, but they certainly benefited from the public welfare of company elites. Was this bargain legitimate in their eyes, or simply tolerated in exchange for prosperity and security? What they settled for, in my view, was more of a sense of "localism" that centered people's loyalties, sentiments, and relationships in a defensive and selective way. A refrain I heard over and over again captures the distinction I am trying to make: "We may fight a lot amongst ourselves, but when our backs are against the wall we stick together." Social tensions, repressed or distorted inward, were hardly resolved in a way that fit the vision that Weir sought, nostalgic historical accounts depict, and critics lament.

For example, race and ethnic relations were a simmering nest of antagonisms with black workers taking the brunt of prejudice and discrimination, inside and outside the mill. Prosperity may have cooled many fires, but paternalism also mitigated racist sentiment by internalizing it, so to speak, into its own worldview. "We don't have problems with niggers here, like they do over in Steubenville," explained one longtime resident. "Everybody's taken care of here." National's discriminatory practices, however, inflamed grievances that many black residents held all along and led to charges being filed by black workers. In early 1982 a consent order was signed by the company that reserved up to 25 percent of apprenticeship slots to blacks and would raise the number of black foremen from 1 percent to 7 percent of these positions in the mill.[71]

Another misjudgment by National during the late 1970s highlights just how much paternalism shaped the lives of women and fused their worlds of work and home. It also reveals how much people had come to accept and rely on traditional mill policies. My neighbor, a clerical worker in the company, explained the "spinster story" this way:

Not many people realize this, but the company used to have this policy that if a woman got married she didn't need the job and she'd be let go so a position would open up, for a man. I don't know why they haven't filed a class action suit. They could, and they might be thinking about it. I don't know. But a lot of women didn't get married because of that, and there's a lot that did but never told the company. It was going on a lot in the '50s and '60s, but probably not as much now, but you never really know.

Well, we [clerical workers] never were represented by the [ISU] but in the late '70s, oh, 1977–78, National started pushing a little too hard. We felt we needed a union to represent us and the USWA came in and thought they'd try and get a foothold [in the mill] by organizing us. I was for the USWA, but if they didn't get in then at least the ISU. . . . [T]he USWA came in second by a couple of hundred votes. It was close. I wanted the USWA because I thought they'd be stronger, but the ISU was better than nothing.

And you know how it all happened? National wanted to cut lunch break for the clerical workers. They felt that an hour was too long and that half an hour for lunch was enough and they could get more production. *Well, this got people angry that otherwise could have cared less for a union and pretty much wouldn't have voted for one.* These were old ladies who'd worked there for years. There are a lot of older widows and spinsters working in clerical and they needed that hour for lunch to go home and care for sick relatives or elderly family members. It turned out that this group was the swing vote. So we got a union because of something like a lunch break [emphasis added].

It was not a "lunch break" that precipitated unionization, but rather a break with the moral economy that Weir and Millsop had fostered and to which workers and their families consented. National had overlooked (perhaps ignored) the link between work and home, mill and community, that paternalism nurtured and in the process began undermining the "moral economy" that grew alongside this order. This normative order was based primarily on the commitment and obligation that Weir and company elites demonstrated to the mill and community. National Steel could not (because of an increasingly competitive global economy) and would not (because of its relentless pursuit of higher rates of profit) uphold what Weir and Millsop had forged.

Finally, production speedups and extra effort in the mill had historically been *local* sacrifices that benefited *local* people. National and its stockholders were a distant, impersonal abstraction for most people in town, far too removed for the sacrifices workers used to make and were being asked to make now. Where families and family life were bonded to the company and millwork routines, National Steel was a giant bureaucracy. Its inflexibility and insensitivity had gradually eroded any sense of mutual obligation and responsibility that once existed between the company and its workforce. National's reign began to elicit some faint and sporadically expressed notions of economic justice that over the years had become deeply held assumptions. In a literal sense, ending the story by closing the mill was National's final and most direct breach of this moral economy. But its announcement in 1982 to significantly reduce operations opened another story, and it set in motion years of conflict that Weirton had not seen since the 1930s and 1940s.

Chapter Three

Forced Choices II: "Buy It or Lose It"

The mills lay silent month after month, under a sky that had never been so clean and blue before. After a while it was hard to remember what it had been like when they were working, the smoke and dust, the glare in the sky at night, the men streaming in and out. Going into the mill was like entering a deserted city. There was no movement, no sound.

Outside the walls idle men lingered like ghosts, staring at the quiet buildings, the vacant roadways, the weeds showing green against a pile of metal rusting in the yard.
—Thomas Bell, *Out of This Furnace*, 1941

I t came with no warning. Few people in Weirton suspected that as production records fell, so too might the sprawling mill that had supported a community and the surrounding region for almost seventy-five years. On a cold and cloudy March 2, 1982, workers and area residents opened their newspapers to a more chilling statement by National Steel chairman and president Howard M. Love: National would cease investment in its Weirton division. Suddenly, the mill that had started National

Steel was expendable; its 1 percent profit margin on $1 billion sales in 1981 was not enough for a parent company that was now moving away from its traditional emphasis on steel production. The announcement abruptly ended Weirton's favored status within the National Steel empire that E. T. Weir had created in 1929. Metaphorically, the stepparents were cutting loose their distant children. For many in town it was more like abandonment.

Before the day ended, one option would become the *only* option for workers and residents alike—buy the mill, or lose it and a way of life that had endured for generations. In his press statement Love proposed a worker buy-out (through an Employee Stock Ownership Plan) as a "preferable alternative" to either selling the plant to another buyer or downsizing to a finishing mill. National's proposal set in motion an ESOP agenda that local management and union leaders then earnestly pursued. But was it a "preferable" alternative? For whom? And how would a worker-owned mill be organized and operated?

Unexpectedly, a small group of millworkers and community activists vigorously contested the nondemocratic and secretive nature of the worker buy-out. Given the crushing economic pressures of the 1982 recession, a conservative political climate at the height of President Reagan's tenure, and legal institutions that favor property rights over human rights, such calls for industrial democracy faced daunting obstacles. And at the local level, a history of elite domination and paternalistic authority left most workers and townspeople without any collective memory of civic democracy or *any reason to think that democratic participation was even possible*. In this atmosphere the rhetoric and symbolism of "community" served to deflect, not rally, support for more rank-and-file involvement; traditions of localism, family, and mill nepotism cast such democratic impulses as threatening and unwise.

Local elites were poised to fill the empty shoes of past patriarchs, but they too faced forced choices within the boundaries and constraints imposed by financial institutions and ESOP consultants. As I show, even though paternalistic institutions reinforced the role of elites in negotiations with National, it was not in the dominant or symbolically meaningful posture of a Weir or Millsop but rather by default. Under these circumstances, rank-and-file workers followed civic and union leadership not because they necessarily agreed with them but in defense of their jobs, their mill, and their community. Ultimately the structural opening for an alternative to traditional forms of authority gave way to *bureaucratic* rather than democratic worker ownership.

Worker ownership, then, became a "forced choice" insofar as the ESOP that emerged dominated all other options as the only financial—and *moral*—option for workers. In saying this, however, let me emphasize I am not insisting that if only people had taken a (the right?) moral stand would democratic worker ownership have emerged. On the contrary, National's decision evoked bitter antagonisms and moral debates that were rooted in Weirton's paternalistic past and continued after ESOP. Indeed, these conflicts were central to the growing frustration toward ESOP years later that preceded a protracted struggle for control of the company in the 1990s.

But demands for more worker involvement during the negotiations were strongly resisted and alternative ESOP structures were systematically ignored or discredited by local mill officials, town elites, and ESOP consultants. Eventually, the terms of the ESOP were not chosen by workers, their families, and residents, as much as they were *accepted* amidst a thickening atmosphere of uncertainty, powerlessness, and fear. In the words of one worker, "What they're telling us is to either buy it or lose it. That's not a big choice, is it?"

The Context of Choice

Had National Steel not offered the mill to its employees—like many troubled steel companies including USX, LTV, and Bethlehem—other options facing workers would have been more compelling. Leaving Weirton to find other work in the area or in southern states like Texas, the Carolinas, or Florida was restricted to those with little chance of being recalled to the mill or those who never intended to work there long. But for most, selling a home in town was about as unlikely as buying an affordable one elsewhere. And leaving for a job also meant leaving a family behind, the thought of which evoked the bittersweet emotions of people's "sense of place." Choked with tears, one woman illustrates the love-hate ambivalence that I heard so often.

I used to say I never liked Weirton. If I get a chance to leave this dirty grimy town, I was going. Somewhere where the soot and the smoke and all that wasn't here. Then you go somewhere and come back and you say, "Oh, God, I'm home," you know? It's almost pathetic. And then when we really thought we're going to have to pack up and leave this home that I've complained about for years cause it wasn't all the things I wanted . . . when you think of closing the doors and packing up and leaving—oh, God, I'm gonna cry—but to leave it all, it just scares me to death. 'Cause I know I can't take my brothers and sisters with me, I can't take my mother, I can't take my grandmother. It's like this whole thing [the potential plant closing] has the ability to take your family away from you, to take your home—no matter how small it is—and you have no choice. And it scares me to death.[1]

People were scared, "terrified," some said. Leaving a town that had so systematically celebrated and enforced the virtues of family and community left many people torn between "holding on" to what they once had and "letting go" to start over again somewhere else. "The people don't want to leave here," insisted one worker. "They don't want to be bothered." As his wife nodded in agreement, she spoke solemnly of this collective attitude.

The majority of people in this valley have been born [here]— their fathers and that have lived here and they think this is the only place to live. That you have to make a living here and you have to survive here. They don't realize that there's a big world out there and they could go out and find other jobs. They're just programmed to do one thing and be in one place and live one type of life. That's all I can figure out.[2]

Starting new jobs with smaller companies in nearby Pittsburgh was an option that many workers I met had considered and tried. But even those who had found other work during layoffs were drawn back to the mill when a job opened. Attending college or technical schools was an option more young people in town had decided upon in recent years, but many still returned to the mill because "the money was better." And although a number of workers held side jobs "working under the table," such work was never a serious alternative to a *career* in the mill. In Weirton, nothing paid as much nor was as stable as working in the mill—until now.

Buying a Troubled Industry

In a way, selling the mill to employees was itself a "forced choice" for National, which sought to escape from what it viewed as a sinking ship in a sea of red ink. As I noted in the previous chapter, National began diversifying during the 1970s into Savings and Loan operations and aluminum manufacturing (Weirton's chief competitor in the beverage and food container market). And finding an outside buyer was also unlikely, given a troubled domestic steel industry, wage and benefit costs of an aging workforce, and necessary mill modernization.

More directly, the shutdown liabilities (for example, severance pay, unemployment benefits, operating losses, underabsorption of corporate overhead) and pension obligations National would assume under a plant closing or steady downsizing made these options exorbitantly costly. Estimates varied, but National faced between $420 million and $770 million in shutdown costs and unfunded pension liabilities.[3] On the other hand, it stood to make a windfall by selling the mill to the workforce and maintaining a supplier relationship with the newly formed company. Clearly, then, National's financial interests strongly favored a worker buy-out.

As the 1982 recession deepened Weirton Steel was holding its own, but barely. Historically, the company had been a leading producer of tin products, primarily for the container industry. During the 1970s half of the mill's output was in tin products with remaining production comprised of assorted sheet and strip products. But aluminum and plastics steadily moved into the container market during this period, reducing the size of the tin market. Company sales suffered, but not as much as other firms, which many attributed to its highly regarded quality and service record. While the recession reduced industry operations to 40 percent of capacity, Weirton appeared to be better off than most judging by the size of its active workforce relative to other firms. Industry observers also considered the plant as one of the most technologically advanced in the domestic steel industry. It housed two of the largest basic oxygen furnaces in the country and one of the largest and most sophisticated continuous casters in the industry.[4]

On the other hand, parts of the mill were antiquated or operating poorly. The coking operations that produce the fuel necessary to make steel were practically useless due to faulty construction and improper operating procedures. At an estimated cost of between $125 million and $200 million for renovation, this was undoubtedly a serious consideration in National's desire to sell the mill. Even with functional coke batteries the plant still faced Environmental Protection Agency (EPA) deadlines on other parts of its operations. Federal lenience won the plant only a few years reprieve before EPA-mandated investments would be required for the blast and basic oxygen furnaces.[5]

By all accounts, the impact of a downsized mill would be devastating for the town, surrounding region, and the entire state of West Virginia. Not only was Weirton Steel the town's dominant industry and employer, it was also the largest employer and taxpayer in the state of West Virginia. By March 1982 the company's workforce numbered about 11,500, though no more than 8,500 were employed due to layoffs the previous few years. Reducing the mill to a finishing operation would mean fewer than 2,000 jobs where once up to 14,000 had received paychecks. More, the "ripple effect" on local businesses and suppliers was tragically vivid to anyone familiar with Youngstown or metropolitan Pittsburgh. Almost half of the workforce lived outside of Weirton and neighboring communities in Ohio and Pennsylvania faced an equally harsh prospect.[6]

Likewise, losing the tax base that Weirton Steel had provided would further undermine municipal services in this, and other, aging industrial towns throughout the Ohio Valley. "It would practically kill this valley if the mill shut down," said Adam Dalessio, mayor of Follansbee, a small town south of Weirton. "I hope they can do something up there. If they don't, Weirton's dead."[7] The mill was so dominant that many people could not imagine life without it. As Weirton's mayor put it:

Without Weirton Steel there is no Weirton. Weirton Steel is all our lives and our children and grandchildren. It was here before I was born and I hope it will be here many years from now.[8]

One Side of Paternalism's Legacy

Lacking any strong, locally respected leaders like E. T. Weir or Thomas Millsop one might expect a general sense of despair following National's announcement. Studies of communities that have faced severe economic decline or sudden industrial or natural disasters have routinely documented such normlessness and isolation among residents.[9] Indeed, local businessman Eli Dragisich described the shock of workers and residents as "sheer panic."

> People want to know if they will lose their homes or their jobs. If we pull together and avoid irrational, emotional, and reactionary thinking, the situation may prove beneficial in the long run. Unless the people pull together now, the situation could have tremendously negative effects.[10]

But on the same day of National's announcement, Weirton division President Jack G. Redline issued a statement supporting worker ownership. Saying "it is vital that we do this," Redline evoked the collectivist "we" but he represented a much smaller group.[11] Local management and the ISU executive committee had begun discussions and by March 4 the Joint Study Committee (JSC) was formed with Redline heading a management group and President Richard Arrango heading the ISU.[12] Without any public forum or union meeting to inform workers and discuss their actions, the JSC assumed the role of "official" representative of workers in negotiations with National towards the formation of a new worker-owned company.

Immediately, local merchants, and local and state politicians voiced their support for an ESOP. West Virginia Governor Jay Rockefeller visited Weirton and rallied with local officials around the idea of saving the mill. Local banks pledged their support for any possible worker buy-out and Mayor Donald Mentzer said the city administration would do "everything we can to assist Weirton Steel."[13] Community leaders formed a "Share Our New Beginnings" Committee to raise money to help pay for the necessary feasibility studies, lawyers, and consultants. Women's clubs hung yellow ribbons throughout town, and eventually the town raised almost $800,000 with the largest contribution of $20,000 coming from the Starvaggi Company (the largest local employer next to the mill). The Weirton

Chamber of Commerce sponsored a "We Can Do It" campaign and in less than a month solicited $1,800 for a feasibility study. Governor Rockefeller also contributed $125,000 from the state treasury to the ESOP effort.[14] Finally, area media reinforced the ESOP option by quoting leading experts such as Corey Rosen of the National Center for Employee Ownership, and New Jersey attorney and ESOP consultant Alan V. Lowenstein as supporting ESOPs in general, as well as one in Weirton. Soon, media reports of optimism and defiance followed the public despair of a few days earlier.

Newspapers outside of the Weirton-Steubenville area were far more critical of National Steel and skeptical of its ESOP proposal. In a March 8, 1982 editorial the *Pittsburgh Post-Gazette* commented, "We would like to be supportive but, frankly, somehow we cannot help but be disturbed by some of the implications of the Weirton proposal."

> Is a corporation's real commitment only to maximization of profits? What is its responsibility to its employees, to the communities in which it has plants and to the nation as a whole, for whose defense establishment and security steel is so vital a part?[15]

The *Pittsburgh Press* was similarly skeptical. "National's sales pitch smacks more of a grand gesture than a viable alternative to more employee layoffs or, even worse, eventual abandonment of the Weirton plant."[16]

Nor was everyone in town as sanguine about National's proposal. Joe Mayernick, a local businessman and Weirton Steel stockholder, announced plans to lead a proxy fight against National Steel's board of directors.

> They've got the money [to modernize the plant]. They just don't want to put it into steel. They'd rather put it elsewhere. I question, as a stockholder, why Weirton Steel management did not explore the possibility of a proxy fight in order to keep Weirton Steel affiliated with National Steel.[17]

Mayernick did not rule out an ESOP, but he felt "it's not fair to the valley to say it's close or buy the plant. This [proxy fight] is an option that should be considered."[18]

But if a stockholder proxy was briefly considered—by Mayernick, if few others—it was never seriously explored or supported. For some in town, National Steel and division President Redline deserved gratitude, not a proxy fight. In a letter to the editor of the *Steubenville Herald-Star* one worker wrote:

> I'm sorry, Mr. Mayernick, but I cannot agree with you. . . . National has done us a favor by letting us stand alone. . . . I firmly believe that we owe men like Jack Redline and George Stinson our deepest respect and gratitude, for I suspect that it was through their efforts that National even offered us the opportunity [to buy the plant]. The entire upper Ohio Valley has a stake in Weirton Steel. We cannot afford to let it die.[19]

Indeed, the prospect of a worker-owned mill held far too much appeal to be cast aside so easily. The idea of buying the plant awakened collective sentiments that National had systematically ignored during the 1970s and early 1980s. Worker ownership resonated with the community and family ethos that paternalism had cultivated so forcefully decades before. Perhaps, it seemed to many, the destiny of Weirton would again be in the hands of local people working for themselves and not some distant and impersonal corporate bureaucracy.

From one perspective this was the positive legacy of a company town. Most accounts of the prospective ESOP—from news journalists to academics—seemed to agree that paternalism left a "social fabric" conducive to the success of worker ownership because it would better enable, and ennoble, the sacrifices, commitments, and difficult relationship between labor and management that lay ahead. Though popular, this interpretation is also misleading for it overlooks the social divisions and class-generated antagonisms in town. As the previous chapter showed, Weirton was born of industrial conflict and matured through bitter struggles over the loyalties of townspeople. If social relations were indeed as "close-knit" as this perspective holds, they were more specific to class and family position rather than characteristic of the community as a whole.

Instead, paternalism left local institutions that more immediately supported alliances *among elites* rather than workers and residents in general. As Thad Radzialowski has argued, the "strong local orientation" of executive management on the JSC may have won a last reprieve for the mill.

> The managers were as upset as the workers by National's decision [to divest Weirton] and the previous years of neglect. The management representatives on the Joint Study Committee spoke for a young and aggressive group of employees, the majority of whom had risen from the ranks and/ or were the sons of Weirton workers. The speedups, the break neck driving of the workers and the production records during the late seventies and early eighties had, according to one former management employee, represented the attempt by the local managers to show the parent company that Weirton Steel could still be competitive and should be saved. The decision to stay and fight rather than move on was, in large measure, the result of the overwhelmingly local origin of the management. The ESOP offered this group a new opportunity to show that they could make Weirton Steel a going concern.[20]

This "local orientation" that Radzialowski refers to captures a key aspect of paternalism here: its capacity to embrace class divisions within collective sentiments of community responsibility and obligation. Local elites vigorously supported ESOP while defending the sacrifices it might entail, and their positions in the mill and community favored them as the legitimate representatives of "the community." But if local management and town elites were visibly concerned about saving the mill, it is still unclear how much *they acted* from a *different* local orientation than workers.[21]

In their zeal to rise to the occasion the JSC excluded those workers upon whose future they were bidding. The "strong local orientation" of Weirton's working class, though cut from the same cloth, was not the same as management's. Not surprisingly, local officials on the JSC acted more like "managers" than citizens in negotiations with National. Likewise, ISU leadership followed management's lead as they had in the past. In *Friendly Takeover* (1995), James B. Lieber argues that "contrary to popular belief, management and the union at Weirton were not in bed together."[22] But if antagonism between the ISU and local management had grown since the 1970s, there were few signs that their 'marriage' of thirty years had ended. Indeed, during the negotiations there was persuasive evidence of a reconciliation. Together, they pursued an ESOP agenda that narrowed, and ultimately eroded, the prospects for democratic worker ownership.

The "Administrative" ESOP Agenda

By early April the JSC began hiring several New York–based consulting firms to assist in the ESOP negotiations. McKinsey and Company, Inc., which had done recent studies on the European steel industry, was hired to do a market and feasibility study. The JSC agreed to National's recommendation of Alan Lowenstein, a New York lawyer who had negotiated the ESOP at GM's Hyatt-Clark bearing plant in Clark, New Jersey, to negotiate the ESOP transaction with National. He was joined by Jack Curtis, a San Francisco lawyer who had served with the U.S. Senate Committee on Finance and had contributed to various ESOP laws.[23] For legal issues the JSC hired the law firm of Willkie, Farr and Gallagher, and consultation on pension valuation and options was provided by the firm of Towers, Perrin, Forster and Crosby.[24] Finally, the investment banking firm of Lazard Freres, which had played a key role in the New York bailout during the 1970s, was retained to help the new Weirton Steel finance the buy-out.[25]

The general outlook of these consultants defined the ESOP agenda that the JSC adopted during negotiations and that dominated public debate over the nature of worker ownership. This liberal "administrative" perspective is perhaps best reflected in the presence of Felix Rohatyn on the Lazard Freres team. Rohatyn, well known for his role in averting New York City's bankruptcy, has also gained attention for his views supporting an industrial policy based on a "tripartite economic development board" composed of representatives from business, labor, and government. His vision of reversing America's decline in a competitive international economy is based on the idea of a "partnership" between various sectors of society that would be facilitated by government councils and committees.

This "partnership," however, is primarily a bureaucratic model that does not speak to or engage popular democratic practices in industrial reorganization. As Robert Bellah and his coauthors argue in *Habits of the Heart* (1996), this approach does not bode well for labor or a more democratic reorganization of our political economy because it

> depends heavily on the administrative structure of government, rather than on popular representation, and would thus bring technical and managerial experts to increased prominence.[26]

Indeed, from the outset the JSC and its Wall Street consultants assumed an administrative posture toward the negotiations that emphasized the financial logistics of the transaction over and above the form and structure of the ESOP. Their major concern was "Will an ESOP work?" rather than "What type of ESOP do we want?" As the negotiations unfolded this approach excluded more democratic structures from serious public debate by trivializing their efficacy and denouncing such proposals as a threat to a successful buyout. The JSC increasingly evoked an ideology of "only the experts can save our community" to discredit its opponents and defend its role as the legitimate and "prudent" representative of mill employees and residents.

Again, James B. Lieber argues that there was far more conflict and diversity of opinion among the JSC and its consultants about how best to pursue an ESOP at Weirton. He notes, for example, conflicts between the philosophies of Alan Lowenstein (favoring a traditionally managed company) and Jack Curtis (who leaned more toward labor) that often erupted into acrimonious sniping, occasionally in public. Or the arrival of Harvey Sperry of Willkie Farr & Gallagher that fostered Jack Redline's exit. Or the tug of war within the ISU and between more militant and outspoken ISU officials and their legal consul David Robertson on the JSC.[27]

My argument is not that the ESOP agenda was a conspiracy of like-minded scoundrels, for it is clear that the *individuals* involved were neither demons nor saints. And though Lieber's account suggests many "mini"-conspiracies, I see the ESOP agenda as a cultural orientation towards industrial and economic reform that directed *collective* action, irrespective of personal intent or desire, toward a bureaucratic version of employee ownership that emphasizes technical expertise and equity ownership above democratic membership as the guiding organizational principles. Though Rohatyn may be considered a "friend of labor" by some, I am not persuaded that his solution is because it assumes that labor (or even communities and local governments for that matter) can be an equal partner with capital. This may have been more likely during the 1950s when labor was organized and stronger, but it is not now. Nor, do I think, an equal partnership between business, labor, and community is likely in the near future. Until power is also equally shared, too many interests will be ignored and too many voices silenced.

The sale price for the mill was as yet undetermined, but its book value was $370 million. Estimates of its market value varied between $150 and $200 million with future capital needs edging upwards of $1 billion over 10 years.[28] The final price would depend upon negotiations, the fate of a sizable pension plan, and any potential National supply contracts. Still, two things were clear to all involved; any new company would have to invest heavily to modernize the plant, and workers would have to make some form of concessions. With $560,000 initially budgeted to fund the consultants, everyone anxiously awaited the results of McKinsey and Company's three-month feasibility study. It was a study that would raise more controversy than it settled.

Divided Loyalties

Within weeks hourly workers appeared more divided and less enthusiastic in supporting an ESOP than local media earlier suggested. Instead, there was a good deal of skepticism and doubt. Was this a trick by National to escape shutdown costs? What about pensions? Can National be trusted after the last ten years? These were just a few of the questions asked by a rank-and-file that did not know who to trust. The first signs of their ambivalence revealed the fragile nature of the ISU's legitimacy at the intersection of paternalism and class in Weirton.

For example, after so fervently supporting an ESOP, union leadership was embarrassed when less than 10 percent of its membership contributed to fundraising drives for a feasibility study.[29] This was uncustomary for workers who historically had been forced to donate to charities and community projects, but it also indicated how uncoerced voluntarism buckled under economic hardship and that many workers may have felt that "someone better off" should chip in.

Then, on March 23 and 24, the ISU held its first public meetings at St. John's Arena in Steubenville to inform workers of the proposed buy-out. When asked to vote for a bylaw change that would release $500,000 from the union's strike fund for the study, less than half of the ISU's 7,000 working members rejected the measure, 1,550 to 1,406. A disappointed ISU president Arrango felt that "the 4,000 people who didn't vote thought it would pass. I think they would have voted in favor of it." He then added:

> It's all up to the members. If they want a job, they'll have to
> pay for it one way or another. We'll just have to get back to
> the problem right away, because the problem still exists.[30]

But the "problem" Arrango saw paled compared to the lack of trust between the union and its membership. While it was becoming commonplace in America for union leaders to tell their members, "If they want a job, they'll have to pay," the ISU leadership underestimated its members' sentiments and fears. The ballot asked members to pass two amendments with a single vote, one allowing use of $500,000 in strike funds for a feasibility study and the other reallocating $6 of a member's $10 monthly dues from the strike fund into general operating expenses (the union faced a large operating deficit).[31] If this procedural tactic mirrored congressional antics in passing legislation, it also rekindled worker distrust and skepticism toward ISU leadership.

According to the union's own analysis, members saw the need to raise funds for the feasibility study, though many opposed withdrawing money from the union's $1.6 million strike fund. As I noted in the previous chapter, this fund began to grow for the first time during the 1970s when National began its shopfloor assault on the workforce. Under the circumstances, it is not surprising that members were wary of reducing this fund by one third. The ISU also admitted that there was opposition to reallocating dues from the strike fund into the general operations coffers. Workers may have agreed that a feasibility study was necessary, but rebuilding the strike fund came before any administrative and consultant costs. At this point, the rank-and-file hardly viewed themselves as "partners" in the ESOP negotiations and they insisted on defending what remained of their collective security as a class. Workers also evoked paternalistic custom by insisting that future ISU meetings to discuss ESOP issues be held on company time rather than their own, as had been policy under Weir and Millsop.

Another vote was set for May 21, but the "misunderstanding" that a *Steubenville Herald-Star* editorial claimed was not political, was indeed the first sign that ISU leadership was more closely aligned, in perspective and action, with management on the JSC than with its membership. In this case, the unilateral decision making that typified ISU-management control over workers under paternalism raised an unexpected objection. Prior to the second vote Arrango admitted,

> We did what we thought was right the last time, *but we talked to the guys in the mill and this is the way they wanted it*. The big thing the last time was that the guys wanted to be able to vote for each issue [separately]. They felt we were trying to pull something over on them [emphasis added].[32]

The revised amendments established a one-year time limit during which all of the monthly dues collected would go into the general fund. Given that it was not part of the first ballot, this time limit on dues reallocation was surely as important to workers as providing them separate votes. Rank-and-file concerns, however, did not translate into a significant collective challenge to the ESOP agenda, nor to the dominant role of the JSC. Jim Zarello, a UAW union leader who had been active in an ESOP at Hyatt-Clark a few years earlier, was brought in to speak to union members. "I got a very strong impression," he recalled, "that there was minimal [employee] involvement in the buy-out process."[33] In his view, local politicians and the business community were much more involved in efforts to save the mill, not the workers.

An Unexpected Challenge

With the JSC's swift formation and its recruitment of ESOP consultants, it appeared that matters would be taken care of like they always had—by mill officials and town elites. But following

National's announcement a small group of millworkers arose in dissent and the Weirton Steel Rank-and-File Committee (RFC) began its own series of formal meetings with workers. The group's initial organizing grew out of the Committee for Justice, a poverty law and advocacy organization located across the river in Steubenville, Ohio. The Committee for Justice shared its facilities with the RFC, which proved to be a supportive environment, but this isolated the RFC from the community of Weirton and as the negotiations evolved, geographical distance became politically and symbolically distant as well.

One of the RFC's most articulate and experienced leaders was Tony Gilliam, a twelve-year veteran of the plant and one of its few black workers. Gilliam had been a prominent civil rights figure in Steubenville, and in 1977 he was appointed to the mayor's Human Relations Commission to investigate citizen complaints about police brutality.[34] Steve Bauman, who had worked with Gilliam for about nine years in the mill's basic oxygen furnace but was currently laid off, joined him as co-chairperson of the RFC.[35] Assisting the group were Steve Paesani, laid off from nearby Wheeling-Pittsburgh Steel and active in an unemployment committee there, and John Lichtenstein, a graduate student in business administration at Yale whom the RFC asked to evaluate the feasibility of an ESOP mill. Finally, the RFC recruited the services of Staughton Lynd, a political activist, writer, and, at the time, senior attorney for Northeast Ohio Legal Services in Youngstown, Ohio. With assistance from Legal Services lawyers from Steubenville and documentary coverage from two New York filmmakers, the RFC emerged early as a challenge that nobody expected.[36]

The RFC held their first public meeting on March 22, three weeks after National's announcement to disinvest and one day before the ISU informed workers about plans to fund the feasibility study from the union's strike fund. Reverend Robert Hutton, coordinator for Urban Mission Ministries in Steubenville, had reserved the Columbia Hall in Weirton and over two hundred workers, their wives, and town residents attended.[37] For RFC members, neither information nor any real rank-and-file participation would come about under the present negotiating conditions. They felt the JSC was not representing workers' interests, but management's, and they doubted the ISU's ability to adequately represent workers in any ESOP transaction. Staughton Lynd also argued that the RFC was legally entitled to represent the rank-and-file because the ISU represented them in the former Weirton division under National, but they were not the exclusive bargaining agent for workers in a possible new company.[38]

During the meeting workers frequently stood to share their doubts about National's intentions and their support for more worker involvement. But as the evening progressed several obstacles facing the RFC organizers became clearer, and they soon found themselves on the defensive. Even if the RFC had a legal right to represent the rank-and-file, their most difficult but important task would be gaining the trust and support of workers who for decades had been coerced, intimidated, even bribed into submission by company and union. If the crowded hall was encouraging, this was precisely where the RFC may have been overly optimistic and least effective. Looking back, one member recalled to me:

> Yes, we didn't get the community support we needed, that's certain. We didn't get into the community like we should have. That [first mass] meeting gave a false impression, people were there out of curiosity as much as sympathy with our goals. With all the cameras there—that was the largest meeting we ever had.[39]

The RFC's critical tasks of forging community alliances and establishing their claim as legitimate "representatives" were reminiscent of the struggle over union representation during the 1930s and 1940s. This time, however, there were no dominant elites *to stand against* nor the absence of a union *to stand for*, as during the reign of Weir and Millsop. It was no surprise, then, when people asked, "Just who are these RFC folks? And don't we already have a union?"

By now, the atmosphere in Columbia Hall was thick with uncertainty and frustration. There were many divisions in the workforce in terms of age and seniority, skilled and unskilled, black and white, employed and laid off. But these divisions only magnified the major controversy over "who was representing who." Tony Gilliam tried to reassure the audience as he spoke of overcoming the patronizing history of labor-management relations in the mill.

> **Union supporter:**   We have an ESOP committee already. Why is this one . . . don't get me wrong. I can't understand why we're having a meeting tonight.

> **Tony Gilliam:**   Again, as I said earlier, we are not attempting to usurp anybody else's responsibility or authority. I think it's time that we start attempting to take charge of our own lives. I'm talking about steelworkers, OK? I think too many times in the past it has been assumed that we cannot understand things, we're not permitted to think for ourselves, things are basically rammed down our throat. This gives us an opportunity to do some research on our own to understand things. Not to have somebody bring us an outline of four or five points and say "this explains it to you." We have an opportunity to do something on our own.[40]

Gilliam tried to balance the RFC's relationship with the ISU, but despite its compromising history with the company, the union held the tenuous allegiance of most workers—it was *all* they had at this point. Even if ISU leadership had raised the ire and doubt of members over the years, it was risky to "jump ship" now.

> **Union supporter:**   You can sign off anytime you want to sign off. I don't know who you represent or where you're coming from. But I'm going to tell you something. You have a union or do you have a union?

> **Tony Gilliam:**   We have a union. It represents us in terms of bargaining for the policies within the mill, for our working conditions, things of that nature. We do not have a union to represent us in terms of business deals. We're talking about business deals with our money, coming out of our pockets. Business deals that we did not elect union officials to represent us [in]. Again, we are not picking on the union or management or anybody else. We're talking about bringing steelworkers together for the purpose of understanding things for ourselves.[41]

Such diplomacy could not, however, dissuade those who felt they were already represented by the ISU. Though skeptical of the ISU's autonomy within the JSC, workers were more so of a small group that nobody knew anything about and who seemed to be raising more dust than settling it.

The RFC also faced a tradition of localism that undermined its appeals for community support. While the RFC consisted primarily of area residents and millworkers, paternalism had rendered people wary of "outsiders" and this lowered their standing in the eyes of many workers. As one skeptical worker wondered, the track record of these outsiders was not reassuring either.

> **Worker:** I think that us going against them and not joining together forming one major rank-and-file is a big mistake. . . . Mr. Mann [speaker for the RFC], you're from Youngstown Sheet and Tube Briar Hills works. . . . I think they shut down, did they not?
>
> **Ed Mann:** Yes.
>
> **Worker:** You fought really hard down there. Maybe you should have stuck together, you'd have fought a lot harder. And also Mr. Lynd, you represented Youngstown in the negotiations?
>
> **Staughton Lynd:** Yes.
>
> **Worker:** They got shutdown?
>
> **Staughton Lynd:** Yes they did.
>
> **Worker** (smiling): Thank you. (*Scattered applause*)[42]

The RFC faced structural barriers at the local level (paternalistic institutions and customs) and national level (the power of lending institutions) that hardly encouraged democratic organizing in Weirton. At no time did they publicly oppose a worker buyout, but they did question National's motive to "let us buy the mill." And though committed to a democratic ESOP and union, their primary concern was generating information and debate about any potential ESOP.[43] As workers left the hall shaking their heads, the RFC's first public meeting ended, but not its challenge.

Changes in ISU Leadership

While awaiting the completion of the feasibility study, the RFC sought a more visible role in the ESOP negotiations. But despite having their letters to the editor printed in area newspapers, local media were clearly disparaging of RFC efforts. According to a March 25 editorial in the *Steubenville Herald-Star*, the RFC was "a group that has the potential to throw a monkey wrench into the sensitive work" of negotiations with National Steel.[44] More, the RFC had "implanted a measure of fear into the average worker . . . a fear of placing trust in the company management and union leadership." The editorial ended with an observation that, unwittingly and unintended, aptly dismissed the RFC's challenge against a noble history of paternalism.

> And it's unlikely that any 25-member committee would ever
> have the ability to tear down what has been 77 years in
> building, that unique spirit that can and will make a success
> out of the very real crisis the company now faces.[45]

By now it was unlikely the RFC would tear down paternalism, which had been gradually eroded by National during the 1970s. Indeed, their very presence signaled a structural opening paternalism had sealed for thirty years.

The "unique spirit" noted above was also being tested from other corners with an upcoming election for ISU president and shop stewards slated in three months. The lack of trust evidenced by the rank-and-file's earlier snub of Arrango was confirmed when his leadership was challenged by ten candidates. His two most formidable opponents were Walter Bish, a former conductor on the mill's railroad who had served as a union steward for six years, the last three on the ISU's executive committee, and Mike Hrabovsky, a crane man in the blooming mill and a more militant shop steward. Hrabovsky was skeptical of National's intent and management's role on the JSC whereas Bish was far more supportive of both local management and an ESOP. Neither candidate considered Arrango capable of leading the union through the negotiations.

On June 22, 1982, Arrango barely edged out Bish, 1,611 to 1,147 respectively, with Hrabovsky barely finishing third with

536 votes. But without a majority of votes, Arrango faced a runoff with Bish scheduled three days later, which he lost, 1,641 to 2,715. Likewise, practically the entire ISU leadership was replaced as sixteen of eighteen committee members lost their seats, including Hrabovsky who also lost a bid for the Steel Works One post.[46] The election clearly signaled rank-and-file disenchantment with their representatives, but did it also indicate their enthusiastic support of an ESOP? As James B. Lieber argues,

> In fact, it was in the average hourly's interest to pick someone clearly in favor of an ESOP in order to preserve jobs, who was bright enough to master financial complexities, and articulate enough to communicate them to the workforce.[47]

I agree that protecting jobs was most important to workers and that they felt Bish might deliver. And their rejection of Hrabovsky (as too militant) and Arrango (as incapable) might also be considered clear evidence of pro-ESOP support. But I am far more skeptical of Bish's commitment to preserving jobs and his role in the negotiations. For instance, the ISU refused to allow laid-off workers a vote in the election and they most likely would have favored an ESOP (and Bish) if it meant a chance to be recalled. According to ISU bylaws, laid-off workers with recall rights were ineligible to vote in union elections.[48] The RFC joined John Gregory in his request for a change in this policy and another election. When the ISU leadership rejected them, the RFC filed a complaint with the U.S. Department of Labor.[49]

Also, as Lieber himself notes, the company vocally supported Bish over Arrango, despite the National Labor Relations Act forbidding management interference in union elections. "Weirton management liked Bish," he writes, then quoting company president Jack Redline, "We did what we could to get Bish elected. Wherever we went we had a good word to say about Bish."[50]

Finally, wanting to save jobs (whether or not this *alone* was in workers' interests) is not the same as supporting an ESOP nobody knew anything about. The rank-and-file wanted to save jobs and ESOP appeared to be the only way, but they also wanted better representation in the negotiations. If Bish's election and the ISU leadership turnover were signs of pro-ESOP sentiments, they were also a collective rank-and-file call for more information and *protection as a class.* Bish may have appeared to represent these concerns at the time, but appearances are often misleading as workers learned during his first and only term as ISU president.

Narrowing the Terms of Debate

On July 26, 1982, McKinsey announced the results of its anxiously awaited feasibility study. Their findings generally supported the viability of a worker-owned steel firm on the basis of "conservatively" estimated market and sales projections and a $1 billion capital improvement program over the next ten years. But the study also raised much controversy over recommendations dealing with three basic issues: employment levels, wage and benefit concessions (including the status of current pension obligations), and stock distribution and employee voting rights. McKinsey recommended:

1. The number of salaried employees be reduced "immediately" and that total employment be cut to approximately 7000 by the late 1980s.

2. All employees [labor and management] would have to take a permanent 20 percent reduction in wages, salaries, incentives, and benefits *in addition to* a 12 percent reduction for "no more than 4 years" to build an equity base so the new company could obtain short-term financing for capital improvements. [No decision had been made about National's pension obligations under an ESOP.]

3. Workers should decide "as individuals" whether or not they wanted to be employees of the new company—there would be no vote on the proposed ESOP, or on the 32 percent reduction in compensation.[51]

Saving jobs was perhaps the most important concern of rank-and-file workers, but just how many and whose? Workers bristled at the high management-labor ratio in the mill (estimated at 2 or 3 to 1) and they were especially antagonistic toward National management. Workers wanted them out under a new company before any hourly layoffs.

And how much would these jobs cost? Capital improvements were clearly necessary, but how much could workers *afford* to save the mill and their jobs? Was a concession of practically one third the value of their wages and benefits reasonable? And on what basis? The data and calculations for what came to be known as the "32 percent solution" were contained in a Confidential Appendix that McKinsey refused to release because of concern that its disclosure would undermine Weirton's competitive position with other companies. A pension analysis was also pending, so workers still did not know the status of their pensions nor who would be responsible for funding them in any new ESOP company.

More importantly, it remained unclear how stock would be allocated or how voting rights would be exercised under the proposed ESOP. Stock and voting issues encompassed employment and compensation levels insofar as they determined how those questions were decided. But the issue of control was never as prominent in public debates as was the issue of wage and benefit concessions. Nor did it evoke the passion and consternation that typified discussions about National management or saving jobs.

The McKinsey study strongly reaffirmed the ESOP agenda that was dramatized during an ISU informational meeting two weeks earlier on July 14. The tension-filled meeting more closely resembled a title-fight between competing visions of worker ownership. In one corner stood the highly favored administrative approach to worker ownership, in the other corner stood the underdog democratic challenge. ISU lawyer David Robertson articulated the ESOP agenda when he argued that it was "an individual choice" to join the new company or not.

Pension rights and whether to join the new company are decisions that nobody can vote on and take a majority vote on. A simple majority cannot work. We'll have better information later, but there won't be a vote to force people into an ESOP company. Each one of you will have to sit down and decide what you want [and] whether you should move on or get out. Collectively we have no right to make these decisions for those people.[52]

Later during the meeting workers in the audience questioned whether the JSC and National management were "in bed" proposing an ESOP that benefited National but not Weirton Steel employees. One heated exchange left no doubt of the animosity and distrust that characterized labor-management relations in the mill. Standing with arms folded across his chest and looking up incredulously toward the stolid panel of ISU leadership and New York consultants, a worker addressed Ron Bancroft of the McKinsey feasibility study team:

> **Worker:**   National Steel will not get to read the feasibility study? Is that correct? Is Mr. Redline on the Joint Committee? Mr. Redline is employed by National Steel. What if Mr. Love [National president] asks Mr. Redline what's in the report?
>
> **Bancroft:**   If he does that you have to question your choice in your president.
>
> **Worker:**   I'll bet three months wages that he'll give them that report.
>
> **Bancroft:**   I can't comment on that, but there is an element of trust . . .
>
> **Worker** (angrily):   We don't trust management! We've taken the shaft for the last 25 years!
>
> **Bancroft:**   I understand, but if it's [ESOP] going to work, both sides have to bend and you need some trust. If not, it's not going to work.[53]

This worker was not dissuaded, nor did he accept the "business as usual" outlook that consultants and the JSC had adopted. For ESOP proponents, "trust" has become the buzzword for what they see as the normative foundation for a successful ESOP company. But trust requires the proper material conditions and at least a vague anticipation among those involved that relations engender some degree of reciprocity. For over a decade National policies had undermined the contested trust that workers had settled upon under paternalism. As this speaker and his fellow millworkers stood defiantly at the microphone, alternatives to a corporately endorsed ESOP agenda were systematically rejected as unfeasible and ill-conceived, if not unimaginable.

> **Worker:**   You're talking about employees buying the company. Now there is a thirty to seventy percent ratio between employees punching the time clock and management. Then, if this thing is going to work, why can't we, the employees, buy the company and hire the management? It's our company. Management is National Steel.[54]

As Bancroft cautioned against losing valuable executive and sales experience under such an arrangement, Jack Curtis, a consultant on ESOP design, interjected with what has become the corporate substitute for industrial democracy: "employee participation."

> We've put 150 ESOPs around the country. The most critical factor is that you participate. Most companies in ESOPs are smaller companies. If you don't have 100 percent participation, you're not going to maximize the benefits.[55]

At this point, "employee participation" and "worker ownership" were still vague to most workers. But when their questions gradually hinted at a vision of a more democratic ESOP, ISU officials and consultants redefined worker-control issues in terms that dismissed workplace democracy while reaffirming the value and necessity of a conventional organizational hierarchy between labor, management, and executives. Harvey Sperry, of the law firm Willkie, Farr & Gallagher, reminded the skeptical audience of their "proper" role in any new company, even going so far as to define for workers what "they wanted" in such a company:

> **Worker:**   How will profits be distributed?
>
> **Sperry:**   It's a management decision. Let's assume the company makes a lot of money and wants to distribute to its shareholders—
>
> **Worker:**   Are we going to be equal partners? Will we be considered self-employed?

Sperry: Let's clarify the term ownership. You can't confuse ownership and being an employee. At home, a shareholder. At work an employee. Management's role is to manage and that's what the owners of the company want. You want management to do the best they can and you'll be working to make the company a success.[56]

As if to summarize the dominant ESOP ideology and its bureaucratic orientation, Sperry's "clarification" epitomized the trajectory of ESOP since March 2. The slogan "workers by day, owners by night" simply, but accurately, expresses an agenda that separates issues of control from issues of equity. As political discourse, it reveals how the language of industrial reform accommodates and neutralizes competing visions of industrial democracy and worker ownership.

Symbolically, the phrase disarms the oppositional threat posed by any sympathies toward more radical restructuring of industrial organization under the rubric of employee participation. Within this model of industrial reform "participation" replaces democracy as the operative term and thereby redirects debate away from the inevitable *political* nature of industrial organization. "Worker participation" becomes a matter of efficiency, of effectiveness, of "fine-tuning" existing social arrangements rather than a matter of balancing power and resolving competing interests. In other words, the language adopted by the JSC and outside consultants signaled nothing earthshaking as far as changing conventional industrial relations. Rather it reaffirmed the ideological dominance of liberal industrial reforms by again placing workplace relations under the guiding directives of efficiency, technical application, and the cult of expertise.[57]

The meeting provided ISU leadership with another opportunity to deflect any vague sentiments among workers that they might become more democratically involved in the new company and their union. As if to trivialize and dismiss these concerns among workers, and especially the RFC, ISU legal council Dave Robertson added,

We're not talking about starting a Mom and Pop shop. You have to resolve in your mind to get the best of the top business people on the board, people who understand steel and high finance. It cannot exist as a popularity contest.[58]

Here, Robertson echoed the view of many critics of industrial democracy: that you cannot operate a business under competitive market capitalism by having workers make decisions about things they do not understand. You need specialists, you need financial experts, and most of all, you need a group of enlightened managers to make these decisions. But what Robertson overlooked was that workers *did* understand this and that there were *many* "top business people" one could hire. As the above worker insisted, there was no economic reason that employees could not hire these people and then vote on whether to retain them or not. "Popularity contests" were not reserved to labor, for surely the ESOP consultants and members of the JSC were "popular" in some circles, among certain interests. Still, Robertson correctly saw that Weirton Steel would never be the same as when Weir and Millsop held the reins. The mill had been very much a "Mom and Pop shop" for over seventy years, but now things would be different. Now it was time to run the mill "like a business"; enter the specialists and experts, exit democratic worker ownership.

Mobilizing Public Sentiments

Community leaders, local businesses, and editorial writers from area newspapers all endorsed the McKinsey study as the only "feasible" alternative for workers, area communities, and the entire tristate region. But the stakes were high, and workers were confused over the details of the buy-out and they still did not know the status of their pensions. Amid the public endorsements of an ESOP and McKinsey's recommendations, clouds of unease descended upon people who did not know who, or what, to believe. As one laid-off worker lamented,

Here I am laid off from Weirton Steel talking about an ESOP and here I'm watching the [Pittsburgh] Steelers play football on TV and they just come off a 51 day strike for more money. They're striking for more money and here I am just trying to stay even. And [Weirton workers] are taking a 32% cut and [the] Steelers are striking for more money! I can't understand whether some people's gonna get rich and some poor out of this. I just can't figure out what's happening in my life. Why all the big changes? Who's making the big changes in my life?[59]

The wife of another worker expressed her despair.

I resent living in limbo. Everything focuses around the mill and what's happening. Can't concentrate on anything else. That's the way it always is but we live under the impression that we can look to the future and what we'll do 6 months from now, [a] year from now.[60]

And she later added,

This is like a natural disaster area in a way. It was just *boom*, it was here and took over [original emphasis].[61]

This mixture of confusion and powerlessness was hardly assuaged as the JSC and its consultants promoted an atmosphere of urgency over completing the negotiations. "National wants an answer as soon as possible," Harvey Sperry warned workers at the ISU informational meeting. "The longer we wait, the more problems there will be."[62] Speaking to Weirton's Rotary Club, William Doepken, general manager of industrial relations and a JSC member, put it bluntly: "It boils down to two choices. It's either jobs or no jobs, a new company or a shutdown. If you prolong the decision process, it only creates more problems."[63] Nobody wanted problems, but people did want more information. And if McKinsey's study was greeted with open arms by the JSC, it was met with clenched fists by the RFC.

When the JSC and ISU both publicly supported McKinsey's view that joining the ESOP was "a matter of individual rights" not a matter of majority decision, the RFC immediately began a petition and leafleting drive demanding that workers be allowed to vote on the ESOP and any wage concessions. Then on August 26, only two weeks after the RFC campaign began, the ISU and JSC reversed their position and announced that these issues would be voted on. Perhaps this was a sign that pressure by the RFC could be effective and that the JSC might bend and accommodate some dissent—if it existed.

Dissent did exist, and not only from the RFC. By late September RFC members began receiving reports that a conflict was brewing between ESOP design consultants Jack Curtis, Alan Lowenstein, and management members of the JSC. Curtis was reported to have clashed with John Madigan, vice-president of industrial relations, over the structure of the ESOP. Curtis wanted more employee input and involvement, something Madigan did not find desirable.[64] Then, shortly after McKinsey's findings were announced the JSC terminated the services of Alan Lowenstein, National's choice for ESOP design consultant. One report claimed he was fired because he recommended that Weirton division president Jack Redline become a salesman since he was not qualified to be president of the new company.[65] And according to one RFC member, "one of the apparent reasons" for Lowenstein's departure "was his opposition to immediate vesting of voting rights for workers."[66]

Despite the RFC's optimism that their actions were bringing results, Tony Gilliam saw the recent moves by the JSC and union to extend voting rights for workers as opportunistic at best, if not deceitful. While the ISU steadfastly refused to change its bylaws to accommodate the Gregory-RFC grievance with the NLRB over voting rights for laid-off workers, they appeared to be doing just that for an ESOP vote. It is quite possible that the JSC and union leadership were courting public opinion and positioning themselves against the RFC. But the JSC was also acting under conditions that compromised their intentions as much as their capacity.[67] With Weirton Steel still negotiating over the terms of decade-old consent decree for discriminatory hiring practices, and with the NLRB complaint over union voting policies, the JSC may have viewed another legal struggle over ESOP voting as a costly delay, one that would impede negotiations with National and seriously jeopardize the new company's image in the eyes of potential lenders and existing customers. This did not, however, keep the ISU from filing a lawsuit to hold National Steel to its pension and severance obligations for up to 500 recently laid-off workers.[68]

And even if the JSC's decision was calculated to secure a pro-ESOP vote, it was still responsive to popular demands and democratic ideals. A survey at the time by sociologist Arnold Levine showed that 92 percent of laid-off workers favored the ESOP plan. As Levine put it, "They harbor the hope . . . that employee-ownership will mean recall to their jobs at the mill."[69] The JSC could also argue that they had planned to permit a vote all along, thus claiming the RFC's issue as their own while criticizing them for interfering with delicate negotiations. Still, after five months, neither the JSC nor RFC had mobilized public sentiment in their favor.

Seeking Allies: The Courts and the Clergy

The RFC continued its public criticism over the lack of information being provided, but the JSC and its consultants refused to release any of the McKinsey report's Confidential Appendix. As autumn arrived the RFC challenged the rationale of such drastic cuts in an extensive leafleting campaign, and on October 13, 1982, they filed suit in U.S. District Court in Wheeling, West Virginia, to have the appendix made public.[70] The suit also asked for forty-five days to study the information and seek a second evaluation of the conclusions before any vote on ESOP.

During a press conference, RFC legal counsel Staughton Lynd stated that the lawsuit was not intended to delay the proposed buyout and that workers had a legal right to all information bearing on any decision to purchase the mill. "I think it is important not to regard the lawsuit as for or against the ESOP plan," insisted Lynd. "This is a democracy lawsuit. We think that if people are to take a vote that they need to have the information necessary to cast an intelligent vote."[71] And Steve Bauman reminded reporters that the union paid for the study from its strike fund and therefore workers owned it and had a right to see it. "They asked us to take a 32 percent cut in wages without substantiating the arguments with data."[72]

The "32 percent solution" also raised serious concerns about the impact such concessions might have industrywide. Staughton Lynd cited a *Wall Street Journal* article that stated that Weirton workers may receive wages and benefits about 10 percent higher than the level provided for in the basic steel contract. Asking for another 22 percent cut beyond parity with other steelworkers,

Lynd argued, was "in effect to invite the workers at Weirton to scab on the rest of the steel industry," something that could potentially lead other companies to demand concessions from their workforce.[73] This would eventually negate any initial cost savings, leaving workers in the position of having to take further cuts to regain any advantage from the original cuts.

Furthermore, the RFC argued that the 32 percent concession reflected questionable calculations and mismeasurement. McKinsey justified the cut in wages and benefits because Weirton was "*not* one of the low-cost producers" in the industry and the cut would bring the company's labor costs more in line with other domestic steel producers. The RFC countered that if labor costs were computed on the basis of dollars per ton of steel, rather than dollars per hour, National would have the *lowest* labor costs in the industry. Even though labor costs at National's various divisions were unavailable—Weirton's was in the Confidential Appendix—the RFC argued that the difference could not be too great because of Weirton's sophisticated basic oxygen furnace and casters.[74] They also questioned McKinsey's analysis regarding capital improvements and whether some of these were necessary.

Another concern was the status of the pension fund. One alternative being discussed was for the new ESOP company to assume National's pension liabilities in return for a lower sale price on the mill. But the RFC noted this would place an enormous burden on a new company already facing exorbitant capital improvement costs, and it might also drive older, experienced workers to seek early retirement rather than risk losing their pensions. This would lead to further concessions on the part of active employees who would then be responsible for contributing to the unfunded liability that was estimated at $102 million. And in the event of an involuntary plan termination, the ultimate responsibility for paying benefits would fall to the Public Benefit Guaranty Corporation (PBGC). But this pubic institution was unlikely to pay full benefits and with the recent string of bankruptcies (White Motor, Braniff, International Harvester) the PBGC was on the verge of insolvency itself.[75]

With the lawsuit, the RFC challenged the JSC's role in the negotiations, the terms of a worker buy-out, and the apparent impotence of their union to more actively represent rank-and-file interests. ISU legal council David Robertson responded to the lawsuit by stressing how the institutions central to a "workable" ESOP would confirm McKinsey's analysis.

> Whether the 32 percent number has any credibility with the employees of Weirton Steel is obviously very critical. However, I think the employees should not lose sight of the fact that these numbers will be examined by potential lenders who would expect to have a company constructed with a cash flow sufficient to repay loans with interest on a long-term basis. It's obvious to me that the McKinsey study is going to be under close scrutiny by the investors, bankers, customers and, of course, the employees.[76]

Ironically, Weirton workers *were* key investors, especially given they were being asked to "invest," as the McKinsey study termed the concessions, practically one third of their compensation. But financial institutions were dominating this ESOP transaction and their investment, not labor's, carried more clout. Meanwhile, ISU president Bish assured a restless workforce that "we have and will continue to give all the information to the members that we can give. We're committed to doing that."[77] Perhaps they were, but ISU leadership appeared to have as little information as it had autonomy. In the months leading up to the RFC's court date the ISU offered no alternatives to its members, and failed to seriously question McKinsey's findings.

Up to now workers were wary both of the RFC and being seen attending their meetings, so the group gained most of its publicity through extensive leafleting. Leaflets inevitably came across the desks of JSC members and consultants, alerting them that workers might know more and be more skeptical than assumed. And RFC leaflets also reached area ministers who occupied a symbolic and visible position in the institutional life of Weirton and the surrounding valley.

Local religious leaders would be important allies if the RFC were to reach into the community of Weirton and surrounding towns. After months of silence they too were beginning to ask questions and the JSC lacked information. Now they wanted to talk with the RFC who saw the meeting as an "opportunity to paint the picture as we see it."[78] But the RFC would have to paint more than a picture of how they "saw things" if they were to gain support from area clergy.

Unlike other industrial towns with recent or impending plant closings (such as Youngstown or Pittsburgh), area churches had never
been aligned with labor activism and were themselves the benefi-
ciaries of a good deal of paternalistic welfare. And while some area
ministers were known to be sympathetic to the RFC, it was unclear
just how sympathetic they were. The leaflet campaign had already
expressed RFC views on worker democracy and their critique of the
ESOP negotiations and McKinsey report. In a meeting with clergy,
the RFC would have to make a strong case for the *efficacy* of their
challenge to a JSC-managed deal with National. They would also
have to convince local clergy of their critical role in the negotiations
without giving the impression they were only needed as honorable
spokespersons for RFC views.

As the RFC went to federal court, their meeting with area religious leaders became a key opportunity to gain a credible ally
against incredible odds. In saying this, however, I do not mean to
portray this meeting as some "turning point" that, if properly nav-
igated, would have brought the RFC instant leadership status.
This would be granting area clergy more influence over workers
and residents than even they felt they had. Still, local churches
could reinforce RFC calls for more public involvement in the negotiations and more information from the McKinsey study.

"Business Is Business, Morals Is Morals"

By contrasting the ministers' meetings with the RFC and JSC one
can view the legacy of paternalism and the RFC's difficulty making inroads into the major institutions of community life. Not only
was the JSC already established in the community, but they also
displayed a "calming reassurance" and deployed tact where the
RFC was considered "the underdog" and relied on passion. The
JSC and church leaders also shared a fundamental, and understandable, outlook that was not held by the RFC; they feared
what an image of conflict and division might mean to lending institutions and customers. For their own reasons, both groups
wanted the mill saved and were looking for consensus, not debate,
unity, not power struggles.

Initially, area clergy supported the ESOP agenda, but with
McKinsey's recommendations and the paucity of information they

increasingly faced more anxious and confused congregations. When a small group of church leaders met on October 20, 1982— one week prior to their meeting with the RFC—two issues dominated the discussion: how to gather more information, and finding ways to help their respective congregations. Apart from these concerns, however, there was common agreement that the church's role was to bring about solidarity, as much as information and comfort.

Likewise, church leaders did not want to be perceived as being either critical or pessimistic about a potential worker-owned company. This made gathering information uncomfortable when learning the fate of other communities, notably Youngstown and Pittsburgh. Yet the risk of courting pessimism paled compared to overcoming the lingering paternalism that still griped townspeople, including area clergy. As the RFC learned at its first mass meeting, information from sources outside Weirton was of dubious merit and the ministers were well aware of this.

> **Minister 1:**   I think there's really an unwillingness to let anybody come in and tell Weirton-Steubenville—give them any advice. Because of the, what do you call it, fear of outsiders? Because of this entrenchment here. That's really prevalent.

> **Minister 2:**   Extremely paternalistic society that we live in here. Paternalism is rampant, it takes four or five years to get established in the community. Anybody from the outside is perceived as being—certainly at least frowned upon.

> **Minister 3:**   That's right. If you don't have roots in the area, you're questioned.[79]

Ironically, despite such misgivings about the defensive localism that paternalism had bequeathed, religious leaders were the standardbearers of paternalistic authority; their spiritual calling was "to care for our steelworkers" and "unify" the community around saving the mill. Their status meshed closely enough with that of the JSC that any criticism of the ESOP agenda might impugn not only the JSC, but perhaps them as well. The cozy relationship between church and company of the Weir-Millsop years persisted and left religious institutions compromised. Church leaders worried about upsetting mill officials, and as the following exchange reveals, they did not want any misinterpretation of either their actions or loyalty to the company and ESOP agenda.

Minister 1: It's almost as if when you raise an issue of diversifying that you're raising an issue as being in opposition to the ESOP. I don't think any of us would want to say that. I think we all want to see that work.

Minister 2: I already indicated that to [Weirton's public relations director]. And said that I did not want the company to come out with a negative opinion of what we were doing. And I was going to sit down and tell them. What and why. Hopefully that would cut some of the negative response.

Minister 3: How'd he respond to that?

Minister 2: Fine. We've been honest with each other. And I enjoy him.

Minister 4: [The management representative on JSC] also knows that we're really in favor of [ESOP]. We've had prayer service and such at the church that show the concern and [that we] want it to go.[80]

The caution of religious leaders grew from their historical alliance with Weirton Steel as much as from their role in the church. And where some ministers were insightfully critical of paternalism's legacy, their shared impulse was to support the JSC and pursue a nonconfrontational stance vis-à-vis the ongoing negotiations. This is what the RFC faced when they met with area clergy one week later on October 27, 1982.

For the Sake of "Democracy"

The RFC appealed for pastoral support by standing against the "human misery" brought on by plant closings and deindustrialization. This was certainly a moral issue that the ministers respected, but when the RFC also attempted to make a history of union culpability and insurgent democracy moral issues, clergy members found things a bit murkier. "We have a right and a duty to participate" in the ESOP negotiations, argued Tony Gilliam.[81] "The moral issue," added Steve Paisani, "is the right of employees and the community to participate in the formulation of what will come about in the new company."[82]

The RFC was addressing the upholders of morality so they understandably argued for the virtue of their position. The problem, however, was that local clergy already agreed that the misery wrought by economic events was immoral. If anyone knew that the forces of evil were strong in the world, it was the church. But in their view, if one could not change or eliminate evil, then one had best not cause *more* misery by failing at something that was unlikely to succeed in the first place. As one minister saw it:

> I don't generally disagree with where you're coming from at all. But I've generally found where you're trying to put forth the kind of thinking and politics—and there's a lot of that in there—that you are doing, that you inevitably get labeled and you inevitably run up against some real centers of power that go beyond just labor and management. I sense in the end it's how much power you can generate, how much leverage you can generate that will determine your successfulness. I just wonder where do you see the power coming from. You've talked about this suit in District Court—which I'll be very anxious to see how that comes out—that's a big test of your effectiveness—But what other kinds of sources of power do you feel as an organization that you have to put some leverage on this whole situation.[83]

A fellow minister saw it perhaps a bit more categorically:

> Your issues being a fight against management which is typically conservative, an entrenched union which is fairly conservative here, a workforce that has been built around paternalism, and the financial community that is conservative. Seems like that's a rather dangerous thing to tackle.[84]

Another minister wondered if the RFC challenge might not divide workers instead of empowering them, and he felt that they needed to work more closely with the ISU.

The union and the Rank-and-File Committee are really shaping up to be on opposite sides of the fence. [Voices of assent from fellow ministers] And what that does of course for the worker who is a member of the union—whether he be working or unemployed—who may also be in sympathy with what you're doing, that person's power doesn't exist. Because both sides are draining that person. They're caught in the middle in other words. I wish there was some way to reconcile that.[85]

For religious leaders, it was not the RFC's democratic principles that were in doubt, but rather the wisdom of pursuing them "recklessly" against such structural odds. Could they succeed in democratizing the negotiations and the company that followed? Could they challenge the ISU's leadership without weakening what little power workers had? Was the risk of taking on National and banking institutions worth losing the ESOP opportunity, however suspect it might be?

Indeed, as RFC members argued for more rank-and-file involvement in the negotiations and a more democratic ESOP, they were met with the clergy's goal of unity. When the RFC charged the ISU with negligence and dishonesty over the years, religious leaders saw both labor and management as responsible for deteriorating relations in the mill. When the RFC criticized the JSC over their handling of the negotiations, religious leaders voiced concern over presenting an image of unity to lending institutions and customers. When the RFC defined a democratic ESOP in terms of more worker authority and autonomy on the shopfloor and representation on the board of directors, religious leaders returned to the "nervousness of this division between workers and their union representatives" and how important it was to "bridge that gap and get greater communication—irrespective of what management does or doesn't do."[86]

Clearly, the RFC agenda conflicted with how area clergy viewed their role in the community. For church leaders, their first priority was to deal with the afflicted, not the affliction. As one minister conceded:

I've learned in meetings with management and union membership—talking about ESOP. So far, in the little bit of politics that I know about, it's a well orchestrated script—with no conclusions. As I look at it, in terms of pastoral work—I'm talking about laid off people, families affected, people hurting. I really could care less about how it goes—structure, procedure. . . . How do I deal with people who are hurting? With possible hurt? With layoffs? As far as I'm concerned, in the area of the church, this is where we need to be addressing what do we do.[87]

But on another level, democratic practice collided with the *ideal*, if not the norms, of "community." The open dialogue and debate among divergent interests that is, ideally, characteristic of democratic government contradicted a traditionally informed image of community, where respect for authority, nonconfrontation, and value consensus prevailed. The ministers felt that the RFC had not approached the community properly, that they were too confrontational for their own good. When one minister asked why the RFC could not trust (then) company president Jack Redline, Steve Bauman angrily criticized Redline's behavior and motives since returning in the late 1970s.

Minister: Are you aware that it's precisely that attitude of hostility that may prevent the dialogue [you want]?

Bauman: Well, it's a question of the power which you originally came down to. If they feel that the working man is entirely powerless then there is no dialogue and things go exactly the way perhaps you'd like to see them go.

Minister: You can't do anything about what they think. You can do something about how you approach them and make your demands. I'm simply suggesting that while the goals and aims of your group are right on target as far as I'm concerned, I think your strategies are weak. I think that your strategies, especially in the area of communication, need to be thoroughly examined if you're going to accomplish the goals you expect to accomplish[88]

Tony Gilliam interrupted to explain the dilemma facing the RFC, and anybody else who dared question the JSC or negotiation process, a dilemma the ministers themselves had discussed at their first meeting. In the process, he also spoke to the contradiction between democracy and the normative order of community in Weirton.

> **Gilliam:** You think what we're saying is right on target, [but] you question the way we're saying it. I put to you that no matter how we said it, we would be criticized as being troublemakers and people interested in throwing this thing off track. Simply because we're asking good, solid questions. For that reason—I understand it may be a rumor—there was a leaflet circulating through the mill that came from management calling the Rank-and-File Committee a bunch of troublemakers and advising workers not to pay attention to us. It's almost unpatriotic—considering Jack Redline's position and all the green ribbons, it's almost unpatriotic to ask any questions here.
>
> [Portion omitted]
>
> **Minister:** I think you have to take the issues you have more directly to the people—specifically the people outside of the worker population.[89]

The minister had correctly pointed out that the RFC had not made inroads into the community of Weirton nor other towns nearby that were equally affected. What he did not say, and perhaps did not know, was how to support democratic participation among people for whom "community" meant a history of subordination to paternal authority and intolerance of any dissent. Even if RFC members refrained from "using inflammatory language that gets you nowhere," as one minister advised, dissent could not be avoided and was in stark contrast to years of paternally informed conceptions of "community."

For the Sake of a "Deal"

Five days later on November 2, 1982, church leaders met with the JSC, represented by ISU legal counsel David Robertson and union president Walter Bish. In the end, Robertson and Bish reaffirmed the ESOP agenda over any other possible options, justified the JSC's role in the face of what they saw as widespread worker apathy, and joined religious leaders in their desire to avoid creating divisions in the workforce or community.

Robertson took the lead during the meeting, as was indicative of his role throughout the ESOP negotiations.[90] In outlining the JSC position, his was a more restrained and complicated version of negotiations than that of the RFC. Saying that "a lot of things [are] uncertain, some in our control, many outside it," Robertson raised question after question about the potential financial and organizational issues facing any future ESOP.[91] Then, responding to a question about whether the McKinsey study and the confidential appendix could be trusted, Robertson argued that what was most important was not so much what the study contained, but that a reputable firm such as McKinsey and Company performed it. In his view, impressing lending institutions and potential customers that an ESOP could work was the "bottom line" and McKinsey's status helped. "Those are the people who count," he explained. "When they say it's a solid enough deal to go with, then I have to believe. End speech."[92]

The JSC appeared more interested in "making the deal" than in the details of it. The prestige (popularity?) of ESOP consultants seemed enough to gain the trust of the JSC, even if not the RFC's. And when discussion turned to the role of rank-and-file workers in the new company, the ISU's conciliatory role in the negotiations became even clearer. For Robertson, the "financial package" for a worker buy-out preceded any questions over workplace democracy.

> **Minister:** My understanding is that ESOP's work well when there tends to be good participation from the ranks— from the bottom up, so that people who are investing in the company also feel that they are being talked to, consulted. Do you think we're doing well in that process at this point?
>
> **Robertson:** I don't think we've done anything with it yet, cause we don't know whether the deal's gonna work. You're focusing on the cart instead of the horse.[93]

As Robertson saw it, talk of worker democracy might undermine negotiations and frighten off lending institutions and customers. The Weirton ESOP stood to be the largest worker-owned company in the country, and with the scale of such an undertaking in a competitive market it was imperative not to get carried away with such lofty principles. "I understand that the whole ESOP movement is worker democracy," he assured the church leaders,

> I am not oblivious to the participatory workshop, participatory democracy issues in an ESOP. I have asked McKinsey and received volumes of material on how you open those lines of communication. You're in a very traditional business here.[94]

But local clergy saw little "communication" between the JSC and workers who were becoming more fearful as the months passed. One minister expressed the doubts held by the assembled clergy over how the JSC was responding to a concerned and uninformed workforce.

> **Minister:** My response is to say—I'm not putting the cart before the horse because I think you have to have participation and acceptance of the workers and I hear a lot that we may be losing the battle even before we've begun the war. I don't know what you're hearing, but I hear a lot of my people who are scared to death.
>
> **Robertson:** What do they want to hear, Tom?
>
> **Minister:** I'm not sure they want to hear anything so much as they want to be talked to. And there is nothing going on.[95]

At this point the estrangement between ISU leadership and rank-and-file workers, evidenced by the earlier union vote over funding a feasibility study, resurfaced. "I don't know what more we can do," lamented union president Walter Bish. "They say they want to be talked to. We give meetings. Why don't they come?"[96] More, Robertson added, written communication was clearly ineffective.

> I have learned in 10 years that you do not make any progress by writing things. I have asked people in meetings— "did you read this?" "I never read that crap. I throw it away." So? I have personally written four complete newspapers and

a twenty-six-page book since April 1st. And the union has spent $15,000 in printing. That medium is not working.[97]

Oddly enough, written communication did seem to work for the RFC in their leaflet campaign. But the ISU president and legal counsel saw rank-and-file apathy, not powerlessness. They viewed "dissenting" calls for workers' rights (for example, voting, more information, and a democratic ESOP structure) as complicating their negotiating position with National. As negotiators in a business purchase, they perceived debate over alternatives an unreasonable and unwise burden; better to follow the reputable experts than discuss such risky issues as stock allocation, voting rights, and board membership.

> **Robertson:** [If you] give options, it becomes too divisive. I respect what your saying. You can ask for anything you dream of. If I put an issue out there for an option to increase the sense of participation, which is sadly lacking, albeit, what do I do when I create divisions with the union over real issues which I cannot later put back together?
>
> **Minister:** Discomfort you feel over that is akin to the discomfort the men feel—question is, how you deal with it?
>
> **Robertson:** I think they feel it because we haven't gone to them yet and said here's what the professionals recommend.[98]

The JSC's concern over "divisions within the ranks" may have grown from their role as negotiators, but it was shared by religious leaders who also sought unity in the community. For both groups, public dialogue and critical debate threatened this solidarity, or at least the *image* of it. And if both groups saw the solution in different terms—for Robertson it came down to "the [union] steward's ability to sell a contract" whereas one minister called for "winning rather than selling" workers—both also wanted to avoid fueling any conflicts.[99] As the meeting ended church leaders agreed to convey any information to their congregations the JSC made available. They had not offered the RFC such support, although they did offer to arrange and mediate a meeting with the RFC that the JSC rejected. It appeared, as one minister lamented during a final meeting of clergy one month later, that "business is business, and morals is morals."[100]

The Limits of Dissent

On October 28, 1982, several months into the negotiations, the RFC entered U.S. District Court in Parkersburg, West Virginia, with enthusiasm and hope. But they left without the Confidential Appendix, a trial postponement until November 6, and an important reminder of the limits of legal strategies. Lawyers representing the JSC, ISU, and Weirton Steel argued that a decision had not been reached on what ESOP package employees would be offered or whether they would recommend the 32 percent wage and benefit concession. At the second hearing the court denied the RFC request for information contained in the appendix. Calling the suit premature, Judge Charles Haden II also agreed that all union members had a right to see anything that was not "absolutely confidential," adding, "I can't imagine what that would be."[101] He then advised that when an ESOP vote was finally scheduled the RFC could reargue their case.

Was the RFC's day in court a "defeat," or was there more to the litigious clouds forming over Weirton as 1983 approached? The court hearing did publicly confirm ISU negligence in its responsibilities to rank-and-file members. Under oath, ISU president Bish admitted that the JSC had never taken notes during meetings with ESOP consultants, nor were minutes taken for JSC meetings. Bish also conceded that he had not read the pension report prepared by consultants and he testified that his entire knowledge of the ESOP proposal came from just two slide-show presentations. He never read, nor desired to read, the McKinsey study appendix, nor did he ever ask McKinsey to justify the 32 percent give-back. David Robertson also had not seen the McKinsey appendix.[102] In other words, the union representatives on the JSC "team" did not read nor have access to crucial documents for a deal in which they were co-negotiators.

The hearing also provided important information apart from the data and calculations in the Confidential Appendix. ISU leadership was further discredited when a JSC lawyer said that it was likely that only 5,000 to 6,000 jobs would remain under an ESOP company.[103] Bish had never questioned nor challenged these estimates—about 2,000 jobs *less* than initially projected—but he continued nonetheless to enthusiastically support McKinsey's recommendations.

Finally, the RFC felt that legal pressure was having an effect insofar as the JSC began to make offers they might not have otherwise (for example, more in-plant meetings, more information, ESOP voting rights). For the first time, the JSC said in court they would disclose some of the McKinsey information that had been considered confidential. Exactly what that was remained to be seen, but in closed chambers Judge Haden offered to review the appendix and help decide what information should remain secret. When the RFC agreed to this proposal, legal counsel for the JSC, ISU, and company all refused.[104]

On the other hand, the hearing ultimately confirmed the JSC as the sole representative of the Weirton workforce, a role they would continue without serious challenge. Even with the ISU further discredited and the court acknowledging workers' fiduciary rights, the RFC still did not have the "victory" that might have mobilized wider public support. Instead, the JSC used the court hearings to cast the RFC as meddlesome, claiming that interference with delicate negotiations only disrupted their "timetable."

Without the appendix, the RFC and workforce still did not know if a 32 percent cut in compensation and perhaps 5,000 jobs were a reasonable price to pay for saving the mill. With the appendix challenge silenced, the JSC began holding regular in-plant meetings through union stewards and they mounted an extensive public campaign in the community. As the JSC's "timetable" accelerated, RFC leadership saw a fleeting opportunity for ESOP alternatives fade rapidly. "This is one of the best shots ever that workers have at controlling the mill," said a dejected Tony Gilliam,

> if people [would] just slow down long enough to look at it. . . .
> If our union was worth . . . anything at all, we could tell National, "yeah, we'll take the mill off your hands, but we'll do it this way, and this way, and this way," and make the best deal possible for workers. And if National says no, then we buy it ourselves, [perhaps using] eminent domain. That would be an alternative. Let National shut it down and pay us millions

of dollars in severance pay and pension liabilities . . . and then let's simply purchase the mill directly for ourselves.[105]

Yet even with a legal victory, it is unlikely that the RFC would have drawn many more supporters at this point. The hearings also revealed how fear, rather than unity, was becoming the key element in securing a "deal with National." Nobody, including Judge Haden, wanted to be held responsible for derailing the negotiations and losing the mill. As they prepared a press statement on the hearings, two RFC members reflected upon the growing "fear factor" that made any opposition to an ESOP threatening.

> **Member 1:** [It's] just like the only thing they (JSC) can say if anything screws up is "it was the Rank-and-File Committee's fault." They're certainly not going to say "we spent a half million bucks and blew it."
>
> **Member 2:** . . . blame it on us . . . and the judge was concerned about that himself. He doesn't want to be blamed for causing the mill to close. Regardless of whether that would be the case or not. He doesn't want anyone to be able to put that blame on him.
>
> **Member 1:** He even said that if anything goes wrong, somebody who doesn't want it to be their fault is going to say it's our fault . . . back in chambers.[106]

Given the larger context of industrial decline and economic uncertainty nationwide, and the growing anxiety among workers and residents, it is not surprising that critics of the ESOP increasingly became marginalized and isolated—there was too much at stake. And in a community where dissent had been systematically intimidated and silenced, the RFC may have been heroic up to now, but to go much further courted foolishness.

At the Institutional Margins

Ironically, the factors for the RFC's limited success also account for their inability to mobilize more support from both workers and the community. Their membership, marginal position in the

community, legal strategy, and demands for community participation in a democratic ESOP, revealed how up to now "community" had become an ideological weapon *against* democratic
action as well as an institutional barrier to it.

The RFC's core leadership of black workers had previously engaged in legal action against the company (McKenzie's suit
against discrimination) and the police department of Steubenville
(Gilliam's countersuit against police brutality). While this provided the RFC with experienced leaders, it also undermined their
efforts to unite an overwhelmingly white workforce behind their
goals. Racism was institutionalized inside the mill (for example,
National's discrimination consent decree), but it was also no
stranger to the civic life of Weirton or Steubenville.

Likewise, as the RFC became more active, red-baiting increased. Over time, more people began to view them as "just
a bunch of dissatisfied agitators" and meddlesome outsiders.
Though the RFC was largely indigenous to the Weirton mill,
some of their outside members did play key roles.[107] For example,
Staughton Lynd brought a history of left activism as well as labor
law expertise to the RFC. As a local politician recalled when
asked about the RFC, "Yeah, they had that socialist Staughton
Lynd come in and spread his bull around. Nobody here wanted to
listen to a socialist." The JSC's outside consultants also faced local distrust of Wall Street, but people had little choice in supporting them—the JSC and National decided that months ago.

So as negotiations moved into 1983, RFC members found themselves fighting a negative public image as much as the JSC. "We
don't have the best reputation going over there in the mill," said
one member. "We're everything from the Judas Goat to the Com-
munist Party."[108] Even more damning were efforts to link the RFC
with the United Steelworkers, or what Weirton workers still refer
to as the "CIO." Despite having no affiliation with the USWA, rumors circulated that the RFC was being funded by the USWA and
a related group that was forming at Wheeling-Pittsburgh Steel.
"We ought to be careful about that," insisted a concerned RFC
member, "there's a lot of that talk in the mill. That's why we have
to be sensitive about this."[109]

But red-baiting only cultivated an already fertile atmosphere
of distrust and caution, one that had made many workers and residents reluctant to attend RFC meetings. Reflecting upon this,

one worker's wife spoke of how even she felt compelled to censor her feelings and thoughts:

> Even my [husband] said that he was afraid—he'd like to know what [the RFC] had to say—but then he always felt as though people were watching who went to these meetings and who were going to be the troublemakers. There was rumors at first that they were going to start cleaning out the mill. And guys that didn't do their job or did something they didn't like, they weren't going to have a job. They were going to find out a way that they could get them out of a job. [My husband] was afraid of it. He didn't want to do anything that could appear in any way as though he were shaking a finger at the company. He wasn't going to risk that, and maybe other people felt the same way, I don't know. Even I sometimes think stuff I say I shouldn't say, 'cause maybe they'll find a way of getting him out of the mill, based on something I did.[110]

And what did she think of the RFC's role during the negotiations? Her account illustrates how people viewed RFC activism from the shifting frameworks of class, race, and community.

> He [Tony Gilliam] had a bad reputation being a troublemaker. I think everybody was sitting back to see what happened. To see if they could blow up enough stink—If they coulda been—I think if there woulda been more of them. And if they had had a bigger mouth and they weren't hushed up as quickly—maybe something more would have come of it. But because of the one guy that was heading it had a reputation for that—whether it's true or not 'cause I don't know him but from my husband talking about him—the way men felt about him—that he was just an idiot—and it's hard to tell what he's doing it for—that he just likes to start trouble. I don't see anything wrong with [the RFC] wanting to see the appendix. It's just another way of hiding something. But it seems naive to me that they thought they could get it. Especially when they were a small group. They were going to be hushed up fast. You know this is a free country but it's not that free, you know. If big business or something like that

wants to keep something from you they've got the money, the manpower, and the lawyers and everything else, that they can do it. . . . If they had been a more prestigious group. If they had been leaders maybe of the union or leaders within the mill. Guys the other guys liked. . . . But since he was someone that screamed prejudice at the drop of a hat—some of the men felt—they just didn't want to be bothered with it. They just felt it was garbage and going to get them in trouble.[111]

If the RFC enjoyed some early institutional support in town, it faded gradually over time. Initially, they were able to use the Knights of Columbus Hall and the Catholic Madonna High School in Weirton to hold meetings. The RFC held public committee meetings on Tuesday nights at the St. John's Lutheran Church in Steubenville, yet they were rarely attended by anyone but a small core of RFC members. And organizers planned to form local chapters in Weirton and nearby towns, but these never emerged.

By contrast, the JSC utilized their institutional position in the community to carry their ESOP agenda to residents, business, and civic groups. Presentations were given to the Rotary Club, Weirton Jaycees, as well as with various clerical associations, political and business associations, and different Lodge groups in town. And even if they were not always convincing, the JSC still dominated public arenas from which to reinforce their ESOP agenda. After a presentation to the Women's Club, the mill-worker's wife quoted above remarked of her experience:

I went to it out of curiosity. . . . [But] when they first started out with the wonderful people of Weirton and what a fantastic town this was and how famous we've been for years—then they showed the film of how it all started eighteen months ago—I felt like they were taking your emotions and pulling you through all of this. And setting you up to the way they wanted you to react. As though—I felt *manipulated!*[112]

And where initially the local press announced RFC meetings or printed their position statements and letters to the editor, this too began to change as the negotiations entered their second year. The RFC got fair treatment at first, said one local journalist, but "I doubt [it] now." Like others in the valley, he explained, reporters "feel like their whole future surrounds Weirton Steel, so they want ESOP to succeed. That's got to be in their minds, and in the minds of their superiors."[113] Finally, as noted earlier, the JSC "resurrected" the support of a loyal but questioning area clergy. Any doubts they may have held during the fall of 1982 were now silent and they became active in fundraising efforts as they reassured congregations from the pulpit.

Splintered Protest and Class

If the RFC did initiate worker involvement in the ESOP negotiations, it was specific to certain groups that also focused their efforts on litigation. After one year of negotiations, fifteen lawyers variously representing five legal cases stood empty-handed awaiting court judgments.[114] Local solidarity in the name of "community" was proving more fragmented than either myth or ideal would have it.

In early April 1983 a lawsuit was filed by 171 workers, all at least forty years old, who sought protection of their pension benefits. John Spoon, counsel for the pensioners, had learned that steelworkers would be asked to pay for their own major medical insurance under a new ESOP, something that National had provided up to now. He noted that workers over forty were being encouraged to retire even without knowing the status of their pensions.[115]

Then, on April 7, 1983, former ISU president Richard Arrango filed unfair labor practice charges against the ISU and company with the NLRB. Arrango claimed that the JSC-negotiated deal with National violated NLRB codes because management personnel infringed on the ISU's collective bargaining rights. Things were fine, argued Arrango's lawyer Eugene Green of Youngstown, when the JSC was studying the feasibility of the plant, but they violated labor law when they began negotiating with National for a buy-out (a point Staughton Lynd argued one year earlier). Calling themselves the Concerned Steelworkers of Weirton Steel, Arrango co-chaired a group of 500 workers who indicated a desire to combine their suit with the 171 pensioners.[116]

Alongside earlier legal actions—the ISU suit against National Steel over pension rights, the McKenzie discrimination consent decree, the RFC-Gregory suit with the NLRB over ISU voting rights policies, and the RFC Confidential Appendix suit—it now seemed that everyone was suing someone but getting nowhere.[117] As the plethora of litigation mounted, it also appeared to more than a few people as a fatiguing and defeating waste of time. As one worker recalled, "The RFC had some good points, and some of the lawsuits were good, but after a while it got to be too much." Even RFC members recalled that "things got out of hand" with the legal cases, many of which were unwise and unnecessary. Perhaps Staughton Lynd put it best when he surmised:

> Probably the most important thing for lawyers, unions and workers—to say to themselves and write in capital letters at the top of the bathroom mirror is DON'T LET THE LAW BECOME A SUBSTITUTE FOR POPULAR STRUGGLE. Nothing wrong with the law. It can make a contribution. But it can't take the place of a people's movement. I think we learned that again in this situation [original emphasis].[118]

Had litigation "become a substitute for popular struggle" or, in this case, a fractured form of popular struggle? As I noted in chapter 1, scholars have routinely noted the difficulties in organizing workers of paternalistic company towns, and also recall the legal battles waged against Weir during the 1930s and 1940s only to result in a company union. Echoing Lynd, Lawrence E. Rothstein has argued that a "myth of legality" can sap worker militancy and organization, both of which are necessary for successful legal opposition.[119]

On the other hand, organized militancy combined with legal strategies do not guarantee success either and litigation may be the only avenue of opposition possible under unfavorable circumstances. The fragmented litigation did suggest more than "malcontents" at work for there was clearly more opposition to the ESOP agenda within the workforce than previously thought. Instead, it signaled widespread discontent and frustration that might, as Rick Fantasia suggests, reemerge later in a more unified, collective "culture of solidarity."[120] That it was fragmented and unable to coalesce into mobilized dissent is hardly surprising given the emergent class, ethnic, and age divisions that paternalism had contained up to the 1970s. And even if the JSC, ISU, and National did more to exaggerate than reconcile such divisions, how much responsibility did the RFC bear for its inability to confront and mend them?

Though other groups sought precisely what the RFC had been demanding for over a year, the RFC could not mobilize a coalition that might have more effectively altered the ESOP agenda. On the one hand, differences within the RFC hindered their efforts to establish broader appeal. Core members each brought different degrees of passion and political sophistication to their otherwise united ESOP dissent.[121] With National's surprise announcement and the JSC's swift formation, the spontaneous response of a diverse RFC meant that personalities had to jell as group strategies were being defined and enacted. Often this was reflected in public displays of frustration and anger that hardly flattered the RFC in the eyes of potential allies (recall the minister's denunciation of Bauman).

On the other hand, the RFC made no serious effort to join forces with Arrango's Concerned Steelworkers or, to my knowledge, the pensioners. By the time other protest groups emerged in spring 1983, the RFC had become too entrenched and disillusioned by their struggle to move toward any alliance with their critics. Where Arrango's group saw the RFC as "dangerous radicals," RFC members recalled Arrango's early endorsement of the JSC-led ESOP until losing the ISU presidency to Walter Bish in July 1982. They tended to view the Concerned Steelworkers as nothing more than "narrow-minded opportunists, interested in little more than quarreling with the incumbent union leaders."[122] Similarly, Staughton Lynd had urged from the beginning that supervisors and management were critical allies in forming any ESOP.[123] But the RFC did not actively recruit lower level management employees to their cause, nor did they issue public reassurances of management's continuing role in a democratically structured ESOP.

Overcoming these impediments, however, would not alone have translated local sympathy with RFC principles into mobilized action. At one level, workers directed their anger at National Steel and company executives. A July 1983 survey of Weirton employees found that 74 percent held National Steel responsible for problems at the Weirton Division, and 33 percent blamed the Division's own executives.[124] While this might suggest there was widespread support for local management, it also says nothing about employee approval of their role in the ESOP negotiations. In my view, balkanized protest signaled collective disapproval of both management and the ISU.

For the JSC and local media, dissent was seen as a threat to the "community" rather than a democratic right or a legitimate means to pressure National for better sale terms. Against the collective sentiments of corporate betrayal and "shoddy mismanagement," responsibility for Weirton's crisis was becoming "localized" and instead of National Steel being held responsible, dissenters were seen as ignoring *their* responsibilities to Weirton and the Ohio Valley region. Challenging the ESOP agenda now risked impugning one's membership in some idealized "community." For one "pro-ESOP" steelworker, this was a disturbing development and in a letter to the editor of a local paper he reminded readers:

> The Weirton Steel men are not "dissidents" just because they disagree with National Steel. Jesus was considered a dissident in his time. An opinion is not always correct just because it is held by the majority of the public. You must stand up for your own rights. The Weirton Steel men are only asking for what is in their contract. What is wrong with that? ESOP will not be ruined by the lawsuits. The Weirton men have not held up the vote. They have not been given anything to vote on. . . . National Steel obviously has the upper hand in this situation and they are using it to scare people. . . . The Weirton men or anyone else in this community have not asked for this to happen. The green-eyed monster of National Steel's major stockholder and administrators are causing this. . . . It should not be Weirton Steel employees versus the community. We should all be working together to fight the real culprit affecting so many other industries along with our mill—big business' lack of compassion, understanding, and loyalty.[125]

If an ideology of "community" that placed loyalty and compassion over higher profits might have unified opposition against National Steel, it was now evoked to silence dissent and tarnish those who challenged the ESOP agenda. To paraphrase Richard Sennett, community had become "uncivilized," turned inward and defensive in response to impersonal forces beyond any one group's control.[126] As fall approached, people just wanted the negotiations to end and for life to return to "normal." Only the former would come to pass.

The Final Deal

Throughout the spring and summer of 1983, one vote date after another was scheduled—and missed. Still, an "ESOP deal" was close at hand as negotiations moved forward despite the pending legal cases. During these final months preceding the September ESOP vote, important elements of the negotiations settled into place.

In December 1982, the U.S. Department of Labor ruled in favor of the RFC-Gregory complaint over ISU policy denying laid-off workers the right to vote in union elections. Attorney David Robertson insisted that the union would stick by its policy (established in the early 1950s) and that the Labor Department would have to file suit to overturn the election.[127] The Labor Department recommended that the ISU elections of June 1982 be voided and that new elections be held, but it also specified that officials chosen in these elections could continue in office until early 1984, at which point the ESOP decision would be settled.[128]

Then, in April 1983, workers learned that they might not face the "32 percent solution" in concessions. According to consultant Lazard Freres & Co., hourly workers would face a 19 percent cut because National had agreed to accept certain pension and health care costs not included in McKinsey's original estimate.[129] This figure fell more in line with the RFC's view of a reasonable negotiating proposal (based on a 6 to 7 percent reduction to industry levels and a further 12 percent to build equity), but for them, the lower figure did not signal hard-fought negotiations as much as it did the spurious character of McKinsey's original recommendations. The RFC continued pressing for an injunction to release "all of the data" in the appendix.[130]

Another contested issue was the status of pensions and whether National was obligated to honor supplemental payments should the mill close down after the sale. Many workers feared they would be ineligible for $400 in supplemental benefits should chronic layoffs after the sale substitute for a plant closing. In late April 1983, U.S. District Judge Robert Maxwell denied a request for a preliminary injunction to halt the proposed sale saying that an injunction at this point would cause the ESOP "to fall apart."[131]

Despite the ruling, litigation over the pensions was bringing pressure upon National Steel and most likely assisted the JSC's negotiating position.

Finally, Weirton division president Jack Redline announced in late March 1983 that he would retire if not chosen to head the new company.[132] While many workers and residents supported Redline, his announcement signaled that the JSC and ESOP consultants—not National—would decide who to recruit for executive positions in the new company. A board of directors and CEO for the ESOP was still unknown, but the JSC held veto power in this process at best. Writing in the *Nation*, Don Goldstein argued that Lazard Freres acted independently of the JSC and lending institutions in selecting the company's board of directors and president.

> The six [outside] board members who were supposed to have been named by Weirton's creditors were appointed by Lazard well before the banks had been identified. Not long after that appointment, Lazard hired former president of Copperweld, Robert Loughhead as the company's new chief executive officer, before the labor and management representatives on the board had been chosen.[133]

And James B. Lieber notes in *Friendly Takeover* that "the first group of directors chosen were the six independents who in turn would choose the CEO. Lazard made the recommendations with input from Willkie Farr and McKinsey."[134] Given their role in the negotiations, it is reasonable to conclude that consultants wielded decidedly more influence in these choices than the JSC.

With Robert Loughhead now at the helm[135] the public rhetoric of ESOP as a way to "save jobs" had gradually given way to assertions that workers could actually make "big money" through profit sharing and stock ownership. By late August final sale documents were made public and workers were given until September 23 to consider their "all or nothing choice."

A "Yes" Vote for Hope

On September 23, 1983, Weirton Steel employees voted on three issues: contract concessions, the new pension plan, and the ESOP. A steady stream of workers flowed into the Millsop Community

Center, some wearing hard hats after being bused from the mill. When the last ballot had been cast, an overwhelming 89 percent of mill employees—including some 2,371 laid-off workers—voted in favor of all three issues.[136] Amid the public celebrations and smiling faces, the Ohio Valley finally breathed a collective sigh of relief. On January 11, 1984, twenty-two months after National first set in motion the ESOP agenda, Weirton Steel became the country's largest fully worker-owned company.[137]

Yet behind the glowing pronouncements of JSC officials and company president Robert Loughhead, not everyone was pleased to be a part of "history in the making." According to Arnold Levine's July survey of Weirton workers, 75 percent favored creating an ESOP but 85 percent felt that they "don't have much choice." More, 28 percent judged the final purchase terms, especially the compensation cut, to be "unfair."[138] For others, the disclosure document was far too complicated to understand. As one worker speculated:

> I think [the disclosure document] overwhelmed [workers]. They figured anything that was that thick that they had to read, had to be right. . . . So many of them said you had to be a lawyer to understand it.[139]

Another voiced the powerlessness so many others felt as he pondered the recent vote:

> I didn't want to see the contract I had, the benefits negotiated away. The ESOP was presented, it was the only alternative presented to us. You almost had to take it. It's been all one side, what are we going to do, it's over now. Now all we can do is let it go, and you have to take what comes.[140]

Sitting back in his chair, hands rubbing away the frustration in his eyes, another worker doubted how much rationality and reason went into the vote.

> In all good sense I don't know how anybody could vote "yes" the first time around, cause let's face it, 90 percent of the people in that mill are so confused now that they don't even know one little thing that's going on, how the hell can they in good conscience vote a contract that's gonna decide their whole life and their future.[141]

What were the sale terms even workers felt they had little choice but to accept? The total purchase price came to $386 million: $66 million for the mill, $127.7 million for current assets (ore reserves, steel inventory, accounts receivable), and $192.3 million in liabilities. To retire the debt, employees would pay $74.7 million to National immediately, then issue two promissory notes at 10 percent interest to National, the first note for $47.2 million due in 1993 and the second note for $72 million due in 1998. The interest on these notes would not come due until Weirton Steel reached a net worth of $100 million, and the first installment on principal was not due for six years. From the Citicorp Consortium credit line of $120 million the company would draw $80 million for the initial cash payment to National, and $5.3 million to pay its consultants.[142]

National Steel also agreed to fund a trust to cover all pension costs owed retired employees as well as the pensions earned by active workers during the period they were employed by National. National agreed to continue retiree health benefits, and they agreed to remain responsible for all pension costs and shutdown benefits should the ESOP fail within five years after November 1, 1983. Exactly what constituted "failure" was unspecified, and National's obligation was binding only if workers honored a strict wage freeze and did not strike.[143]

Just where were wage levels frozen? Also approved in the ESOP vote was a union contract that called for a 20 percent cut in wages and benefits, and an end to the pyramiding of overtime (a paternalistic practice of compounding overtime hours at double time or more). On average, ISU hourly members took a 14 percent cut in wages, or $4.88 hourly pay, and almost a 5 percent cut in benefits. Salaried union members took a $4.14 hourly wage cut, and Guards Union members gave up $3.97 per hour. Salaried employees lost approximately 19 percent of their pay and 2 percent of their benefits—on average, $2.07 per hour for managers, and $1.27 per hour for nonmanagement, nonunion employees.

Did National concede more than it had originally intended? And how much of this resulted from JSC/consultant bargaining or the protests from the RFC and other groups? Clearly, National did not dictate the terms of sale even if they avoided exorbitant plant closing and pension liabilities (including future pension obligations for an aging workforce). And the JSC/consultant negotiators *did* have an interest in forging financial terms that they felt the new company could support. The mill's sale price of $66 million was 22 percent of a listed value of $300 million, and the 20 percent compensation cut was considerably less than McKinsey's original estimate.[144] National announced losses of up to $386 million from the fourth quarter of 1982 through July 1983, about $150 million from employment-related costs such as protected pensions.[145] The JSC/consultant negotiators also responded to National's reorganization as National Intergroup in February 1983 by securing a pledge from the new corporation to underwrite the Weirton pension trust.[146]

At the same time, legal protests and general discontent signaled to National, the JSC, and ESOP consultants that workers might be a "tougher sell" than imagined. The extensive public relations campaign directed at workers and residents suggests more than a little concern over a skeptical audience. And the litigation over pensions, an ESOP vote, and the right of laid-off workers to vote on a proposed ESOP were successful to some degree. Staughton Lynd has argued that the initial 32 percent compensation cut "appears to have been, not a financial estimate" of what concessions were necessary to make the mill competitive, "but a political judgement of how much the traffic would bear, of how much could be extracted from Weirton employees."[147] For Lynd and other RFC members, the reduction was due to their efforts to obtain the McKinsey data and *publicly* analyze its recommendations. With the data still confidential it is difficult to judge how the final compensation settlement was achieved, but the lower wage costs did put Weirton workers slightly below labor costs at other USWA plants.[148]

Workers were taking a risk, but for most it was "the best" they could get. They bought a mill that McKinsey estimated required some $1 billion capital spending over ten years to modernize. They bought a mill with a staggering debt to repay—from their own concessions and future profits. And they bought a mill with an environmental reprieve, but not an escape. All of this was balanced by the new company's lower production costs, ESOP tax advantages, historically high quality in tin plate products, and a niche marketing strategy that would benefit from pending capital improvements.[149] But Weirton workers also had to settle for much less in the way of control over a company that, in principle, they owned. Under the ESOP provisions, they would become "owners" with some equity, but little actual control.

Second-Class Owners

Perhaps the key "selling" point of the ESOP agenda was its nod to workers' pecuniary interests. To soften the blow of heavy wage concessions, the ESOP included a profit-sharing plan that would begin when the new company reached a net worth of $100 million. At that point one third of the profits would be distributed to employees, and when net worth reached $250 million one half of annual profits would be disbursed. To McKinsey's claim that concessions were actually an "investment," workers would see a "return on their investment" through profit sharing, if the company were successful.

Profit sharing, then, became the most tangible means whereby workers became "owners" in the company (see chapter 6). Just prior to and after the ESOP vote JSC members and consultants routinely issued highly optimistic profit-sharing projections. As one worker observed, "this thing started out to save jobs" but "Valdiserri and them pounded awful heavily on trying to convince people" they stood to make good money under an ESOP. The drawback of the profit-sharing policy, however, was it would inevitably compete with the costly capital improvements necessary for a successful company. A projected 50 percent profit-sharing formula would, in all likelihood, be reduced in the face of future modernization costs and loan repayments. Like other worker buy-outs, another forced choice loomed ahead for Weirton's worker-owners: take an increased profit-sharing check or reinvest in the mill.

Workers would also have to settle for proportionately less equity in the company than management. Ironically, the three major consultants—Lazard Freres & Company (financial), Willkie Farr & Gallagher (legal), Ludwig & Curtis (ESOP structure)—initially recommended that stock should be allocated equally. In an October 29, 1982 information pamphlet that workers chided as "the comic book," consultants explicitly stated: "Although other ESOP's allocate stock based on formulas involving compensation, seniority or other factors, we think equal allocation is fairest and best.[150] But by the summer of 1983, this egalitarian proposal was quietly dismissed in favor of compensation-based stock distribution. On July 5, the three consultants issued a memorandum to the JSC—but not to workers—entitled "ESOP Structure: Allocation of Stock, Distribution of Stock, and Voting Rights." This memo stated in part:

We originally recommended that each year every employee should receive an equal amount of the total stock allocated. . . . [Now] we think Weirton should allocate stock in proportion to compensation.[151]

This critical reconsideration was never discussed publicly and was unknown to most workers even as they voted. Seven million shares of the new company would be issued and 6.5 million held in an ESOP trust holding account (with some 500,000 retained for bonuses, incentives, etc.). The company would then make annual contributions to the trust until it paid off the initial $300 million stock value. As the note is repaid, an amount of stock equivalent to the payment moves from the holding account into the employee account *in the same ratio that each employee's annual compensation relates to the total annual compensation paid by Weirton Steel.* Under federal laws, proportional distribution was required to be eligible for ESOP tax breaks.[152]

More importantly, the ESOP provided that no stock be distributed to employees for five years, and only then if this would not depress the company's net worth below $250 million. According to the July 1983 memorandum to JSC members, this was "to preserve the independence of the Board of Directors."[153] Not only were workers blocked from voting for board members, but, as Staughton Lynd argued, stock distribution after five years presented them another "forced choice" of whether to sell stock publicly or hold a majority interest. As the July 1983 consultant memorandum stated, "Weirton will not be able to afford full distribution [in 1988] unless Weirton stock can be sold to people other than employees of the Weirton ESOP."[154] The memorandum then advised that when workers vote on this issue "they approve public ownership." But converting the company's stock to a public stock issue would, as Lynd put it, "dilute ownership of shares, and destroy the last vestige of worker control in the corporation."

In order to obtain stock allocated to their individual accounts, workers will have to agree to give up control; but if they insist on retaining control, they may not be able to exchange their shares for cash. . . . It is inevitable that all but a handful of workers, if forced to choose between their economic interest and a very attenuated form of control of the company will opt for ready cash.[155]

Leading up to this point, worker control would be "attenuated" indeed, and it was on the issues of voting rights and the board of directors that the hierarchical character of the ESOP agenda became structured into the new company. Of the legally mandated protections, the ESOP provided workers with full voting rights on issues such as amendments to the corporate charter, mergers, sales of corporate assets, and liquidation of the company. Yet, here the ESOP trustee must vote all shares as instructed by the workers and all unallocated shares *in the same proportion as the allocated shares voted.*[156] With the unequal distribution of stock according to compensation this would still be an unbalanced exercise of voting rights. However, an additional safeguard was included beyond legal mandates by granting workers full voting rights on (1) amending or terminating the ESOP, (2) the initial public sale of stock, and (3) any sale of stock by the trustee in a tender or acquisition offer. In these cases voting rights would be exercised on a one-person/one-vote basis and would require a majority of workers vote for an issue to be approved.[157] All other decisions were in the hands of the board of directors which, along with its organizational form as given in the ESOP provisions, precluded any significant control on the part of workers until January 1989 at the earliest.

Of the twelve initial directors, three would be union representatives (Bish, Robertson, and former UAW Vice-President Irving Bluestone) with six "independent" representatives joining Loughhead and management.[158] Willkie, Farr & Gallagher and Lazard Freres & Company each appointed their own representative to Weirton's board in the person of Harvey L. Sperry and Eugene J. Keilin, respectively. Financial and corporate interests were well represented on Weirton's board, perhaps overrepresented to appease the banking consortium underwriting the buy-out,[159] and they would face little interference in running the company for at least five years, including having the power to nominate their own successors.

Furthermore, according to the disclosure document, even after stock is distributed the majority of board members—the "independent" representatives—must not be either Weirton employees or affiliated to any labor organization or union.[160] In effect, the "choices" workers could look forward to when voting what stock they *might* have in five years were circumscribed by the ESOP terms they had very little choice over now. "It was the best we could get," sighed one hopeful but resigned worker. "It was either buy it or lose it." They bought the mill and began an era that would challenge the legacy of paternalism and the "community" they once knew.

P^{art III}

Workers by Day

Chapter Four

Forced Choices III: Employee Participation

Industrial democracy will not come by gift. It has got to be won
by those who desire it.

—Louis D. Brandeis, 1915

For Weirton Steel's new president and CEO, Robert Loughhead, worker ownership was never intended as a bold move
toward industrial democracy:

Everybody understood going into this venture that the organization would be operated as a business. So in a sense, the
people are workers by day and owners by night. It may be a
social experiment, but it's not an experiment in socialism. It
doesn't necessarily have to be run any differently than any
other organization.[1]

The phrase "workers by day and owners by night" embodies a
management strategy, embracing the contradictions inherent in
running a worker-owned company no "differently than any other
organization." Employee participation is the core of this strategy

that is ultimately an effort to reform how work is *managed* within a conventional corporate hierarchy. Employee participation did not fundamentally alter the division of labor or the distribution of power, nor was this desired by company officials. "The idea is to establish capitalists," said former president Jack Redline. "We fervently hope to add 7,000 capitalists to the rolls."[2]

Loughhead shared this view and he was clearly not embarking on "an experiment in socialism." Instead, officials negotiating the ownership transfer introduced an elaborate set of programs they hoped would more fully integrate workers into a steel company that, at least on paper, they owned. Profit sharing and stock ownership were key elements of a worker's "ownership" status, and I deal with these issues in more detail in chapter 6. In this chapter I analyze how an employee's status as "worker" was reinforced through participation reforms that ostensibly claimed to enhance and elevate that status in the organization.

Employee participation, or what was formally called "participative management," involved group decision-making through which workers suggested and implemented ideas about improving their jobs or their product. The Employee Participation Group program (EPG)[3] was the centerpiece of reforms along with an elaborate Internal Communications program (discussed in chapter 5), which was the official medium of communication in the company, presenting employee viewpoints and statements by senior management regarding company developments and policies through print and video media. Together, EPG and Internal Communications formed the core of the "new" industrial relations at Weirton Steel.

From some accounts, Weirton was considered a pioneering example of this industrial reform movement in America (see chapter 1). Just how does employee participation here shed light on the debate over the "new industrial relations"? During my research I became familiar with EPG through interviews, both in groups and individually, with the program staff and workers. I attended EPG meetings and a training seminar for prospective group members, and I reviewed company literature outlining the program and the progress of EPG groups throughout the mill. Unfortunately, I was unable to observe or systematically document how employee participation operated in the labor process of steel making. That perspective is critical in any structural analysis of how the labor process is affected by employee participation, so my conclusions are more tentative at this level.

Nonetheless, my interviews and observations of group meetings strongly suggested that workers exercised a narrow range of decision making within the "problem-solving" orientation of EPG. From this orientation, participation is a *technical* process directed toward problems that have *technical* solutions, which is consistent with the general pattern of employee participation throughout American industry.[4] There are, however, problems in the workplace that are political, normative, and moral, which "problem-solving" does not address. Problems of this nature are endemic in industry, but EPG either ignores them or treats them as technical riddles, solvable through the rationalized procedures of group problem-solving and more effective communication.

My data do illuminate a much neglected aspect of participation reforms—its culture, or what it means to the people involved. If, as both supporters and critics seem to agree, these reforms have emerged in the context of a global reorganization of industrial production, then the normative order of industrial authority must also be changing—or at least it will have to in order to legitimate the relationships that are gradually becoming institutionalized. The normative basis upon which authority rests will have to be modified in order to sanction and dignify how work is organized and performed. Otherwise these changes will likely evoke conflict and discontent that ultimately undermine their value in raising productivity and restoring economic health.

By discrediting traditional managerial methods, proponents of employee participation have undermined the legitimating principles upon which such control has rested over the past century.[5] In other words, a new "social contract" is necessary to support the symbolic foundation upon which *trust* in the workplace can be generated. However, as I noted in chapter 1, most participation programs have not significantly altered the power relations that constitute labor-management relations and corporate hierarchies. Consequently, at Weirton Steel the organizational hierarchy had not been changed so much as the *ideology* of organizational relations. The resulting discontinuity was reflected in frustration and conflict within and between both labor and management. If the manifest function of employee participation was to solve problems of productivity and efficiency, it brought with it problems of a different nature—a crisis of authority.

Participation by Decree

As the ESOP negotiations drew to a close, employee participation was promoted by company officials to assure the new "worker-owners" they would have some voice in their company. Exactly what that meant, however, was never clearly stated. The term "employee participation" was vague enough to say virtually nothing, yet cover everything. But it did evoke a hazy idea that workers would play *some* role in running the company and have *some* voice in how they performed their jobs. What role and how much voice came from the higher circles of management, the ISU, and outside consultants assisting the new company.

According to the JSC, a major criterion in selecting a new CEO and board of directors was their commitment to employee participation. Robert Loughhead accepted the position, according to one board member, because "a large employee-owned company was the perfect environment to prove that employee participation could work."[6] Eugene J. Keilin, of Lazard Freres and Company, had worked closely with the JSC and became one of the initial six outside members on the board of directors. As Keilin put it:

> Loughhead isn't just interested in QWL (Quality of Work Life)—gives a speech—and then it doesn't happen. . . . He's done it. And he plainly believes in it. The firmness of his belief is one of the things that persuaded the Board of the candidates presented to them that he was the right guy to pick.[7]

Upon his arrival to head the company on August 8, 1983, Loughhead spoke of the "great opportunities" that a worker-owned mill presented, one of which was employee participation.

> It is the wave of the future. I believe that. I'm committed to it. Things are never going to be the same again at Weirton. We're going to live under a new set of rules, we're going to operate differently and we're going to think differently. We

have to, because we're dealing with involvement in its purest sense. I have said many times that I think employee participation might be management's last chance to grab the brass ring and correct some of the ills that have plagued us for probably three decades. If we don't do it now, we might not get another chance.[8]

Loughhead praised employee participation in speeches to colleges, community organizations, and industry associations. Although his rhetoric was somewhat strained, he was certainly interested in improving labor-management relations. Still, the "brass ring" was there for top management to grab, for *them* to cure the "ills that plagued American industry for decades." And executive vice-president Valdiserri claimed that all levels of management would continue "working together" with the union as they had done during the ESOP negotiations.

We think, and I speak for everyone in the plant . . . that one of the key ingredients to making this thing a real success is that we involve the workers and get their ideas, their comments, their considerations on how the plant should be structured, should run. After all, they've got all the experience working that machinery and we want to take advantage of it. We in management certainly want to do that.[9]

Mr. Valdiserri may not have reflected the views of all 900 management personnel, but he did reveal, no doubt unknowingly, just how well employee participation might support management interests: "After all, they've got all the experience . . . and we want to take advantage of it. We in management certainly want to do that." Critics of the "new industrial relations" could not have said it better.

Top management was joined by the six-member ISU executive committee represented by President Bish, who fully endorsed employee participation and pledged union cooperation in the programs. But like the negotiations, the "independent" status of ISU leadership with employee participation was, again, in doubt. Commenting on the Weirton case, William F. Whyte and his colleagues at Cornell questioned the integrity of the ISU on the eve of Weirton's ESOP.

While the Independent Steel Workers Union at Weirton is cooperating with management on the employee ownership project, it remains to be seen to what extent a union that has been dominated by the company can break out of the paternalistic relationship and become a worker-controlled force for a democratically managed, employee-owned company.[10]

While it is not clear exactly what role the union played in designing the participation reforms, their compromising position with the JSC during the negotiations suggests that they were "followers" here as well, not leaders.

On this point, a possible exception was Irving Bluestone, who had been an outspoken proponent of union involvement in Quality Work Life programs, which, along with his former affiliation with the UAW, was undoubtedly a factor in his being asked to represent labor on the board.[11] Bluestone supported worker participation and he encouraged unions nationwide to adopt these reforms. His public views seemed consistent with a more democratic version of unionism.

> The notion of unionism is to bring into the workplace not only decent standards in the economic life of the workman and his family, and decent working conditions, but to bring some measure of democratic values. The notion of industrial democracy is what unionism is all about.[12]

Bluestone also envisioned a more democratic workplace.

> If a worker is a free citizen in a free society outside the workplace, involved in making decisions within his family and his community, why then should he be deprived of all those rights when he works in the workplace?[13]

Yet despite these sentiments, Bluestone was not dealing with an independent, democratic union nor was he at the helm of an experiment in industrial democracy. Furthermore, pressure by lending institutions against any significant change in the company's management structure rendered any progressive rhetoric increasingly hollow. Whatever democratic possibilities employee participation engendered, they were subordinate to the interests and support of financial institutions who had no illusions about what type of company they were funding. As board member and financial consultant Keilin put it, "This is not industrial democracy, it's worker capitalism. Just like any other company, stockholders do not make day-to-day decisions."[14]

These, then, were the sponsors and architects of employee participation. Rank-and-file workers did not propose the idea, nor were they exactly sure what it all meant. And even with the overwhelmingly vote for an ESOP one could overhear workers murmuring about "having more control in our company" and "getting rid of National Steel management." These sentiments reminded top officials with even the slightest inclination toward "management as usual" to press ahead with programs that might relieve such concerns. The company soon hired the Pittsburgh-based consulting firm of Kirkwood and Associates to help implement employee participation.[15]

During the first three years of worker ownership, CEO Loughhead spoke frequently of how employee participation was the bedrock of Weirton Steel's early success. Regional newspapers, national magazines, industry journals, and even television talk shows emphasized the company's participatory orientation as the cutting edge of industrial relations.[16] It was symbolically important that Loughhead credit and pay respect to "our worker-owners" and this was a strong theme in company public relations. But the public relations of Loughhead and the company also served as a platform for a much heralded case of a company where "enlightened management" and "progressive thinking" were saving a steel company, a community, and, indeed, a region. Not a few people I spoke with felt that employee participation conferred more status on those who initiated the program than on those working under it. As one millworker put it:

We have the best board of directors anywhere and I don't know what's going to happen with them. The only reason we got them was because this ESOP was so big. They all wanted a piece of history. They only wanted the prestige. That's all they're here for and they're a good group. We were lucky to get them, but I'm not sure how long they'll be around.

ISU attorney David Robertson reaffirmed this view in response to early concerns by workers over compensation levels for Lough-head and other board members.

These men are all of such status, with such distinguished careers, that money is not the incentive. . . . They're here because they want to see it work, but I don't think they signed on for a charity case.[17]

In other words, the symbolic message of these reforms had as much to do with displaying a magnanimous and enlightened outlook of company and union officials as it did with improving productivity, product quality, and labor-management cooperation. Executive support for the reforms was essential, and this was clear to everyone involved, especially the workforce. Consequently, the structure of employee participation at both an organizational and an operational level must be seen in this context.

The Structure of Employee Participation

Organizational Structure

At an organizational level employee participation involved many programs that operated independently but often overlapped. Employee Participation Groups (EPG) form the core of these reforms, whereas Statistical Process Control (SPC) and the Operations Improvement Program (OIP) were started about the same time but involved fewer workers.[18] A steering committee, composed of four representatives from union and management, set EPG objectives along with four adjunct steering committees that oversaw participation in specific areas of the mill.[19]

The EPG department was headed by a department manager and consisted, at the time of my research, of seven to ten full-time group facilitators (with some part-time facilitators) and a few secretaries. All of the facilitators applied for their positions through a millwide selection process that generated between four to five hundred self-nominations. A steering committee, headed by the company and union presidents along with four representatives from both management and union, then selected facilitators in three phases. Three were hired in 1981 (under a similar program initiated by National Steel), four in 1985, and three in 1986.[20]

The role of facilitators, according to an EPG newsletter, was to "help provide company resources to the group and help the [group] leader organize the group meeting."[21] Facilitators assisted EPG groups in following formal procedures and guidelines, but they also acted as a "go-between" for workers and management and they helped groups prepare management presentations of their ideas. They ran the EPG training program and were involved in national associations and seminars dealing with industrial relations reform. Facilitators, therefore, played a critical role in promoting employee participation to workers, management, and outside institutions.

ISU president Bish was part of all EPG steering committee work and union members were on the EPG staff advising on projects that involved areas of union jurisdiction, such as work rules, wages, and scheduling. "We are half union managed in this department," explained a senior facilitator, "the EPG movement, the EPG philosophy is embraced by the union." Yet EPG was not part of the collective bargaining agreement and, as often happened, participation led to instances that raised questions about the spheres of influence of the union and EPG. On the other hand, management did not "fully embrace" EPG, contrary to executive claims, and it had no formal veto mechanism on projects except their personal rejection of EPG projects.

EPG Groups

The average group size ranged from between six to twelve workers. Each group self-selected a group leader who chaired group meetings and coordinated project activities. Often groups had co-leaders either to share responsibilities or due to shift work. After group leaders were selected they attended a four-day leader seminar for further training.

Groups met once a week for an hour and often meetings were scheduled before and after a shift because continuous production units cannot be shut down. Meetings were held inside and outside the mill wherever there was a convenient conference room available. Yet meetings accounted for only a part of the time workers spent on EPG projects. Much of the information gathering, data and cost analysis, and preparation of management presentations workers did on any one project was incalculable, as was the time they spent off-hours on a project. It was not uncommon for group members to attend meetings on their off days. Occasionally the company sent group members to safety seminars or to visit suppliers and customers throughout the country to improve and coordinate product specifications and quality standards.

EPG members also received time and a half wages for the hour they spent in meetings. "A lot of people in the mill, 1,500 to 2,000 people are putting in 41-hour weeks," one facilitator stated, "and that time and a half comes out of our budget, it doesn't come out of their department's budget. We pay them for that. It's easier to track the costs of the program."[22] It might be easier to track what EPG costs but, as I discuss later, *interpreting* these costs proved more difficult for facilitators.

Prior to forming an EPG or becoming a group member workers were required to attend a three-day training session, for which they were paid their regular wages. The training was conducted by the EPG department manager and one or more facilitators. "Basic" or "Launch" training instructed workers in fundamental group dynamics, the principles and techniques of group problem-solving, and what "problems" they could legitimately address. It also presented, according to one facilitator, "a little bit of an overview on how participative management came into being. Call it the history of management."

Finally, employee participation was a voluntary program and this made the Weirton case different from others. Elsewhere employee participation has been involuntary; either imposed throughout the organization directly by senior management or negotiated as a part of a union collective bargaining agreement.[23] At Weirton, EPG was formally based on incentives rather than coercion or contractual obligation. Facilitators often tried to organize departments of the mill without any EPGs, but they had only the authority to persuade, not demand. In this context, the "philosophy" of EPG assumed an ideological cast that I describe later in this chapter. Likewise fellow workers could be important advocates—indeed, they could potentially exert tremendous pressure on workmates. Yet when it came to employee participation, EPG members I spoke with seemed to respect the decision of those who opted not to join.

EPG at Work

How successful, then, was voluntary employee participation? As chapter 1 noted, research shows that employee participation *combined with* worker ownership leads to improved productivity. I will discuss financial measures that balance the costs of the program with the savings from EPG projects and track long-term improvements in mill productivity in chapter 5. But the voluntary aspect of Weirton's EPG does provide a window into the collective attitudes of workers. On the basis of EPG membership and retention of groups and group members, EPG was not as successful as company officials and EPG staff proclaimed it was.

Three years into the program over 1,600 employees had completed the training session, and this number had risen to 2,000 by 1988. The number of employees who completed training, however, overstates the actual number of workers active in the program. In the summer and fall of 1986, there were 94 active EPG groups,[24] but the number was probably closer to 100 if one includes unlisted groups. Based on an estimate of 12 members per group, only 1,200, or 14 percent, of the approximately 8,300 employees in the company were active EPG members. Nearly nine of every ten workers did not participate.[25] Furthermore, 400 workers, one quarter of those trained, left the program or never formed groups after training. Using a more reasonable figure of 8 to 10 group members, employee participation involved 800 to 1,000 workers, or 10 to 12 percent of the total workforce, with almost half of those trained leaving the program.

According to a senior facilitator about eighteen groups had become inactive since the program began in 1984. "They no longer meet for some reason or another. Some of it was the chemistry just wasn't there. In other instances departments have to be rearranged, or transfers, retirees, various reasons."[26] Why certain groups disbanded, or why some parts of the mill (or better put, some parts of the steel-making process) resisted forming groups were thorny problems facing EPG staff. Although facilitators optimistically noted that the program was growing slowly, the number of workers that did not form groups or disbanded after training suggests that more than transfers, retirements, and the like were at work. More likely, many employees quickly became frustrated and "burned out" with the program because of the contested nature of authority in the mill.

Clearly the number of active EPG members was low, even considering the voluntary nature of the program. Skepticism toward management intentions ran deep within the workforce and EPG faced a difficult task in persuading workers to form groups and then maintaining them after they organized. But EPG also reproduced "workers by day" through the "problem-solving" process and this conflicted with the alleged status workers acquired under the reforms, a contradiction that routinely confronted and frustrated workers in the program.

Participation as Forced Choices: Type I Problems

At an operational level employee participation was based on group "problem-solving" that followed an eight-step process.[27] If not currently involved with a project, groups continued "brainstorming" for other ideas to begin working on. The eight steps were:

1. Identifying and defining the problem
2. Analyzing the problem—finding causes
3. Generating possible solutions
4. Evaluating solutions through testing
5. Selecting the best solution
6. Developing an action plan or management presentation
7. Implementing solutions
8. Follow-up

At any point group members were encouraged to voice their opinions and suggest ideas, but they had to reach a consensus before moving to the next stage. A consensus was defined by EPG training literature as "general agreement" with the following elaboration:

> You as a member of a group in a meeting may not be in total agreement with a decision, but where consensus is used as the criteria for determining what decision a group shall make, you buying into the consensus is saying, "okay, I can live with it."[28]

Accepting a decision was more important than agreeing with it because moving to the next stage required completion of the task at hand. But even though each step of the problem-solving process organized participation within narrow parameters, the process still had the potential to exaggerate contradictions in the program and call into question authority relations in the mill.

Completing the first step was the most crucial factor in managing this potential because it was here where legitimate "problems" became defined. The EPG program defined "problems" at three different levels, of which only the first two need concern workers:[29]

Type I: Those which we (as a group) have control over. In other words, the groups members themselves have the authority to make a change or the turn foreman in the group has the authority to implement a solution.

Type II: Those which we have no control over but can influence someone who does have control over them. In other words, the group members or the foreman in the group don't have the authority or the expertise to implement a solution but could go outside the group or up the chain of command and influence the proper person or persons that do have the authority.

Type III: Those which we have no control over and have no influence with anyone who does have control. In other words, highly improbable of solving.

This problem typology reflected a conventional hierarchical division of labor between rank-and-file workers, administrative and technical staff, and management. As for those problems that workers had control over, Type I problems focused primarily on immediate job concerns of a technical nature. The emphasis on "problem solving" directed workers to specific technical areas of the production process and product quality such as modifying a work procedure, tool usage, mechanical improvements, or quality control. Safety issues were also emphasized.

During the spring and summer of 1986 EPG groups were focused predominantly on technical improvements in the production process, product quality, and the work environment, or

Type I problems (Figure 4.1). The primary goal of problem solving was on increasing the overall *efficiency* of the labor process; essentially an adaptation of the Japanese form of industrial organization, *kaizen*, which means continuous improvement in productivity.[30] But as Mike Parker and Jane Slaughter have shown, this quickly becomes "management by stress" where "physical, social, and psychological [stress] rather than management orders and decisions . . . regulate and boost production."[31] As one of the more militant union officers saw it, workers were being told to do things "twice as fast."

> They are doing more work with fewer people. Where three people used to do a job, I think two people are doing it.[32]

The goal of work speedup was embedded in the structure of EPG and was manifest differently in any given project. EPG groups had to demonstrate some reasonable cost savings to justify project implementation (a point I will return to when discussing EPG and productivity), and decreasing labor time was a key factor in this estimation. After convincing department and senior management of their idea's "bottom-line" value workers could begin implementing their project, which they were also responsible to check routinely afterwards.

Work speedup was routine at the Weirton mill throughout its history and had generally been celebrated under the banner of "production records" and the public adulation surrounding these feats. The key difference with EPG was how work speedup was generated: through an intensified and more highly structured system of *group think and sanctions*. EPG members were encouraged

Technical Improvements	57
Workplace Reorganization	25
Communication	15
Team Organization/Brainstorming	8
Safety	7
Total	112

Figure 4.1.   EPG Projects by Type of Activity, 1986

Source: EPG Newsletter, *Spring and Fall, 1986*

to set aside their personal grudges and informal codes of work behavior in favor of collective action based on formalized and highly
regulated procedures. Those who insisted on their point of view or
failed to compromise were then subject to peer pressure within
the group to join the consensus. They may not have liked it or
agreed, but they would "live with it."

A Note on Problem Solving, Skills,
and Worker Autonomy

Apart from culling the production-related skills and knowledge of
workers, EPG claimed to promote new skills and knowledge. Participation in EPG was said to require and develop different sets of
skill.[33] They included: (1) identification skills; (2) data selection
skills; (3) communication skills; (4) analysis skills; (5) planning
skills; and (6) decision-making skills.

Did workers actually learn and employ new skills in the course
of problem solving? This question was difficult for me to investigate since I did not observe any EPG projects from beginning to
end. Even if I had, the definition of "skill" and its meaning for
those practicing it are thorny issues at best. But if we define skill
as "a creative response to uncertainty based upon experience and
talent,"[34] workers may have developed new skills through EPG, although this was more likely to occur in the skilled crafts than
among production workers. A genuine skill upgrading that was
more widely distributed among workers would entail some form of
multi-crafting or job rotation, and workers resisted this during my
research.[35] For most rank-and-file workers there was probably little in the way of new knowledge and skill development that they
did not get in high school or college (which many had attended) or
on the job. Instead what they learned was how to formulate craft
knowledge into the language of scientific knowledge that could
then be used to increase and standardize productivity and quality.
This was most characteristic of the Statistical Process Control program, in which a smaller but more highly trained group of workers
used statistical analysis to monitor the production process.[36]

On the other hand, the "skills" associated with small group interaction (1, 3, 5, and 6) were directed in a bureaucratic manner
toward monitoring group members. Actually, they could be more

accurately considered techniques that managed group interaction in reaching a series of consensuses and completing projects. These highly structured tasks routinized group interaction, reducing participation to collecting and documenting technical data. These techniques did not increase a worker's capacity to respond to unique events. Rather their intent was to reduce the occasion of such events in the first place.[37]

Did workers exercise more autonomy on the job through employee participation? In technical areas EPG groups appeared to have some autonomy in modifying their work environment and influencing the production process. Even critical studies of employee participation have confirmed that workers do exercise more influence in altering how a job is performed or in modifying the tools to do it.[38] Occasionally, EPG groups worked on larger projects involving other groups or with officials of the town on projects that affected government services. Groups might also contact and visit customers and suppliers in the course of a project that brought them a degree of autonomy in getting material and making products.

But this autonomy was exercised within the bureaucratic context of EPG and the limits of the problem-solving orientation. Under these conditions, workers faced choices that were systematically curtailed by the rules and routines of participation. First, they had to choose problems whose solutions were technically given; only problems that led to a technical "fix" were allowed to be considered. And as the following section shows, like rank-and-file workers who routinely complained to me about management—"Too many white hats in this mill," "Why can't they just tell us what to do and leave us alone"—EPG members were also critical of what they considered the wrong kind of management participation.

Participation as Forced Choices: Type II Problems

Under the technical problem-solving orientation of EPG it was imperative that group members did not stray far from this agenda, otherwise meetings bogged down, enthusiasm waned, and tempers flared. But choosing projects inevitably led to differences of opinion and often heated debate. Issues falling within the Type II and Type III problem categories were often raised by employees who were intent on getting something done but also by those who were disgruntled or dismayed. In either case, it was here that "problem solving" revealed the structure of power relations in the company—something that was not easily ignored.

Type II problems were frequent, said facilitators, and for the most part they were manageable. But these situations aroused more than just the ire of many EPG members. On occasions where EPG groups relied on technical staff and management personnel, assistance was not always forthcoming. Inevitably groups faced bureaucratic obstacles and delays, and the limits of their autonomy became very apparent. As one exasperated EPG member told me, "We've been waiting for two months now and we made a good case for these trucks and here we are two f——ing months later and still no trucks. Now we've been telling [the facilitator] about this for a long time. What does it take to get anything around here?" It was quite common, I was told, for groups to wait months to get materials, tools, or even a response from management to ideas and suggestions. All facilitators could do was meet with the parties involved and try to expedite the process. Delays due to organizational inertia frustrated both group members and facilitators. "The bureaucracy kills us," lamented one facilitator. "That's got to be our biggest problem here. What can you do?" This problem, however, was not included in the EPG typology, and for good reason. Confronting bureaucratic inefficiency would mean questioning the position and role of facilitators, the structure of EPG, and ultimately the entire Weirton ESOP.

What about those cases where groups had good ideas but were not being heard? EPG had no formal authority to coerce or reprimand unresponsive management, and EPG groups had to persuade management of the cost savings of their suggestions. However, workers could go "up the ladder" and appeal their case to higher-level management and executives if they felt they were encountering unnecessary resistance. This feature of employee participation was very appealing to group members (as I discuss in chapter 5) and gave the impression that workers had indeed gained status in the company.[39] As one facilitator explained during a group interview:

> In EPG you're brought face to face with technicians, engineers, management, and supervisors, to explain the ideas and

if you get a negative response this must be accompanied by some explanation of why the idea wasn't accepted. If workers don't like the refusal of lower level management and supervisors they can go higher in the company to make their case.

I was told by another facilitator of occasions where uncooperative managers were "let go" due to repeated complaints by EPG members and staff to senior executives. Without documentation I could not judge how often this happened, but there were sound reasons to suspect that these cases were extremely rare. During my research, management personnel had yet to be cut to the levels suggested by McKinsey and Company studies in 1984 and again in 1987. Workers' grievance about "management dragging its heels" was confirmed by a senior facilitator.

> There's still resistance, mostly passive resistance. Nobody wants to stand there and openly—there are many cases where supervisors are energetic group members or leaders. There are also as many cases where supervisors have gone through the training and don't complete it. That's okay at this point in time. We'd like to see more participation from the salaried, *but the culture isn't such that it permits that.* Everyone decides that things are getting better when we do see more salaried participation. Right now, a supervisor sees his role or the way he models his role to be more vital in the workplace or on the line, than in an employee participation group [emphasis added].

For this facilitator, then, the problem of management resistance rested with the "culture" of the mill, not with the structure of EPG and the relations of power in the mill. If only *attitudes* need to be changed, Type II problems could be resolved through the appropriate avenues of "influence." The point here was that EPG members had to rely on facilitators to routinely involve and encourage intransigent managers and supervisors before they could complete many projects. They could not rely on their union in these disputes because it had no jurisdiction in these areas. Even when facilitators could effectively mediate in Type II problems, workers rarely extended the range of their participation beyond strict technical domains.

Participation as Forced Choices: Type III Problems

With Type III problems, workers reached beyond the boundaries of EPG only to have their hands slapped and their initiative blocked. The labor process involved much more than technical issues concerning how steel was made. It also entailed political and normative aspects of production relations in the mill. Problems originating in the organizational hierarchy also impaired efficiency and needed to be addressed, but EPG groups could not address these issues or seek solutions to problems they saw as equally, if not more, relevant to their immediate jobs.

A cornerstone in reproducing "workers by day" was the role of group facilitators in *avoiding* these "distracting" episodes by keeping groups focused on the task at hand. During one meeting a worker raised the issue of the rights of workers as owners, and on this occasion the "problem" cut right to the central contradiction I noted at the beginning of this chapter: that a conventional hierarchy was retained despite workers owning the company.

> **Facilitator:**   Let's talk about some things that can get in the way of our perception—
>
> **Joe:**   It's not our mill. Why can't we go into our foremen's meetings?
>
> **Facilitator:**   Management does have a right to manage, Joe.
>
> **Joe:**   Let's put workers—a little EPG—on the board of directors. Then we would have a voice.
>
> **Another worker:**   The union is our voice.
>
> **Joe:**   It's not our union because we don't have a union. Our union sold out! *We* are the union! *We* are the company!
>
> **Facilitator:**   Let's not discuss this anymore or we could be here all night.[40]

The facilitator then gave workers a task involving cardboard puzzles (presumably the "cause and effect chart" described in a training pamphlet) and insisted there be no talking. In this case—one I was told was not infrequent—workers' perceptions were "clouded" by issues with no technical solution. Groups were often frustrated or critical of management but they were discouraged from discussing it during meetings. An exchange during another meeting shows how workers raised problems they had with management and how facilitators tried to keep things "on track."

> **Group Leader** (perturbed as he reads a message from the floor supervisor):   T. said he didn't want anybody from the group leaving EPG early and going to the showers. He said we're not setting a good example and that we should set a good example for the other workers.
>
> *(No verbal response, but a few men smile
> as they shake their heads.)*
>
> **Group Leader** (after a few moments):   Personally, this upsets the shit out of me! You know, I'm down at the Chevy dealer, or down at the market, and these guys are always getting served first. I'm waiting in line and this white-hat comes in and still goes before me. Now, I'm not going to cause any waves, but if T. wants *us* to set an example, *they* should set an example. I don't know why we should set an example!
>
> *(Heads nod amid murmurs of approval.)*
>
> **Group Leader:**   This is what T. said to me and I'm going to pass it on to you *(nodding to the other group members)*. I'm not telling you what to do. You're not children. I'll let you decide how you want to handle it.
>
> *(All the group members look to the facilitator
> for his views on the issue.)*
>
> **Facilitator:**   Well, this is regulations, and you have to abide by regulations.
>
> **Group Leader:**   This is bullshit and it irks me. And I want you to know that I've told everyone.
>
> **Facilitator:**   Well, we can't deal with that anyway, so let's move on.[41]

This exchange was also an poignant example of how mill and community life overlapped in Weirton as a group leader defended his group from a supervisor's "out of line" directive by referring to indignities workers face daily outside the mill. The group leader insisted that a problem between management and workers was normative—"if T. wants us to set an example, they should set an example"—to which the facilitator responded bureaucratically, "this is regulations." Such instances where workers defined problems that lay outside the acceptable range of issues were clearly important. But if these normative conflicts ran parallel to the technical problems of any EPG project, they were not subject to any technical solution.

Facilitators normally viewed these disruptions as "griping," something they considered time-consuming and beyond their sphere of influence or duties. They "distracted" workers from the problem solving they should be doing (though, again, these problems were not unrelated to the production process and product quality). Therefore, groups were systematically discouraged from discussing problems regarding labor-management authority and EPG did not prescribe any recourse other than a facilitator who might pass this discontent on to specific management personnel. Instead, EPG staff deferred these problems to either the union or the labor relations department in the mill (see below). Facilitators tried to manage these situations, but when they could not—which often happened—they insisted that the group move on to more modest problems.

Facilitators tried to avoid these hot spots by encouraging groups to consider problems that, in a sense, did not cause problems. These were projects that had a strong chance of being implemented and completed relatively quickly. This was important to all groups, but especially for newly formed groups that needed to complete a project to justify their time and efforts. Failures threatened to undermine workers' commitment to EPG, and project delays sapped the motivation and goodwill of even the most dedicated EPG members. Thus, facilitators supported projects that they felt were doable over more ambitious ones. As one facilitator explained:

> The last thing the group does before it leaves training is they brainstorm a problem. That's one of the last things people do in training. We take that problem list back to the workplace

and that becomes the list we're supposed to work on. As they work through this list, they pick the simple problems to start with, solve the simpler problems then move on to big problems.

Facilitators denied shaping workers' choices, claiming that groups "work on problems that [the] group has selected, not problems that have been brought to them." Still, they were not passive observers, even by the formal definition of their job title. Facilitators depended on successful groups to convince other employees that EPG "worked" and was worth trying. "We've had a lot of success with the projects. We've got a lot of projects on line," one facilitator told me. "We had a lot of early successes and people got interested in EPG by seeing other groups succeed." The odds of success increased, however, when workers exercised restraint in choosing problems. If nothing else, facilitators acknowledged projects that they judged to have a high chance of success (that is to say, those that generated the least resistance from management).

Still, some groups insisted on testing these limits. During one EPG meeting I attended, a group of nine women chose for their first project a problem concerning a promotion policy among the salary excluded (this group was *not* represented by the ISU). After reviewing a list of easier problems—putting up mirrors to help see around corners, fixing up reception areas, and replacing a lighting fixture on an elevator—a group member spoke about comparable worth issues and higher pay for the added responsibility that her group had recently taken on. As she put it, the criteria for hiring into salaried positions were vague and the group wanted "a more consistent policy so that fairness might prevail where women are concerned in promotion matters."

This problem might otherwise have been rejected by a facilitator, or at least strongly discouraged in most other groups. But such a bold use of EPG (I was aware of no other group addressing any issue of this kind) was apparently tolerated because this group could not be referred to the union to settle the dispute. "They sure picked a tough one to tackle first," mused the facilitator as we left the meeting. "They probably should have taken an easier problem first, just until they got started, but they were unanimous about this. We'll see."

Their test, however, was short-lived as the group dropped the project shortly after this meeting. According to the group's co-leader, they decided that the hiring policy was "a department thing" and that their project would only benefit the group. Instead, they began working on something that was "beneficial to the entire company and not just us." Their research on Weirton Steel's accessibility for the handicapped was accepted for implementation and they were later invited to discuss their work at a Seattle conference as the company's representatives. The group was not pressured into dropping their initial project, explained the co-leader, and group members were unanimous in the decision. Although their concern for the "greater good" of the company reflects the spirit of EPG, their initial project suggests that the structural limits of EPG could be exploited only in the interstices of corporate and union institutional control.

Employee Participation and the Union

According to an EPG training pamphlet, "the (E.P.G. Steering) committee or employee groups will have no authority to add, detract, or change the terms of the Labor Agreement."

> The key is working on work-related problems. The group must avoid the problems which are under the jurisdiction of the company-union agreement. There are proper channels for these problems.[42]

Problems concerning wages, scheduling, profit sharing, stock ownership, investment, modernization, and the like were not under the purview of EPG. Likewise, problems having to do with labor-management relations such as discipline and supervision were dealt with through union grievance procedures and the company's labor relations department. Yet, despite being instructed that EPG focused on "work-related problems," it was precisely such work-related problems that often fell within the jurisdiction of the company-union agreement. In these cases the problem had to be resolved in a manner that preserved the integrity of both EPG and the union while maintaining the narrow parameters of the "problem-solving" orientation.

Separating the functions of EPG from those reserved to the union might appear to preserve the autonomy of workers' institutional representative. In principle, this follows the conventional wisdom of EPG proponents in industry, labor, and academia.[43] From this perspective, unions represent workers in the company and protect their interests *as workers*. Yet unlike other unionized companies with extensive participation policies, Weirton's EPG was not part of a union contract, nor were there any contractual provisions that precisely defined the role of the union in EPG or its veto power concerning EPG projects.

The union's role was most ambiguous at the shopfloor level where technical problems often overlapped with union contract provisions. Here facilitators played a crucial role in mediating this sensitive area by defining the problems that could be considered by groups. As one facilitator put it, "EPGs can work on anything with the exception of contractual issues. That's the forbidden sign." When I asked why, he explained:

> Well, because so many of those issues involve labor law. That's one reason. Another reason is there's already a union that exists in the workplace to address those issues. We don't want to represent ourselves as being union busters or out there to take work away from stewards. And we are half union managed in this department. The EPG movement, the EPG philosophy is embraced by the union.

If the program's philosophy was embraced by the union, and the union's president was on the steering committee, then why not have some provision written into the labor agreement? How were cases resolved where participation infringed on areas covered under the union agreement? According to the facilitator above, EPG either negotiated around the issue or avoided it altogether.

> Sure, not only are there a lot of cases, there's a lot of gray area. The boundary doesn't have a lot of definition. So that's one of T.'s [a union facilitator] functions, if an area should surface that has union ramifications he clarifies and we advise our groups "no, you can't go into that." Scheduling, for instance, rescheduling a crew to maximize profitability, re-

duce costs, could be a terrific idea to a point. The point is where you start affecting overtime, Sunday premium, things that are addressed in the contract.

In the area of work rules, the boundaries of EPG and union jurisdiction were most ambiguous yet sensitive. And it was here that the EPG systematically undermined traditional union protections. The facilitator explained the conflict and his role in the following way:

A group may come up with an idea, and make a pretty good case to buy a truck for their department, say a flatbed. It's a fine idea until it has to be determined who's going to drive that truck. We have a trucking department, they're entitled to drive that truck, but this department wants one of their own riggers or pumpfitters or whatever driving that truck. Now it's a contractual issue and the [union] has to get involved, it has to be defined. We touch on these issues [during the training session] and explain that we don't allow groups to work on problems that are contractual in nature. We say because it is so ill-defined, so nonspecific, as these situations arise we clarify them.

This problem was magnified without a collective bargaining agreement that formalized how such situations should be dealt with. On the other hand, the absence of such a provision afforded the EPG staff and union officials ample opportunity to manage these situations with as little resistance from workers as possible. These "gray areas"—arguably the most sensitive with which EPG dealt—actually favored a negotiated resolution that tended to "bend" the union contract language. The facilitator's judgment in "clarifying" problems of a contractual nature and the flexibility that characterized the union-EPG relationship minimized this potential obstacle.

The union facilitators said they saw no conflict of interest and that EPG did not threaten the interests of workers. "Yeah, I don't see this group and that group and that group," a union facilitator assured me. "I see people." This populist rhetoric was readily appealing to everyone I spoke with, but even if workers too spoke in these terms they also talked about "us" and "them," workers and management. The rank-and-file were wary of possible changes in work rules, and for good reason. In private discussions, all facilitators agreed that "archaic" work rules were an obstacle to EPG reforms. They viewed EPG as a neutral system of organizing information and of generating knowledge that did not, or at least in principle *should not*, undermine the union's role in representing workers. The fact remained, however, that EPG did involve organizing the labor process and it inevitably intersected with areas formally under union jurisdiction.

Ideology and Employee Participation

Workers were formally introduced to employee participation during a three-day training session conducted by the program manager and one or more facilitators in the company's general offices. "Basic" or "Launch" training presented the "philosophy of participative management," techniques of group problem solving, some fundamentals of group dynamics and, in the words of one facilitator, "a little bit of an overview on how participative management came into being, call it the history of management." After three years of EPG over 2,000 employees had completed the training session and more were scheduled when I attended my first meeting.

I have argued that EPG had not changed the basic structure and priorities of industrial organization, but it did seek to change the *ideology* of industrial relations. The "philosophy" of EPG took on an ideological cast precisely because the program was voluntary and workers had to be persuaded to participate. This ideology upholds a technocratic vision of the workplace where the knowledge of workers is mobilized in the interests of higher productivity. The EPG training session communicated this ideology, reinforced the distinction between workers and "those who really have the power," and subtly reminded trainees of their place in the organizational hierarchy—one remained a worker-by-day. Contrary to the claims of EPG staff that employee participation united labor and management, and despite efforts to flatter workers by treating them like "owners," I saw just the opposite during a training session in July 1988.

The Training Session: Learning One's Place

The general offices are located "up on the hill," on the eastern out-skirts of town about a mile up from the river valley and mill. The offices were built when National Steel assumed control of the Weirton mill and the expansive grounds are lush and well kept. Marble pillars reach upwards as one walks up the main entrance steps to the reception lobby. Noticing a sweeping staircase leading to the second floor, I was struck by how much the corporate hier-archy was symbolically represented in the spatial relations of the mill and executive offices. Within this symbolic topography, as one descended the hill toward the mill, one encountered differences in prestige within the workforce. People in town and millworkers considered the general offices "up on the hill" a prestigious work site, even if one's position did not warrant such a distinction. For example, clerical and secretarial employees working there held higher status than similar positions either in the mill or in the old general offices next to the mill.

My impression was further confirmed during a Fourth of July fair on the general office grounds. I noted how convenient it was that people could park on the lawns of the general offices to at-tend the fair. A friend laughed and explained that when National owned the mill, "they wouldn't let anyone near this place, unless they worked here. I mean, it was off limits." I joked that if you own it, you can at least park on it, but the significance of his re-marks was not lost to me. Opening the general offices to workers and townspeople represented an important public display that the mill was their mill, and holding EPG training there symbol-ized a new egalitarianism at Weirton Steel.

But the white collar–blue collar distinction remained, and as the training session began it became very clear who worked where. The training was held in an old executive dining room and coffee, tea, juices, donuts, pastries, and a variety of fruits awaited trainees when they arrived at 8:00 a.m. They were also provided a lunch allowance to use in the cafeteria. Compared to the mill, this was a pretty classy affair. Many workers, who had completed the training, called it "one big perk." "So this is how the other half lives," quipped one trainee as we poured some coffee. The EPG manager's opening remarks seemed to confirm his observation.

First of all we want to get a little bit of perspective, some idea of how we got to this point. We're talking about a change in the way we do business. The very fact that we've got this group up here . . . talking about how we do business. You see, that's a change right there. George, would that have occurred to you a few years ago? Do you think that would have been possible, to come up here and sit here in what used to be a manager's dining room? This was the executive dining room back in the old days. You know the *regular* people ate over there and the executives ate in here, and the vice-presidents ate over in the next place. But, to have this up here, to have this group up here sitting down together talking about how we do business . . . that's a pretty big change [emphasis added].

As heads shook from side to side it appeared that nobody could imagine the privilege of sitting in an executive dining room talking about "how *we* do business." Every rank-and-file worker I met talked about mill business in the mill, sitting at their kitchen table, on their front porch, or at their favorite bar. This is what struck me initially as the session began.

The appearance of privilege, however, could not obscure the fact that these were "hourlies," not executives; workers, not owners. Slowly, this contradiction took bolder shape: we were told that we could stand up during the session if we were not used to sitting (a privilege only a production worker could appreciate); we could use the phone whenever we wanted—we didn't need to ask—and we could walk around outside if we needed to at any time during the sessions. For employees who "were used to working in the fresh air," or those who often needed to escape the fumes and chemicals of the mill, the contrast between these freedoms and their daily work routine was absurdly ironic. "Go ahead and snooze if you need to," a fatuous facilitator assured us trying to be gracious. "Take a few winks." This not too subtle reference to local criticism that workers sleep more often in the mill than they work (see chapter 7) seemed to trivialize the training. Although courteous, this facilitator's halting demeanor intimated a patronizing attitude that seemed to set the tone of the session. These were *workers* and they were being trained how to be better ones.

These remarks were not the only reminder of a worker's place in the company. The introductory segment of EPG training covered an historical overview of how management—the "oldest profession," joked the training facilitator—had evolved. The presentation reaffirmed a management perspective on efficiency in manufacturing and industrial organization. From the facilitator's account, the history of work had been one of progressive development in how "machinery, material, manpower, and method" had been organized to improve productivity. Conflict (though rarely mentioned) and low productivity stemmed from poor organization and misguided management, not from a conflict of interest or struggle for control and autonomy. EPG was the contemporary solution to an historical culmination of past mistakes. From this account, then, participative management was "enlightened" management and would soon replace any archaic conventions that hindered industrial progress. As history, this was a coherent story, although one that conspicuously left out labor resistance and workers' organized struggles to manage their own affairs at work. At this training session, no worker spoke up.

The "philosophy" of participative management, outlined in EPG literature and emphasized throughout the training session, centered on three themes: (1) workers have valuable knowledge and ideas that *they* must use to increase efficiency and improve productivity; (2) a successful organization requires the cooperation and coordination of all its members—particularly between labor and management—in achieving these common goals; and (3) participation is based upon the use of scientific methods. As these themes were elaborated during the session, the ideology behind this philosophy became clearer. Each of these themes reinforced the "worker by day" orientation of EPG and upheld a technocratic vision of workplace reform that focused on rationalizing the labor process. Mike Parker has argued that the ideology of employee participation combines two essential elements; "new forms of work organization are socially and technologically determined," and "this new form of work organization is good for everyone involved: consumers, managers, owners, and particularly workers."[44] To these I would add that under employee participation, an expanded image of the "knowledgeable worker" has to be balanced in order to justify the hierarchical structure of corporate bureaucracies and the ambiguous role of management in this structure. As I will show in chapter 5, this ideological balance had not been achieved at Weirton Steel. First, though, I shall elaborate on each theme.

"The Knowledgeable Worker"

At first glance, the theme of "knowledgeable worker" seemed to represent a cumulative step in the evolution of previous management ideologies and a significant departure from Taylorism and Mayo's industrial relations. Under EPG the worker was cast as a "responsible holder of knowledge" motivated largely by the intrinsic value of applying that knowledge in work. This conception replaced Taylor's notion of the worker as a competitive individual in the industrial machine who is motivated primarily by extrinsic rewards (money) and Mayo's view that "human relations," group solidarity, and social prestige were the main factors motivating workers.

Unlike Taylorism, which took account of workers' knowledge but sought to expropriate it to management, EPG sought to mobilize the cognitive potential of workers in shopfloor decision making. The idea was for employees to generate ideas that they then developed and implemented to cut production costs and improve efficiency. EPG emphasized how satisfying work became when workers could think for themselves in group decision-making.

This theme was heard early in the training session. Speaking of the challenges facing the new employee participation program, the manager of EPG asked trainees,

> How do we recombine the planning of work and the performance of work? How do we logically put those things together to become productive, to make work satisfying?

Reversing a process that Taylorism elevated to a science seemed like a progressive step in restructuring the labor process. But as Reinhard Bendix notes in his seminal *Work and Authority in Industry*, the ideology of Taylorism granted *management* the role of bringing "science and the workman together." Managers would also be subject to the dictates of science, but in the end (with adequate training) they would hold the knowledge and skills needed to impose scientific methods on the labor process and on workers.[45]

Under EPG, the worker was no longer viewed as subordinate to science, nor did management "naturally" hold it exclusively. Instead, workers were potential users of science, and in some cases were more knowledgeable than management. As we will see, the strongest appeal of employee participation lied in these references to more autonomy for workers and more respect for their suggestions, ideas—their minds. This was a significant departure from the images of workers put forth by Taylor and Elton Mayo, who emphasized the emotive, "nonrational" character of workers and group behavior. And just as Mayo stressed that both managers and workers had emotions and group solidarities (although trained management could set these aside while at work), employee participation held that both workers and management were knowledgeable and could exercise scientific control over the workplace.

As Shoshana Zuboff rightly notes, this conception of the knowledgeable worker undermines Taylor's and Mayo's justification of management's exclusive right to control the labor process and "can offer a substantial challenge to managerial authority, particularly on the shopfloor."[46] If workers are as smart as management, can learn what management knows, and in some cases know more than management, what gives management the right to manage? EPG was on fragile ground here, as management resistance and worker skepticism about the reforms suggest. The second and third themes of the EPG ideology sought to resolve this incongruity.

The Bureaucratic Ethos

The role of worker-by-day was further reinforced through a bureaucratic ethos underlying employee participation. From this perspective, the organization was still stratified on the basis of knowledge and specialization, and formal rules and standardized procedures constituted the most efficient means to coordinate such large-scale activities. But if specialized knowledge was still considered the key criterion of hierarchical position, under employee participation *role competence* was as important as technical competence. As the EPG training facilitator explained:

> How do we create an environment that allows each of us to contribute to the extent that each of us knows that we are already capable of? That's a big part of the frustration.

Ideally, management created an environment where workers contribute to the extent that they are already capable of, and this reinforced a division of labor based on management's additional knowledge of the organizational "big picture." Workers became valued not only for their physical labor, but also for their mental labor; their minds should be used, not abused. But as *responsible* knowledgeable workers they must also recognize their capabilities and participate according to their qualifications. Though their position in the labor process was reaffirmed, their status was dignified by the philosophy of EPG. This enhanced image of workers could coexist with their subordinate position in the corporation in part because EPG extended qualities to workers previously associated only with management and in part because EPG stressed the "compressing" of corporate hierarchies down toward workers. As a training facilitator put it:

What we see today is a reinventing of the corporate structure, a change in the way business is approached, a change in the organization of work, a change in the way we manage, a change in the relationship between those that work and those that manage. If you look at a very successful organization, typically it's going like this rather than the old pyramid structure. Yeah, maybe it's losing its shape of a pyramid, but it's made up of problem-solving groups at the bottom. It's much lower in profile.

But if the organization may be changing, bureaucracy remained as a neutral and complex entity where members were easily alienated from each other and from the goals of the organization. EPG claimed to reduce alienation by involving workers in group decision-making and by workers playing out their *proper* roles. All of this, explained the facilitator, rested upon effective communication.

You see, in this type of an organization you have a different focus. It becomes the job of the senior heads of these organizations to not just identify what the goals of the organization are, but to communicate the goals of the organization at every level of the organization. Everybody has got to know what the place is about. . . . This organization focuses in on output. Define that output, what does it look like, what do you need to make, how much of it, what are the quality standards of it, what do the customers want, what do they expect. What do we have to do to meet those demands? This is the survival of our organization, to communicate that to every level.

Ideologically, EPG reified the organization as a system with its own needs that had to be obeyed. Organizational forms had to respond to changing political and economic environments or cease to exist. EPG claimed to decentralize and delegate decision making while simultaneously opening lines of communication that held together a successful organization. Though hierarchy per se was discredited, EPG accepted bureaucracy as necessary and said that "what we need is more bureaucratic structures to reform this mess." From this perspective, conflict and misunderstanding were not the result of different "interests," rather they could be effectively resolved through *more efficient* communication. The assumption of this view was that disruptions to the system were technical in nature, not political or moral. "Better communication" was seen as a key tool in building trust between labor and management. Trust, however, requires much more than words and technical information. It is also based on deeds, on actions. Likewise, too much "open and honest" communication between unequals can also undermine trust, especially when different interests are expressed. This brings us to the final theme of the EPG ideology.

Participation as Scientific Technique

The final theme of employee participation rested, as the EPG manager put it, "on the use of data, fact-based decision making, not opinion-based decision making, the analysis of facts and applying them right to the process."[47] Because bureaucracy was "apolitical" and its nature unquestioned, EPG appealed to science in an effort to analyze these neutral forces, harness human potential, and integrate workers within the organization. Science was the methodology of employee participation, as it had been of management control under Taylor and Mayo.

Just as Taylorism did, employee participation claimed to apply science to the labor process and the relations of production. However, where Taylorism sought to impose the methods of science on the labor process and over workers, employee participation involved workers themselves in doing so. EPG took the form of "worker research" where problem-solving groups "gather data," analyze "facts," and facilitate information "input" and "output." In other words, workers became pseudo-scientists *and* the objects of pseudo-science.

This emphasis on science also encompassed group dynamics. And much like Mayo, who felt that a managerial elite could "detach" themselves from emotional and "nonlogical" thinking through systematic training, EPG insisted that workers too could "detach" themselves with the proper training and techniques for group interaction.[48] According to the training literature an employee participant's role in group meetings was defined in terms of controlled and disciplined interaction. Participants were encouraged to "state opinions and feelings honestly," but they had to "stay on the agenda item," "avoid communications which disrupt the group, such as sarcasm and humor," and "approach the task on the basis of logic, not individual judgments." Separating logic from individual judgment strains even the most rigid definitions of science, but EPG's emphasis on objectivity also intimated a technocratic ethos that sought to rationalize the labor process, and it reflected the concern of EPG staff and proponents about anarchy, politics, or personal grudges being acted out through the program. In other words, the essence of Taylorism resurfaces in this final theme as the principles of "scientific management" are replaced by a science of "participative management" that intends to rationalize conduct in routinized ways.

Summary

These, then, represent the three major elements of the employee participation ideology: (1) an expanded image of the "knowledgeable" worker who has valuable ideas about improving productivity and product quality, (2) the organization as a system with its own needs in which everyone must contribute *their part* to fulfilling, and (3) the principles of science guide worker participation and the internal dynamics of the organization as a whole. According to EPG training, employee participation constituted a "new style" of management and a more effective organization of the workplace. Trainees were being told they were still "workers" by day, only smarter and more responsible. Still, a hierarchical and more bureaucratic workplace remained, and this was the major problem facing employee participation and worker ownership in Weirton.

EPG training introduced employees to the boundaries of what constituted legitimate "problem-solving" and it provided a set of techniques directed at technical problems that presumably had no political and normative implications for the people involved. Yet as I have shown in this chapter, employee participation revealed the political nature of labor-management relations and often touched normative sentiments that extended beyond the workplace.

The training session also reminded employees of the distinction between their role as a worker and as an owner. In this respect, it did not educate employees about the financial status of the company, nor did it prepare them in any way to understand and make decisions in this area. Company finance was central to their roles as worker and owner; an area bearing on many decisions workers would face in the future (modernization projects, profit-sharing formulas, public stock sale, etc.). But this was not part of the training agenda, nor were there any classes available to workers who were interested in learning more about corporate finance. Instead, this was considered a specialized, competitively sensitive area reserved for company executives, management, and accountants, not something workers should, or could, be educated about.

EPG training also avoided any serious discussion of the role of the ISU or questions about control and conflict stemming from labor-management antagonisms. Facilitators "touched" on union-EPG relations, but they did not spend much time discussing this issue in training. Instead, they would "clarify" these situations "as they arise" on the shopfloor. I was told by a training facilitator that the group I observed was a "quiet one" and that often trainees can be very vocal and critical of the program. Of that I have few doubts. But the training was highly structured and tightly focused on group problem-solving techniques and this left little time for much else.

As ideology, however, EPG was not without its contradictions and ambiguities, the most serious of which lied in its most appealing theme; the idea that workers could "think" and act "responsibly." Participation resonated with workers' desire to suggest ideas that were seriously considered and implemented. But in claiming to extend decision making to workers, EPG risked upsetting the assumptions and expectations of both labor and management. EPG training, operation, and structure all attempted to manage higher worker expectations that many feared would come with worker ownership. As the next chapter shows, this concern was only partially confirmed. Though worker expectations about participation were quite moderate, EPG had nonetheless undermined familiar assumptions about how work was done and how authority and trust were sustained. For all its explanations and justifications for industrial reform, EPG lacked an adequate normative order to complement its model of a labor-management "partnership." The absence of such a normative order left many questions about authority and power ambiguous, opening the way for challenges to the EPG program and, indeed, the entire ESOP at Weirton Steel. To explore this more fully I turn now to my interviews with facilitators, managers, and workers, and I look more closely at the role of internal communications.

C^{hapter} F^{ive}

A Fragile Trust: The Normative Order
of Employee Participation

Labor doesn't trust management and never will. Management
doesn't trust labor, and never has.

—Weirton Steel employee, 1987

I n 1987, the EPG department operated from a building directly across from the mill on Main Street. The building was
part of the old general offices in what used to be the center of
town (before a mill overpass relocated the central business district south). The two-story structure needed repair, and rain and
snow had gouged the gravel parking lot. Ironically, for a department with so much paperwork, there was no photocopy machine.
Debbie, the office manager, crossed the street to an adjacent
building for copies. "We need one," she smiled, "but the walk is
good for me, gives me a chance to get out of the office." More than
once I was warned to look out for large rats lurking in the rest-
room. "It's not pretty," a facilitator sighed, "but it's ours!"

He could have been just as easily referring to the EPG program
instead of the building. As I talked with facilitators it became

179

clear that employee participation was *their* program because they had more at stake in its success than either EPG members or the company executives. Facilitators made up a small group but they occupied a critical mediating position between labor and the technomanagerial personnel in the mill. They were also the chief spokespersons in the company for employee participation and were involved in a national network of associations and organizations that promoted the "new industrial relations." As one facilitator commented,

> We spent a lot of time with John Simmons [author of *Working Together*], he's coming in to speak. We have occasional meetings where we get as many of these people as we can. Guest speakers come in. There's an international organization called International Association of Quality Circles, IAQC, the name's going to be changed shortly to something else, taking out the quality circle part and putting in participative management.

Their position in the company, however, was quite awkward given the very structure of EPG and the organizational hierarchy. Employee participation still had to prove itself to executives, management, and rank-and-file workers, and the reforms still faced the "the bottom line." Under ESOP, labor-management relations were more directly mediated by a technocratic-administrative class,[1] and those running EPG represented aspiring members of this class. They viewed employee participation as "better than" both traditional management structures and the role of unions under these structures; a critique of capital-initiated mass production industrial organization as much as of union-negotiated collective bargaining and work rules.

In this chapter I examine the contradiction between the status of a "worker by day" and worker ownership by looking at the views of facilitators and workers, and the Internal Communications program. For facilitators, the key to overcoming the problems facing EPG was better *communication*. But as I argued in the previous chapter, something more than information and knowledge must be "communicated," and EPG staff did not articulate a normative order that resolved the contradictions both management and labor felt between their positions in the corporate hierarchy and the ideology of employee participation. Instead they sought to mediate tensions through what I call "industrial therapy," a form of organizational intervention that sees the *culture* of the workplace, especially attitudes and identities rather than hierarchy and power, as the major problem facing labor relations reform.

For workers EPG led to frustration and criticism expressed in moral terms and that drew from a normative order that was regularly evoked alongside their moderate expectations of the participation reforms. Ultimately, these moral codes were not so much opposed to employee participation as they were critical of the organizational hierarchy and its contradiction to the spirit of participation. EPG validated workers' belief in their value and contribution to the company but it also magnified conflicts that were rooted in shopfloor traditions and working-class culture.

Finally, an elaborate communications system functioned as a form of "internal public relations." As an ideological medium it did not dominate the definition of employee participation and worker ownership, but it existed alongside alternative sources of information and interpretation that competed for the hearts and minds of workers. Ironically, EPG's emphasis on honest communication was met by growing skepticism among workers, further reinforcing their frustration about worker ownership during the late 1980s.

Facilitators as Industrial Therapists

Initially, I was taken by the loose, jovial nature of the EPG department, the relaxed atmosphere, the leisurely pace of work, the bantering and razzing. The staff displayed a camaraderie and esprit de corps that reinforced bonds of solidarity and distinguished their position within the company. But EPG facilitators also functioned in ways that reflected the seemingly impenetrable bureaucratic nature of industrial organization and worker ownership at Weirton Steel. From my interviews and observations I began to see EPG facilitators more as "industrial therapists" whose role was to help labor and management *adapt* to a changing global economy through less antagonistic and more cooperative workplace relations. In this regard, the marriage counselor who helps estranged spouses become better "partners" is an apt analogy.

I elaborate on this industrial therapist metaphor by considering the "mission" of EPG facilitators and the language of reform, the subjective nature of their job and the "facilitator personality" that they believed made an effective facilitator, and their emphasis on "honest" communication and belief in training and education as the foundation for successful employee participation. Facilitators resembled therapists in their sense of detachment from political and moral conflicts as they dealt with antagonistic "feelings" resulting from "misunderstandings" between labor and management. They were committed to changing how people thought about themselves so thcy could "get along" in a changing workplace. And much like therapists, they offered their clients interpersonal, group "techniques" for resolving strained workplace relations.

The "Mission" of Facilitators

Facilitators formed a small group whose "mission," as one put it, was untested and controversial. They repeatedly expressed an unwavering commitment to EPG and sincerely believed that it was a progressive and necessary transformation in industrial relations. In their view EPG marked a significant departure from previous reforms and was far ahead of anything of its kind—or anything they had ever seen at Weirton Steel. "What we're doing here" stated one facilitator, "is way beyond what's ever happened here."

> You look back 10 years ago and see how far we've moved, you wouldn't believe it. It's just been great. We've made good progress but we can't do it all. We're stretched as it is, but we're working hard to get our programs implemented.

But in my interviews with facilitators, I never received a clear explanation of just how EPG was different from past industrial relations reforms. In fact, what distinguished it from earlier reforms was more a matter of degree than of kind; the basic bureaucratic framework continued to define employee participation.

> **Varano:**   You mentioned earlier that the quality of worklife program that was in place here just prior to the ESOP has changed a bit in an employee-owned corporation. How?

Facilitator: Let me give you some definitions. QC, quality circles, groups of workers and their supervisors meeting weekly to solve quality problems. The theme of QC is quality.

Varano: Quality of what?

Facilitator: Product—this narrow and closed. . . . [I]t's more like SPC than anything else now. QWL, quality work-life, the difference is in the name, groups of managers, supervisors, and workers meeting weekly address problems relating to the worklife, the quality of their worklife. A lot of gingerbread types of things, like locker rooms, air conditioning, things that make the quality of worklife better.

The next definition would be human resources development. Work on the organizational level, organizational development. Yes, you're probably familiar with OD [Organizational Development] work, changing organizations to become more effective organizations. Sometimes you have to look at the organizational structure, flatten an organization, change it. That's organizational development kind of work. We're going to make some changes in the actual structure.

Not only that, you're changing methodology. Okay. EPG, or what we call EPG—you see it called a lot of other things—it addresses all of the above. The quality, the quality of worklife, the organizational development aspects, all those types of things [are] rolled into what is now called employee participation, employee involvement. Okay. So when we talk about QC's, talk about QWL's [Qualityof Work Life], we're talking about specific entities or a participative group that has specific properties.

The [QC] movement has matured into full-blown participative management philosophies and it's gone—what they're trying to do is take employee participation from one hour a week meetings to a forty-hour philosophy.

On the surface, this elaborate explanation is quite vague and never conveys exactly what EPG is all about or how it had developed into what facilitators said it is. But his account reflected the strong bureaucratic orientation of participation reforms and its long tradition in management circles. Only now the range of programs that were so "focused and narrow" and that reproduced the specialization associated with bureaucratic organizations were "all rolled into one."

The language of reform expressed above has a clinical tone and is characterized by pseudo-scientific phrases—"you're changing methodologies" to cope with "specific entities" with "specific properties." The jargon of employee participation (and acronyms that accompany it) rival that of any scientific or therapeutic discipline. And conceding the irreversible transformation underway, EPG is potentially a "forty-hour philosophy," a set of principles that will encompass and guide the entire labor process and employee relations from shopfloor to executive offices.

The idea of worker participation as a "forty-hour philosophy" was perhaps the most striking outlook of facilitators and it conveyed the detachment therapists claim is necessary for effective therapy. I asked facilitators if their role in EPG groups was necessary or if groups could operate autonomously. In what might first appear to be an excessively disinterested and modest response, facilitators all agreed that EPG could eventually function without them. As one explained,

> As the natural leaders in the group emerge . . . we bring them back off site for four days of leaders training. The idea is to eventually enable the group to function without a facilitator, to stand alone—that's what we call it, stand alone group— able to function as an effective problem-solving team in their work environment without weekly visits from a facilitator coming around making sure management and workers are cooperating, participating, and jointly trying to solve problems.

During an EPG meeting I asked workers if they thought their facilitator was necessary or if they could function effectively without him. The facilitator was present and this may have inhibited them, but in this case they unanimously supported his role at meetings and agreed that his help was indispensable. As we saw in chapter 4, EPG members felt that they needed facilitators to help them deal with management. They realized that to get anything done they had to stay within EPG boundaries or see their time wasted and their ideas rejected; facilitators reaffirmed these boundaries and validated appropriate participation. Still, after the meeting, the facilitator appeared puzzled and he insisted "they could do it without me." He actually seemed disappointed that they expressed such dependence on his role in the group, much like a therapist would regard group or client dependence.

What Made an Effective Facilitator?

Recall that facilitators were chosen from within the company. All had mill experience and rose through the ranks, and they knew many workers personally. But an effective facilitator required more than a familiar face with the appropriate personal history, and more than formal education and specialized knowledge. Jim, a facilitator for almost three years, worked irregularly in the mill before finishing his college education with various academic credentials: an associate's degree in industrial engineering technology, a bachelor's in business, and a master's in counseling psychology and human resources development. "This [EPG] is human resources development work," he explained. "It's precisely what I was going to get my master's for." Still, for Jim, formal education was not important in becoming an effective facilitator.

> All of us don't have master's degrees. Some don't even have degrees. It's more of a personality type than—ah, you have to have a facilitator personality, I suppose, [be able to] work well with people, a lot of people skills. You have to have those skills for training, keen knowledge of group dynamics, those types of things.

According to Jim, the key to a facilitator's role lay not with education, social ties, or mill experience, but rather with "something inside," a "personality" type, someone with "people skills" who was able to "work well with people." Jim's assessment of what made a good facilitator emphasized the same qualities that Elton Mayo attributed to the manager of the 1930s, although, for Jim, this "personality type" could not be taught—you either had it or you didn't. This characterization also underscored the difficult task facilitators had assumed—to affect the attitudes and behavior of people under conditions that structurally restricted and impeded this goal. "Psychologizing" the role of a facilitator, as Jim does, illustrates the industrial therapist metaphor, but it also captures two dimensions of the basic structural contradiction of employee participation.

First, "people skills" and a "facilitator personality" are vague terms that refer more to the ambiguities of their job than any personal quality or character trait. The facilitator's job was in many ways a "thankless" one because it was very difficult to attribute the consequences of EPG to anything *facilitators* had done. Objective measurements of facilitators doing their job were hard to come by, and Jim recognized this.

> We are on course. Yeah, we're on a bumpy road, but we're not as unfocused as we appear. People perceive us to be completely unfocused. [Our job] is not crystal clear. We're flying on instruments all the time, but the commitment is there.

When asked if he knew why EPG was successful, Jim revealed the "bumby road" of the reforms. As I noted in chapter 1, despite methodological shortcomings, some studies do show employee participation improving productivity, but in relation to reducing labor-management conflict, research is far less conclusive. In 1986, Jim explained, the company spent $1.6 million on operating EPG, the Operations Improvement Program, and Cost Accounting Reduction Effort.

> Those three programs saved, after Treasury and Accounting got done with their figures, $10.6 million for the corporation. An equivalency of $330 million in sales is what we gave back to the corporation.

A further breakdown of the savings from EPG in particular was unavailable, but it should not be surprising that EPG projects saved the company money. As I showed in chapter 4, EPG projects were "chosen" based on some potential cost savings and group presentations to management emphasized this. It was also possible, however, that *more* savings would result if ideas that management rejected had been implemented. Likewise, management resistance to the program—"dragging its heels"—and festering labor/management conflict may also have limited the potential cost savings of EPG reforms. It was also unclear whether workers would continue forming EPG groups or keep existing groups operational if the company began posting financial losses rather than gains (as it had up to 1988) or if the amount in profit-sharing checks decreased.

In other words, both labor and management might have squabbled over a project that saved money, but this hardly reflected the spirit of cooperation and partnership that EPG sought to encourage alongside improved productivity. Actually, as we will see, EPG was more of a "tug of war" between labor and management. In this context, facilitators were at pains to identify attitudinal or behavioral changes resulting from EPG as the source of these "bottom line" savings. In Jim's mind, some things were best left unmeasured.

> **Varano:**   How do you measure a cost savings due to attitude changes or behavioral changes?
>
> **Jim:**   All we measure is what we can measure, direct cost savings as it relates to implemented projects. That's what we're talking about. This cost savings wouldn't exist if there hadn't been—if attitudinal changes hadn't occurred at some point along the line. All the intangibles you can't measure.
>
> **Varano:**   It would seem kind of rough to really get ahold of that figure.
>
> **Jim:**   We've explored I don't know how many attitudinal surveys, or ways to try to measure attitude change, and without exception every single one of them you encounter you have to measure hard core items. Everything has to be factored binomial, something occurred or doesn't occur, and that's all you can measure. Meeting attendance, we're going to track meeting attendance for the last half of this year. One of the facilitators is changing groups to align ourselves more with area management. When we do that, how do we know where the impact is? Well, about the only thing we can figure, the only thing we can measure is the meeting attendance. We're not sure how it correlates. We don't know what the correlates are.
>
> **Varano:**   Yes, we're getting into that gray area now.

Jim: The position we take is all those things are things best not measured at all. Why bother?

Varano: Well, because of the expense of the program, and because of the emphasis put on it by the company.

Jim: MBA's have a real tough time [with EPG]. See, that's where the commitment comes in. You gotta believe. That's why it [EPG] has to be recession proof.

This strong personal "commitment" facilitators had in the program underscored the ambiguous nature of their positions and responsibilities. Lacking any quantitative evidence linking changes in workplace *culture* with EPG cost savings, "you gotta believe" that what you were doing was right. There were certainly many "good" ideas that had little empirical evidence to support them, and in a corporate bureaucracy one had to be very persuasive without such evidence. Facilitators had to persuade labor, management, and the board of directors that EPG was "right." Cost savings from EPG projects were the only indication of EPG's bottom-line value, but these figures alone were not enough to convince workers and management of the normative virtues of employee participation that were "recession proof."

Secondly, "people skills" and a "personality type" reflected the emotional labor facilitators performed when coping with the recurrent conflicts and disputes that developed in group meetings. Their job was to bring people together under a common goal, people who otherwise were fragmented by an elaborate division of labor and distrust. Although EPG focused on solving *technical* problems, facilitators felt their job required talents and personal traits that extended beyond observable skills and technical competence. As one facilitator intimated, the emotional labor facilitators performed required they have that "something extra."

Sometimes we're brutally honest with the workers, the people we come in contact with. We see that as being extremely important, deal with people in an open and honest fashion. If somebody's bullshit, we tell them. We've been consistent. We haven't wavered at all. We had a lot of early successes and people got interested in EPG by seeing other EPGs succeed. We've had this commitment. Our people are made up of varied individuals from different backgrounds. We're extremely dedicated. This week my employees' meeting was at 6:00 in the morning. My latest meeting will be from 11:00 to 12:00 at night. We're in the plant at all hours. We're tenacious. A lot of reasons for our success has been because of our department. There's a lot of adjectives that come to mind: dedicated, tenacious, ruthless. In any given moment I can be conversing with a janitor in the mason department and an hour later with the president of the corporation. And people all in between. We're very flexible, very agile people.

Facilitators were brought face to face with divergent interests, experiences, and power that were structured in the organizational hierarchy. Being "flexible" and "agile" was important as they constantly moved between rungs on the company ladder, but also because they saw their job as bringing these groups together in cooperation. In their view, facilitators had that "something extra" that allowed them to get along with everyone in the company from janitor to president. How then could workers and management develop this agility, this flexibility, if employee participation was envisioned as a "forty-hour philosophy" minus the assistance of facilitators?

Precisely because their task was structurally impeded, facilitators also had to be "dedicated," "tenacious," and "ruthless." Their emphasis on "brutally honest" communication further reflected a view of the workplace as uncongenial and unyielding, but where divisions between workers and management could be overcome with "tough talk." "Better communication" has become the sine qua non of industrial relations reforms and employee participation, and this was no better illustrated than in how facilitators viewed the union.

Facilitators and the Union

Another aspect of facilitators' optimism about EPG that validated their emphasis on communication was how they minimized or ignored the degree of stratification in the mill. As they saw it, Weirton Steel was not separated by divisions between workers and management, administrative and technical staff; it was composed of people. "I don't see this group and that group and that group," said one facilitator. "I see people." This populist outlook, so often invoked by E. T. Weir and Thomas Millsop, reduced structural divisions to personality characteristics and framed how facilitators viewed labor-management conflict. By reinterpreting mill stratification in this manner, facilitators were more prone to viewing problems in the mill and with EPG as a matter of *culture*. Thus, it was attitudes and "outlooks" that had to be changed and this could be done through training and improved communication. As a union facilitator put it:

> At first people thought [EPG] was trying to break the union, but we've put 2,000 guys through the training and there's groups signed up more than we can handle. It's working real well. Management's got to give a little, but so do the workers.

Even union facilitators agreed that archaic work rules hindered effective participation and would inevitably be replaced by more flexible arrangements. All facilitators felt that the ISU had to "change with the times," but they also insisted that areas over which the union had jurisdiction were "off limits" for EPG and that they were not trying to replace the union. The key in dealing with the union, according to facilitators, lay in better communication and including them on all major projects. A senior manager in the Operation Improvement Program put it this way:

> In our particular case the union doesn't give us any hindrance whatsoever. The biggest thing is just get 'em on early on, tell 'em what you're doing, here's what you're heading for and here's the benefits. And in the majority of cases you have very little problem with the union. We've found that whether it be union, hourly people, executive, management, salaried people, if you just explain to them what you're doing and the rationale behind it, 90 percent of the time that's your problem. We bring the union on board first, to let them know what's happening.

Though represented on the EPG steering committee, the ISU had been bypassed on some key projects and management studies, which caused some turmoil in the mill. During the second

McKinsey management study, a pilot project was initiated to assess the feasibility of reorganizing work areas and redesigning management-staff relations so that each department (sheet, tin, strip mill) functioned more or less as an autonomous production unit responsible for itself, rather than having to report through a companywide chain of command. According to a senior facilitator:

> There were supposed to be some union changes that they were supposed to incorporate into the pilot project gainsharing. This is a system whereby the maintenance people working on these production units would receive incentive on production as well as the operators. So there's a giant rift out there in this plant. That incentive was to be quality-based, not productivity-based. There was supposed to be broad-based job descriptions, a lot more latitude in what you could do, multi-crafting, all those things. At the last minute the union pulled back.
>
> [For what reason?]
>
> Because, in my opinion, and it's my opinion only, McKinsey did some unethical things. They went into the plant, they called meetings against the wishes—the meetings weren't against the wishes of the executive committee, but the timetable was. When they went in and talked to the people on the floor they tried to bludgeon people with their concepts, which are good—good, sound, solid concepts—but their means of delivery were rotten. When that happened, there were probably two or three instances, we found that the union pulled back their support and said that "we're not going to support anything that we have to do when it involves a change in the contract, and the reason we're not going to support this is because you McKinsey people did this and this and that."

The problem here was not that the project was unsound, or that workers resented potential infringements on their autonomy and job security, or that it threatened union interests. Rather the union "pulled back" because "good, sound, solid" ideas were not properly communicated to workers—"their means of delivery were rotten." Here again, facilitators considered their interactive talents and sociable predisposition prerequisites of "open and honest" communication and successful EPG reforms. As one facilitator told me sternly during a group interview:

> If we don't have an answer, we don't give one. We don't pull any punches. We don't paint any glory pictures here. We tell it like it is. We give them a truthful answer if we know it, and if we don't, we don't say anything. We stress pulling people together.

As industrial therapists, facilitators saw *all* groups—labor, management, and the union—as divided and threatened by misunderstandings and unfounded fears, not by the power structure in the mill. "Pulling people together" came from truthful communication that respected these relationships but did not seek to alter them. This may have characterized the views of facilitators and union leaders, but why was it so hard to "pull" management into employee participation?

Employee Participation and Management Resistance

All facilitators praised the rank-and-file's support of EPG. Management, however, was another story. Despite earlier claims by executives that management was "behind employee participation 100 percent," most were still reluctant to endorse EPG by cooperating with projects or workers. Managers attended the same training session as the rank-and-file, and according to one facilitator, of the 2,000 trainees "probably a quarter of that is management." Some lower-level managers were considered model participants and they received a fair amount of publicity in newsletters and weekly videotapes. These, however, were the exceptions and EPG faced a major hurdle involving more supervisors and department managers. As one facilitator put it:

> There's still resistance. It's mostly passive resistance. Nobody wants to stand there and openly—there are many instances where supervisors are energetic group members or leaders. There are also many instances where supervisors have gone through the training and don't complete it. That's okay at this point in time. We'd like to see better participa-

tion from the salaried, but the culture isn't such that it permits that. Everyone decides that things are getting better when we do see more salaried participation. Right now, a supervisor sees his role as being more vital in the workplace or on the line, or sees the way he models his role is more vital in the workplace or on the line, than in an employee participation group.

Management had good reason to be suspicious of EPG and their reluctance to embrace it was not surprising. The fate of American managers during the 1980s and 1990s has been no more secure than that of labor as corporate downsizing has also "streamlined" mid-level management positions. Many have lost jobs, experienced blocked mobility, and suffered financial setbacks.[2] Weirton Steel was no exception and there was widespread concern among management personnel that their jobs were "on the line." When National Steel announced its disinvestment in 1982, department managers and shopfloor supervisors were as fearful of losing their jobs as were hourly workers. The first McKinsey study in 1982 reaffirmed these fears by specifically recommending that management personnel be reduced. Four years later a second study reiterated this finding and it was clear to everyone that cutbacks were in the offing. Rumor constantly kept management looking over its shoulder and cast a shadow of suspicion over the participation reforms. Many in lower- and mid-level management felt that EPG complicated their view of the correct way to manage and undermined their ability to perform their jobs so they could save their jobs. The following example illustrates their dilemma and the resistance EPG facilitators faced.

Hal, a manager from the pollution control department, had been at Weirton Steel for just over twenty years and he was not overjoyed with the EPG reforms. "Everyone's got an axe to grind," he said. As we sat in his office Hal sarcastically recited the various EPG programs by their acronyms, his tone and pace blurring the letters into a meaningless string of sounds that made no sense to me. Perhaps employee participation made no sense to Hal, but the programs had become a hot topic in town after the fervor over the ESOP settlement had subsided. Hal felt he had a job to do and all this "hoopla" over EPG was not only distracting, but disturbing because it raised the idea of employee involvement in areas previously reserved under management discretion. In a guarded tone, Hal assured me that management authority was not undermined by EPG, nor would workers make decisions over issues they were unqualified to address.

Workers participate in the everyday shopfloor decisions that affect the immediate job situation, but they do not participate in the decisions of capital spending, financial operations, or the *actual operations of the company* [emphasis added].

The rank-and-file worker on the shopfloor, Hal explained, "doesn't know enough about the business of a steel mill" to make these types of decisions. "They make decisions about what they know best, and management makes decisions on what they know best."

On the one hand, then, employee participation appeared to threaten Hal's job; EPG was moving forward at the same time management faced impending cutbacks. On the other hand, EPG challenged Hal's authority on his job. There was a clear division of labor in the mill and he was adamant that workers should stay in their place. He considered the reforms "much ado about nothing" and superfluous to what was necessary for a successful mill. In this respect, Hal's views had much in common with other critics of employee participation (myself included) who saw it as more symbolic than substantive reform that did not alter the basic organizational hierarchy of power. If this was the case, Hal wondered, why was there so much fuss over it?

Hal was not worried that rank-and-file workers would try to take over the company and make decisions that were management's to make. That was unlikely. His major concern was keeping his job and this meant making steel and making it profitably. The idea that workers might have a voice in how the company was run—"the actual operations"—was absurd to a man who felt his job threatened not by workers making decisions, but by the plant closing down because it could not make enough high-quality steel on time for demanding customers. The participation reforms did not hold much credibility for Hal because he was skeptical about how valuable these programs would be in producing steel. Rather, what bothered Hal was that employee participation held him personally, and management in general, responsible for the troubles facing Weirton Steel. In this respect, Hal was representative of many in lower- and mid-management who felt that EPG challenged not only their assumptions regarding labor-management relations but their sense of competency as well. Their jobs were on the line, but so too was their authority in the mill.

Overcoming Management Resistance

Many in management resented the idea of cooperating with workers. But as facilitators saw it, EPG only challenged *how* managers had always managed, not their *right* to manage. Consequently, just as facilitators had to reinforce the "worker by day" orientation for labor, they also had to reassure management that they retained "the right to manage." However, if EPG was a "new" way of managing, then what "rights" did management have? For a senior manager in the Operations Improvement Program, they simply misunderstood what EPG was all about.

> Well, that's where their [mid-management's] misconception comes in. We say participative management is a tool to allow middle management and executive management to make the proper decision. *It's a tool, that's all it is.* It does not impair executive management's right to manage. He still has that right. You see, this is where we keep getting screwed up. He thinks he doesn't have that right anymore. He still has the right to manage. *He just doesn't have the right to mismanage.* You can't get that point through to him. For whatever the reason, middle management feels that if I got six people in the room, I have to have a consensus of opinion to do what's right. Whereas five people might want to do things one way and one might want to do it another, it's that manager's responsibility to evaluate everything that's said, and he just might feel that the one guy has the right way to go, and then that's it. He's got to make his decision. But that's a cloudy issue. That's what tears at a lot of people [emphasis added].

The problem of mismanagement was not about "rights," but responsibility, not position, but accountability. Management had been given "a tool" in EPG to manage better and they should not misuse it. They were being held accountable for productivity as they always had and retained their authority over the production process and labor. However, for managers like Hal, they were now responsible for programs to which they were opposed and which they felt undermined their ability to manage properly. As one OIP manager saw it,

> I think it's total resentment that you see from middle management that they feel you're stepping on their toes, or they don't like to be held accountable. We have a real sophisticated tracking program in place. We know by month who's falling behind and where these projects should be, and you have that accountability. We build that accountability into it. This, in turn, gives us problems with our middle management because they've never had their feet held to the fire. We've had instances where we've had to go to the steering committee and say, "Joe Blow's giving me problems. He's falling behind. He don't give a shit. It's probably advantageous for Mr. Loughhead to give him a call," which he has. When you start doing that it builds resentment.

Like the "worker by day," the position of management was as secure or insecure under employee participation as before, only now the autocratic management style of the past had to be replaced by a style that "fit" contemporary industrial and competitive realities. Rather than "commanders," this new style placed managers in the role of "listeners" or, as Shoshana Zuboff writes of the contemporary manager, an "educator and learner."

> Their aim is to expand the knowledge base and to improve the effectiveness with which data is assimilated, interpreted, and responded to. They have a central role in creating an organizational environment that invites learning and in supporting those in other managerial domains to develop their talents as educators and learners. In this domain, managers are responsible for task-related learning, for learning about learning, and for educating others in each of the other three domains.[3]

Clearly, this was not easy for facilitators to convey, but they were at pains to do just that. And again, as with the union, overcoming management resistance depended on improving communication and fostering a "better understanding" of employee participation among managers. As the OIP manager correctly pointed out, the form of managerial authority was shifting, even though management's position over labor remained intact.

> They have a feeling that it threatens their authority. They have this misconception about employee participation. You know, employee participation is really allowing your people to participate, to speak out. It's not a thing where you have a vote and majority rules. In other words, say you are my manager and I as an hourly person say, "Hey, I have this idea, Just hear me out." If it helps you make a better decision, fine, but the ultimate decision still stays with management. But, see, *that part was never clear*, and so consequently management and a lot of foremen feel like they're being threatened [emphasis added].

With these "misconceptions" cleared away, facilitators were confident that they could "bring people together," that is, bring management and labor together. For them, the only way to clarify these issues and allay the fears of managers was by more effectively communicating the idea of EPG. Just a little more honest communication and the antagonistic parties could (re)unite. But might not *too much* honesty intensify, rather than ameliorate antagonisms?

This was reflected in facilitators' criticism of how the company had dealt with management personnel. Whereas EPG was voluntary for rank-and-file workers, management was intimidated into the EPG scheme of things. "They tell them you *will* do this," explained a facilitator, "and that's not the proper way to deal with management." Clearly this "strong-arming" contradicted the message facilitators were trying to present while also reinforcing management's worst fears about EPG. Facilitators insisted that you could not change attitudes by forcing people. "That's why we think it's important to get supervisors through the training" a facilitator explained.

> Then they at least know what's going on. They know what to expect. Their expectations are more in tune to what is

happening. They know what the problem-solving process is. They know that groups are supposed to bring them solutions of problems. So our major goal is to get all these supervisors and workers working together solving problems. Our sub-goal is getting [management] trained so at least they're aware of what's taking place.

Again, effective communication was considered the critical factor for involving management in employee participation. Facilitators stressed how EPG required open and often "brutally honest" communication, but as I showed in the previous chapter, such openness and honesty in EPG meetings was intolerable and undermined the controlled nature of the problem-solving process. Within the industrial therapeutic metaphor, however, this was not unresolvable—therapy involves both the controlled expression of emotion and its resolution through enhanced awareness (self-education through problem-solving). Working together not only meant physical coordination of the division of labor; in the "participatory" workplace it now entailed a verbal and emotional coordination, making the role of facilitators much like industrial therapists.

Workers and Employee Participation

With barely a quarter of the labor force involved in EPG, most employees were less than enthusiastic about employee participation. At best, there was widespread ambivalence toward the program and people had to be "won over" to it. During interviews workers were often contemptuous of EPG, claiming that it was just another management scheme to "get more for less." Workers were protective of the skills and autonomy they had secured over the years and, in the words of one facilitator, "many areas in the mill are real tough to break through." And as I noted earlier, many people had become frustrated and had dropped out of participation groups.

For their part, the EPG members I spoke with supported the reforms and most saw an improvement over how things "used to be." Employee participation brought about added frustrations, but group members felt that in time their talents would be used more effectively to benefit the company. These favorable attitudes toward employee participation were not unusual nor surprising.

Research has consistently shown that workers support the idea of
participation and see in it an opportunity—and a rare one at
that—to suggest and implement ideas about improving production and their work environment.[4] Indeed, most workers I spoke
with (both group members and nonmembers) thought the *idea* of
employee participation was a good one. "The concept of worker
participation is great," said a bundler in the tin mill. "Most of the
guys like the idea, Charlie, get me? You follow me?" Well, not exactly. What was their idea of worker participation? How did workers view this "new way of doing business"?

For seven EPG trainees I met, that "idea," that "concept," was
still quite vague when they attended their first training session.
When asked by the presiding facilitator why they came and what
they expected from EPG, most of them wanted to know more
about the program they had heard so much about. As a boiler-
house worker put it:

> I'm here because, well, all the guys I work with, they came
> and they said there's a lot of things, they all liked it. They said
> it was real interesting. They said go and find out for yourself,
> so that's why I'm here, just to learn a little bit about it.

These workers decided to join EPG because "word of mouth"
heightened their curiosity and maybe there was something to all
this talk about participation. For everyone the program sounded
interesting and was ambiguous enough to evoke many possibilities as to what it might entail. And for the most part, this range of
possibilities coincided with the "worker by day" orientation that
EPG reinforced.

But perhaps the most striking outlook among the trainees was
their interest in how EPG "got things done." This concern reflected not only their view of management resistance but also
their experience with bureaucratic obstacles—the very obstacles
that EPG reinforced and extended.

> The tin mill welders have never had a group before. . . . I'm
> hoping that by my tin mill participation and, ah, the partic-
> ipation by other people in the group, we can get something
> accomplished to save our company some money. (welder in
> the tin mill)

The reason I joined EPG was basically I was wondering how they get anything accomplished. I joined the group to find out if there is an effective way to ask a question without putting someone directly on the defensive. [People] do tend to get defensive, like [they think] that you're trying to find something wrong with their personal work performance. That's my main purpose. In other words, how can you get effective answers without people feeling that their job is in question? Seems like there's more talk than action everywhere. (central storage worker)

With only few exceptions, the workers I spoke to held *moderate* expectations of what the participation reforms might lead to. They did not expect to participate much beyond their immediate work environment, nor did they desire this. Rather they were satisfied to have more voice over how they did their jobs and they felt redeemed by the program's respect for their ideas and suggestions. This outlook, or "job consciousness," is characteristic of worker attitudes in other cases of employee participation.[5] But if Weirton workers appeared to accept their role as "worker by day," they were still frustrated with employee participation. Why? EPG did not resonate completely with workers' conceptions of industrial hierarchy or with their views of authority relations in the mill. It was here where I first began to see how workers drew upon a traditional normative order to criticize and challenge worker ownership and where EPG's failure to summon an appropriate alternative surfaced most clearly.

On the one hand, workers accepted EPG's emphasis on the knowledgeable worker and organizational ethos, but they tended to question what constituted legitimate knowledge. Their criticisms of the mill hierarchy were couched in norms that defined an appropriate display or use of authority; norms based not only on the knowledge superiors claimed, but also *where* this knowledge came from. Furthermore, although their enhanced status did not expand their sphere of decision making, workers felt it *should* at least permit them more autonomy in their job. In this respect, workers held superiors responsible for upholding the principles of EPG. They did not expect power but rather fairness.

At the same time, workers interpreted the organizational hierarchy from a perspective at odds with the bureaucratic ethos that

EPG endorsed. Specifically, they favored management that had "risen through the ranks" over the "outsiders" that National Steel had hired in the 1970s. Here, the outlines of a normative order rooted in the community, as much as the mill, began to emerge where "loyalty" and "nepotism" competed with bureaucratic criteria and the "bottom line." These moral judgments were calling into question shared assumptions about the basis of authority in the mill that EPG did not resolve.

This normative code resembles the "indulgency pattern" characterizing labor-management relations of a gypsum mine studied by Alvin Gouldner in *Patterns of Industrial Bureaucracy*.[6] There, a pattern of traditional norms governing workplace routines, rule-alterations, and authority relations was undermined when management changed and new supervisors failed to abide by custom. Gouldner's analysis focuses on how this process unfolded in the gypsum mine, though he suggests that the origin of these indulgency patterns are in part derived from community life outside the mine. My analysis seeks to bring out more clearly how similar patterns I observed in Weirton arose from the *intersection* of mill and community life. More, just as Gouldner shows how the disruption of these indulgency patterns led to a wildcat strike in the company he studied,[7] my analysis in the following chapters suggests a similar trajectory in Weirton. An initial glimpse of this pattern is found in workers' views on EPG.

Views from the Shopfloor

Over time I came to know a few workers quite well and our discussions oriented me to the frame of reference employees used to interpret the EPG reforms. Sal, Pete, and Bob were all married and homeowners, and although they were hardly a representative sample of the employees in EPG, they were still diverse in terms of their age, jobs, skills, seniority in the mill, and wage rate. Consequently, their similar perspectives on EPG were all the more striking and suggested that the normative order they evoked was more commonly shared than not. All three were enthusiastic group members when I first met them in fall 1986, although by summer 1987 they were beginning to have serious doubts.

Sal worked on the tin mill bundling line, and after forty-three years in the mill he was approaching retirement. Bundlers packaged large steel rolls for shipping after a large crane lifted the rolls to a bundling station. "It's not a desirable job," he said speaking of his job. "We don't have people knocking down doors trying to get into our department."

> It's hard work, Charlie. Not many people want to work that hard. You know, when a guy with average intelligence and a little bit of ambition walks into the mill, he cases the joint, right? He makes up his mind what kind of job he wants to have. Not too many pick the bundling line.

For Sal, money made this job worth his time. "I wanted to go to college, lot of my buddies did. But the money went home." Then, he rubbed his fingers together, "It's the money, Charlie. What else is there?" Sal earns about $39,000 a year, a little more with overtime and a double shift or two.

Initially, Sal was against the ESOP and skeptical of EPG. "But as things went along I started to get optimistic about it. I thought it had a good chance of working out if we all worked together." Then, clenching his fists together, he said, "But we all have to work together or it's not going to work." Though it troubled him, Sal respected those who did not want to join EPG.

> Just the other day I was talking to a supervisor about the EPG and he said it was a waste of time. I looked at him and said, "You've got a bad attitude." But that's the way it is with a lot of guys. They feel why should I contribute with ideas when I know they won't do anything about them. Well, I want this thing to work. At first I was skeptical, I was against it. But then I thought it was a good idea and I've been going to the EPG and OIP meetings and giving it my best. I'm an optimistic guy, I try to look at the bright side of things. And I want this mill to work, especially for my two daughters.

Pete worked on a maintenance crew and had been in the mill for about twenty years. After a two-year apprenticeship, Pete worked as a first-class welder for eight more years before becoming certified (certified welders were insured and were called upon to weld high-pressure pipes). He had always wanted to work with his hands and this is what led him to become a welder.

> I like to make things and see something when I'm done. It gives me a feeling of accomplishment. I can see what I produce. I never thought I'd do anything else, and I didn't like school and [had] no ambition to go any farther.

With overtime Pete could make up to $50,000, and although he liked his job and took great pride in his skills, Pete abhorred the health problems and threats he confronted as a welder. "The heat, dust, and fumes can get bad and I don't like that part of it. But I get all the safety equipment I can get my hands on. I wear the earpieces and glasses, everything I can. At least I don't have the high-frequency humming in my ears."

Pete was first in line when EPG began in 1984. "Before ESOP we had 'quality of worklife circles' so I was familiar with employee participation. And when we started the training program I wanted in. I didn't want to manage, but I wanted to help solve problems in the mill any way I could." As Pete considered those who rejected the program, he noted,

> It's voluntary and a lot of guys think it's a waste of time, that nothing will come of it. They say, "What are you doing, you're crazy," stuff like that. They give you a hard time. There's always going to be about 10 percent that won't go along with it, but you just have to get a tough hide and commit yourself. You have to stick by your guns. If you really think your idea is the way to go, then you have to stick with it and try to convince the others it's the way to go.

I had heard this 10 percent figure once before from a mill tour guide referring to the "bad apples" in the mill, yet from my estimate almost 75 percent of employees were still untrained and not EPG members. Realizing the difficult task ahead, Pete was ready for the challenge.

> We're trying to change attitudes, also, not just floor space. And by doing it, by proposing something and going ahead

with it, people begin to believe in themselves and that they can make a difference, that they play a role. But you have to do it, not just talk about it. It's those small grassroots movements that will make it go. A little here, a little there, it's a way of life and it gives you a sense of pride that you could do it.

Bob had worked in the mill about five years as a millwide pipe-fitter. "Each department has their own maintenance crew and construction workers for the small jobs in their area. But for the big jobs in the mill we go in." After starting in 1973, Bob was laid off in 1975 and not rehired until after the ESOP began in 1984. During this period he worked for a lawn-mowing business and even after resuming his mill job continued to do a little on the side "for some extra money and just in case something happens." Bob liked his job and spoke enthusiastically about his crew and their performance. "It's amazing how complex a job will be, people moving around and overhead all at the same time, pulling cranes and all. Boy, when it clicks, it's great!" With a little overtime, Bob could add almost $10,000 to his annual earnings of about $26,000.

Like Sal and Pete, Bob too felt that EPG was important to Weirton Steel's success and could make a difference if more employees supported it.

I'm going to the EPG meetings because I want this thing to work. I tell the guys that I don't want to go back on the streets and work thirteen hours a day for $50 again. We have a good thing going here and I want it to work out. A lot of the guys grumble, a lot of the older ones, and they say, "What does it matter? They're going to do what they want anyway so why should I bother?" But some of them are coming around, and I even raise hell once in a while.

The views of these workers partially coincided with two elements of the employee participation ideology: the knowledgeable worker and the bureaucratic ethos. First, while a successful mill was the most often cited reason for supporting EPG, what appealed most to these workers was the opportunity to suggest ideas about improving the production process and product quality. For each of them EPG dignified the knowledge they had acquired over the years and supported their collective involvement in deploying this knowledge. As Sal's wife once confided, "Sal likes EPG because he gets to take part in it, he gets to participate and suggest things." Yet Sal also realized that this opportunity came only in the context of recalcitrant management.

> You know, I've worked here 43 years and I should know a little about what's going on. The employees know how to run things. They have good ideas on how to make things work better, but try telling management that.

In Pete's view, employee participation could have been implemented long ago if not for management resistance.

> The steel industry really missed out in getting ideas from workers. [Edward] Demings went to Japan and suggested the idea of quality circles and they jumped on it, but we couldn't do it here. We really missed out because the workers have a lot of ideas on how to make things better. But management wouldn't listen. You had to do it their way or no way at all.

Other workers shared this view. "Big Mike," a production worker for fifteen years, spoke of how well EPG could work with a little more support and a little less management "foot dragging."

> Yes, they have EPG here, and things get done through it. But it's a slow process. It takes a while to get things done. You see, we still have National management working here and they don't act on things very fast. Before ESOP you couldn't get anything done. You'd tell them something or suggest something or an idea and they'd sit on it for a month letting it go through their heads, then they'd say it was their idea and you wouldn't get any credit. At least you get some credit now.

Despite management resistance, workers found solace in knowing that they could contribute to the company with their intelligence as much as their muscles—and be recognized for it. This was something that was denied them in the past when management's philosophy had been "hire them from the neck down." By discrediting this element of traditional managerial thinking *at least in principle*, EPG elevated the importance and value of craft knowledge and brought dignity to the working lives of many mill employees.

The second way in which the views of workers meshed with the EPG ideology was in their consensus on the need for an organizational hierarchy. As the views expressed by workers above illustrated, EPG boosted workers' self-esteem, but it did not alter their subordination to management. Nor did it completely challenge how workers conceived of their position in the mill hierarchy. In general, workers agreed that management was necessary for a successful company. According to Pete, "You have to have management. Someone has to give orders and someone has to take 'em." A thirty-five-year-old electrician with seventeen years in the mill explained it this way:

> I don't have anything against supervisors. Most guys talk about what assholes they are, how they're no good. That's most of the talk, but they're okay. They don't want paycuts, either, and are looking out for their jobs, too. Everyone's looking out for themselves, the hourlies and supervisors. But you gotta have good supervision. You need someone to tell you what to do. If they tell you what to do and let you do it, everything is okay. But you need good supervision.

Workers realized that management could not be simply eliminated altogether from the labor process, but for many, like Pete, things had changed.

> Under [former president] Redline's management style, they'd all go into a room at the Holiday Inn and he'd tell them, "Okay, boys. You're the boss down there in the mill and what you say goes. Anyone doesn't follow your orders, they'll answer to me." Under Loughhead's management style, he'd say, "You're the boss down there, but let me tell you something. Nobody knows that job better than the guy who works it, and you'd better listen to them and put your heads together to get results and if not, you'll answer to me." Now that's a different style, isn't it?

Yet for others, some things never changed. I asked Big Mike if workers would vote out management they disliked after the stock was distributed. He looked at me with exasperation, as if I should have known better. Status and power were clearly two different things.

> You can't vote these guys out. Look, you can say what's on your mind and be critical, but you can't get rid of them. Hey, you better be critical. Anybody who isn't, it's his own fault. But you can't get rid of these people. There's a lot of dark places in that mill. You ever worked in a mill or industry?

I answered no and with a serious stare Big Mike shook his head. Looking down, he reflected on the nature of industrial authority that EPG claimed it would overcome.

> In this place you take orders from the guy on top of you. They tell you what to do and you do it. They pay supervisors to think, they pay hourlies to work. That's the way it is. After working like that for a long time these guys get fearful. Fear—it stops you from wanting to think, from developing your mind. The EPG's are trying to get these hourly guys to start thinking and it's not that easy. You're fearful of stepping out of line. But when they get going on it, it works pretty well. It's an uplifting experience, getting to use your brains.

Workers spoke proudly of using their "brains," not only in EPG problem-solving, but also to overcome management resistance. Often they would recall such incidents when evaluating the participation reforms. One evening at a local pub Bob spoke confidently of how he always questioned management in EPG meetings and was "not afraid to stand up to them." During his layoff Bob attended some college and his chemistry classes helped him confront management.

> I always come prepared. I do my research and they're not used to that. Like when we work on the blast furnace. It gives off these two chemicals [which he named, but I could not pronounce, much less recall, them] and when they mix you get

sulfur fluoride and [?]. Well at [certain parts per million] it can kill you in 30 minutes and [certain parts per million] it can kill you in 2 minutes. I called up a friend of mine who's a chemical engineer and asked him about what could happen and then presented my case to management. (*He laughs.*) They didn't know what to do. Guys working up there get bloody noses and fever blisters, and their lips swell up real big.

Pete recalled a similar experience with his EPG work crew.

We wanted to see how far Loughhead would go with this EPG. So we drew up a plan about how the company could do some work cheaper and better by not contracting it out. It took us a year and we did it on our own time. We found out how much it cost, the materials, and then showed that we could do it better and cheaper, and save the company money. It wasn't easy and we worked hard on the proposal, but when we presented it to the executive board they couldn't say anything. They said they'd get back to us and a month later we got it changed. They accepted our proposal!

Pete and Bob expressed more than how satisfying it was to think on the job. They also described just how EPG provided them with an "opening" through which they could challenge management inertia and prove *themselves* as much as the effectiveness of their ideas. Employee participation did not replace antagonistic labor-management relations but instead bureaucratized this relationship whereby workers could challenge management on questions of knowledge and fact over a restricted sphere of influence.

To exploit this opportunity workers had to mobilize evidence supporting their idea. Consequently, EPG reinforced worker consent to the mill hierarchy by inducing them to perform this mental labor, often on off-hours, under the guise of cooperation, but also as a "game" *against* management. This "mental game" resembles the "game playing" that Michael Burawoy described by which workers reproduce their subordinate relationship to management in the labor process.[8] Through a process of "making out," workers gain incentive pay for reaching production quotas but also regulate their labor (and others') so as not to raise the quota level. Burawoy notes the many functions served by this "game workers play," most importantly how this process both obscures and generates consent to capitalist relations of production.

For Pete, Bob, Sal, and others, their role in EPG as "worker by day" also involved a mental game of sorts that mitigates their experience within the mill hierarchy. "It's fun to play with their heads," redeeming to "show you were right," "uplifting to use your head." But while this mental game constitutes workers' consent to organizational hierarchy it also involves a *critique* of the bureaucratic structure and criteria of authority it embraces.[9] The key contradiction of employee participation—the tension between the respect it bestows on workers and their continuing subordination as "workers by day"—resurfaced throughout my interviews. Sal's lament underscored this contradiction:

> Everybody has ideas in their heads about how to make things work better, but they don't listen. You'll give them an idea and they say they'll think about it, then they put it on the back burner, and a few days later forget all about it. They drag their heels on most of the ideas you give them.

When I suggested that management was probably afraid of "losing their turf" and relinquishing too much of their authority, Sal became defensive. His comments reflected how sensitive the issue of knowledge was for many workers and demonstrated how central it was to their conceptions of the industrial hierarchy.

> That's exactly it. They think they know more than us and they don't have to listen to us dummies. They think we're stupid and say, "Why should I listen to you?"

Who, then, had to sacrifice more to make Weirton's ESOP successful, labor or management?

> They do. They have to *drop down to talk to us*. It's no skin off my nose to talk with them, but they have to listen to us and it's not that easy for them, so they brush us off [emphasis added].

With his hand sweeping under his chin, Sal's gesture spoke loudly to the "hidden injuries" of class that Richard Sennett writes about as characterizing the social psychology of class relations under contemporary capitalism.[10] Management had to "drop down" to workers rather than workers meeting management at their level. "Shit, we didn't have any authority to begin with so what do we have to lose?" For Sal, any authority workers gained was because management had to answer to company executives if they undermined the spirit of cooperation promoted by EPG. This spirit, however, evoked the status injuries that intellectual intimidation had inflicted upon workers. "They think we're dumb, that we're stupid. Well, we're not. We know!"

EPG and the Normative Basis of Worker Criticism

The legitimacy of EPG rested upon recognizing and dignifying workers' knowledge of the labor process and work environment in the context of a bureaucratic hierarchy. But workers' frustrations with employee participation were rooted in more than management resistance. Employee participation had called into question the very nature of labor-management relations without effectively dealing with the shared assumptions in the mill regarding authority that, to borrow a phrase from Shoshana Zuboff, "seem to be eroding rapidly without anyone ever having agreed to let them go."[11] In the Weirton mill, these assumptions shaped definitions of a "good" or "just" mill hierarchy; assumptions that were rooted in the intersection of mill and community life. In other words, workers consented to industrial hierarchy but they also evaluated and judged that hierarchy based on community-based criteria that employee participation evoked, but that conflicted with the strict bureaucratic ethos of EPG. The outlines of these criteria are illustrated in how workers defined "good" supervision and legitimate management authority.

First, workers felt that the respect that EPG bestowed did not mean more autonomy on the job. As EPG affirmed their sense of expertise, workers judged management on its willingness to abide by this same criterion. Angrily, Big Mike sounded a familiar criticism from workers:

The thing I don't like is having three supervisors standing over you. If you go into the mill, you know what you have to do and how to do it. Everyone has a job to do and they do it. You gotta have good supervision, but after they tell you what needs to be done, then leave us alone.

For Big Mike good supervision meant that management did not interfere with labor or insist on validating that a job was being done properly. If EPG claimed that people who did a job knew best how to do it, then having a superior constantly checking on them was belittling and a sign of distrust. It reminded labor that their celebrated status as "knowledgeable" worker was capable of being revoked at the whim of management. Therefore, workers came to see their status as "achieved" not "ascribed"; something that management confirmed but that was not characteristic of them personally or as workers, as EPG claimed.

Workers also complained of too many management personnel in the mill. This grievance is not uncommon among workers in most types of employment, but at Weirton Steel it took on greater significance because two McKinsey management studies had both recommended reductions in management personnel, yet nothing had been done about the number of "white hats" in the mill. Often, as Sal did one evening, workers referred to these studies when criticizing the company.

You see, things have changed. What's different now is that management isn't safe from layoffs like they used to be. Before, they never got laid off. This has been going on a long time. I'm used to layoffs. Hell, I didn't know if I'd have my job when I got back from my honeymoon. But the salaried never had to worry. They never got laid off. But now it's different. The management study said the same thing the first one did. Management has to be trimmed. We spent all that money to find that out, again. But for three years they dragged their feet.

Exasperated, another worker put it this way:

Look, they had this study done on management which said that about 140 guys were useless, so what do they do? They bump them down to hourly. The same study said to get rid of about 900 hourlies. Now that's bullshit! We were trimmed down. It's a big smokescreen. You can't figure out what's going on, and they won't let you know—or they make it real hard to find out.

The fact that management personnel had not been reduced to the levels suggested by the company's own consultants raised doubts in the minds of many workers that the very principles of EPG were being undermined, sabotaged, or just plain ignored. This weakened the fragile trust that workers had in the reforms and made them skeptical that anything would actually change.

But reducing management was not as clear and simple as it might have appeared. Another source of worker frustration was the distinction between "inside" and "outside" management. Workers often expressed bitter hostility toward "outside" management that arrived under National Steel's stewardship during the 1960s and 1970s when "things clamped down" and more autocratic methods were instituted. As Big Mike explained:

Look, you got this college guy, he goes to WVU [West Virginia University] and majors in forestry. Then he comes to work here and they put him in—right in telling people that's been here a long time how to do something that they know how to do better. You're not going to tell a machinist how to fix a grease joint. They know! Like I said before, and some of the guys brought it up when this new president came in, hey, if you're going to hire new supervisors, take them from inside, from the work groups that know what's going on. Hey, some of the guys in here can tell from the sounds of the mill what's going wrong. They know just from listening how things are going and if something's going to blow or whatever.

Workers repeatedly criticized middle managers and shopfloor supervisors for not living up to the principles of a meritocratic organizational hierarchy with which they themselves abided: knowledge and performance. As Bob explained:

They pull in these guys from Detroit or wherever and they just scan over the place and think they know what needs to be done. How can they? Some of these supervisors and outside engineers sit in their offices all day and never come into the mill. We get blueprints from them to build something and it just won't work, it can't work. So we send them back and we do this a couple of times before anything gets done.

Bob's general criticism was not only that "outsiders" were brought in to manage but they did not bring the *appropriate local knowledge* to manage effectively. For Bob and Big Mike, this knowledge came from working in the mill, not from textbooks and college courses. Those who did not "work their way up" held less legitimacy as superiors. But "working one's way up" meant more than practical experience in the mill. It also was based on residence in the community and a sense of place that evoked normative obligations and moral approval. As Sal put it:

The guy working in the mill knows more than them. Hey, these guys work over their jobs day in and day out. Don't you think they know how to work that area best? You know, this mill was built from the bottom up. You know Millsop? Well, he worked his way up and that's how this mill operated. Generation after generation from the bottom up. You didn't have all these guys from outside coming in and running things like we do now. Yeah, I've worked here a long time and I should know something. You don't need a degree to know how to work the mill. You learn by working there.

"Good" managers started out in the mill—and in the community—and *lived* their way up the corporate hierarchy. Outsiders arrived in the mill without demonstrating either their competence on the job or *their loyalty to the community*. Many workers had fathers or relatives in management, but they were born and raised in Weirton. They held more favor in the eyes of workers and there was a place for them in mill hierarchy. Here, the criteria of effective and legitimate management authority rested both on meritocratic principles and community norms that emphasized loyalty to the community rather than to the bottom line.

At the same time, with the mill's survival at stake workers were growing ambivalent towards community norms that upheld nepotism and a sense of loyalty. For one worker whose father worked in management, it was a matter of "weeding out" bad management who found their way in the mill because of inside connections.

Some of the management people are real worried about their jobs. A lot of them got in because they knew someone, but they don't know a thing. They were shoved away, someplace out of the way so they wouldn't screw anything up and they don't do anything and make $30,000. Maybe they make coffee all day.

And as another worker bluntly stated:

There are a lot of people working in this mill that got where they are because they knew someone. The problem is they don't know or do shit.

Workers straddled these two competing criteria of meritocracy and loyalty. They conceded that knowledgeable people should be in these positions, but they also knew that a lot of management personnel "got there because they knew someone" and not much else. Mill nepotism and the "favors" that were exchanged back and forth over the years had, in the eyes of workers and residents alike, left many people in supervisory-managerial positions "who don't belong there." Workers and residents simply found it very hard to balance how they, their friends, and family got into the mill, with their concern for economic survival.

A Failure to Communicate

EPG promised to open channels of communication between workers on the shopfloor and "the big shots up on the hill." This was very attractive to workers who often told me how they could talk to anyone in the company, even board members and CEO Loughhead. For Sal, Pete, Bob, and others, EPG personalized authority in a way that contrasted with the autocratic and impersonal methods of National Steel management. This also resembled the "chummy" workplace that many recalled from the earlier days of Millsop's stewardship. The opportunity to meet with top management and discuss issues had a strong emotional impact on workers who only a few years earlier were denied access to the executive offices "up on the hill."

Yet in the few years since ESOP had begun, skepticism and doubts began to puncture this earlier optimism. Pete echoed the views of many workers with whom I spoke when he thought about the progress of employee participation and the dialogue it afforded with superiors.

> When it first started I think we were getting the straight scoop. In plant meetings we were able to meet face to face with Loughhead and other top management. And we could ask anything we wanted to, and a lot of us did, and he'd answer us. But lately I'm not so sure about it.

Bob saw it similarly.

> I mean, you could ask anything you wanted. And if your supervisor wouldn't listen to you, you could go all the way to the top. At least someone up the line would listen. Loughhead used to come into the office and answer any questions you had, face to face. He might not tell you the truth—most of the time he probably didn't—but he'd give you an answer.

Going "up the line" and speaking to executives "face to face" was very important to these workers and was evidence that they could overcome middle-management resistance. This was a sign of the new status workers assumed through EPG and it helped validate the program in their eyes.

Often these discussions between workers and top management became heated when individuals became unduly confrontational. Some older workers felt this was an abuse of their opportunities to meet and speak with executives and as a result undermined EPG. Sal expressed disdain for younger workers who were apt to be disrespectful. Referring to one incident where workers and CEO Loughhead became embroiled in a shouting match over Loughhead's compensation, Sal's comments revealed not only the contradictory experience of the "worker by day" role but also the rupturing of a paternalistic order.

> Things are different now. When I was young and in the mill I'd do what I was told. But now they're smarter, I guess. They don't put up with things like we did. Yeah, maybe Loughhead isn't worth the money he makes, but it's not right to talk like that to him. I'll disagree with him, but for

God's sake, show some respect. You don't go cursing him and screaming at him like that. All he did was yell right back. That doesn't get us anywhere.

These incidents not only sidetracked group members from exercising what influence they could, but also cast them in an unsavory light. In what became a subject of awkward humor workers often referred to EPG meetings as confrontational and chaotic. Bob summed up this recurring irritation rather graphically when he invited me to a group meeting one day.

The meetings are working out, but they can get out of hand. A lot of mother-f——ing goes on and guys get hot. Then we get off the track and guys are yelling at each other. You'll have to come to some of the meetings and see the rank-and-file at work (*smiles*). You can talk to them all together, but I don't know how much you'll be able to get, it can be pretty hectic at times.

The perception among workers that "open" and "honest" communication had broken down in the mill brought the contradiction of employee participation to the surface. The early optimism in worker ownership and employee participation was severely challenged in the context of structural conflicts that were revealed again and again over time. "Trust" and "goodwill" yielded to distrust and skepticism as the "worker by day" role contended with organizational realities that had not changed.[12] More importantly, this growing apprehension in the workforce cast a pall of unreliability on all sources of information and "communication." In this context it is important briefly to consider the Internal Communications system in the mill.

Internal Communications: Public Relations at Work

Company officials considered Internal Communications (IC) as central to a successful ESOP. Like EPG, it also answered directly to the board of directors and its staff had to consult with them before printing or broadcasting anything to employees. A senior manager oversaw a small production crew, two writers, a video producer and his assistants, and secretarial staff. IC had an institutional history beginning in 1934 when the company started a newsletter in response to organizing efforts by AAISTW and later by the CIO (see chapter 2). But the post-ESOP communications system was far more extensive than anything anyone could recall.

Like EPG facilitators, those in IC felt their department was a fine example of "how far ahead we are of anyone else" in implementing an employee participation program.

We blew our horn last year, the '86 ESOPs Association in Washington. But at the '86 convention there was a communications contest. In four different categories we were so far ahead of all the ESOP organizations in overall categories we were taken off the roll. Everywhere you went after the contest was over, when they saw Weirton Steel on your name tag, no matter who you were as a representative of the company, they wanted to talk to Weirton Steel, communications, employee participation, that kind of stuff.

IC produced a weekly newsletter and monthly bulletin covering various developments in the mill, new technologies being implemented, market conditions, and examples of workers improving some aspect of making or marketing steel. It prepared features about different departments and ongoing modernization or repair operations throughout the mill. The senior manager was also considering starting a Weirton Steel museum with memorabilia he had collected.

IC also produced weekly videos to "inform and educate" workers about developments on the shopfloor as well as more general matters about the company as a whole. Workers could view videos either in EPG meetings or on monitors located throughout the mill. Although only one of a number of information mediums used at Weirton, the weekly video was perhaps the most celebrated method of what I call internal public relations. For workers, on the other hand, *News and Views* contributed to their skepticism and ambivalence about worker ownership. It was something to watch and listen to (any information helped), but workers also felt it needed to be sifted through carefully, for what was said and *not* said.

Internal Communications and "Objectivity"

Internal Communications could be considered the "life blood" of
the EPG program and the ESOP in general at Weirton. It brought
"news and views" to all departments, but it also served as an ideological mechanism; the "last word" regarding problems or controversies. Like EPG facilitators, the staff of IC claimed to be
impartial in their job. When controversy arose over one issue or
another, they saw themselves as a beacon of objectivity. One staff
member assured me:

> We're objective! We present the good with the ugly. We make
> sure our employees are well informed and hear all sides.
> We're not here to resolve those issues. We don't get in be-
> tween and try to sway one side or the other. We're here to in-
> form them of what's going on and what's the truth. I don't
> think we should be in the middle of it.

But staying out of "the middle" of controversy was never simple
and IC staff recognized that self-censorship was often the most
prudent path to protecting their claims to neutrality.

> Now you have to watch what you do. It gets messy. We're
> here to print fact. We're here to print the truth. We're here
> to inform and educate. And we're not here to get into any
> messes or to support one side or the other. People will accuse
> us of that, but it's not true.

Many of the IC staff had worked in the media industry, either
for local newspapers or television stations, and they frequently
appealed to journalistic principles during my interviews with
them. But quite often they found their faith in objectivity and
their interest in a "good story" undermined by forces beyond their
control. As a staff member admitted:

> You can't be totally objective with what you want to say be-
> cause there are always hands in the approval process, the ed-
> itors, editing stories. That's good and bad because sometimes
> they save your butt if you've taken a piece of fact and you're

wrong. But sometimes there's something missing that's perfectly good that should be released, that somebody wants pulled, or somebody wants to change it and not tell. Although it's a truth, it's not the whole thing, you know. There are certain things you can't tell, because of market conditions and competition and that sort of thing, and I know that. *But there are just some problems within the ranks, especially within the management ranks, that some people just don't want to tell.* And you'd like to get those stories out and it's frustrating because you know you got a good story. It's something that people should know and you just can't get it out. *It gets political.* I don't know. Maybe it isn't, but that's on page five or six [emphasis added].

IC's claim to objectivity, however, persisted despite the clear political obstacles facing them. As IC personnel saw it, that made their job even more challenging and reinforced their commitment to an ideal of neutral, "hard news" reporting. But even if IC did not set the agenda for any particular EPG meeting it still framed organizational and shopfloor issues as *bureaucratic* problems that required technical solutions, not political choices. IC reinforced the "worker by day" orientation, but it was not "the last word" on either company developments or controversy.

Internal Communications attempted to reassure workers that the company was being managed properly. But it gradually met the same skepticism and distrust that characterized labor-management relations in the mill. As one staff member explained:

At first nobody would talk on camera or to the communication department. Then it started to get better and a lot of people talked. But it's gotten worse recently, I don't know, maybe the past seven months. I don't know why.

After years of National Steel intimidation and indifference it was not unreasonable that workers would shy away from talking "on the record." Also recall that when Weirton Steel finally became worker-owned the rank-and-file were "cautiously optimistic" about the mill's future and opinion was mixed over the hard-fought terms of the ESOP. Many workers admitted having to "warm up" to the idea of speaking up under the IC spotlight. But as some people attested "some things did begin to change" under ESOP, including their willingness to talk with IC staff.

Nonetheless, IC had to deal with the same basic contradiction that EPG facilitators faced. As workers gradually discovered that their "worker by day" status left them without any *effective* voice, power, or security, they withdrew their trust. For example, IC had also established an intramill "hotline" where workers could call anytime for information or to report on problems in the mill. Intended to enhance "employee communication" (one staffperson put hotline use at about seventy-five times per month), many workers saw the hotline as another way the company induced people to "rat" on one another, thus a form of surveillance that was more intimidating than inviting.

If things had "gotten worse" for IC staff, it was undoubtedly due to a series of controversies (discussed in chapter 7) beginning with a mill scandal in December 1986, the surprising announcement of CEO Loughhead's retirement in February 1987, and some unexpected pay raises to certain groups later in the spring. As these events unfolded, IC became a source of information that workers I spoke with approached cautiously and skeptically. It had become merely one of many sources of information competing for the hearts and minds of workers.

Competing Voices

An obvious source of information was the union, but ISU leadership had gradually lost whatever credibility it held since ESOP. After a bitter debate during one union meeting about pay raises the company granted to some employees with "critical skills" (see chapter 7), a former union steward explained: "The guys don't care anymore. They never show up to union meetings, and they never read anything you give them." Many workers I spoke with agreed, but they also added angrily: "You can't rely on the union. Half the time they don't know what's going on."

Another source of information was local media. But, here, too, everyone I spoke with had their doubts. Initially, I was surprised by how skeptical people were of the local newspaper, but over time I began to understand why. Simply put, it just conflicted too much with what people either personally experienced or knew from other sources, including newspapers from neighboring towns. People recognized that the "good and dirty" news, what was *important*, was not covered in any newspaper and they had other means of learning what "really happens" in town.

This brings up a third source of information that workers and residents relied on: informal talk between workers, families, and friends in town.[13] Even in a small town like Weirton, everyone did not know everyone else. But almost everyone did know someone who knew someone else. Interpersonal networks in town linked different workers in the mill with various sources of knowledge, and these sources often gave conflicting accounts that had to be evaluated. The credibility of this information depended on the position and prestige of the source from the view of the individual. Workers I knew had their favorite "sources," but they also sought information from people they considered closest to the issue in question. This inside knowledge was not always completely accurate or trustworthy, but it did provide an alternative means or framework by which to evaluate competing accounts.

On the other hand, this led to the infamous "rumor mill," which, in the eyes of everyone I knew, was as prominent in town as the steel mill. Rumor served many functions in town. It enhanced sociability as a source of excitement and a means of inclusion in the community. Spreading rumors, or having heard them, involved people in the ebb and flow of everyday life that defined community membership. "People like rumors," explained an EPG secretary. "They enjoy hearing them. Sometimes people make them up just to hear them go around." A facilitator added: "You know what we used to say was a good rumor, if you can start it in the morning and by the time you leave you've heard it from someone."

Both EPG facilitators and IC staff emphasized that a big part of their job was dispelling rumors by "going to the source." Yet the problem here was that all sources—including IC—were questionable and people stitched together a credible version by weighing them all. In this respect, the ideological force of internal communications rested on adding to the complexity of viewpoints rather than enforcing a dominant outlook.

Finally, there was a lively underground information network that operated in the mill. Workers often showed me documents and letters that had been circulated and that either contradicted official company statements or were critical of company policy. Many workers had access to confidential documents by virtue of their jobs, and mimeograph machines were available for reproduction. Clandestine distribution of this material kept sources hidden, but copies routinely found their way into homes and bars throughout town.

One mimeographed letter given to me by a worker illustrated the growing distrust and skepticism among workers toward "official information." Dated October 3, 1987, the letter was addressed to Herbert Elish, who had recently replaced CEO Robert Loughhead. It read, in part:

> Since you took your case [favoring labor force reductions] and appeal to the news media, I would like to have the same opportunity. Mr. Elish, you seem to forget that the employee owners of Weirton Steel are also your employer. We pay your salary and you should have had the decency to have had a companywide meeting or departmental meetings to inform us and explain to us what your plans were before you went public with them. We would have respected you more if you would have given us a chance to digest them first. It was an outrageous and irresponsible act on your part. Where is all of the co-operation and communication that ESOP was supposed to be built on?
>
> The morale among union employees is at an all time low. We are left out of the decision making process and either misinformed or not informed at all. Management's need to hide or suppress the truth is continuing to grow.

The anonymous author also captured the confrontational tone that many workers expressed during my interviews and informal discussions. But critiques of the power structure of the mill, such as the above, were seldom raised publicly. Though submitted to the local press, I never saw the letter reprinted. This underground medium was not accepted unquestionably but it often reflected the deepest sentiments of workers. As the worker who handed me the letter put it, "Not many guys would agree with everything in here, but it speaks for how a lot a guys feel."

Given these competing channels of information, it was unlikely that the ideology of employee participation was "embedded" in or imposed on workers. With so much information being distributed and debated, and none of it complete or wholly reliable, workers could be forgiven for experiencing "information overload." This is more or less what an IC staff writer said when commenting about how workers felt they had been denied important information during the ESOP negotiations. Referring to improvements within internal communications, he noted:

> If we'd have had this type of program we have now, we would have had information going out to them in droves. They wouldn't have known what to do with it.

But IC's inability to foster the expanded and bilateral communication it considered necessary for effective employee participation was based upon the same contradiction EPG facilitators faced, an ideology that emphasized an enhanced worker status and an organizational hierarchy that failed to support it. More, IC was unable to provide a coherent and symbolically resonant vision of what worker ownership *should* be in a town like Weirton. Support for participation reforms had to reach beyond the executive offices "up on the hill," and beyond mere rhetoric and company propaganda. It had to reach "worker-residents" as much as worker-owners.

By 1987, such support was still left wanting. Management continued to doubt the effectiveness and fear the intrusions of employee participation; resistance followed. Worker optimism in a "new way" of working was structurally impeded and symbolically hollow; cynicism built. As one worker saw it, some things never changed. "Labor doesn't trust management and never will. Management doesn't trust labor and never has." Likewise, a normative challenge persisted despite attempts to define the "worker by day" in narrowly technical/bureaucratic terms. This challenge stressed loyalty to the community, people before profits, and fairness over position as the criteria for exercising authority in the mill. And as the next chapter shows, these sentiments were also at odds with conventional market-centered versions of worker ownership.

Part IV

Owners by Night

Chapter Six

Class and Worker Ownership

I can tell a snow job when I see one, and this was one.

—Weirton Steel employee, Third Annual Shareholders Meeting, 1987

If the slogan "workers by day" accurately depicted the role of rank-and-file workers on the shopfloor, the phrase "owners by night" was far more ambiguous in accounting for their role as owners. As chapters 4 and 5 demonstrated, worker ownership did not entail worker control. "We still have management. We still have a board of directors" was Robert Loughhead's pointed response to questions about worker control. "This is not codetermination."[1] Nor were employees being prepared for a more active role *as owners* when the five-year prohibition on voting rights expired in 1989. "We haven't done a great deal with that," admitted Loughhead.[2] Likewise, ISU shop steward Mike Hrabovsky conceded that his co-workers "will never have control. How are they going to? Management will never give up the right to manage."[3]

True enough, but as I showed in chapter 5, workers were ambivalent about the issue of control. Hrabovsky again echoes the sentiments of people I had spoken to: "What would happen if steel

227

workers ran their own mill? I'll tell you. It would be a fiasco!"[4] But if nobody expected employees to run their own steel mill, what did worker ownership *mean* to millworkers and residents of Weirton, West Virginia?

Publicly, the rank-and-file were "owners." Local billboards and media reinforced the idea of "employee-owners working together" while the national media framed Weirton as the most recent example of how employee stock ownership was making "worker-capitalists" out of "working stiffs." In statements by company executives and public relations officials "the idea [of worker ownership] is to establish capitalists." During the ESOP negotiations, former company president Jack Redline "fervently hoped" that a Weirton ESOP "would add 7,000 capitalists to the rolls."[5] After four years of worker ownership this had not happened, nor was it likely to.

Worker Ownership and the "Equity Solution"

Formally, the ESOP granted worker-owners a right to *equity* in the company through stock distribution and profit sharing. According to advocates of employee ownership, equity redistribution motivates employees to produce more efficiently, to dedicate themselves to the firm, and to endure sacrifices because they now have a financial stake in their company's future success.[6] Stock allocation gives workers a long-term interest in their company beyond hourly wages, benefits, and whatever emotional rewards or craft pride their jobs provide. Proponents consider this extension of property rights a new motivation for workers because their labor is now more closely linked to the current, and future, value of their property.[7]

Profit sharing is the second pillar of equity-based worker ownership. Although profit sharing does not always entail a distribution of company stock to employees, most worker-owned companies or ESOPs (private and public) have some form of profit-sharing plan as part of their compensation package. For ESOP proponents, annual or semiannual profit-sharing checks (normally computed according to individual or craft rates of compensation) provide an additional reward necessary to maintain the motivational benefits of worker ownership.[8] "Owners" deserve a return on their investment, and so some regular and significant "payoff" is considered necessary, as a reminder of one's ownership status, but also, as in cases like Weirton, to offset any wage concessions made at the on-set of ESOP or the concessions made to management on the shop-floor (for example, changes in work rules or job combinations). The ESOP agreement set the profit-sharing pool at 33 percent of yearly net profits, rising to 50 percent when total assets reached $250 million. Profit sharing replaced stock dividends because worker stock was held in an ESOP trust until the five-year waiting period expired. At that point, sometime in 1989, employees could elect to sell stock publicly, after which dividends would accrue—given a profitable company.

The Limits of Equity Redistribution

Profit sharing and stock ownership were important to workers, but I saw no evidence that these *financial* enticements were ei-ther making capitalists out of wage laborers or increasing work-ers' commitment and favorable attitudes toward the company. On the contrary, it became very apparent that workers remained working class, in behavior as well as outlook, and that, if any-thing, ESOP was a focus of contention for workers and residents alike. And while the view that profit sharing and stock ownership motivates employees is a difficult one to assess empirically,[9] re-garding the Weirton case it was suspect for a number of reasons.

On the one hand, the motivational effects of equity redistribu-tion are difficult to measure against the reported surge of enthu-siasm following the buy-out. Like other ESOPs during what has been called the "honeymoon" period, it is quite reasonable to ex-pect a highly motivated workforce after eighteen months of fear and anxiety over the fate of the mill, but this is not the same as being motivated by anticipation of a financial payoff or some at-tenuated form of ownership. Following the ESOP vote there were indeed many workers who, as one millhand put it, "thought they were going to be millionaires." But if these *aspirations* were widely held, so too were the *expectations* of workers who doubted the sincerity of company officials and were equally skeptical of whether the current value of their stock would match its value if and when they cashed in.

More, the unequal distribution of equity based on compensation and the formula for dividing the annual profit shares made many workers suspicious of foul play. Profits were to be divided among five groups: rank-and-file workers under the ISU; the Independent Guards Union; clerical and technical staff; salaried classified;[10] and professional, management, and executive personnel. Each of these groups received a cut of the profit-sharing pie based on the "ratio of their salaries and wages to the total eligible profit-sharing salaries and wages of the company."[11] Although each group decided how its share would be divided, workers were upset over the formula for initial group allocation and they felt that profits should be divided equally among all groups. According to a clerical worker from the payroll department who "sees the numbers":

> Say the clerical workforce numbers 800 people and out of a $100 million payroll they receive about 8 percent of that in wages, then we get $8 million. But management might number less but account for 15 percent of payroll so they receive $15 million to divide. That's not how we wanted it, but the union didn't push to change it and now we're stuck and people are angry. It should be equal. They [the union and company] tell us that we okayed the contract [and this arrangement]. But we didn't. We thought it would be *equal*. Now we're in arbitration and have been for quite a while [emphasis added].

The rank-and-file's desire for equal distribution was further reflected in how they divided their allocation from the first profit sharing in 1986. The union groups divided 80 percent of their allocation equally with 20 percent divided according to seniority. In contrast, executive personnel divided 37 percent equally, 46 percent based on seniority, and 17 percent based on relative compensation; management divided 35 percent equally, 37 percent based on seniority, and 28 percent based on relative compensation.[12] Interestingly, rather than enhancing their individual accounts (as one might expect of budding capitalists) rank-and-file workers favored equal distribution, even over seniority status.

Further, workers increasingly doubted that profit sharing would be raised to 50 percent from 33 percent of net profits when total company assets reached $250 million. The 50 percent figure was pushed strongly to workers as they approached the ESOP vote in 1983 and it constituted a central element of the "worker ownership=worker motivation" theory of ESOP promoters. But rather than view this as financial compensation above and beyond their regular wages, workers saw it as a way to *regain* wages they had conceded to save their jobs. If the prospect of an elevated profit-sharing percentage was a motivating element, it was only in the context of making up past losses, not accumulating future financial gains.

Finally, it is more likely that the financial interest workers have in a successful steel mill rests not so much on profit sharing and stock ownership per se, than on the stability of their jobs in the mill and the wages they earn. To the extent that profit-sharing dividends and share distribution rests on compensation and seniority status, *and not on membership status exclusively*, the financial stake workers have in the company is no different than before ESOP; jobs and wages are what workers desire and they have an interest in securing as much of both as they can.

Consequently, as "equity solutions" to the problems of industrial efficiency, productivity, and cooperation, profit sharing and stock ownership are not substantively new motivations for employees. Rather they merely add to the logic of preexisting capitalist relations of production where elaborate wage structures and the bureaucratic hierarchy that supports these structures remain intact. Stock ownership and profit sharing alone do not alter an employee's interests as a worker but instead reinforce those interests and the structural motivations underlying them.

The "equity solution" of worker ownership, then, was neither equally applied nor a significant departure from "business as usual" at Weirton. And when the rank-and-file played at the role of "owners by night" they were again reminded that they were *workers* first and foremost, owners only in name. Workers may have held few illusions about a democratic ESOP, but they were steadily becoming disillusioned with the bureaucratic one they had. This was never more clear than when the symbolic and structural clashed one night at the annual shareholders meeting. On this night, worker-owners were participants without a voice, spectators from the sidelines.

Owners by Night . . .

I was granted permission to attend the third annual shareholders meeting not by worker-owners, but through a network of elite influence. After speaking with a former local politician, he arranged a meeting with a future mayoral candidate who then called a senior company official who allowed me to attend the meeting after confirmation from his superiors. "I'm going out on a limb on this one," cautioned the company official. "Nobody other than some media people and stockholders are allowed in and you'll have to walk in just like you were a worker. And you can't ask any questions, only workers can ask questions." At the meeting, only two workers did ask any questions; in their dramatized role as "owners by night," the rank-and-file knew their place.

For company officials, the shareholders' meeting was perhaps the most appropriate opportunity to spotlight the mill's early success and its ESOP-participative structure.[13] Upon entering the Millsop Community Center I walked through the front lobby and hall where product displays and company promotional exhibits were neatly arranged. Given that only shareholders (employees) and local media were invited, these props served more as a reminder of something they already knew, or at least should know; Weirton Steel was the largest fully worker-owned company in America (at the time) and it produced high-quality products for many nationally known companies. As I curiously surveyed the tables, people shuffled by with but a glance.

The contradictions of a worker's symbolic role as "owner by night" appeared again as I moved into the center's gym where the meeting would be held. Upon a large wooden floor stood a few hundred folding chairs facing curtained tables centered by a podium and microphone. The gym bleachers angled upwards on either side of the chairs, and in the rear of the gym were televised videos and more promotional displays on EPG programs, the company's newest technologies, as well the history and successes of ESOP. I climbed high up the bleachers where I might gain the best view of the meeting and write notes without being too conspicuous.

As people filled the gym, the division between management and labor emerged spatially by where they sat. Even a cautious judgment based on people's attire suggested that management and union officials (wearing suits and ties) took seats on the gym floor while workers (wearing jeans, plaid jerseys, and casual dress) gradually filled the bleachers. Amid a steady drone of murmuring I looked about me and noticed that hardly anyone from the bleachers was talking. Down on the gym floor I could see heads moving back and forth, gesturing and smiles, but in the bleachers I was struck by the blank faces, expressionless, neither skeptical nor impressed. As they waited, workers occasionally cast a wandering glance down the bleachers for a familiar face.

Company president and CEO Robert Loughhead began the meeting by introducing board members seated at the front table. After a pro forma nomination and selection of board members, which included voting them shares of company stock—workers could not vote on these issues for another three years—a few of the board members spoke briefly on the company's progress and future challenges. Loughhead then returned and remarked on how Weirton's ESOP was a noble crusade against both doubt and a hostile environment encroaching from all sides.

He began by denouncing the "naysayers" and critics of the company. Faring especially poorly were the academics and "bookwriters" who, in his view, talked a lot but did nothing.

Books are written on what Weirton is doing, but *real* companies are doing *real* things. Real things come first, not the other way around. We do things and then they write about it, and we must continue to do so.

Loughhead's rhetorical appeal to pragmatism and hard work, and his contentious framing of academic work seemed geared toward a "working-class" audience, but workers did read those books and they did have real questions about the company. Loughhead then added that "with all the closed plants because of lack of efficiency and no profits, we can't depend on outside forces for our survival, we have to be competitive on our own." Ironically, it was precisely because of outside forces—federal and state financial aid, tax relief under federal ESOP legislation, EPA leniency, favorable court rulings, not to mention Citicorp loans and ESOP consultant services—that Weirton's ESOP was born and continued to survive.

The ideology dominating Loughhead's speech, which resurfaced in interviews with workers and residents alike, bore a striking resemblance to a Darwinian "survival of the fittest" outlook.

Again, the collectivist "we" evoked a spirit of inclusion (rank-and-file, management, and executives "working together as a team"), but it also *excluded* everyone not employed in the mill or not living in town or the immediate area. Not unlike the paternalistic days of Weir and Millsop, Weirton was portrayed as isolated from and threatened by outside forces; the mill and town would have to rely on its tenacity and solidarity to survive and prosper.

Here, an ideal of "community" was deployed to connote collective interests and collective sacrifice, but it was a community on the defensive, almost like an armed camp awaiting enemy attack.[14] If competition with other mills and steelworkers throughout this industrial valley meant Weirton's success at their expense, that was an unfortunate, but inescapable fate. There was no other choice—Weirton Steel had to survive. Most people I spoke to were uncomfortable with this outlook and "wished it didn't have to be this way." But if workers and residents reluctantly conceded this view, company officials embraced it vigorously; a "survival of the fittest" ideology of ESOP set an urgent and threatening context justifying their role in directing company affairs.

Resigned Dissent

After a short film celebrating the company, its products, new technologies, and the cooperative spirit of its worker-owners, Loughhead asked for questions from the audience. After prolonged silence a heavy-set man emerged from the back of the gym. Apparently he was well known judging from the dispersed laughter and jeering that followed him to a microphone on the gym floor. "Well," Loughhead noted, "I should have guessed that *you'd* have something to say." Referring to the capital improvements looming ahead, the man asked pointedly:

How we gonna finance this thing? You mentioned that there's a lot of closed plants and boarded-up buildings around, but if you come after my pocketbook you'll see *my* house boarded up.

This, Loughhead replied, was "in the hands of a long-range planning committee" composed of management and union officials. Their recommendations were not expected for another few months

when, as Loughhead put it, "we'll have to make a collective decision." What he meant by "collective decision" was unclear, but the
planning committee would set the framework for that decision,
not rank-and-file workers. Silence resumed as the man walked
away shaking his head.

Another worker then stepped up and asked about the second
McKinsey management study. Again, outsiders were intervening
into company affairs and this troubled workers with whom I
spoke. "The McKinsey people have caused a lot of fear and rumors
in the tin mill about being laid off," the speaker said. "What's the
deal with them?" Over a steady murmur rising from the bleachers
Loughhead replied, "It's tough to stop rumors," and he made no effort to stop this one.

> I can't go into what they're doing now, but they should be fin-
> ished soon. . . . If you don't want to talk about the wage
> structure, I can't go into this. We can talk about jobs and job
> redesign, but I can't go into the McKinsey study now.

This terse exchange stilled the audience, with Loughhead ap-
pearing even a bit condescending at times. From the shuffling and
shaking heads in the bleachers it appeared that workers were not
only dissatisfied with the whole affair, but they also feared speaking out in view of union officials, management, executives, and local media. After asking for any more questions, Loughhead
quickly adjourned an annual ritual that fewer and fewer worker-
owners even cared to attend.

Ironically, as I climbed down from the bleachers hoping to ask
someone what they thought of the meeting, a news reporter with
a cameraman asked me for my opinion of the event. Replying that
I may not be a good person to ask, I noted his frustration finding
anyone who would talk; at least six people politely turned him
down. As the crowd slowly dispersed, I noticed a casually dressed
man moving toward me. We stood together for a moment looking
up at company officials talking with one another at the head table
when I asked him about the meeting. "This was my first," he said
tilting his hand from side to side, "and will probably be my last.
It was just a big show. They set it up just right, planned perfectly."
Saying that I had expected to hear more workers asking questions, he smiled and shook his head, "This meeting was a show."

It's not like that, what you heard tonight, in the mill. The
lines between management and the workers are still clear
and tight. They don't budge an inch and they balk at significant suggestions. It's like hitting heads. They have their own
way of doing things and they'll do it their way. It's just like it
was before the ESOP with National. It got better there for a
while, but it's starting to harden again.

He conceded the company was making money, although he did not
know how "with all the waste." And as far as he was concerned,
collective action was a waste as well.

I'm looking out for myself. I take care of my own problems.
Look, you can't get ten people to stand together on an issue
here [in Weirton]. It's not like Poland. Now that's solidarity.
But not here! I'm not educated, only out of high school, but I
like to read and I read a lot, and I can tell a snow job when I
see one and this was one.

If the shareholders' meeting was a "snow job," workers were beginning to see through their role as "owners by night." Up to now,
worker ownership had forbidden them any significant role in decision-making, and equity distribution and the structure of control continued to separate company elites from rank-and-file
workers. Ideologically, Weirton's ESOP was portrayed as a struggle of "us against the world," a "mission" that was being carried
on under the most difficult circumstances and against all the
odds. In the gym that evening a different struggle appeared to be
emerging as both company and union officials found themselves
being questioned by an increasingly disgruntled workforce.

. . . Workers at Heart

Even if people agreed that worker's control would be a "fiasco,"
they were equally skeptical of how management and executive
personnel ran the company. "You want to know what it's like at
this mill?" asked a slabyard inventory clerk after an interview.
Opening a dictionary on his desk, he pointed to the word "snafu"

and laughed, "That's what it's like down there, one big snafu—situation normal all f——ked up!" This sense of unease and doubt was common to workers, management, and residents alike. Although their accounts differed, everyone eventually spoke about the mill in some manner. "This town obsesses about that mill" sighed a nurse from the local hospital, "and I can't stand it. Everywhere you go, every party you go to, sooner or later talk turns to the mill." Not a few people nostalgically wondered if things were not better before the ESOP when Weir and Millsop directed National Steel, the mill, and the town.

As the company posted a fourth year of consecutive profitable quarters, workers and residents still wrestled with the meaning of worker ownership *in the context of their changing relationship with the mill.* Worker ownership was, as one worker's bitter humor attests, a "snafu" only in comparison to what people considered "normal" before ESOP. It is in this context, where class and community intersect, that worker ownership is meaningful for workers and residents alike. And it is here that a *moral* dimension of ownership begins to take shape, judgments of right and wrong concerning the roles of different participants in the town's dominant institution.

Working for a Living

Contrary to public relations by the company and local media, workers were still "workers at night" as well as "workers by day." This contradiction disturbed many people who could not understand why the rank-and-file continued to "act like workers." Millhands, in their view, did not think or act like they thought owners should. "They have to wake up down there and run it," sighed one mill retiree, his disappointment hanging like the ruffled linen over the kitchen table where we sat. "All they care about are boats and highs," laughed a close friend after we met his highly intoxicated friend from the tin mill. "When profit-sharing checks come out in the summer," I was told, "it's one big 'hoopie-Christmas' and everybody spends every penny."[15] For a local financial investment consultant, this tendency among millworkers to *spend* their profit- sharing checks rather than *invest* in stocks and bonds was discouraging.

It's tough to convince them that a safe investment is wiser than spending everything they get, or putting it in a low interest bank account. I know a lot of these guys well, but I can't get them to trust me that I can make them more money in the long run. They don't look that far ahead, and they better if they want that mill to keep going.

Far from becoming capitalists, as the third year of ESOP unfolded, rank-and-file worker-owners were still working-*class*; they identified with and lived according to their job and the wages it brought them. Their daily lives were dictated as much by the shifts they worked as by their desire for more overtime and less management. The distinctions workers drew between "we" and "them" on the shopfloor carried over to the bars scattered throughout town. Everyone knew the nightspots where the "college crowd" gathered and the pubs where millhands drank and practically any wager could be made. If profit sharing did motivate rank-and-file workers it was in their desire to consume or save, not to invest. And for the most part they consumed among themselves and apart from the town's professional-managerial class.[16]

Nonetheless, the rank-and-file did display an attitude that reflected an investment they felt they had in the company. Rarely did I meet a worker who was not concerned about waste and efficiency in their department or in the company as a whole. When it came to product quality and customer satisfaction, workers were more outspoken than management. More, their concern for modernization projects and mill competitiveness was reflected in the only two questions asked during the shareholders meeting.

On the one hand, these attitudes cannot be wholly attributed to their new financial status as "owners" simply because they were common among workers *before* ESOP. They are also common to many workers in companies that are not employee-owned or that do not have profit-sharing programs. Perhaps workers were more likely to talk about these issues more often and openly than before they became worker-owners. But this does not mean that their status as owners has led to these views being more commonly held. Rather, these views that workers have always held have become more salient and accentuated because their jobs, the mill's capacity to provide jobs, and the compensation for these jobs are all on the line. Workers interpret worker ownership in large part from their position as wage-earners in the organizational division of labor.

On the other hand, as I spoke with workers about the mill, its progress, and its future (and not about ownership, per se) it became increasingly clear that they did hold a conception of ownership, one that was rooted in a mode of reasoning that drew upon moral considerations as well as economic ones. This mode of reasoning, or moral economy, informed and guided workers in their interpretations of company progress and policy. Weirton's moral economy consisted of a set of principles and priorities, norms and obligations that defined and explained the proper economic functions of town elites, mill officials, workers and residents, and what constituted acceptable and unacceptable economic behavior. These assumptions of right and wrong, so deeply held and seldom challenged until ESOP, set the symbolic parameters within which workers conceived of, and acted out, their compromised role as worker-owners.

The Moral Economy of Ownership

Even if holding company stock and receiving profit-sharing checks did not make capitalists out of workers, their conception of themselves as owners did provide the symbolic means to press for demands born of, and shaped by, a moral economy of paternalistic origins. In other words, workers did not act like capitalists, nor did they even think like business owners are "supposed" to think. Instead, they challenged the rational, calculating, profit-seeking logic of ESOP from a cultural heritage rooted in their working-class position in a paternalistic company town. Likewise, they selectively adopted the status and outlook of owners only when it furthered their arguments against company policy or defended their class interests in the mill and community.

This moral economy did not arise with ESOP but took shape during Weir's and Millsop's stewardship over the mill and the lives of townspeople. Under this paternalistic code, mill organization, compensation levels, mobility, and labor force size were governed by elite efforts to control the working, civic, and personal lives of a labor force (recall the spinsters in chapter 2), strategies that pursued profit and expansion but also entailed obligations to a benevolent, though autocratic, version of community. In all, this moral economy emphasized notions of the common weal that had served Weirton for generations but that were no longer accepted unquestioningly by elites, the middle class, or rank-and-file mill-workers.

The essence of this moral economy is captured in one criticism I heard again and again from workers and residents alike. As one worker put it,

> People think that National Steel *owes* them something, that National will bail us out if things don't work out. They've got to realize that this is our mill and we have to make it work.

Routinely, people spoke of National's *monetary* debt to the work-force. Under the ESOP provisions National was legally obligated to buy steel, supply coke for mill furnaces, and assume financial liability for closing costs and severance pay should the mill fail within a five-year period, or until 1989. National was also oblig-ated for all employee pensions assumed during its tenure. But the refrain "National owes us something" also spoke about a *norma-tive* debt, an obligation that National had reneged on by threat-ening to close the mill. Here, the word "debt" refers to the breakdown of reciprocity between National officials and a Weirton workforce that felt betrayed. Workers had upheld their end of the bargain by setting production records throughout the 1960s and 1970s despite what they saw as National's hardline management strategy. Townspeople proudly claimed that it was they who had built National Steel and for this they felt that they deserved a kinder fate. In this context, National Steel was *morally* obligated to Weirtonians who felt that were it not for them National would not even exist.

When I began to think about the anger and frustration ex-pressed by workers, management, and residents in this context I began to see how their moral judgments of one another derived as much from paternalism's demise as from the onset of worker own-ership. Not only did National Steel "owe" something to townspeo-ple, the mill and those who now ran it owed something to workers and residents alike, *to the community of Weirton*. This was illus-trated in an angry letter to Loughhead's successor (see following chapter) that was informally circulated in the mill.

Our community means nothing to you. How long will you stay at Weirton Steel? Is this an opportunity for you to get richer and then return to your family in a few years and still receive an outrageous financial benefit from Weirton Steel? That is, if it still exists. . . . What is your personal contribution to the survival of Weirton Steel Corporation?

Worker ownership was meaningful, then, only in the context of people caught between "letting go" and "hanging on" to familiar norms regarding economic relationships that had been so thoroughly fused with community institutions and family life. Under paternalism, economic relations were defined by notions of the mill as a family where company policies and practices implicitly, as well as explicitly served to unite work and home. Where in the past the mill provided social services and extended civic noblesse oblige in the form of labor power and building materials, today it no longer performs this role. Where the mill once supported generations of Weirtonians by employing and promoting family members, post-ESOP labor force reductions and the outsourcing of jobs and major construction projects had shattered any pretensions that the mill was a family affair.

Under ESOP, this vision of the mill as family was being replaced by one that saw the mill as strictly as "business struggling to survive," a rationally structured organization that must follow the harsh and impersonal rules of the marketplace. From this view of the mill, work and family had to be *separated* rather than united. It was the structural and symbolic separation of mill and community that elicited moral disapproval, but in subtle and often indirect ways. The paternalistic norms governing economic relationships were being redefined and recontested as worker-owners coped with a company that was becoming more bureaucratized in its pursuit of economic survival. At the same time, it appeared to be less humane, less concerned with the plight of workers and their families, and less responsible to the "common weal" of Weirton. The tensions created by this separation of mill and community, and how people tried to resolve them, are the subject of my next chapter.

Chapter Seven

The Moral Economy of Worker Ownership

> How do you fire a widow who's handicapped and needs a job,
> even if she's unqualified, but everyone wants to look after her?
>
> —Weirton resident, 1987

When I asked people about worker ownership directly—
what it meant to them, what they expected it would be or
thought it *should* be—they never had a clear, definitive
conception of what it was all about. They knew that the town's survival rested upon a profitable mill and that everyone would have to
endure some sacrifices. The community would have to "pick up the
slack" where the mill once carried the load. They also knew that
worker ownership was more than simply an economic affair, but it
was still vague and evolving after three years of ESOP.

Over time, however, I began hearing an informal dialogue
among workers and residents that was not always about worker
ownership per se but still expressed how people were trying to
make sense of it in the context of local life. These conversations per-
meated social life in Weirton, from the bars scattered throughout
town, to the many family dinners I shared. When heated debates

243

erupted, people often became upset because these conversations evoked moral sentiments about the mill, workers, and ultimately worker ownership; judgments about what was right and wrong with the changing relationship between the mill and community. Several themes routinely emerged that together made up the contours of a moral economy through which people rendered interpretations and judgments where "worker ownership" was in some way being implicated, defined, or debated. Gradually I noticed discernible frames of reference as people moved back and forth between a utilitarian-individualistic market morality which ESOP had reinforced and paternal-collectivist moral codes that arose alongside it during the Weir-Millsop decades.

In this chapter I examine the contested nature of this normative order through a series of "conceptual vignettes"; analytical sketches of issues and events that emerged over the course of my research. First, I show how controversy over compensation in the company reflected a deeper confusion in evaluating *the value of labor.* I then look at company theft in the context of a locally centered, collectivist version of *property rights.* Finally, I consider the growing ambivalence toward *nepotism* and *local control* in the mill and the community. Together, these vignettes demonstrate how events and company policies undermined local customs and normative codes that people relied on in constructing a meaningful and morally relevant view of worker ownership. Furthermore, as class antagonisms sharpened, people were moved to debate the relative merits of an egalitarian and locally responsive ESOP over the bureaucratic one they had.

The Value of Labor

The issues most often debated among millworkers, company management, and residents alike revolved around the value of labor. Whether it be workers upset over the salaries of management and company executives, or residents and local businesspeople dismayed by what they saw as "spoiled and overpaid" millworkers, ESOP had evoked a steady controversy over how much people were paid for their job, and if they—or their job—were worth it. This dispute focused on the top of the corporate hierarchy—CEO Loughhead's salary and stock options—as well as the middle levels of the company—a series of unexpected pay raises for select mill personnel in the spring of 1987. Ironically, antagonism towards millworkers followed major wage and benefit concessions agreed to by all salaried and hourly employees under the 1984 ESOP terms.[1]

Sleeping in the Mill

The value of rank-and-file labor was debated through an informal commentary over "sleeping in the mill." Initially I considered the pointed, yet often humorous accounts of workers sleeping in the mill a lighter, more trivial topic of people's attention. But it was more than that. Despite only anecdotal accounts of how prevalent the practice actually was, people routinely referred to sleeping in the mill when discussing rank-and-file compensation. This suggests that the phrase "worker-owners who sleep on the job" was an exaggerated depiction that embraced various strains of local discontent toward millworkers for their abuse of *paid time* in the mill, whether it be extra long breaks, arriving late for a shift or leaving early, reading the paper or, as one worker put it, "making coffee all night." If rank-and-file workers were being called upon to justify the value of their labor, this dialogue was also assessing their obligation to the larger community in the absence of paternal oversight and benevolence.

People working outside the mill commonly saw steelworkers as privileged and chronic complainers, overpaid and underworked. A local financial consultant said adamantly,

> Nobody can tell me that they put in a full eight hours. Four, maybe six, that's all. They find a cozy place somewhere and snuggle up for hours. I know, I worked there once.

The owner of a hair salon expressed similar misgivings. In her view, millworkers were "spoiled."

> They get great benefits. I don't get that. I have to pay for my medical and retirement. They don't know how much that stuff costs. They don't know how good they have it there.

It was much the same for a garden nursery owner on the outskirts of town.

> They're paying people too much. An eighteen-year-old can come out of high school and make 25 grand as a laborer, *a laborer*. Are you getting me? That ain't right.

A young woman cashier at the local K-mart store agreed but offered some conciliatory reflections that I had also heard from others.

> It used to kill me when I found out they paid $25 an hour to push a broom. I interviewed for a summer job, but there were no openings. I figured that the money was good and I could make some money for college. I'd work there for a summer, but just to make some money for college. *But it's not something I'd do for a career*. It used to bother me that they'd complain about having to give concessions. But I understand all the bitching and moaning now. They don't want to give up something they've had for so long taken away [emphasis added].

Contrary to the years when a mill job was an expected, even desired, course for most Weirtonians,[2] it seemed that nobody working outside the mill would like to work there now, at least not for the rest of their lives. Nonetheless, for those employed outside the mill, millworkers seemed to have things pretty good overall. They had good wages, good benefits, and more than enough time and space to "snuggle up" if they wanted. As people working outside the mill saw things, for the company to survive and benefit *everyone* in town, millworkers would have to be more reasonable over compensation and more responsible on the job. Public disapproval reflected people's anxiety over their own occupations and economic future, but it also served to remind workers that they had a moral obligation to the town. Mill practices and community welfare were linked, people reasoned, only not like they once were under paternalism. Workers' labor was being reevaluated in light of their newly bestowed, though largely symbolic, "ownership" status and sleeping on the job simply represented the most flagrant assault on townspeople's sense of what worker-owners *should* be doing.

Workers were not ashamed of their compensation, even if people tried to depict them as greedy and irresponsible. Millworkers admitted they were well paid and they ardently defended themselves against what they considered petty and naive attacks. "I work my butt off in that mill," said Sal angrily in response to the view that workers were overpaid and underworked. "Let them come down and work in the mill. It's hot in the summer and cold in the winter, it's loud, it smells, and it's dangerous." Then, rubbing his fingers together, Sal calmly explained,

> I chose the job I got because of the money. The money, what else is there? I could have had a cush job pushing buttons, or I could have had all daylight, but the jobs that required you to work paid the best. That's why I picked bundling. Hell, I can make about $39,000 a year, and with overtime and double shift I can make up to $50,000. Maybe not now, but I could. It's not hard work, but when you get home you know you've worked a hard day, it's physical labor.

Sal's outlook was representative of skilled and unskilled workers alike, and it was not uncommon during interviews for workers to show me a pay stub confirming their income. More, every millworker I spoke with emphasized how important overtime was to reaching the peak yearly wage. As Pete, a welder, explained,

> With overtime a welder can make up to $50,000 and some can make a few thousand more than that. Without overtime, maybe about $35,000. About 60 percent [of welders] go for light overtime, while maybe 40 percent go for the six-day week. Some go for heavier overtime, but for the past few years we've worked six-day weeks because management doesn't want to hire on new welders. It's not hard physical work, but you work the hours.

But along with wage concessions ESOP also brought reductions in the overtime that workers customarily relied on. One worker after another lamented to me that "since ESOP there's just not enough overtime." Ironically, far from the public criticism that they hardly worked, Weirton's rank-and-file complained that they could not get more work, those extra shifts that brought in the "big money" that people outside the mill found unreasonable under the circumstances.

Despite such public denouncements and lacking any systematic documentation of hours spent sleeping on the job, I was surprised to hear so many workers admit that sleeping in the mill was, more or less, commonplace.[3] Even a highly respected retiree spoke fondly of how "in the old days" he often sought a comfortable place to nap during his shifts. And more than a few workers explained the conventional mill wisdom that warned against sleeping on the floor: "Gases in the mill tend to settle near the floor, so find a bench." During a weekly mill tour that the company offers, our tour group happened upon a sleeping worker perched high above his workstation. The group was amused as his friend tried to wake him, but it also affirmed their preconceptions; even in a noisy mill there were plenty of quiet corners for napping.

Defending themselves, workers pointed to "lazy" managers who "might make a pot of coffee, then hide somewhere all shift doing nothing for thirty grand a year." Even when they conceded that among the rank-and-file there were "some guys in here with a bad attitude," workers also condoned sleeping as long as people did not abuse the practice. "Sometimes," one millhand explained, "somebody just has a bad day, a fight with the wife, sick kids, whatever. So you cut the guy some slack. But some guys you gotta kick 'em in the ass."

For workers, then, sleeping during one's shift should be regulated by fellow workers who know better what is, or is not, acceptable behavior in the mill. Management was clearly in no position to judge, especially given the view among the rank-and-file that they were not much better. And people outside the mill were equally unworthy to pass judgment: "How can they know if they don't work here?" More, as one retiree speculated, the value of other jobs seemed just as dubious. After saying that I taught at my college, he offered the following observation:

> And teachers, they get $17,000 to start and they work five days, get Saturday and Sunday off, maybe work eight hours a day, sometimes less. That's too much. Some of them aren't that good. And we have to pay for it.

But as familiar as these responses were, it was not until a comment by Sal that I began to see a connection between paternalistic customs and the current disputes over the value of labor. "Nobody can work two shifts without sleeping on the job. It's impossible." For Sal, sleeping and overtime went hand in hand. And everyone—millworkers and residents alike—did agree that *overtime* did not always mean *overworked*. Sleeping in the mill was neither a personal flaw nor collective abuse, but a product of mill organization under paternalism. Indeed, the grievance of residents that the mill supports "overpaid workers who sleep on the job" can actually be seen as a response to the paternalistic legacy of mill overtime and overstaffing policies. The moral controversy over the value of workers' labor, then, was also about changes in the structure of mill and community life.

When Sleeping Worked

From the 1940s through the 1970s the high compensation levels of Weirton steelworkers were always based upon the company's lucrative overtime policies and extra shifts (see chapter 2). Likewise, during these decades the company could also afford to overstaff the mill in exchange for worker loyalty and obedience. Overstaffing may have varied, given production surpluses or a slack market (temporary layoffs were not uncommon throughout the Weir-Millsop years), but the practice was supported through nepotistic hiring and layoff policies, policies that may not have been "economically sound" but that ensured a ready and loyal labor force inside as well as outside the mill. If paternalism "found a place" in the mill for many because it could afford to, this practice also ensured the long-term control of labor—and this too was profitable.[4]

Though recollections of retired workers and townspeople alerted me to these paternalistic policies, further support comes from employment level data (see Figure 7.1).[5] In 1933 Weirton Steel employed approximately 10,000 workers at its three plants (Weirton, Steubenville, Ohio, and Isabella, Pennsylvania), and by 1937—a year of deepening national crisis during the Great Depression—employment climbed to 12,000 employees with about

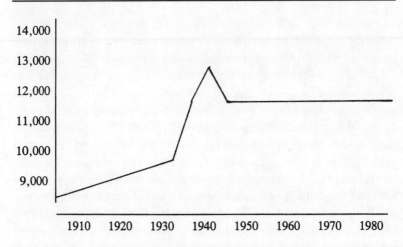

Figure 7.1. Labor Force Levels 1910–80[1]

Source: Weirton Daily Times, *1933*; New York Times *1933–1950*; Weirton Steel Bulletin *1950–1980*

Note: Estimates include the company's Isabella, Pennsylvania, mines prior to 1937.

10,000 working in the Steubenville and Weirton plants.[6] Employment rose steadily through World War II and peaked in 1942 with 13,000 employees before settling at 12,000 in 1944. Then from 1950 until the early 1980s employment levels varied slightly between 11,000 and 12,000 employees. Thus, from to late 1940s to the early 1980s, employment at Weirton Steel remained relatively constant.

This rather stable employment level would imply that business conditions were also relatively stable, yet this is far from true. Despite the Great Depression and labor strife, Weirton Steel was growing and hiring. Wartime production led to increased employment, and labor strikes in the steel industry during the 1950s kept employment high as Weirton Steel filled orders originally placed with idled companies. Yet employment levels reached a relatively high benchmark during the 1940s at 12,000 workers and never declined below 11,500 employees through the 1960s and 1970s. One might expect a lower benchmark figure following the war and labor peace in the steel industry, but even if the company and its market grew steadily into the 1960s, one still sees no significant increase in employment. This employment stability, even during the 1970s when imports grew and domestic production slumped, suggests that Weirton Steel carried a bloated labor force it could use when necessary.

Also suggestive is evidence of the overtime hours worked by Weirton steelworkers compared to the industry average workweek. At the height of the Great Depression and CIO–Weirton Steel litigation in 1937 the company's own figures showed that while it met the industry standard 40-hour week, in June of that year its employees averaged 43.1 hours.[7] Furthermore, liberal overtime policies were enacted throughout the 1940s and 1950s as employment stayed stable (see chapter 2). For example, a 1951 agreement between the ISU and company provided for overtime pay to be computed based upon "less than a full eight hours worked to be counted as a full day worked for such overtime purposes."[8]

But the most direct evidence that paternalism contradicted economic rationality and "good business sense" regarding overstaffing was testimony given by company president Thomas Millsop himself during hearings before the National Labor Board in 1938. Answering charges that Weirton Steel maintained a system of intimidation, discrimination, and arbitrary discharge of CIO sympathizers, Millsop admitted spending $5 million in sixteen months to retain old and loyal employees on the payroll. With the introduction of new "continuous process" technology in producing tin plate the company found itself with outmoded hot plate mills employing some 3,200 workers. "We had to adopt it to compete, or get out of business," Millsop explained.

> Yet the chief concern of Mr. Weir was for the old and loyal employees. Other employers merely posted notices telling the men they were through. But we didn't do that. We went before the [National Steel] board of directors and urged these outmoded mills be retained *in the full knowledge that it was bad business judgment. We wanted these workers provided for*. Mr. Weir hoped somehow he could make the old mills pay [emphasis added].[9]

A reluctant board agreed to keep a few of the mills, and this employed some of the workers who would otherwise have been laid off. "But," Millsop added, "we went further."

The corporation had a $5,000,000 appropriation set aside to finance an expansion program over a five-year period. Mr. Weir insisted that this fund be made available immediately, and he expended it in a period of 16 months for construction work to furnish employment for these men.[10]

Even in the midst of the Depression and facing modernization costs for new hot mills, Weir still had enough money and exercised enough power among the National Steel board of directors to "provide" for loyal workers as he fought, intimidated, and fired CIO supporters. If there was an economic logic to these "make work" employment policies it was clearly focused on the long term and was sustained by an unyielding (irrational?) passion against outside union representation.

Overtime and overstaffing institutionalized paternalistic benevolence that "took care of our people," cultivated worker loyalty (and dependence), and ensured a labor surplus in times of need. But these mill policies also gave rise to and supported the custom of sleeping in the mill. At the very least, workers were not discouraged from a nap they considered well deserved and appropriate. Again, while there is no way of knowing how much sleeping occurred, everyone I spoke with conceded it happened often enough. Much like the "indulgency pattern" noted in Alvin Gouldner's analysis of gypsum miners, sleeping was a form of leniency that superiors extended to workers.[11] And while the practice likely varied with the nature of the job and work shift, sleeping was also regulated by co-workers who either looked the other way, looked out for supervisors, or used the practice for their own ends.[12]

Under paternalism sleeping worked. It was an accepted, even if seldom used, mill custom that valued ready, loyal, and productive labor. With ESOP, however, sleeping on the job—and every other imaginable inefficiency on the part of labor—conflicted with a more bureaucratic company and its rationalizing EPG reforms. The idea of workers "sleeping in the mill" also contradicted townspeople's conceptions of responsible worker-owners and served as a symbolic target for moral judgments of rank-and-file labor and their responsibility to the community.

But in denouncing worker behavior and what they considered undeserved compensation, people appropriated the norm of paternalistic obligation to community without acknowledging how that same norm was central to overstaffing and overtime policies that supported sleeping. Likewise, rank-and-file workers defended themselves from their position in the mill ("they don't work here, how do they know?") but without any clear reference to the paternalistic origins of such conduct. Not until attention refocused up the organizational hierarchy did workers adopt elements of Weirton's moral economy to protest and evaluate the value of executive labor. If rank-and-file workers were on the 'hot seat,' so too was CEO Robert Loughhead.

How Much Is a CEO Worth?

The Loughhead compensation controversy highlights larger debates over how to measure, evaluate, and compensate professional and managerial labor. It was not simply a local issue but merged with a growing national debate as the 1980s ended.[13] Public reports of CEO compensation had provoked criticism from many corners over the high ratio of American CEO's to employee compensation, especially in comparison to foreign competitors, and in particular Japanese executives.[14] As labor, especially in manufacturing and heavy industry, suffered through over a decade of wage and benefit concessions this growing discrepancy between the highest and lowest paid employees in corporate America raised questions of *economic fairness*. It also signaled, despite claims of how teamwork and sharing (both sacrifices and rewards) were the wave of our industrial future, that the higher circles of corporate life were still more highly valued.

    In Weirton, workers' sense of economic injustice derived in part from their expectations following ESOP. Even if some workers considered him merely the most conspicuous example of an overpaid board of directors, Loughhead personally came under attack for what many saw as an exorbitant and unjustifiable salary and bonus package. As Bob, a pipefitter, explained:

    I was talking to my dad (who was in management) and he said Loughhead made about 1 million dollars last year, plus the $250,000. [Was that fine with Bob?] Well, no, not really. When ESOP went through we were told he'd be making about $250,000 and we figured if he could turn it around it was worth it, but not this much. If the workers could vote on it, they wouldn't vote the CEO that much.

This controversy eventually reached the pages of the company newspaper, *Independent Weirton*, in the spring of 1987. In its opinion section, the paper printed the responses of twelve workers to the question, "In terms of dollars and cents, how much is a CEO worth to the corporation?"[15] A few thought Loughhead's compensation was fair.

At least $250,000.

He's worth his weight in gold if he can produce and get this company operating profitably and efficiently.

For a corporation of this size, I don't have a problem with the salary Mr. Loughhead presently makes or the structure of his salary.

I don't think you can put a dollar value on it. If his credentials qualify him for the job and he has a reputation for the getting the job done, we should pay him whatever he's asking for.[16]

However, there was still an unmistakable leaning among respondents in favor of an annual salary less than the $250,000 reported by the *Independent Weirton*.

I don't think it should be as much as we have been paying.

He's probably worth about half of what we're paying now.

I figure about $150,000 a year, depending on his experience and expertise in the steel business.

About $75,000 if he's good. If he does a good job, then give him a bonus. Deduct for his ESOP, too.

$100,000 a year, [and another] I'd say $5,000.[17]

Having accepted deep wage and benefit concessions and a five-year pay freeze, and concerned over future concessions to help finance pending modernization, workers were especially leery of executives who failed to shoulder their fair share of the ESOP burden. In the context of company slogans calling for "working together works," the rank-and-file were quick to apply this populist spirit to executive compensation. Company officials were not unaware of these sentiments among workers, and the straw poll cited here was one way of managing these concerns. According to the company paper, this "admittedly unscientific survey" showed that Weirton's worker-owners were ill-suited to make such judgments.

> [I]t is clear that the employee-owners of Weirton Steel need to educate themselves, not only about their own jobs, but also in terms of what it takes to ensure the long-term success of a corporation. Those who fail to bat an eye at the millions earned by professional athletes, balk when a CEO make hundreds of thousands. . . . Few employee-owners would argue that as consumers, you get what you pay for. However, many seem reluctant to apply that maxim to the leadership of their own company.[18]

Workers were *not* "reluctant" to pay their CEO a high salary, but they were unsure of how much to pay him, how to judge what was fair and reasonable, and who should decide. Likewise, workers were unsure of just what they were getting in a CEO. In Weirton, CEO compensation raised moral questions about the relative statuses of labor and leaders under worker ownership.

Status and Compensation

Under paternalism executive pay, like the rank-and-file's, was never a serious issue for anyone—Weir and Millsop were not figures who invited this kind of public scrutiny. It was Weir's mill, so whatever he took in compensation was unquestionably his. And Millsop was so adored by townspeople that they might have paid him anything to continue running the mill and the town.[19] However, when it came to the criterion by which to judge the value of a CEO, workers found themselves grasping for credible guidelines. Was it right to pay the CEO of a worker-owned company so much? Was it right to pay *this* CEO so much? Commenting on the opinion survey in the *Independent Weirton*, Sal felt that $160,000 was "in the right ballpark."

> I mean, in other major companies they make a lot more than that, but in a small company like ours, that seems to be about right, maybe a little small, but in the right ballpark. I mean, Loughhead makes what, $250,000? That's about right. That's about what they should make.

Sal felt that some of the opinions in the survey were "way out of line" and that some of the respondents were "nuts" for suggesting that a CEO should be paid much less.

> One guy said that the CEO should make $60,000 a year and that it should vary according to profits, just like our profit-sharing checks. Now that's crazy! Hell, some of the guys in the mill make close to that. This guy must have been making close to $40,000–$45,000 and he says that. Come on! How do people come up with that? I can't understand the reasoning behind that. Sometimes I wonder how these guys think.

The "reasoning" Sal wondered about justified minor, if any, differences in compensation on egalitarian grounds. This "principled" approach was something Sal considered too extreme, an approach that seemed to penalize rather than reward labor. Though vague ("in the right ballpark," "seems about right,"), Sal emphasized comparisons with workers at Weirton Steel and CEO salaries in other companies to arrive at an estimate of what a CEO "should make," criterion also used by the *Independent Weirton* in its framing of the CEO compensation debate. But this market comparison or "reference group" approach to judging compensation still left unanswered the question of whether other CEOs were overpaid and whether the discrepancy between executive and rank-and-file rates of compensation was acceptable, much less fair.

When asked how CEO pay should be decided, Sal laughed and then pointed to what he and other workers had always been judged by: "Performance! By performance!" Other people also saw merit as a key criterion, but defining and measuring a CEO's performance remained quite obscure. Where workers can see what they produce and where productivity is routinely measured to judge labor's value, this is not as easily applied to what CEOs do. Among service workers, administrative workers, and others whose occupation results in less tangible products, labor and its value are not amenable to such seemingly objective calculations. "My job is not as important as the guys on the shopfloor, production workers," conceded one clerical worker. "You can't see what I make, but they make what we sell, our bread and butter."

But even if one uses comparative measures or, say, sales figures or market share to arrive at CEO compensation, how does one account for high and rising executive compensation in the face of falling profits, failing companies, and a faltering U.S. economy?[20] When I asked these questions, workers looked beyond purely economic factors in deciding what a CEO was worth. As Sal put it, CEO pay was "decided by the board of directors," and if it was still unclear just how they came to a figure (other than by comparisons with other companies) it was clear that they had the power to decide.[21] "[Our CEO] doesn't have *that* much power," added the clerical worker cited above. "The board of directors is probably more responsible for what goes on."

> I don't agree with those high salaries. That's way too much. Nobody deserves that much, and the CEO doesn't have that much power. The board of directors does. So we pay all that for image. It's like I told you before, image is real important, especially to customers and banks.

Status, as much as any objective account of their productivity, was a factor that had to be calculated into the value of a CEO. But status is not easily determined (if at all) by rational calculations. Weir and Millsop held status in Weirton though, as I noted in chapter 2, for different reasons. Loughhead's status in the eyes of most employee-owners was fragile and wavering into the third year of ESOP. He had to "earn" respect among the workforce and in the community, but his compensation was still determined by the board of directors. Pete elaborated on this theme, adding that workers had very little choice over the matter. And even if they could decide, workers would still have to pay for the "right guy" as CEO.

Well, I'm willing to pay him something, I mean, what good is it without my job. If we don't have someone who can run the company, then my job is on the line. [Loughhead] didn't have to come here. He was well off and could have retired, but he wanted a little piece of history so he took on the job. I remember when he talked to some workers at an in-plant meeting and they questioned his salary. He said, "Now wait right there. I never asked for this salary. You offered it to me. So don't get angry with me," and he was right. We need someone who can run this company and who the banks and customers can trust. We have to keep their confidence, especially now when we need loans. No, I'm willing to pay someone, if they're the right guy.

What the controversy over executive compensation revealed was the *unraveling of class, power, and status* that had been sewn together under paternalism and where there was no question who "the right guy" was or how much he was worth. Four years after ESOP both the basis of leadership as well as its monetary value were being seriously questioned as class divisions became more transparent. As one "concerned employee-owner" wrote in a letter to the editor of the *Weirton Daily Times*, the company survey on CEO compensation was a "very clever piece" that was not only misleading, but also demeaning. Criticizing the survey's facts and the company's logic of comparing CEOs, the writer angrily noted,

This same article goes on to tell us, "it is clear that the employee-owners of Weirton Steel need to educate themselves not only about their own jobs, but also in terms of what it takes to ensure the long term success of a corporation." Personally, I take this as an affront and an insult. This sort of "talking down to" type of statement only magnifies a situation that is growing between those of us in the mill and those of you on the hill.

Besides being the best workforce in the steel industry, I would say that on the whole we are one of the better educated ones. Perhaps, though, we are one of the most gullible! I believe that the time has come for some real questions to be asked and some up-front answers from the people we employ to manage our company. It is time to put a stop to the cleverly worded stories, the rationalizing, the deceptions and devious manipulation of the backbone of our company. That backbone is the employee owners of Weirton Steel.[22]

Although executive compensation was decided by the board of directors, this controversy anticipated a renewed challenge by rank-and-file workers in the years ahead. Unconvinced by "comparative" and "performance" standards in judging what was fair compensation for those who led the company, rank-and-file workers looked to an egalitarian ethos that had never been called upon to judge the status of company or town elites. It too failed to adequately define an appropriate *financial* value for mill leadership under worker ownership. With an increasingly bureaucratized mill, the egalitarian ethos was tested again in the "critical skills" controversy.

Critical Skills, Critical Mistake

"Why do they go and lie to the workers," asked a clerical employee from the payroll department. "They make people mad!" And workers were incensed over pay increases for some management and hourly personnel in the spring of 1987. In their view compensation rates were to be frozen during the first five years of ESOP and they were outraged as word spread about the raises. According to company and union officials, the raises were necessary to keep people with "critical skills" from leaving Weirton Steel for a higher-paying position elsewhere.

The workers I spoke with were not impressed. At a union meeting that spring, ISU President Walter Bish faced angry workers seeking an explanation. As he tried to calmly explain his support of the pay raises, Bish was soon defending himself, and not very successfully at that.

> **Bish:** These people have critical skills and we need to keep them, especially if we're to get a bank loan for the capital improvements. Under the ESOP agreement we're obliged to maintain high-quality management and we can't be going to the banks for extensions and new loans if we keep on losing people with critical skills. We need to pay these people.

Worker: Well, tell me, what exactly is a critical skill? Can you give me a definition of what a critical skill is?

Bish: A critical skill is something people have who can go out on the open market and sell it. They can find work easily on the open market—

Worker (interrupting):   Well, give me an example.

Bish: Well, like accountants, engineers—stuff like that is considered a critical skill, and we need to keep these people to maintain quality.

Worker (angry and clearly unconvinced):   I can show you hundreds of guys in that mill who have critical skills, and without them that mill wouldn't be running. Don't bullshit me Walter, don't bullshit me!

There was also confusion over pay raises that some hourly workers received. Bish explained that the raises for "about 1,100" hourly workers were "due to job combinations and upgrading of job classifications, which is all legal under the ESOP provisions. Read it and you'd see that!" By now Bish was shouting at workers as much as they were at him, and his defense of the "critical skills pay raise" policy was alienating him ever further from a skeptical rank-and-file. As the worker who invited me to the meeting put it, "Most everyone feels he's in over his head. He really doesn't know what he's doing and is sort of learning it as he goes along." ISU leadership optimistically took office during the ESOP negotiations, but by the third year of ESOP they had steadily lost the confidence of even the most supportive rank-and-file workers. Bish's justification of the pay raises not only echoed that given by company officials, but workers considered it an irreversible breach of faith, perhaps his final undoing as ISU president. Bish would lose his bid for reelection the following year.

Over the next several weeks everyone I spoke with viewed the raises as a flagrant abuse of the spirit, if not the letter, of Weirton's ESOP and worker ownership. For the rank-and-file, the five-year pay freeze was supposed to apply to everyone, regardless of their position in the company. And if it did not, it "ought to." As the worker above who wrote to the *Weirton Daily Times* noted, the raises constituted a moral breach where the value of labor was to be—at least for five years—subordinate to an egalitarian ethos of "sharing," both rewards and sacrifices.

> When the grand idea of ESOP was conceived for Weirton Steel, it was carefully put together so the burden would be shared equally just as the rewards were to be shared equally. Alas! That grand idea has been violated in both a fair and moral sense.[23]

While the policy seriously undermined this egalitarian interpretation of the ESOP agreement, workers still tried to reconcile the breach by focusing on specific circumstances that framed the pay raises in a larger context. However, even when they did consider other factors, most remained puzzled and dismayed. Pete is a highly skilled welder, and even though he is willing to accept the pay raises, he also wonders just what a "critical skill" is.

> When the ESOP started everyone believed there would be no raises, across the board—not even any talk about compensation. And then this thing happened and a lot of guys feel they've been taken. I feel that way. So we all want an answer and nobody's gotten a good one yet. If only they'd tell us and explain why. We're not all capable of running a multimillion-dollar company, so you need to keep some of these people and pay them, otherwise they'll leave if they're offered more money. But [management] has to make a good case about it, and they haven't yet. Most of those raises were in Industrial Relations and that's a joke.

A computer printout of salary payroll that was confidentially provided to me (though I was told that copies were circulating in the mill) listed exempt personnel who received raises of between $350 and $500 a month according to a handwritten note at the bottom of the page. Although the list was incomplete (I was told it represented only one third of the "critical-skill" pay raises), it showed that a majority of the raises went to Industrial Relations personnel.[24] Of the 26 names listed, 17 were Industrial Relations representatives.[25]

Pete's outlook on the situation reflects what many other workers told me. Even though he was willing to hear the case for raises, he seriously doubted that Industrial Relations personnel had such "critical skills," by any definition. Dave, a clerical worker, agreed and added that the market criteria in awarding the raises were equally dubious.

> There was not supposed to be any pay raises, but then they go ahead and do it and say they were promotions. Sure, some of those positions probably were critical, but so are a lot of jobs in the mill. And to say that they'd get another job somewhere else if they didn't get more money? They're making good money and they're not going anywhere. They couldn't get a better job somewhere else any more than anyone else. No, that was a bad move, and the timing was terrible.

Workers saw no justification for the raises on the basis of "skills" nor on the basis of an individual's "marketability." And they found the pay raises especially unjust after seeing their own profit-sharing checks shrink in the spring of 1987 compared to the first distribution in 1986.[26] Except for company officials and union leadership, employees from production worker to clerical and secretarial staff agreed that the pay raises were a critical mistake.

For the most part, people employed outside the mill shared the disillusionment of millworkers. They, too, were surprised at the policy and they worried about its impact on worker productivity and morale. Though residents tried to evaluate the raises from the vantage point of their occupations, it was still difficult for people to specify which skills were increasingly valuable and thus worthy of exceptions to the compensation freeze. Even when people made distinctions between jobs requiring abstract knowledge and technical skills with those associated with craft knowledge and physical skills, it was hard for them to judge the pay raise policy.

Lacking any clear and convincing job-related criteria to justify the raises, people looked elsewhere much as many workers did. One response was to consider the "image" that Weirton Steel was presenting to customers and banks and how important keeping their trust was to keeping their business. In this context, the pay raises may not have been justified on the grounds put forth by company and union officials, but they were a necessary evil under difficult economic conditions where everything (even image) mattered.

On the other hand, even when people found it difficult to define the skills involved in any particular job (even their own), they all rested their opinions on some version of the work ethic that they assumed was characteristic of *all* jobs. The pay raises did not so much reflect critical skills as they did a degree of personal desire, self-motivation, and, perhaps most importantly, voluntary adherence to work. A neighbor reasoned this way when commenting on a family friend who was among the Industrial Relations representatives listed for a pay raise. "Maybe he deserves a raise," explained Ted as he compared his friend to a production worker who lived down the street. "The guy next door is forced to work hard, Bud isn't and he still works hard."

The point here was not that one person worked any harder than the other—this is as difficult to quantify as skills are—but that one had little *choice* compared to the other. In a world of "forced choices" where every job takes its toll and everyone is apt to think that they are "overworked and underpaid," those most morally deserving of exceptions, privilege, and rewards are those who choose to work hard. My neighbor cast virtue on those who appear to have escaped the "iron cage" that Max Weber envisioned in *The Protestant Ethic and the Spirit of Capitalism*: "The Puritan wanted to work in a calling; we are forced to do so."[27]

This emphasis on individual virtue was most satisfying when people also viewed management and executive personnel as working for something other than themselves, say the welfare of the mill or the community. But it was hard for everyone, especially rank-and-file workers, to agree with the notion that if these virtuous people were not well paid they would leave the mill for greener pastures elsewhere, precisely what the company argued in favor of the policy. All bureaucracies make this argument in order to keep their executives and professional staffs, but in Weirton it contradicted workers' egalitarian vision of ESOP and it conflicted with a moral economy that emphasized obligations to the general welfare of the mill and community.

After three years of worker ownership people were beginning to question an impersonal, unjustifiable, and unequal distribution of rewards and sacrifice. This eventually led the company to hire a psychologist who conducted an attitude survey of some 3,700 employees in April 1989. According to James B. Lieber's account, its results indicated significant confusion over the value of labor and widespread skepticism about fairness in the company.

> Only 16 percent of the subjects agreed with the statement: "I understand how pay is administered in this company (how salaries are determined, who is entitled to an increase, etc.)," while 64 percent disagreed, and 20 percent were "neutral." Similarly, only 7 percent believed that "pay is administered fairly in this company," while 74 percent disagreed. Only 20 percent of ISU employees favorably perceived an "opportunity for advancement," while 55 percent viewed the situation unfavorably. Thirty percent approved of the record of promoting from within the company, while 53 percent objected. Only 15 percent of the sample supported the statement: "When sacrifices are necessary to meet business needs, all levels and parts of Weirton Steel share equally in the sacrifices." Sixty percent disagreed, 25 percent strongly.[28]

Lieber also notes that the survey showed overwhelming support for the company and "satisfaction with the job itself," and that 90 percent "felt a mutuality of interests with their employer and agreed with the statement, 'The better Weirton Steel performs as a business, the better it is for employees like me.' "[29] I too found that workers supported the company, liked their jobs, and wanted the company to succeed as a business. And workers did see a "mutuality of interests with their employer" to the degree that it was the *mill* that employed them. What they questioned was how this business should be organized and the value of labor was central to a growing debate in which the bureaucratic structure of ESOP contradicted egalitarian principles and people's sense of community obligation.

Property Rights

Just before the critical skills pay raise controversy erupted, a mill scandal was uncovered that revealed yet another legacy of paternalism. On Christmas Eve 1986, a brief article appeared in the "Local Scene" section on the front page of the local newspaper.

> Three Weirton Steel employees were fired Tuesday after an audit committee investigating the mill's traffic department concluded that individuals had engaged in conduct that is not in the best interest of the company, a spokesman said.[30]

Three employees were "terminated" and one "officially reprimanded" though none were identified. Some of Weirton's worker-owners had ripped off the mill—and gotten caught.

The rumor mill in town was soon hotter than the mill's blast furnaces. Who did it? What did they do? How did they do it? Were the guilty being properly punished? My landlady heard that the main culprits were an elected city official (who also worked part-time in the mill)—"a crook, just like his dad"—and a company executive "who's always had a trashy mouth. I never did like him." Other townspeople also heard these individuals were in on the scandal, maybe even CEO Loughhead. One worker, whose father worked in management, doubted that Loughhead was involved but he agreed that executive-level personnel were responsible.

> My dad said no [to Loughhead's involvement] and so did our shop steward, but rumor has it that he was. He may have had a hand in it, but I hope not. They were sending damaged steel rolls to customers and then selling them for half price besides selling them good rolls. Well, we never saw the bad rolls come back, so some people were starting to get suspicious.

According to this worker and others, some executives were getting kickbacks but nobody could, or would, verify who. The company's investigation and its results were not made public as executives tried to resolve the infraction 'in house.' Even the ISU leadership sought to 'cool out' the rank-and-file during a union meeting in January. "It was pretty crowded," one worker recalled of the meeting, "and a lot of guys were asking questions, but Bish said that they had a [union] investigating committee looking into it and they'd get back to us. Then he moved on to other things. We still haven't heard anything about it."

Similar to other cases of corporate crime, the company sought to manage whatever negative impact the scandal might have on its relations with customers, suppliers, banks, and competitors. But in Weirton the scandal also revealed coexisting assumptions about property as a collective resource and as an individual right. "Stealing" evoked different moral judgments when property was viewed as a collective rather than private resource, and the scandal forced people to reconsider yet another paternalistic custom that now contradicted the interests of worker-owners and community residents alike. At the same time, however, the scandal crystallized class sentiments that stealing from the mill had once served to repress.

All in the Family

For some people, the investigation signaled that the company was acting responsibly. "Yeah, it's good they cleaned that up. It shows that the people running the show want this [ESOP] to work." Yet for others, the scandal sent the exact opposite message, that, in fact, the people running the show were crooks and above the law. Said one worker,

> We'd get strung up for that shit, and they get off. Sure, maybe they all got fired, but they should have made all this shit public and prosecuted them. Hell, they stole from us!

Yet as I listened to people discuss the scandal, it also became clear that stealing from the mill was far more widespread than this single incident—or at least the *perception* of it was. And company theft was not limited to management and executive personnel; rank-and-file workers took credit for a number of schemes. Practically everyone had their own story to tell about pilfering from the mill. Quite often, I was told, this practice involved more than swiping a pencil or pair of gloves. One worker grudgingly confided to me his role in abusing company credit cards.

> Another thing that was going on was that some guys were using company credit cards and going to [a southern state] and not reporting it. They'd run up the bill and have a good time on the company but were not reporting it as pleasure. The IRS was in on this and it's really scared some people.

You could call it a kickback. No, not really—well, yes, it was a kickback, I guess, but I went on some vacations down there and the place was plush. It had everything. Yeah, I guess I'm guilty of that, too, and should probably stop that, too. I think that won't happen again.

Although he expressed remorse over his involvement, this worker was also ambivalent that what he did was wrong. "Everyone did it," I was told again and again, and even if people did not steal, the practice was still condoned through an informal code of tolerance and permission. Another former millworker, who moved from Weirton to later become a corporate merger consultant, recalled "how it was in the old days."

Supervisors or foremen would build houses from mill materials. They had a scrap steel thing going where people were padding their pockets. It was endless. The thing is everyone did it, and they all had a hand in something. And if they didn't, they'd look the other way. It was accepted. And I wasn't blameless, either. I'd take tape, a pair of gloves, whatever. But it got into big bucks sometimes. Things have gotten better. They've tightened it up a lot.

Indeed, stealing from the mill—much like sleeping in it—had become institutionalized under paternalism. This again resembles an element of the indulgency pattern Alvin Gouldner noted in the gypsum mine he studied, what he called "government jobs."[31] With the mill considered as a familial arrangement an informal code governing the "use" of mill property was respected by management and labor alike, and this code recognized that the mill was "ours" as much as E. T. Weir's or National Steel's. Besides, how could one "steal" from one's own family?

From this line of reasoning company theft could be redefined as "borrowing," even if the item was never returned. Keeping a "borrowed" item was not a major indiscretion as long as what was taken from the mill *did not leave Weirton.* Under the moral economy of paternalism, using mill tools and mill supplies to repair or modify one's home was an acceptable form of company noblesse oblige. Not only had mill officials set an example by using mill personnel and resources to build Weirton, but they too were not innocent of covert and illicit activities. One may recall from chapter 2, in 1945 the company was found guilty of violating a War Production Board contract by installing an air-conditioning unit at the elite golf clubhouse rather than the mill hospital it was intended for. This and similar indiscretions were overlooked as long as company benevolence via civic welfare continued and workers could occasionally indulge themselves.

This history of institutionalized theft had not evoked the same moral outrage among workers and residents as it might have among outsiders. Such indiscretions were considered local matters and federal intervention was not sympathetically received by elites nor, for that matter, townspeople or workers. Many people saw the intrusion of outsiders and their moral impositions as a threat to local autonomy and independence. Paternalism generated strong bonds between the mill and community, work and home, and it also sustained conceptions of property rights that reflected and reinforced these bonds. Local interpretation of this code still rendered theft of individuals immoral but condoned theft of the mill as tolerable, if not acceptable, in the normative context of collective property.

People moved between both conceptions of property rights as they reasoned about what they deserved from the mill, what they could use, and what they could "get away with." Given the assumption that whatever was taken from the mill would stay in Weirton, people made a distinction between what Marxist theorists call "use" and "exchange" value.[32] Stealing from the mill in order to use the material in town was acceptable whereas stealing in order to exchange mill resources for personal financial profit conflicted with the collective notion of property rights that condoned theft in the first place. And if stealing from individuals contradicted notions of private property, stealing from a large organization that was seen as a family and part of the larger community of Weirton did not.

William Serrin notes a similar pattern in the Homestead mills where workers were often recruited by management to help them use stolen mill materials for home improvements. "No one questioned these actions or the thinking that was behind them. The mill was there, so you *used* it."[33] So it was in Weirton, but my point is that the "thinking" behind these actions drew upon paternalistic notions of collective property rights and was not merely vice, corruption, or convenience. Over time, paternalism generated local consent to stealing as long as "it stayed in the family."

Given this legacy, the scandal inevitably raised questions about the nature of property rights under worker ownership. As one woman who never worked in the mill wondered:

> Why [in a worker-owned mill] would someone want to steal from themselves? But I guess it happens all the time. People take paper clips and pens from work, I guess, so it's everyone.

Although not everyone stole from the mill, the general mood that condoned stealing—"it happens all the time, so it's everyone"—still existed. Indeed, what most annoyed workers was not so much that someone had stolen from the mill, nor even the degree of the infraction. Rather, what the scandal magnified was a double standard that many workers felt existed between executives and management, and labor—"them and us." When workers claimed "they stole from us" they were making a distinction that paternalism had blurred for decades. Despite company efforts to define ESOP as a "partnership" of "people working together," this distinction was sharpening as workers sensed that their rights were not quite the same as management's.

For instance, the rank-and-file routinely submitted to automobile checks when entering and leaving mill parking lots.[34] Many workers considered this humiliating, unnecessary, and another sign of the hollowness of their ownership status. It was also hard to take in light of the corruption that many felt went on "up on the hill." As a worker from quality control put it:

> Hell, everyone takes a pencil now and then, but those guys manipulate the numbers all the time. They steal money and it's not fair that they treat us like criminals!

His brother-in-law agreed.

> I just tell them to go ahead and look, they're not going to find anything. What the hell can I take worth anything that'll fit into my car. I ain't got nothing to hide.

That tolerance of the car searches, however, angered the first worker.

> Yeah, well, that kind of attitude just makes them think it's all right and makes it harder for us to stop that management bullshit.

Many workers felt they were denied the "leeway" to pursue the custom of stealing while management and executives were not equally subject to the same surveillance. And management was in a position to steal much more, more easily than closely watched workers. Underlying class relations, no longer mediated by paternalistic customs, had come to the fore.

ESOP failed to resolve the tension between collective and private property rights. The question "how can worker-owners steal from themselves" made little sense precisely because as worker-*owners* they were not "stealing" anything but rather using what was already theirs. From viewing the mill as collective property under paternalism to viewing it as collective property under worker ownership was not a dramatic conceptual leap. Under ESOP an employee's right to property, whether in terms of profit sharing, stock allocation, or voting, rested on years of service and compensation; on individual rights that stealing contradicted.

Paternalistic traditions, however, also valued *membership* in the community within a collectivist notion of property rights. Yet there was no similar conception of how stealing under worker ownership violated this moral code except in terms of class—"us" versus "them." In other words, workers knew it was wrong to steal from the mill—it was "about time this stuff ended—but they also retained a collective notion of property—"*we* own the mill"—that had been undermined by the structure of worker ownership and the manner in which property rights were exercised. This problem was further illustrated in my final set of vignettes where I look at the norms of community nepotism and local control under ESOP.

Waste Not, Want Not

Before continuing, I want to briefly consider a close cousin to the practice of stealing: wasteful or inefficient use of mill resources. Though not technically stealing, misuse and abuse of mill tools and materials cost the company money in waste, unnecessary repairs, and retooling. In general workers strongly opposed what they saw as tremendous waste and inefficiency in the mill. Repeatedly I was told by EPG members how their project to save materials, time, or effort—in a word, waste—was "stonewalled" by management. Many workers were likewise critical of the wasteful habits of their fellow employees. "A lot of these guys," said a younger inventory clerk from the slabyard, "still think they're working for National Steel. They still think National owes them something. But it's our mill and we have to start thinking that way or we're in trouble."

Although workers were unanimously critical of waste in the mill, I did not find the same antipathy toward either sleeping or stealing, both of which could easily be considered wasteful. How, then, was worker concern with waste reconciled with their defense of sleeping and stealing? I see two reasonable explanations. First, controlling waste was perhaps the number one priority of EPG, whether saving materials, time, or effort. Although everyone condemned waste, EPG members may have been the most outspoken precisely because their efforts were directly focused on eliminating it. Likewise, waste was an issue that workers could use to chastise management for their resistance to employee ideas. The issues of sleeping and stealing were not as useful in this regard because they implicated workers as well. But this still leaves workers having to justify their frustration with waste in the face of informally condoned sleeping and stealing on the job.

Another plausible answer emerges under the moral economy of collective property rights. In this context, sleeping and stealing were both concerned with the "use" value of the mill. Sleeping might be condoned by workers because it was useful for "the guy having a bad day, or with family problems." Besides, as Sal explained, nobody could work two shifts without napping at some point. Stealing was likewise "useful" and, like sleeping, was condoned under the moral premise of egalitarian advantage from collective access to mill resources. Waste, on the other hand, had neither "use" nor "exchange" value. If one used more than one needed or threw away something that was still good, it represented irresponsibility, laziness, or, at worse, indifference. At least if you stole it, you used it for something you needed or wanted. But waste benefited no one, neither the individual nor the collective. Under the logic of collective property rights, waste could be condemned because the community lost what was wasted and nobody prospered from it.

Community, Nepotism, and Local Control

Under market pressures and ESOP's bureaucratic organization workers and residents had to defer to the "bottom line" needs of the corporation and its emphasis on performance and efficiency. Rewards and mobility were *achieved* by individuals through their actions, and individuals were held accountable for those actions. Under paternalism, on the other hand, people gained rewards and mobility as much because of their *ascribed* status in the community as anything they did. In Weirton, getting a mill job and keeping it were strongly influenced by family connections and one's social position in the community (see chapters 2 and 5). In the past, the weakest and most vulnerable were accommodated within a paternalistic order that extended care and benevolence to "our kind" in the face of market pressures toward competition and profitability. Under ESOP the "humane" face of paternalism was absent as one's birthplace and family connections carried less and less influence in the company.

Despite the slogan "We Can Do It—Working Together Works" of company public relations, Weirton's ESOP had no place for nepotistic sentiments and customs. This was poignantly illustrated in controversy over changes in the company's summer work program, CEO Loughhead's retirement, and a mayoral election. In each case, nepotism and localism informed workers' critique that worker ownership was not living up to its promises to serve the interests of workers and the community. In each case, these same sentiments were also being publicly reevaluated and found wanting. After three years worker ownership had not provided an institutional or cultural alternative that might reunite the mill with family and community life.

What About Our Kids?

One way that nepotism was institutionalized and led "generation after generation" into the mill was through a work program that hired the sons and daughters of millworkers during their summer break from school. This program offered premium wages to summer hires and also served as anticipatory socialization for youth who would eventually seek work in the mill full time; it only took a family member or friend to "put in a good word."

But in the summer of 1987 Weirton's worker-owners were informed that the program was being modified. With labor force reductions looming ahead, the summer jobs program seemed more a feeble nod to tradition than necessary for the current needs of the company. Summer hires would be compensated at 70 percent of the applicable contractual rate for the particular job, and they would not be eligible for medical benefits. Still good money for the summer, but there would be less of it for fewer area youth. Only 200 applicants would be drawn from a lottery and summer hires would not accumulate seniority in anticipation of regular employment in the mill.

Hard economic times meant hard choices, but this new policy cut to the heart of Weirton's moral economy. Workers held mixed opinions over the program revisions, but during one union meeting there was still general hostility at the ISU leadership for supporting the changes. When a union committeeman explained that summer hiring "is the company's right and we have no say in that," an exasperated worker bellowed, "but we *are* the owners!" As he turned away in disgust to a cheering audience, another worker stepped up and chastised the assembled rank-and-file for being unreasonable. Given the hard economic times, he asked, and the fact that workers were already hanging on to their jobs after deep wage concessions, how could anyone seriously expect the summer jobs program to escape a similar fate? He then turned back to the ISU committeemen and scolded them for poorly representing the rank-and-file.

Indeed, while it was unreasonable to expect the summer jobs program to continue as it always had, there was still widespread resentment among workers to yet another example of how mill and family were being separated under ESOP. Not only was the pay rate reduced without guarantee of employment after the summer, but workers also felt that the company was ignoring the health and safety of their children. The historic obligations of a paternalistic mill to family life were again being gutted, but this time it was a direct hit upon the children of millworkers.

Here was a policy where the link between mill and family was most direct and profound. At one level, ESOP did not sever that link but rather reinforced it. Most workers, like Sal, agreed that only sons and daughters of mill employees should be eligible for the program.

> Now, we're the owners, so I agree with that, but not paying them like us and no benefits or medical? That's unfair! Hey, it's their kids working in there.

But the policy also revealed that perhaps the link was *too* strong for the interests of workers' children. Though Sal's wife and sister agreed, they also reasoned, "Well, maybe it's a good thing. They'll think twice about going to college." Nepotistic hiring practices were yielding to more impersonal, market forces that people found out of their control. Workers could not resist these forces under ESOP and protect their family as they once did under paternalism.

Let me restate and elaborate this point. While nepotism was a central element of paternalism in Weirton, it was not completely and unskeptically embraced by townspeople. With all its benefits came arbitrary firings and favoritism, minority discrimination, and a management flexibility that could "taketh away" privileges as often as it "giveth." This is one reason most workers, yet few residents, still supported a union; nepotism persisted, but so too did favoritism and discrimination. The ISU regulated nepotism's worst excesses, which brought some stability to workers' lives at work and in the community. As Sal recalled:

> They used to say, "Sal, you take tomorrow off," and I'd take it. I know I had another day coming, but I wouldn't ask when. You just didn't do that. You went along with it because that's how it was. [The foreman] would have his blue notebook and would pull it out of his back pocket—that was scheduling. Now you have to post it and you have some idea of your workdays. Then they also used to give overtime to people depending on if they liked you or not. Now you get it based on seniority, and seniority is accumulated by company time, not how long you worked in any one department.

Workers used to invite their foreman over for dinner on Sunday nights. "That always went on," chuckled Sal. "You wanted to get in good with them." But if personal informality between labor and management aided workers, it could just as often backfire, leaving them without any organizational or legal recourse when they were slighted or treated unjustly. The ISU brought some institutional standardization and a degree of job stability and protection, but it also upheld nepotistic customs that served company interests and reinforced workers' expectations of, and dependence on, company noblesse oblige.

The controversy over summer hiring revealed that the ISU could no longer uphold nepotism, nor had it adequately represented workers' sense of familial and community membership *in the mill*. Rank-and-file anger over revisions in the summer work program did not easily translate into clear strategies or viable alternatives. As worker after worker explained when I asked why they did not collectively fight back against such company "wrongs" as the revised summer hiring policy, "It'll never happen here in Weirton—they never have and never will." Things might be tough, but if you "caused waves," they could always get tougher.

Leadership after Paternalism

On January 24, 1987, Robert Loughhead set off yet another wave of rumors when he unexpectedly announced his retirement as president and CEO of Weirton Steel. The resignation of other top company officials and the search for Loughhead's replacement evoked localist sentiments from workers and residents who saw the real stripes of indifferent outsiders, but it also signaled that "taking care of our own" required more than blind faith in the loyalty of mill officials and trust in their wisdom. These same sentiments, however, discouraged any serious consideration of having someone from town run the company and once again revealed the ambivalence people held toward nepotism and localism in Weirton.

From his own account, Loughhead had planned to retire during his mid-50s but he postponed that decision when the Weirton ESOP position was offered in 1983.[35] He noted that the company's long-range plans regarding restructuring, refinancing, and a massive capital spending program made it "unlikely" that he would remain until they were all completed and that "it would be most unfair to any new chief executive officer to have to come into the picture in midstream, so to speak. It's far better for him to be involved at the outset."[36] One month later, Executive Vice President Carl Valdiserri also resigned his position. According to Loughhead, Valdiserri "was an avowed candidate to succeed me upon my retirement, and when not considered by the board of directors for the position, [he] chose to resign."[37] As the upper echelons of the mill quaked, people wondered why they "really" left and who would now lead Weirton Steel.

Everyone I spoke to insisted there were other reasons for Loughhead's "retirement" and many workers expressed dismay over his decision to step aside before restructuring and capital improvements began. At a Super Bowl party, Sal put it this way as he shuffled me into a garage:

> Don't believe that stuff in the paper. You don't believe that, do you? No, there's more to it than that. Let me tell you. I'll fill you in. I don't want to talk about this in there, but there's more to his retirement than what you read. Yeah, most of the guys like Loughhead, but they like his ideas of worker-participation. They like the ideas he has, but they don't think he should have retired now, not midway through this thing. He should have stayed at least until 1988. You start something, then you leave? It's like a captain leaving his ship in rough waters.

A few days later, Sal's brother echoed the widespread suspicion and speculation that followed Loughhead's announcement:

> It's tough to work under that uncertainty. You got to wonder why Loughhead decided to retire now. It just doesn't seem right, unless things were going wrong.

Not a few people wondered if Loughhead and Valdiserri "had their hands in the till" or at least knew about the recent mill scandal and failed to act. But the rumor most often repeated and widely believed was that Loughhead (and perhaps Valdiserri) were forced out by a faction among the board of directors. The local *Weirton Daily Times* cited an anonymous director who was "displeased with Loughhead's lack of day-to-day contact with operations due to his concentration with the sales aspect of Weirton Steel." Such speculation was "ludicrous," said Loughhead, "nothing could be further from the truth."[38]

Still, speculation continued to grow that Loughhead's relationship with the board of directors had steadily deteriorated. Even Loughhead intimated this in July 1987 when he told the *Pittsburgh Press* of executive disagreements over modernization strategies.

> Over the past few years we have had a lot of complicated discussions on exactly what Weirton's strategy ought to be. We agree on where the company is going to go, but there are different ways of getting there. That's all there is.[39]

But there was indeed more to it, according to directors from the Weirton board who were anonymously cited in a July 29 article in the *Weirton Daily Times*. Questions about the size and method of funding a much-needed continuous caster to produce semifinished steel had "provoked disagreement among directors and managers." The larger the caster, the more difficult it would be to fund, leading to either more concessions or a revision of the profit-sharing formula that was scheduled to increase from 33 percent to 50 percent of net profits. It could also mean a labor force reduction, changes in work rules, or multicrafting to achieve lowered production costs.

Loughhead and Valdiserri had argued for a larger caster, but instead of approving their plan, the board hired McKinsey and Company to reexamine the company's alternatives. For one director the proposal put forth by Loughhead and Valdiserri was too vague, while another director conceded differences of opinion on the board, but said it had nothing to do with Loughhead leaving the company. "Would it be fair to say there was reasonable disagreement? Yes. . . . But to say a great cleavage? No."[40]

Loughhead's "retirement" and rumors of dissension among board members raised concern among worker-owners that their jobs and equity status were again in jeopardy. The labor-cost advantage that Weirton Steel enjoyed by virtue of the 20 percent ESOP concessions was slowly dwindling in the face of modernization pressures. And as the *Weirton Daily Times* noted, rank-and-file worker-owners were again being targeted for more cuts.

One Weirton director faulted Loughhead for the absence of new concessions, saying he gave no clear signal to the union on what measures it would have to take to ensure the company continued as the lowcost producer in its markets.[41]

Given the mill scandal involving upper management, controversy over Loughhead's salary, and the critical-skill pay raises, workers were incredulous over suggestions that they might be asked to bear the burden of capital improvements. This was even more offensive in light of two McKinsey studies showing that the mill was management top-heavy and a general attitude among workers that management was not acting in good faith on their EPG ideas for cost savings. During the CEO search people began to ask who could, and should, run the mill. Leadership in post-paternalistic Weirton was fleeting and suspect. If the experts were not reassuring, then neither was local nepotism.

"Nobody Here Can Run That Mill"

Speculation over Loughhead's successor filled the bars and parks, living rooms and kitchens about town. Though nobody had the slightest notion of who it might be, everyone was certain that "nobody here can run that mill." For workers and residents alike, the idea that someone from town should take the reins of the mill was preposterous. Rumors that ISU president Bish might succeed Loughhead were simply incredible to Sal. "He's not smart enough to do the job. No, he's not the person for that position." Nor did the wife of a grocery store owner think Bish was qualified to handle the job—"I heard they might make Walter Bish president, but I don't know. I don't think he's smart enough to handle it."

Here was a troubling irony—one that people were vaguely aware of but perhaps did not want to admit. Claims that nobody in Weirton was "smart enough" were routinely made by people who otherwise praised the mill labor force and local residents for their intelligence. As I noted in chapters 4 and 5, workers consistently defended themselves against the impression that "management thinks we're stupid" by referring to how smart they were, how much they knew about their jobs, and how many ideas they had to increase production and efficiency.

Likewise, residents and local businesspeople always referred proudly to community members who "know what they're talking about" and were endowed with intelligence or wisdom. The *Weirton Daily Times* never failed to run a story or note the academic or career achievements of townspeople, nor was the *Weirton Steel Bulletin* shy of celebrating the knowledge and skills of workers in what could easily be considered complex and technical areas. However, when it came to someone leading the mill, nobody seemed "smart enough" to handle the job.

Workers and residents alike were concerned about maintaining the good favor of lending institutions and customers, but this does not fully account for their almost uniform insistence that local people were intellectually inferior. As I talked with people, it became clear to me that they were telling themselves this for the same reason given by the grocery store owner above; nobody could imagine making the hard *emotional* choices that inevitably came with running the mill.

> Besides, they need someone from outside Weirton to run things. Nobody from around here would be good in that position. Can you imagine someone from Weirton having to fire someone? It just wouldn't work.

Under paternalism the emotional burdens that a market economy imposes were always mediated by the forceful, yet benevolent oversight of Weir, Millsop, or town elites. Even when paternalism turned ugly (as it often did), people could turn to family and friends, or leave town. Like it or not, everyone knew who was in charge and the emotional burden was in taking care of one another, not firing them. With ESOP, claims that nobody was smart enough to run the mill reflected more the loss of past leadership and its normative obligations than the absence of intelligent and qualified local personnel. Conditions and events since the 1970s generated growing awareness of how strong the localist and nepotist legacies of paternalism still were in Weirton and how difficult it was to redefine and reestablish these bonds within a worker-owned mill. The norms and sentiments of "community" were incapable of "doing business" with worker ownership—at least as community was constructed and reinforced under paternalism.

After spending some $500,000 in search of Loughhead's replacement, the board of directors chose Herbert Elish, a current board member, to assume the position of chairman, president, and chief executive officer. Most people I spoke with held a "wait and see" attitude about Elish in particular, but they were not as reserved over the process and cost involved in his selection. As a clerical worker put it:

> It's funny, but here they [the board of directors] go and have this big search, to New York, and then they pull in somebody from their own backyard, from the board. But I don't know about him, just what I've read. You can't judge him yet, but in six months to a year, then we'll see.

In an anonymous letter circulated throughout the mill a few months later, another worker was far less amused over Elish's selection. This worker also mocked the legitimating principles upon which most people agreed that "nobody from [Weirton] could run the mill."

> You sat on our highly educated, intelligent, and professional board of directors and let management and the board spend approximately a half million dollars to engage a New York company to help find a new president and CEO and then you were selected. This is another exemplary exploitation of management waste.

The goodwill and cautious optimism that immediately followed the formation of ESOP had by now deteriorated to a point where workers and residents no longer knew whom to trust. Just as with employee participation, "trust" was a normative orientation that, however forced under paternalism, had become empty rhetoric under worker ownership. At the same time, residents were coming to terms with a local polity that was no longer dominated by the mill. Here too, trust between leaders and led was on trial, as was the legacy of the benevolent face of paternalism.

Politics as Usual?

In the spring of 1987, amid these mill controversies, Weirton held a mayoral election. Local politics had always been a family affair dictated by mill officials, but in the first election since ESOP the affair was being contested. As my friend Ted remarked one night during dinner, "Weirton Steel does not run politics in Weirton like they used to. Those days are over!"

Perhaps Weirton Steel did not determine political life as it "used to," but nepotism still infused local politics. As a social worker remarked, the current mayor might be "dumb," but "he's a nice guy." Qualifications and political orientation were one thing, but personal charm and social connections were still the key to political position and influence. Recalling her first taste of civic associations, my landlady explained how "all you did was sit around while the cliques made all the decisions and ran the show. I didn't want any part of that, so I've never joined another club." Town council meetings were also pro forma rituals where the agenda was set, and key decisions made, well in advance and normally behind closed doors. As one resident put it:

> I've attended a few meetings, just to see how they worked. But everything was already decided and you just sit there and listen to what they were going to do. They work things out before people get there, then open the doors and let everyone in to find out what's going on.

In many ways Weirton's city election was no different than any other local election in America. Appeals to voters were made on the basis of "what's good for everyone," and previous experience in business and political affairs could be as detrimental to one's candidacy as they were a boon. What mattered most was making the right friends and "scratching" the right backs. In the end, what goes around comes around, and for candidates it was important to get around. Local politics (and, for many people in Weirton, politics in general) was something that the wealthy and "good old boys" ran, and where corruption and vice were endemic.[42]

But under worker ownership the town had to fend for itself, and by the 1987 city elections people were asking what kind of politics they wanted. More importantly, the debate and "gridlock" that precede compromise in a democratic polity conflicted with an ideal "community" that stressed cooperation and harmony. Paternalism supported this ideal of community as forceful and charismatic elites with access to a seemingly endless stream of mill resources would simply "donate" enough (and strongly encourage workers to as well) to alleviate potential disputes, disruptions, or civic need. Now, lacking any credible leadership and facing fiscal austerity, political patronage could no longer be justified against the divergent interests of family, class, and residential area. The mounting ambivalence toward nepotism and localism was illustrated during a public debate between the mayoral and council candidates one night in late April 1987.

Prior to the primary election a mayoral forum was hosted by the Marland Heights Civic Association. One of seven wards making up the city of Weirton, Marland Heights rises high above the mill overlooking northern Steubenville, Ohio, and the Ohio River to the west. Once the exclusive residence of town elites, mill executives and management, Marland Heights had lost some stature over the years as Weirton expanded toward the Pennsylvania border, up through what is now known as Weirton Heights (see Map 1.1 in chapter 1). Weirton's professional class (doctors and lawyers) and local business owners were more scattered throughout Brooke and Hancock Counties, though a favored destination for local professionals was the lush King's Creek Valley just northeast of the mill. Meanwhile, Marland Heights had steadily become more class diverse with more and more skilled and semiskilled millworkers living next door to retired mill officials and their children who have remained. Still home of the exclusive Williams Country Club, Margaret M. Weir Park, and ostentatious Marland Heights swimming pool, Marland Heights was facing the same problems of civic maintenance and renewal as the rest of Weirton.

Upon entering a Lions Club meeting hall I was immediately greeted by two council and two mayoral candidates, one of the mayoral candidates earnestly campaigning for my vote. After explaining who I was, all but the silent mayoral candidate left for potential voters. A very warm and talkative man, he began to explain the key points of his plank (of which renovating the old Weirton Hospital into a senior citizens' home was a priority) and his "high-tech" vision of Weirton's future. After a few minutes I asked if he might gain more votes by discussing these ideas with residents, but he knew he was a "dark horse" in this race. "The cards are on the table," he sighed, gently setting his hand on my shoulder.

> Everyone else has money. I don't really have a chance, just don't have a chance to compete with these people. My friends always ask me why my signs are so small, and I tell them I can't afford bigger ones or all the newspaper advertising they have. The money always wins out and it's a shame, but that's the way it is.

Money may have mattered, but so did connections and this candidate appeared to have neither.

As the debate began close to 125 people had filled the room with many standing against a back wall. After hearing opening statements from all the candidates, two general issues were clearly atop everyone's platform: the need for economic development apart from the mill that would stem the out-migration of area youth, and holding the line on local taxes while maintaining services such as fire and police, parks, and recreation facilities. As for public services, nobody advocated raising taxes and all the candidates followed the familiar theme "We must live within our budget and tighten our belts." Not surprisingly, nobody could—or would—suggest where civic administration ought to be cut, and the issue of fiscal policy was left as a matter "to be studied."

Likewise, the issue of economic development produced few innovative proposals from the candidates. None of them, from what they said or what I read in the local paper, had any clear proposals for stimulating local economic growth other than supporting the completion of an interstate bypass and bridge between Steubenville, Ohio, and Weirton. This, people hoped, would attract businesses wishing to locate just outside the Pittsburgh metropolitan core. Otherwise, the general sentiment remained that "where Weirton Steel goes, so does the town." My neighbor, tired of this "mill or nothing" attitude and local exclusiveness, thought that Weirton was ideally situated to attract people employed at the new Pittsburgh International Airport being expanded northwest of Pittsburgh, but only thirty miles from Weirton. "This is an ideal place to live and raise a family, and we could draw a lot of pilots and airport staff here who could easily commute to the airport. But a lot of people in this town don't want any outsiders, so how are we going to grow?"

Localism proved to be a stubborn legacy of paternalism, and it was not until the question and answer period that criticism of one mayoral candidate revealed how moral considerations about the local economy persisted. As the candidate fended off accusations that he had misused city funds for personal travel, the audience sensed that it was, as a woman next to me quipped, "being taken for ride." Murmuring and laughs of disbelief followed each candidate's effort to distance themselves from any impropriety ever rumored. This led to the emotional issue of casino gaming in town, which evoked the independent, almost isolationist character of local life.

"We Take Care of Our Own"

Although many people opposed bringing in casino gaming, some, even from establishment corners of Weirton, did not. The local paper and chamber of commerce supported it, and although Weirton Steel took no formal position, public relations executive Charles Cronin felt "it's a must. Given the history of this area, it would flourish. West Virginia is out of options. I may have to learn how to shoot craps."[43] Still, most of the candidates either explicitly opposed casino gambling or skirted this divisive issue with the refrain "it needs to be studied." Even mayoral candidate Joe Mayernick, head of the chamber of commerce, was cautious despite his support of casinos a year earlier.[44] But one mayoral candidate qualified his opposition with a startling admission given the tone of the debate thus far.

> I gamble. I gamble, and it's illegal! (*Pause*) You'll see me down there betting football games during the season. I like to lay a few dollars on the game. Yeah, I gamble and it's illegal. But I don't want casino gambling here. It's not right and it would only cause us problems.

Whether a populist appeal to appear "just like everyone else," or a sincere plea for consideration of the "problems" large-scale legalized gambling might introduce to Weirton, the morality of casino gambling was being called into question, but *not* the morality of this candidate's "illegal" bets at local bars. While on the surface this was a glaring contradiction of principle, it was not inconsistent within the moral economy of Weirton.

With horse racing only a few miles north and dog racing thirty miles south in Wheeling, the West Virginia panhandle is a haven for legalized gambling in an otherwise fundamentalist state. But in Weirton, *illegal* gambling had flourished for as long as people could remember. Practically every bar in town operated some form of gambling, from cards, to sports betting, to numbers. And practically everyone—at least among the males in town—made a bet now and then, usually just a few dollars, but often enough hundreds and thousands of dollars. "I can find you six or eight bookies in three blocks," said one steelworker. "Might as well make it legal 'cause it's here anyway."[45] Federal officials periodically cracked down on local gambling, but rarely was anyone convicted. As the former city editor of the *Weirton Daily Times* put it, "I don't recall a single major gambling bust (in Weirton), gambling is accepted here."[46]

Gambling was not only accepted, but as this candidate's admission indicates, illegal gambling was *morally* right as well. Gambling was neither crime nor vice, but a legitimate form of entertainment and chance. And if it was widespread and accepted in Weirton, people were also weary of efforts to bring large-scale legalized gaming into the area. Most opposition to such efforts cited the increasing crime, police costs, and congestion legalized gaming would bring to town. But people in Weirton also preferred to *regulate gambling themselves* for a number of reasons. First, the money wagered on the local betting scene stayed in Weirton and among Weirtonians, something that legalized gaming would steadily undermine. As a Brooke County magistrate and retired Weirton Steel executive put it:

> Our people and natural resources have always been exploited by outside interests. Before John L. Lewis, our coal miners got paid a pittance. Our timber goes to North Carolina to be made into furniture. So here we come again, with outsiders ready to exploit us.[47]

And much like the numbers rackets studied by William Foote Whyte in *Street Corner Society* (1943),[48] gambling was an important source of sociability through which membership and reputation in the community were established and reinforced (something impressed upon me at some cost). More, community control also managed people's excessive betting as bar owners could refuse a patron's bet "for their own good." Casino gaming would not only siphon local funds to outside interests, but it threatened to disrupt social relationships and status markers that defined community boundaries.

Even those who supported legalized gaming expressed reservations about "losing control over it." According to this reasoning, community welfare and local autonomy were of a higher moral order than state or federal laws that people viewed as an infringement on their collective rights to regulate customary behavior. This moral code distrusted outside business conglomerates as well as the heavy hand of federal regulation, so even though casino gaming might be an economic boon to Weirton, people wished to preserve whatever local control they could over gambling. As things stood, casino gaming could not pass the state legislature, and this made it easier for people to avoid this choice while keeping their fragile hold on local custom.

One final incident during the debate illustrated the persistence of local nepotism and the ambivalence it fostered. Following the issue of casino gambling, a young man sitting next to me (and writing notes as feverishly as I) stood up to question the city's hiring practices and the pervasiveness of "cliques and power groups that get their people in." Here was a direct attack upon nepotism and its tension with meritocratic principles. Once a lifeguard at the city pool, the man recalled his enlistment in the air force and specialized aquatics training.

> I learned all there was to know about the water and water safety. So I felt I was extremely qualified in this area and when I got out I decided that I wanted to come back to Weirton and make this my home, hoping to get a position as a lifeguard. But when I applied I was turned down and the position was given to someone who wasn't nearly as qualified as I was. Now, I know this city is run by political groups and cliques and my question to you [directed to the mayoral candidates] is whether this practice will continue or not, and if I can get a job here.

As vaguely as he could, one of the two leading mayoral candidates admitted that although favoritism was a "fact of life" in Weirton he could only promise to moderate it and that hiring for such positions rested with the park board. Such candor appealed to the man and audience alike, and it was in stark contrast to the other candidate who claimed that he was unaware of any nepotism in city hiring practices. This drew a chorus of sarcastic laughs and heavy murmuring from the audience. As he argued that employment should not depend on "who you know" but the most qualified should get the job, his words were drowned out by a rising volume of laughter. Nepotism was entrenched in the institutional workings of city government and most people knew it; nepotism was something that you just "had to live with." Those who moved from Weirton or decided to return after living elsewhere might find such favoritism archaic and an affront to their belief in meritocracy, but if they intended to live here they would have to deal with nepotism.

After the debate I walked outside and again spoke with the "dark horse" mayoral candidate I met earlier. As we talked about the young man who challenged local nepotism he expressed the strengths and limitations of paternalism in Weirton, its enduring appeal and Achilles heel. He spoke of a widow who worked for the city, and even though she was unqualified and "not doing the best job," he wondered, "How do you fire a widow who's handicapped and needs the job, even if she's unqualified, but everyone wants to look after her?" He then became angry at the mayoral candidate accused of abusing travel funds.

He's a two-faced liar, and he lied when he said that he didn't travel other places. I know of at least three other trips he took. He was lying up there tonight!

But when I asked why he did not protest during the debate a smile crossed his face, "You don't do that around here, we're a family."

Summary

Family. Community. These were the ideals that people found wanting as they faced hard economic times and an impersonal bureaucratic ESOP. Though resembling a classic example of "tradition

versus modernity" or another case of "cultural lag," worker ownership in Weirton is far more complex in my view. Paternalism here
was itself a unique combination of tradition and modernity, and it
entailed specific duties, obligations, and patterns of respect that
continue to define and organize life here today. Still, as previous
chapters show, the paternalistic order that National Steel rejected
during the 1970s was being challenged under worker ownership
as well.

Workers had become frustrated with the inegalitarian nature
of worker ownership in the company and on the shopfloor. At the
same time, people were ambivalent about the changing relationship between a once paternalistically organized mill and their
families and community. This was most evident in the subtext of
local life, in the collective rituals and informal discourse over
which customs and traditions to "hang on to" and which to "let go
of." Though not clearly articulated within the rhetoric of control,
the moral economy I have analyzed in this chapter grappled with
precisely that. Broader than the indulgency pattern analyzed by
Alvin Gouldner, and more than just "worker" control, people were
debating the complex interplay of *worker* and *community* control,
as well as the criteria upon which authority rested and by which
it was exercised.

These criteria of community membership, loyalty, nepotism,
and local use of mill resources were once embedded in a normative order that united work and family, mill and community. Under the structure of worker ownership and a more competitive
global economy, however, these criteria had become more ambiguous (if not contradictory) and therefore contested. So when I asked
about worker-control specifically, most workers and residents
speculated that it would be a "fiasco." But as I listened to people
discuss controversial issues I began to understand their ambivalence toward "worker-control" in the context of their conflicted positions in the mill and community. Debates over these issues
carried strongly felt moral views about ESOP and the rights and
responsibilities of worker-owners. Three schematic themes became evident in these debates and directly implicated in how equity and control were organized in the company.

First, the *value of labor* had become ambiguous since ESOP.
Despite significant concessions by labor, criticism of rank-and-file

compensation was epitomized by routine references to sleeping in the mill. This practice epitomized "worker irresponsibility" and was condemned by townspeople on the basis of worker-owners' collective obligation to the public welfare. While this critique was class based (local professionals and business owners arguing that workers should act "more like us"; area wage earners envious of better mill wages and benefits), it also expressed a moral priority of community responsibility that derived from the same paternalistic mill policies that initially produced the custom of sleeping "on the job." In other words, *workers* were being condemned as immoral, rather than the fact that paternalism shaped the value of labor where loyalty and compliance meant more than the hours one worked.

Likewise, ambivalence over how much a CEO was worth arose from the same structural changes that revealed objective discrepancies in evaluating the value of rank-and-file labor, ambiguity that paternalism had once mitigated. As people grappled with the criteria of power, status, and market comparisons, each contradicted their own work experience, the larger regional and national economy, and their sense of fairness under ESOP. Still, workers leaned toward egalitarian principles rooted in class but consistent with their ideals of community when evaluating the value of company executives. Despite company efforts to manage rank-and-file judgments (through internal communications), the controversy signaled that under ESOP workers felt that executive compensation should be subject to measurement, review, and modification.

Debate over the value of labor came to a head with the critical skills pay raises. This was perhaps the clearest example of how the bureaucratic principle of expertise and the role of technical knowledge staff conflicted with both the egalitarian principles workers held of ESOP and people's more general sense of collective obligation to the public welfare. Not only did both workers and residents find it difficult to judge what a "critical skill" was, but the policy demonstrated how the value of labor was being determined by forces outside their control and apart from community norms that were more available and valid than an impersonal bureaucracy.

A second theme, the issue of *property rights* under worker ownership, was also complicated by notions of private and collective property that were once compatible but now seemed contradictory. Stealing from the mill was another practice that paternalism fostered and condoned. It was organized and justified according to a principle of local use by local people where all could partake without rancor or reprisal. The mill scandal over management theft confirmed that stealing could no longer be tolerated under ESOP, even though notions of collective property persisted. But the lesson workers learned was that *they* were held more accountable than management; *they* were checked and watched closely without being able to return the favor. It was not mill theft, but what workers saw as a double standard that contradicted their class interests as well as their notions of community based collective property rights.

Finally, ESOP policies clashed with paternalistic *nepotism* and a stubborn *localism* that once "took care of our own." Even though workers had to concede wages and benefits under ESOP, many were appalled that their children would as well under the new summer hiring policy. This new policy cut to the heart of paternalism, and it illustrated just how dependent on the mill workers and their families had become. But what most angered them was their union's complicity in this policy. If such complicity with the company once benefited workers, it now appeared to harm them and their families. For more and more of the rank-and-file, it was about time for new union leadership that would represent and protect them as workers and members of a community.

Likewise, it was time for new leadership in the company. With Loughhead's retirement people began wondering who would, and could, run the mill. Even though people favored local control, they still could not imagine someone from town at the helm. This was because company leadership involved emotional and moral as well as economic dimensions. "Caring for our own" conflicted with the requirements of running the company, at least as it was organized since ESOP. More, the executive shakeup was viewed by workers and residents as a sign of dissension *among elites*, something local people had never seen (under Weir, Millsop, or even during the ESOP negotiations). This signaled problems in the mill, but it also revealed the fragile nature of elite solidarity and loyalty to the community that was once so solid under paternalism.

As for leadership in the community, this, too, had always been in elite hands but had now fallen in the laps of townspeople. And it was around this issue that traditions of nepotism and localism were most visible. Even as people realized that gambling was illegal they still appealed to a custom of local control that managed it within the boundaries (both geographical and normative) of Weirton. Much like local police "took care our own" local deviance, the custom of gambling called upon an organized and familiar relationship between local bookies and people's betting. And if nepotism and localism once mitigated meritocracy and civic debate in behalf of paternalistic control, they were gradually losing favor under the structurally generated transparency of personal injustice, cliquish avarice, and inefficiency in city government.

A Comment on the Norm of Reciprocity

Before concluding, let me clarify my analysis of the egalitarianism of Weirton's moral economy. Although such sentiments were reflected in the outlooks and behavior of rank-and-file workers there may be an even more basic principle encompassing moral reasoning about worker ownership and economic relations in Weirton—the norm of reciprocity.

Under paternalism, relationships in the mill and community were far from egalitarian. Besides the dominance of mill elites, gender and racial inequality were central to the paternalistic order and worldview. Yet as chapter 2 showed, paternalism also embodied reciprocal duties and obligations between leaders and led; perks and privilege entailed responsibility to the community and public welfare. Likewise, class stratification did not preclude workers from some of the fruits enjoyed by company elites.

Under worker ownership class divisions have become more pronounced and the nature and form of reciprocity between the board of directors, management, and labor was still an open question. As I demonstrated in chapters 4 and 5, rank-and-file workers still thought management—as much as a union—was necessary in the mill. They agreed that "someone has to run things" and they consented to an organizational hierarchy of decision making. But what seemed to be missing was any meaningful reciprocity between company officials and workers—the "trust" issue.

In this context, it was one thing for workers to take pay cuts for the "good" of the company and community, but quite another when board members did not in kind and instead received raises or bonuses. It was one thing when mill theft was denounced—at all levels—for the "good" of the company and community, but quite another when worker-owners faced the daily indignity of routine surveillance while management infractions receded quietly beneath an organizational veil. It was one thing for workers to be efficient and attentive to the company "bottom line," but a constant source of frustration and antagonism when management failed to act on EPG ideas. For more and more of Weirton Steel's rank-and-file, their families, and residents in general, it seemed as though the company could not even abide by its own principles.

Struck by discrepancies between the spirit and deed of ESOP, calls for a more egalitarian (though not more democratic) company emerged and faded in my conversations with people. It was precisely the wax and wane of these sentiments that reveals the tension between the class structure of local life and the paternalistic norms that once mediated it. This tension would erupt in the 1990s as a struggle for control raged through Weirton and confounded those who saw paternalism dissolving class struggle and providing for a quiescent ESOP.

C^{hapter} E^{ight}

The Struggle for Control

We should have a real say, be exercising our right to vote. People want control, we want to control the voting power of the corporation.

—Mark Glyptis, ISU president, 1992

As employee frustration grew over controversial company policies and rumors of executive dissension, people were questioning just how "reasonable" worker-ownership was in the first place. In the summer of 1988, Herbert Elish had replaced Robert Loughhead as company president and CEO, and Walter Bish was about to lose his reelection bid to Virgil Thompson for president of the ISU. "I guess they got rid of their top guy," laughed Sal, "and now we're getting rid of ours." These changes anticipated the difficult and contentious decisions over delayed modernization projects and a potential public stock offering that was fast approaching in 1989. But the leadership shakeup also signaled an impending showdown between a labor force conflicted about its contradictory role as "workers by day, owners by night" and a board of directors that insisted on its autonomy from workers and its direction for the company.

In this chapter I describe how the disruptions of the moral economy I analyzed in the previous chapter evolved from 1988 to 1996 into a full-blown struggle for control of the company. First I show how rank-and-file frustration over company downsizing and job outsourcing constituted class-based opposition that was evidenced in a succession of ISU presidents leading to the most militant union leadership since 1934. I then describe how union leadership began playing a more activist role within the company, both in defense of workers' interests but also in an effort to *redirect* the direction and philosophy of Weirton's ESOP. I examine how the intersection of class and community shaped this struggle for control in which worker opposition eventually led to a blocked public stock offering in late 1993 and hastened Elish's resignation in early 1995. I conclude by discussing how recent developments were still interpreted through a normative order that blends elements of mill and community under worker-ownership.

A Changing of the Guard

When I returned in the summer of 1988, Sal thrust a Bish campaign leaflet in my hands. "I like Walter," he sighed, "but Thompson has a law degree, maybe he's better for us during this period." What struck me most about Sal's comments was not his reference to Thompson's educational credentials but that he felt "we" needed someone who was "better for us." As tensions grew between labor, management, and executives, workers sought to redress what they considered inadequate representation as a class. Though Bish appeared to face no serious challenge, he garnered only 2,034 votes to Thompson's 3,649. The election clearly signaled that workers did not feel like ESOP partners with management, and they were acting that way. "A gap exists between union members and management," Thompson observed, "We need to close that gap."[1] Though reassuring, Thompson, like Bish, would also underestimate rank-and-file discontent and their determination to alter the course of Weirton's ESOP.

With a new union president, workers were seeking stronger leadership and a stronger voice on the board of directors, leadership that could meet the union's new responsibilities under a worker-owned and soon to be public corporation. Likewise, people's "wait and see" posture toward the new CEO, Herbert Elish, was ended when his policy of "reduction through attrition" stoked rumors of impending layoffs and permanent job losses—perhaps *the* major concern of both workers and residents. "Now we know why Elish was brought in," one worker told me. "He's the hatchet man they were looking for."

By 1989, five years after ESOP began, Weirton Steel was still employing close to 8,000 people and posting profitable quarters. The profit-sharing percentage had risen to 50 percent for the 1989 distribution and it appeared that the ESOP gamble had "paid off." But by now everyone knew that appearances were deceiving and workers faced two important decisions that could make or break the mill, their jobs, and their community: modernization and a public stock offering.

To remain competitive the company had to renovate its continuous caster (which forms molten steel into slabs) and its hot strip mill (which processes slabs to customer specifications). Postponing these projects surely contributed to the string of profitable quarters and employee's yearly profit-sharing checks. And raising capital by issuing stock publicly had always been the most likely scenario after the five-year freeze on wages, strikes, and workers' voting rights. With a stock offering, however, workers would dilute their 100 percent ownership of the company.[2]

But like the original ESOP and a close union vote approving job reclassification and multicrafting in 1988, workers again voted to sacrifice some of their equity and some of their control. They agreed to sell 30 million shares of common stock, reducing their control to 77 percent, and they agreed to roll back profit sharing to 35 percent of net profits in order to raise $740 million for modernization.[3] Under the revised ESOP employees still held a majority interest in the company and, more important, they were now voting shareholders. The years ahead would test how much more the rank-and-file would sacrifice before asserting their inclinations for control.

As the 1990s opened, developments took an abrupt turn for the worse. By the fall of 1990 demand had fallen for sheet steel used in appliances and construction, a product that made up half of the company's $1.2 billion in annual revenues. Problems with a new rolling machine cost $18 million to fix and a computer room fire cost the company another $10 million. When it could not meet delivery on 300,000 tons of steel the company was forced to pay competitors $10.8 million to roll slabs it could not finish on its own equipment. All of this contributed to the company's first losses as an ESOP, including $48 million in the first half of 1991.[4] Company stock had dipped to around 4 points from its original public opening at 14.5 points and President Elish eliminated the 16-cent dividend, which cost employees about $280 a quarter.[5]

With the company losing money, and jobs threatened by the modernization projects, insult was soon added to injury. Workers were enraged to find that the board of directors had voted themselves a 47.5 percent salary increase and had extended Elish's contract indefinitely. More, Elish's salary (like Loughhead's before him) was again a bone of contention as workers saw their profit-sharing and stock dividends disappear while his compensation was rising. The pattern of unequal sacrifice that appeared three years after ESOP started continued unabated. In the wake of the public stock offering and recent company setbacks workers began to act.

"Hanging on" to Jobs

If Bish's departure as ISU president was unexpected, Thompson's brief tenure signaled a far more contentious labor force. The widespread, yet silent, unrest I observed in 1986–87 had gradually unfolded into a collective challenge to company executives and their policies. In June 1991 the rank-and-file replaced ISU President Virgil Thompson after only one term by electing Mark Glyptis (a third-generation millworker) on a platform of putting workers ahead of public shareholders. "I don't believe in maximizing profits at the expense of losing jobs," said Glyptis. "You can't throw someone out like an old shoe. If you sacrifice, you're part of the team."[6] Glyptis's victory margin of 3,151 to 1,074 was even more decisive than Thompson's victory over Bish, and in my view, was a clear sign of an emerging class consciousness among Weirton's rank-and-file. Easily the most militant ISU president in Weirton Steel's history, Glyptis vowed to represent workers' interests in job security and he was especially angered by the outside contracting of mill projects even though workers faced potential layoffs and downsizing.

The most egregious example of outside contracting made local headlines in June 1992 when a group of nine worker-owners filed a civil lawsuit against the company for "gross mismanagement by corporate officers and directors."[7] After rejecting their own construction crews, company officials hired an outside firm to build two reheat furnaces for $50 million. With one furnace completed, Bricmont and Associates of Pittsburgh pulled out of the project citing cost overruns and Weirton Steel's refusal to advance more funds, even though it had already paid out the initial bid of $50 million. The suit claimed Elish and other executives were negligent for not investigating Bricmont's qualifications and financial background before accepting their bid, failing to implement capital spending controls to prevent cost overruns, and not requiring a written contract and performance bond before advancing Bricmont $26.6 million for the second furnace.[8]

In seeking $30 million in damages, the workers wanted the money be returned to the company. They also stated in the suit that their purpose was to give shareholders a way to protect the company from "the misfeasance and malfeasance of faithless directors and managers."[9] Vocal support from ISU President Glyptis reflected the views of the rank-and-file who felt redeemed in their long-standing opposition to outside contracting when mill construction workers completed the second furnace in less time and under cost. Vowing to avoid such situations in the future, Glyptis and the ISU began a more active and public role as loyal opposition in the company.

This activism quickly became evident following the Bricmont incident. Months of rumors were confirmed in June 1992 when the company announced "several hundred" temporary layoffs until economic conditions improved. From an ESOP high of 8,300 in 1987, mill employment had already declined (through attrition and early retirement) to some 6,800. Layoffs were bad enough, even if only "temporary," but one month later workers and residents were shocked when Elish announced a board approved program entitled "Assuming Weirton's Future" that called for a workforce reduction of 25 percent, or 1,700 employees, over the next five years.[10] By 1997, the company workers bought in order to save jobs would have lost some 3,000 since ESOP began.

Anticipating the announcement, Glyptis responded by saying the union "philosophically disagreed" that the company's survival rested on indiscriminate job elimination. In challenging the market-oriented bureaucratic ESOP that had been steadily assaulting workers sense of justice and moral sentiments, Glyptis attempted to rescue the "spirit of ESOP" he said had been lost.

The ESOP was never really designed to see how much
money we could make. It was designed to provide us with
work, and to provide work for our sons and daughters. It was
designed to save jobs. People don't think [sacrificing jobs for
corporate survival] is what it's about. . . . The true founders
of this company are the people who sacrificed to make the
ESOP a reality. Everyone realizes this company, like any
other, has to operate efficiently to survive. I'm not arguing
that point, and I'll go so far as to say that often, "getting efficient" means some sacrifices might have to occur. But it's
management's responsibility, if sacrifices have to occur, to
make sure they are imposed equally and fairly for all employees, whether unionized or not. [The union is] dedicated
to making sure if sacrifices have to occur, they are fair. More
importantly, we will strive to ensure management is held accountable for its actions so we have every opportunity to preserve as many jobs as possible to get more efficient.[11]

Holding management "responsible" for labor's interests in jobs
marked a clear reversal of the ISU's conciliatory role in ESOP,
and it contradicted management's traditional accountability to
profits. More, Glyptis extended the conventional notion of worker
"job consciousness" by saying that mill jobs belonged not only to
workers, but to their families and the community. Far from revo-
lutionary, this vision did challenge how ESOP had evolved up to
now and it placed workers and residents above the corporate "bottom line." Worker distrust that had simmered since 1987 was
gradually transforming into action *against the board of directors*
and how they ran the mill.

"Letting Go" of Executive Board Members

In June 1992, the ISU initiated a series of challenges over the
company's organization and direction by asking that longtime
union board representative David Robertson resign his seat on
the board of directors. Robertson, ISU legal counsel and an influential member of the JSC during the ESOP negotiations (see
chapter 3), had served on the board since 1983. But after nine
years representing labor, ISU leaders requested his resignation

claiming a conflict of interest existed because of his law firm's business dealings with Weirton Steel. After initially refusing to step down, Robertson acceded to union wishes one month later and quietly resigned.[12]

One month earlier, during the annual shareholders meeting, outside director Harvey Sperry had also come under suspicion for alleged conflict of interest. Sperry, a partner of the New York firm Willkie, Farr and Gallagher that played a key role in creating the ESOP, revealed that his firm had for the last decade been representing foreign steelmakers, some of whom were Weirton Steel's strongest competitors.[13] CEO Elish explained that the matter had been discussed and that a "majority of the board" saw no conflict of interest with Sperry's serving on Weirton's board.[14]

But a minority of the board thought otherwise, and independent director Phillip H. Smith openly questioned Sperry's role and sought his removal. ISU president Glyptis agreed, saying, "Our membership felt betrayed. Sperry's firm has been representing the people who are putting us out of work."[15] In this dispute, CEO Elish sided with Sperry and during an August 1992 board meeting he was able to sway 9 of 12 members (including Smith) to waive any conflict of interest on the part of Willkie, Farr and Gallagher.[16] "I have no doubt at all about Sperry's loyalty," Elish told *Forbes*, but he apparently doubted that of Smith, who was later relieved of his duties as chairman of the audit committee in November 1992.[17]

By fall 1992 rank-and-file workers had seen about enough and they directed their sights on CEO Elish (this, recall, followed just after the Clinton-Gore campaign hailed Weirton Steel as an example of cooperation and the future of American industry). Following a controversial "Make vs. Buy" study aimed at eliminating more jobs, the ISU held two meetings at the Millsop Community Center on November 17, 1992. Before one standing-room-only meeting, employees gathered to discuss how to stop the study and reverse the direction executives were taking *their* company in. In the words of Richard Burge, a Weirton resident with twenty-three years in the mill:

> The workers want to get rid of [CEO Herbert] Elish. They're talking about strikes and work stoppages. I don't want a strike or a work stoppage. I don't think that's the way to do it.

I think the way to do it is to put pressure on Elish and War-ren Bartel [executive vice-president of operations] to resign.[18]

Rather than responding in a manner that might be characteristic of "workers by day" (for example, strikes or work stoppages), this worker-owner proposed a course of action more appropriate for "owners by night" (for example, pressuring company executives and perhaps voting them off the board). Which course workers pursued would depend heavily on both their union and their membership in the community. Glyptis's election was based on a wave of class antagonisms that resonated with community senti-ments. It was unlikely that worker-owners would endanger *their* company or *their* community by a strike, but it was still unclear whether the ISU could translate collective discontent into a viable challenge that reunited the mill and community.

Challenges to ESOP Leadership and Ideology

In April 1993, just prior to upcoming contract negotiations, Glyp-tis spoke out for more worker control through shareholder voting. Rehiring laid-off workers was a priority, along with maintaining wage and job stability, but in public statements following two union meetings Glyptis also looked toward the company's execu-tive board.

> There was a lot of concern about the board of directors and its actions of late—a fair part of the meeting concerned the board of directors. People want to know which directors are working for the people. . . . [W]e discussed it in quite a bit of detail.[19]

Glyptis urged union members to "become involved" in the contract negotiations, but he also admonished them to attend the May 26 shareholders' meeting and vote their proxies.

> We should have a real say, be exercising our right to vote. People want control, we want to control the voting power of the corporation, but the only way that means anything is if people submit their votes. If you don't do it, you're not exer-cising the controls we worked so hard to gain.[20]

From a "difference in philosophy" to "controlling the voting power of the corporation," Glyptis was adamant that it would no longer be business as usual at Weirton Steel. For Glyptis, the contracting-out issue was "definitely eroding the fabric of the ESOP and what make us a success."[21] He also noted that outside contractors, including some workers for a local business, had been caught photographing equipment and operations hoping to win a contract for work that was being done by mill employees.

> Their people are walking around saying, "We're going to take your jobs." Imagine how the men on the shopfloor feel. This thing has the potential to be very violent.[22]

Not only were rank-and-file worker-owners disaffected over how the company was being run, but so too were many from mid-level management. According to Glyptis,

> A lot of people who haven't said much over the years, a lot of "senior" people, came down to the union meetings and voiced their opinion on how the mill used to be run and how it's being operated today. These are not radical people. Virtually everybody, including a large number of management people, are telling us the same thing.[23]

Aware of the growing dissent over his leadership and company policy, CEO Elish responded a few days later claiming that the "Make vs. Buy" study was aimed at making the mill more efficient and profitable, not contracting out work currently being done by worker-owners. For Elish and other board members, preserving as many jobs as possible was important, but being cost competitive was more important for the survival and future success of the company. As for those in mid-level management who Glyptis said were sending union leaders a different message, Elish took a hardline stance: "If mid-level management is saying something different, it doesn't matter. What I say is what is going to happen."[24]

This dictatorial rhetoric may be familiar to the conventional hierarchy of most businesses in America, but it clearly contradicted the organizational leveling that EPG facilitators claimed was their "mission" (see chapter 5). Likewise, it struck a sensitive nerve among most of the rank-and-file who also felt what *they said* mattered and that it was about time company executives listened. If Elish thought a tough stand would restore order and his authority in the company, he was mistaken. Elish was no E. T. Weir or Thomas Millsop, and worker-ownership in Weirton was not a paternalist order, nor was it a conventional firm in the eyes of its worker-owners.

By the spring of 1993 dissension between the board and workers, and among board members themselves, had reached a fevered pitch. In April a series of "Steel Forums" were held by the company to address concerns about the duties and responsibilities of directors in an ESOP firm. After ten years of worker-ownership it is ironic that such forums were necessary, but in the context of my analysis in chapters 4–7 and with workers and some directors now openly challenging Elish and company policies, it is not surprising. With workers as voting shareholders the forums were less intended to inform and educate employees than to head off any effort to replace Elish at the upcoming May shareholders' meeting.[25] More, in the context of the still pending Bricmont suit (see above), there was also concern over an amendment to the ESOP charter that would limit directors' liability for future lawsuits.

Board members Harvey Sperry, David I. J. Wang, and F. James Rechin led the forums, telling workers and retirees that a director's role is one of being an advisor, someone who evaluates and approves "plans and programs proposed by management."[26] For Wang, a complex business like Weirton Steel, "can become competitive and therefore healthy only if it's managed in a competitive way with qualified managers and directors."[27] These familiar references to competition and qualifications were growing old to workers who agreed in principle, but (as I showed in chapters 5 and 7) not on *how* to be competitive or *what* qualifications were important. Likewise, people knew that *power* as much as technical knowledge was involved in how competitive and healthy Weirton Steel could become.

This was blatantly revealed when, unlike previous forums, the directors responded to written questions submitted by those attending rather than answering questions posed by people standing at a microphone. Elish said the format change was designed to avoid any confusion from people "jumping up and down" to pose their questions.[28] But director Phillip Smith, who had become an outspoken critic of Elish, Sperry, and recent company policies, publicly stated that the change was intended to silence him and his supporters: "They didn't want Phil Smith or any other people to be near a microphone."[29] Greeting supportive workers after the forum, Smith added that it was ISU president Glyptis who urged him to attend the meeting, not the company.

If board members wanted to silence Smith, they could not silence the angry voices of betrayed and estranged worker-owners. On May 26, 1993, Elish was narrowly reelected to the board when holders of 22.5 million shares of stock voted in his favor and 17.3 million shares voted against him. Elish had barely survived, as did an amendment to the restated certificate of incorporation to limit directors' liability for monetary damages in future lawsuits. It passed by a vote of 22.8 million shares to slightly more than 19 million shares.[30] The message being sent was clear, workers were angry. During a question and answer period before the official meeting one worker told Elish to "put his money where his mouth is" by purchasing more stock in the company commensurate with his salary.[31] After responding that he had put his entire career and life at stake by moving to Weirton, laughter erupted from the crowd estimated at between 1,200 and 2,000 people. Threatening to adjourn the meeting if the boos and cheers continued, Elish said he took a large pay cut when he joined the company. The rank-and-file had also taken substantial pay cuts for ESOP and *their* lives and careers were also at stake. If Elish had a choice about coming to Weirton, he was reminded that it was not the forced choice workers faced in 1984.

Confrontation

Late in summer 1993, Elish and the board began advocating for a second public stock offering of 30 million shares to reduce the $500 million debt incurred from recent capital improvements. The stock sale would raise the company's common stock to 60 million shares and provide much needed relief from interest payments approaching $51 million per year, or $1 million per week.[32] But the proposed sale would also mean a further reduction in worker-owners' voting power to 44 percent from 77 percent. The struggle over control that was looming back in 1987 had since matured into a full-blown brawl pitting worker-owners against Elish and the board.

For Elish the stock offering was a "matter of company survival" and workers were "playing Russian roulette with the future of this company" if they did not immediately approve the sale due to favorable market conditions.[33] Not unlike the rhetoric of fear expressed by the JSC and ESOP consultants, Elish claimed he was not being alarmist by alluding to bankruptcy if the company failed to act soon. "[Bankruptcy] couldn't happen next week or even next year. Our cash position is good. But, if we don't reduce our debt, it's going to be inevitable at some point.[34]

And like the negotiations ten years earlier, Elish also framed the stock issue as another "all-or-nothing" forced choice. The company, he admitted, had "no Plan B" and he rejected any notion that there might be alternatives. "This is an extremely serious problem, and to say there is another way to solve it is just not true."[35] But the stock issue was not merely about technical problem solving, it was about also about solving *political* problems, especially the issue of control. As if to implicate worker-owners for their "workers by day" outlook, Elish added that "every business has formidable problems and they can be dealt with if we *act like businessmen* [emphasis added]."[36] In this case, however, it was Elish and his supporters on the board who were being implicated and the ISU responded swiftly.

For ISU president Glyptis, the stock offering was a matter of control and accountability. Accusing Elish of a "propaganda offensive," Glyptis demonstrated that he too could use the press in advancing the views of worker-owners and waging an impressive opposition. As he put it:

> A large number of employee shareholders have indicated that control still remains an important issue, just as it was during the initial public offering in 1989. Since the issue of additional stock authorization was first discussed in early 1992, the union has consistently informed senior management and the board of the importance of the control issue.[37]

To reinforce this position, the ISU hired its own legal counsel to confer on the issue. Then, after an October 16 shareholders' meeting, Glyptis charged that a potential conflict of interest existed because a Lehman Brothers consultant who had been retained by the board to advise on the stock offering sat with Elish and Harvey Sperry on another corporate board. Calling his fellow directors' selection "100 percent wrong," Glyptis found it "appalling that on an issue this important, we can't find a [consultant] who is truly independent."[38]

With the ISU publicly challenging Elish, his supporters on the board, and the bottom-line orientation of ESOP, other workers were also beginning to realize that they too had options they had not previously considered. As I noted in chapters 4 and 6, employee participation training provided no information regarding the financial aspects of an ESOP company, nor had the company done much to educate workers about their role as shareholders. But following the announcement of a second stock offering, twenty-one-year worker-owner Frank Slanchik, an hourly worker in the steelworks crane department, began forming the Weirton Steel Corporation Shareholders Association. Frustrated by vague answers to workers' questions and by the distorted appraisals of worker morale given by Elish at yearly shareholders meetings, Slanchik decided it was time to let "the directors know they are accountable to the shareholders."[39]

Slanchik was particularly upset by the manner in which voting power was being manipulated by board members and their disregard for employee shareholders. Referring to Elish's narrow re-election and the even closer vote limiting directors' liability, he commented:

> What makes these numbers disturbing is the fact that the board hired a proxy company to solicit votes for them and also had special meetings for all salary personnel to sell their position. I thought with these types of voting numbers, the board might consider some sort of action to show the shareholders they got their message. But with the recent purchase of a $7 million insurance policy [for the directors and corporate officers], it's apparent that their number one priority is not the shareholders.[40]

Noting that "even some management people are dissatisfied" and "are afraid to speak up," Slanchik spoke to the legacy of paternalism that had burdened the RFC ten years earlier.

I'm not a radical and I don't expect the association to come off as such, but the association would give us access to the board of directors. . . . I know there are a lot of unhappy people and everyone is always waiting for another guy to start something. Well, I'm tired of waiting, so I decided to put my name on this and go forward with it to see if there is any interest in forming the association. I think it's our silence that has hurt us.[41]

Unlike RFC opposition during the ESOP negotiations, however, Slanchik's association was spawned from the same collective rank-and-file activism that swept Glyptis into office. Likewise, where the RFC was demonized by the ISU, the spontaneous emergence of the shareholders association was supported by Glyptis and ISU leadership. More important, if "saving the mill and the community" distanced workers from the RFC, this very same sentiment supported Glyptis and his brand of confrontation. In both cases, collective action was predicated upon protecting the interests of workers as a class and as members of a community. For years executives had overlooked the goodwill and concerns of worker-owners. They would no longer be silent.

In late October 1993, the board formally voted to authorize 60 million shares of common stock rather than the initial 30 million shares proposed months earlier. In a nine to three vote, ISU board members Mark Glyptis, Phillip Karber, and Robert D'Anniballe rejected the motion and the ISU steward body issued a statement urging all union members and retirees to defeat the proposed stock authorization.[42] With a November 11 voting date set, ISU board members could not support a measure they claimed was vague, diluted employee-owner control, and did not "preserve the relationship between public and employee-shareholders that was created in 1989."[43]

Then, three days later on October 26, independent board member Phillip Smith joined the ISU in opposing the stock offering. Smith, who had earlier spoken out against board member Harvey Sperry on conflict of interest charges, agreed that a stock offering was necessary but that this measure was too vague and did not address the legitimate concerns of workers. Smith urged that the vote "should be postponed so we can work this out, together."[44] If Elish saw no other alternative to the stock offering, his fellow "businessmen" in the ISU and Smith insisted there was and it lay in the details of a plan that would preserve local control.

With the proxy vote only two weeks away ISU leaders, Smith, and Frank Slanchik's twenty-member shareholders' association urged those holding stock to vote against the measure. Soon, accusations against Elish of coercion followed growing opposition to his stock proposal. ISU leaders and Smith held a press conference in which they charged that Elish "is failing the most elementary tests of democracy" by allegedly forcing employees to watch a videotape explaining his reasons for the stock authorization.[45] Speaking from a prepared statement, Smith charged that,

> Elish has put such heavy-handed pressure for a positive vote, many employees—including salary and management—have expressed fear that if they do not vote the way they are being told, they will lose their jobs.[46]

Calling the allegation "a complete fabrication" and "totally repugnant," Elish "categorically [denied] that threats of job loss in any fashion have been conveyed to any employee of this company."[47] Whether such charges were true or not did not matter at this point. Opposition to the stock offering could not be overcome in the days ahead. Two days prior to the November 11 vote, the board scraped the proposal. A major stock offering had been blocked by a more activist rank-and-file and their union, but was a new era of worker-ownership dawning on Weirton Steel?

Throughout the winter of 1993–94 the board met regularly to discuss three major issues: a public stock authorization, a labor contract with the ISU, and board governance. Regarding the latter issue, ISU board members and independent Phillip Smith wanted to separate the positions of CEO and president, which were currently combined and held by Elish. In addition, concern was raised about establishing "a process at the director level to examine and explore matters of board structure and corporate governance."[48] The ISU accelerated negotiations on a labor agreement in the hopes of a settlement prior to another vote on the public stock offering. In public statements by all concerned, it *appeared* that the animosity of the last few years had given way to concerted efforts in achieving a unified direction for the decade-old ESOP steel mill.

Then, on April 6, 1994, Weirton Steel suffered a critical setback when a major fire erupted in a section of the tin mill resulting in seventeen minor injuries and threatening about 20 percent of the company's overall production. The fire damaged one of the three cold rolling mills that processed steel into sheets used in food cans and other containers. The tin mill was the company's biggest source of revenue, having accounted for 90 percent of its $1.2 million in sales in 1993.[49]

Though nothing like the explosion at the nearby Brown's Island coke plant in 1972 that killed nineteen and injured ten, the mill fire was still a major blow to a company that had just posted its first profits since the final quarter of 1990 and was trying to move beyond a bitter proxy fight just a few months earlier. On April 9 the company announced it would lay off 225 workers (210 from the tin mill) indefinitely because of the fire. More layoffs were possible depending on the extent of the damage and the time it took to repair.[50]

Concern about the fire's impact on layoffs and productivity raced through town but both Elish and Glyptis were confident it would have no effect on the impending stock offering. And as people anxiously awaited estimates on the financial costs of the fire and rebuilding the scorched tandem mill, Glyptis reflected the pride and sense of obligation workers had for the mill they had fought so hard to keep.

> The response from employees in other parts of the mill has been overwhelming. Employees have been saying they are willing to donate their time without pay to help rebuild the tandem mill [that burned down]. That shows they genuinely care about this mill and you wouldn't find that determination anywhere else in the world.[51]

The fire had touched localist sentiments that united a workforce and community that had been torn over the contested stock offering. But beneath the surface of public solidarity lay other interpretations of the fire; views that again reflected the strains of a class struggle that would persist well beyond the fire and stock offering. As one worker's wife confided upon my recent visit in 1996, the "big fire of '94" was not some fluke accident but resulted from poor working and safety conditions in the mill.

That mill fire was not simply some freak accident like they said in the papers. My husband works in that part of the mill and he said there was oil so thick on the floor that when the fire started it just caught that oil and ran through that place. Workers had been complaining about that oil for a long time.

The struggle over the stock offering was but a mirror image of deteriorating relations on the shopfloor. If the fire brought unity and determination in the face of crisis, for many it was almost a deadly reminder of executive indifference to the well-being of rank-and-file workers.

Forging a Structure of Control for Weirton's ESOP

On April 13, 1994, the ISU agreed to support a stock authorization plan of 20 million shares that also included seventeen bylaw changes in board governance and the addition of an independent board director. With a vote date set for May 26, the ISU, the shareholders' association, and management combined efforts in securing the necessary 80 percent shareholders' approval for the plan. When the vote was tallied, all issues passed by an 82 percent margin, with a 92 percent approval rating among active and retired employees.[52]

Under the plan, 15 million shares would be sold publicly with 5 million shares reserved for a voluntary employee stock purchase plan at a 15 percent discount spread over five years. All proceeds would be used to reduce company debt and contribute to the pension plan, and worker-owners would also retain about 52 percent of the vote. In addition to bylaw changes in the qualifications of independent directors, another independent ESOP director would join the board. This director would represent *employee* shareholders' concerns and would be selected by a committee comprised of five participants in the company's ESOP program.[53] This director would also sit on the company's nominating committee along with Elish and Glyptis and two independent directors, thus giving worker-owners more voice in selecting future board members.

Although the plan did not separate the positions of CEO and board chairman as many worker-owners had called for, it did include some bylaw changes that reflected key elements of the control struggle waged over the last seven years. One provision that excluded anyone over 65 years old from serving as an independent board member prevented ISU ally 67-year-old Phillip Smith from seeking renomination. Smith said he offered to resign rather than establish a unilateral age limit, but that ISU directors "declined to step up and support me."[54]

It is quite likely that Glyptis and the ISU "declined" to support Smith or oppose the bylaw amendment because of the politics of business rather than business sense. Only two days before the ISU announced its support for the plan, Harvey Sperry announced he would not seek renomination because of the plan's qualification amendments for independent directors.[55] I seriously doubt that these bylaw changes eliminating two principal protagonists on the board were unrelated. The departures of Sperry and Smith were likely a political quid pro quo that was necessary for board approval of the plan.

And in a clear acknowledgment of years of local controversy over the value of labor— specifically the value of a CEO's labor— the plan also included guidelines for a formal, annual evaluation of the CEO's performance that would be used by the Compensation and Management Development Committee when considering compensation.[56] Elish supported the formal evaluation, saying it was neither unusual nor different from policies recently initiated at General Motors Corporation. But for worker-owners this policy and other changes in board governance meant much more. It gave them more influence in determining the value and accountability of a CEO's labor and more opportunities to exercise that influence.[57]

Had Weirton Steel become a different company from the one workers bought ten years earlier? Much-needed modernization improved the mill's competitiveness but also threatened workers' jobs. Bylaw changes in board governance increased the worker-owners' voice on the board, but that voice would still have to contend with competing visions of company policy. Workers and residents had moved one step away from the legacy of paternalism by shedding much of the compliance and powerlessness that it bequeathed. Yet they still held tightly to the ideals of local control and independence that paternalism fostered. When a tentative settlement was announced in the Bricmont lawsuit on June

30, 1994, the ten-year struggle for control appeared to be at an end.[58] Once again, however, appearances were deceiving.

Just four months later the ISU learned that the company was considering raises for about 40 to 50 executive personnel along with changes in the compensation plan for over 1,000 non-union employees. The proposal sent another shock wave through an already skeptical workforce. "It appears to me," said Paul Barnabei, a union steward and chairman of the Steel Works II Division of the union, "that management is using the profits from the stock issue to get raises."

> We have a profit-sharing plan and when the company does well, we all do well. I guess management feels they should make money in times when we aren't making money. I feel it's ludicrous that the company lost money last quarter and they [management] want to give raises.[59]

Mark Glyptis was equally outraged and he vowed to represent workers on this issue. Unlike Bish's accommodation to the "critical skills" pay raises back in 1987 (see chapter 7), Glyptis launched a petition drive against the proposal. He also noted that the rank-and-file were connecting the raises with ongoing efforts to eliminate 700 more jobs through early retirement and they feared that these job cuts were financing the changes in management compensation. "This issue," Glyptis claimed, "has virtually alienated the workforce of this entire corporation,"

> People in this company are upset because management trust has been squandered. They feel betrayed. . . . There is a serious trust problem in this company. I don't think the board understands how volatile the issue is to the company and the workforce. There could be a rebellion on this issue.[60]

Glyptis's rhetorical plea aside, company executives either did not understand the concerns of workers, or they did not care. William C. Brenneisen, senior vice president of human resources, was "surprised there is so much controversy over a decision that hasn't been made," but he added that with compensation plans "the idea is to attract and retain quality management people."[61] Seven years earlier the "critical skills" pay raises were similarly excused and few were persuaded. This time, noted Dave Gossett, a member of the ISU Executive Committee, "even the guys who normally don't get upset are really angry. The people who might sometimes be called the silent majority aren't silent anymore."[62]

In a letter to Glyptis, Brenneisen warned that "any employee or union officer who instigates, authorizes or participates in a work stoppage, walkout or any other impedance of work will be subject to discharge."[63] Rank-and-file opposition, however, would not be deterred. On November 16 and 17, Glyptis and ISU board members Phil Karber and Rob D'Anniballe led a protest of workers who picketed the company's headquarters "up on the hill" during executive meetings on the compensation changes. On November 17, a full-page advertisement appeared in *The Intelligencer* of Wheeling, West Virginia, that chastised executives for the proposal in the face of "gross mis-management," "broken promises," "lapses of executive integrity," and the company's "pathetic performance . . . under the failed leadership of Herb Elish." Paid for by the donations of over 1,000 shareholders, the ad ended with a direct call to "vote against Elish and his cronies at the next annual shareholders meeting."[64] Mounting what pressure they could, the ISU delivered a petition with 4,000 signatures calling for "fair and equal sacrifices" to the compensation committee. Once again workers found themselves fighting for egalitarian principles that were awakened seven years earlier but had yet to be heeded by company officials.

On November 17, the board approved a bonus plan but agreed to discuss the plan with the ISU before it took effect in February 1995. In exchange, union members and shareholders would agree to call off any proxy fights, future protests, and advertisements that berated the company's performance record.[65] Speaking to a crowd of seventy union protestors on the General Office grounds, Glyptis was congratulated for his stand against the pay raises and carried on the shoulders of cheering workers. Contrary to the bitter exchanges between Bish and union members during the "critical skills" controversy, Glyptis had moved in the direction of rank-and-file workers and he was now being carried by a "culture of solidarity" that showed no signs of reversing course.

Then, on January 26, 1995, Herbert Elish announced he was stepping down as president and would serve as board chairman and CEO only until the end of the year. After years of bitter struggle and widespread disapproval, Elish had been "thinking about the right time for a transition to a new management for some time."[66] Richard Riederer, executive vice president and chief financial officer since 1989 and a board member since 1993, replaced Elish as president. He would also be eligible for the chairman and CEO positions in May when a newly constituted board of directors was in place. For Glyptis, Elish's stepping down signaled a "new beginning, not only for the company and its employee-owners, but also for Herb Elish."[67] Unfortunately, but not surprising either, Elish's departure did not usher in a new beginning. Class struggle was not about individuals—it was about a structured conflict of interests, and these still remained.

Two Years Later: The Struggle Continues

"The union should protect workers, not try to run the company. That's management's job and the union has no business trying to make those decisions." My friend and key informant had just picked me up from the Pittsburgh train station upon my recent visit in June 1996. As Ted negotiated rush-hour traffic and the maze of detours from downtown redevelopment, it was hard to tell when he was angry at the union or his children in the back seat who were elated to see me and kept interrupting us. Ted was not upset that the ISU was confrontational because "that's what unions do, that's what they're supposed to do, but they're not supposed to be involved in the business end of a company, that's what management and executives are for."

I knew labor-management relations had deteriorated further since 1994, but I should not have been surprised at Ted's frustration and his belief that the union did not belong in the boardroom. After all, the "worker by day, owner by night" ESOP never intended to empower workers and Ted's views reflected this now as they had ten years ago when we first met. But he also intimated that workers had been exercising *too much* control recently and this unsettled him. When I noted that the ISU held three seats on the board of directors and this justified their participation in executive decision-making, Ted shot back, "Well, they shouldn't be there!"

On this point we disagreed, but I still had to ask whether events over the years had not warranted such a strong ISU role in the company. Even though Weirton Steel was profitable again after years of losses and profit-sharing checks were being distributed, labor-management conflict had remained intense from 1994 to 1996. Indeed, the trend of executive indifference toward rank-and-file concerns continued unabated and at times it seemed intentional. Likewise, these ongoing disputes over company organization and policy had become a more *public* affair as ISU president Glyptis increasingly utilized local, regional, and national media to argue labor's case. This may have effectively united Weirton's rank-and-file with Glyptis's leadership, but it also revealed the troubling confluence of class and community that people found so disturbing ten years earlier. It appeared that debates over the moral economy of worker-ownership had moved from the front porch to the front page of local life.

On February 19, 1995, thirty-five workers called a four-hour work stoppage in the tin mill. The company suspended them for five days and it sued the ISU for $50,000 for lost time and production.[68] The lawsuit claimed the stoppage was in protest of a company policy whereby if workers with seniority refuse overtime shifts, management can use a "forced overtime" schedule to keep the mill running. According to William Brenneisen, vice-president of human resources, the work stoppage was not the first such violation of the union contract under ESOP, and he cited a half-day internal railroad disruption a few years back. "We are trying to stop a pattern of conduct," he explained, "We want to run the business in a businesslike manner. . . . There is a well-defined process for disputes—but not self-help."[69]

The problem, however, was that "self-help" was becoming the only means available to workers who found little redress through the "well-defined process for disputes." Instead, they acted spontaneously and apart from any ISU influence or direction. The temporary work stoppage constituted an alternative to both union-company grievance procedures *and* ISU influence on the board of directors because those channels of opposition had been blocked or become ineffective. In this context, enduring grievances sought other means of expression apart from bureaucratic structures designed to regulate worker resistance.

And rank-and-file grievances included far more than "forced overtime." On April 5, the ISU filed a response and countersuit for $50,000 in compensatory damages and $5 million in punitive damages.[70] ISU president Glyptis argued that the company suit was done "with malice and in bad faith," and he claimed that serious safety problems in the tin mill were the primary grievance of protesting workers (an issue many of them traced back to the 1994 mill fire). In defense of the workers, Glyptis and ISU legal counsel Robert D'Anniballe noted a contract clause justifying "relief from the job" under abnormally unsafe working conditions.[71] But the ISU went further than just defending workers' independent and spontaneous action. They also charged that the company's suit was in retaliation to a more activist union, including: their public criticism of the mill's safety record; their criticism of senior executives and the performance-bonus plan; the union's role in Herbert Elish's resignation; and the union's exercising rights guaranteed under the National Labor Relations Act and collective bargaining agreement.[72]

The work stoppages signaled a new stage in the labor-management conflict of the last ten years (indeed, it marked the first time since 1934 that workers had acted so militantly). But two points should be emphasized that are important in understanding the intersection of class and community throughout this struggle for control. First, these acts of shopfloor resistance *were not* directed by Glyptis and ISU leadership as part of any larger oppositional strategy. Instead, rank-and-file militancy was part of a larger collective "culture of solidarity" that had been forming in response to company policies that conflicted with workers' interests as a class. As the transition from Arrango, to Bish, to Thompson, to Glyptis demonstrates, the ISU was gradually *pushed and pulled* into line by the rank-and-file. Glyptis enjoyed widespread respect and popularity among workers because, as one company official confided to me, "he stands up for them, he's trying to protect and defend what the rank-and-file have. They believe in him."

Second, the ISU had gradually stepped up its use of the media to make labor-management conflict into a public conflict. "Mark [Glyptis] has a pipeline to the press and he uses it," said the company official cited above. "They always want a good story and they'll print anything, even if there's only a glimmer of truth in it or it's taken out of context." But the conflicts at Weirton Steel also reached regional and national media. As my friend Ted surmised, "The guy from *Business Week* must be hiding out in town, there's always something in that magazine." Likewise, as noted earlier, many workers and retired shareholders had bought advertisements in regional newspapers to publicly criticize company executives and call for policy changes in compensation, job outsourcing, safety issues, and downsizing.

This pattern of "going public" with labor-management disputes was disturbing not only to company officials who reasonably feared its negative impact on customers, but also to residents who found themselves engaged in a controversy where it seemed nobody—labor, management, or the community—benefited and everyone "looked bad." As Sal explained, "We used to follow orders and then deal with the problems. They don't do that anymore." For Sal, the younger workers today had an "attitude" about standing up to authority in public that his generation lacked. As one employee who considered himself a "company man" explained,

> In the past when labor and management had problems they'd go into a room, lock the doors, slug it out, then come out shaking hands. They'd settle it behind closed doors. But today everything is done out in the open, through the press or face to face. Everything's aired out in public and I don't think that helps the company.

Concern for the image of the company, though valid, is only one aspect of recent labor-management conflict at Weirton. As the quote above illustrates, publicizing the struggle also upset customary practices and paternalistic norms that once governed the exercise of power and the resolution of mill disputes. The conflict was difficult for people to reconcile with community sentiments that denied class divisions or dissolved them into personality or ethnic conflicts. "Slugging it out behind closed doors" became a forced choice under paternalism when company elites wielded considerably more power and the mill was organized in a considerably less bureaucratic fashion. But with these customs steadily eroded under National and ESOP, conflict had indeed moved "out in the open."

As the employee above added, "This is Mark's style, his approach. It seems to work for the rank-and-file, but I don't think it's good for the company." Using the media to mobilize rank-and-file support *did* seem to be working, but only because workers were collectively predisposed to such challenges in the first place.

Furthermore, the actions of upper level management and company executives to regulate and close off other avenues of protest (EPG, board participation, internal communications), and their continuing indifference to rank-and-file grievances spanning ten years, were central in shaping the ISU's media strategy and Glyptis's "style." With the "well-defined process" (bureaucracy) ineffective, and "slugging it out behind closed doors" (paternalism) a thing of the past, class struggle found alternate and often public forms of expression in Weirton.

Likewise, the renewal of litigation within the company can also be seen in this context. Litigation may be a serious matter that takes long to resolve and seems to benefit no one, but it is also a less disruptive means of conflict that avoids production delays, is less personal and visible than strikes, and serves as a platform for airing grievances and recruiting supporters. And if monetary awards were inevitably returned to the company as the litigants both claimed, I asked people, was not this pattern of internal company litigation like a "shell-game" where the goal was control, rather than money? Over who was "right" and who was "wronged"? Shaking their heads in disgust, people I spoke with viewed the lawsuits as pettiness more than anything; as *childish*, like bickering between siblings. To the degree this view was widespread, it also minimized and redefined class conflict in terms that resonated with paternalism and community norms.

The struggle over worker-ownership in Weirton, as I have argued, grew out of the intersection of class interests and community norms, both of which were magnified and contradicted over the course of ESOP. Rank-and-file opposition was centered on keeping jobs, halting the contracting out of jobs, seeking fairness and equality in the distribution of rewards and sacrifices, and holding company executives responsible and accountable to worker-owners and local shareholders. As these grievances were ignored and the ISU became more confrontational, company policy hardened as executives sought a return to the ESOP agenda of running the mill "like any other business." Contracting out jobs continued alongside downsizing, and new CEO Richard Riederer faced angry worker-owners at the 1996 Shareholders meeting just as Elish had years earlier. With contract talks stalled over issues of job security and outsourcing, the rank-and-file still held a vision of worker-ownership that was at odds with that of company executives.

Indeed, months before I arrived another controversy erupted when a *Business Week* article on ESOPs quoted a Weirton Steel spokesperson saying that "we don't consider ourselves an ESOP company anymore."[73] The article raised an uproar and it affirmed the direction that workers claimed indifferent executives were taking *their* company. Calling the statement "a slap in the face to the ESOP participants," ISU president Glyptis saw it as an insult to everyone in the community who had worked and sacrificed to keep the mill operating. The next day Chuck Cronin, director of corporate communications, issued a press release that said the *Business Week* article omitted some important (and telling) facts.

Although Weirton Steel employees no longer own the majority of the common shares of the company, they do, in fact, own [a] significant percentage (about 30 percent) and their shares represent about 49 percent of the voting power. The majority of the company's stock is owned by the investment community.[74]

Cronin further stated that although the company was now organized more like a conventional corporation than when it was fully worker-owned,

Nonetheless, since the company originated in an employee buyout and Weirton [Steel] retains such characteristics as worker-involvement teams and bargaining-unit representation on the board of directors, it is likely that Weirton Steel will long be identified to some degree with employee ownership.[75]

Exactly what "degree" was still being contested when I visited in June 1996. But Cronin only confirmed that the original bureaucratic structure of worker-ownership had become further entrenched, giving rise to class based opposition that both drew upon and upset community norms and sentiments.

Perhaps the final irony in this struggle for the heart and soul of worker-ownership came after the board of directors unanimously adopted a resolution affirming Weirton Steel as an Employee Stock Ownership Plan during a March 28 meeting. The directors also established a seven-member corporate responsibility committee (which included the three ISU board members) that would "examine the proper role of the ESOP under which the company was formed in 1984."[76] A few months later a message was painted high on a mill wall downtown that read in large white letters: WEIRTON STEEL CORPORATION—AN E.S.O.P. COMPANY. One day as Ted and I drove by the sign I commented about it and he laughed,

> Yeah, the company had that painted because of the flap over whether we were an ESOP or not. But now the guys are pissed because the company contracted the painting out, they said we didn't have anyone who could do the job that high.

Chapter Nine

Conclusion

I n a town where steel mill and community were always inseparable, worker ownership held out the possibility that this relationship might continue. Following the 1960s and 1970s
when National Steel began undermining the paternalistic order of
an earlier era, worker ownership evoked one constant refrain in
pubs, across dinner tables, and in backyards throughout town:
The mill would again belong to the people of Weirton.

But keeping the mill a "family affair" presented its own troubling irony. The emotional sentiments and cultural identities that
located people in a small town of local customs and extended family networks supported the ESOP negotiated in 1984 and dignified the sacrifices it entailed, yet they eventually conflicted with
the bureaucratic organization of worker ownership that they initially supported. As chapters 7 and 8 demonstrated, the norms
and moral codes of paternalism were invoked to criticize and challenge company organization and policy, as well as rank-and-file
behavior as "worker-owners." Though routinely dismissed by
company officials, as well as many workers and residents, as archaic, inefficient, and "no way to run a business," a local egalitarian spirit remained an organizing principle for people in which

company policy and organization were answerable to the community as much as to the "bottom line."

This moral economy was not without contradictions and anomalies. Once mitigated through the power of local elites, strains in this moral order were now exaggerated by changing structural conditions (global competition, mill modernization, civic maladministration and funding) and the absence of authoritative elites. As class antagonisms became more compelling in the lives of workers and townspeople alike, moral judgments about worker ownership, the behavior of employees, and company executives were still filtered through a normative order that de-emphasized class divisions and upheld the priority of community in people's lives.

These structural contradictions gave rise to a disturbing ambivalence over the relationship between mill and community. Lacking any clear indicators (or at least a consensus on what constituted valid criteria) for judging the value of labor, fragilely holding to notions of the company as collective property, and ambivalent toward a legacy of community nepotism and localism, workers and residents evaluated ESOP from the symbolic context of paternalistic norms as much as from rationally calculated self-interest. From this cultural topography of collectivism and individualism, localism and market interdependence, nepotism and meritocracy, people sought a coherent perspective that might reunite the mill and community.

But, the critic might ask (as I too asked townspeople), was it not unreasonable, not to mention uneconomical, to operate a business according to a normative order that supported sleeping on the job, stealing from the mill, and nepotistic organization (with its discriminatory and antimeritocratic effects) of mill and community life? Perhaps, and for many employees and residents, much of the "old ways" had to go.[1] But "reason" operates in a cultural context in which self-interest, webs of emotion, and moral sensibility blend together out of an historically constituted and institutionally structured social life. Reasonable people are "pulled" and "pushed," nudged reluctantly in directions not always chosen, but compelling, nonetheless. As such, people's ambivalence over the relationship of mill and community was an expression of changing structural factors. Customs that were once quite "reasonable" under paternalism's "chummy" mill had become wrong, if not seriously unreasonable, under a competitive market and bureaucratic ESOP. Workers and townspeople were structurally "stuck," almost as if the gates that once swung freely between the mill and community now opened in only one direction—the mill.

How much should someone be paid? For how much work? Who should do the work? Who should—and could—run the company? The town? As they debated the hard decisions facing the mill and community, people still held on to the benevolent principles of a paternalistic order that "took care of our own," blurred notions of the collective and individual, and saw the steel mill as a "family affair." Perhaps some of these "old ways" like extended family, local independence, and community membership, were worth keeping in a worker-owned company—in some form. At the very least, these ideals represented the aspirations and desires of townspeople to keep a human face on the mill they had grown up with and relied on for so long.

In this context, rank-and-file opposition sprang partly from workers' role in, and expectations of, ESOP, and partly from their membership in, and identification with, the community of Weirton. Along with their modest expectations and ambivalent loyalties, workers still held to vague notions of control that derived from the intersection of the mill and community life. I say "vague" because these notions were embedded in consciousness as assumptions (as "taken-for-granted" as their view that "Weirton Steel has always been here, and always will") and partly because of company efforts to narrowly define the parameters of "worker by day, owner by night." Still, traditions of local control and responsibility confirmed and blended workers' roles in the mill and community, shaping the form of class struggle that emerged.

Undoubtedly, volatile market conditions, costly modernization projects, and capital funding are all serious problems facing Weirton Steel, but these are problems for most, if not all, of American industry. Likewise, problems of equity distribution and job retention will remain sensitive matters. The company's net income was up from $35.2 million in 1994 to $48.8 million in 1995, while the third largest profit-sharing payout of $24.1 million (or $2,500 average per employee) was distributed in 1996.[2] Still, even with recent financial success, controversy and conflict continue.

The Lessons of Worker Ownership
and Participation at Weirton Steel

Worker Ownership

Worker ownership at Weirton Steel was initiated by capital and, like most other cases of employee ownership, was neither intended nor structured to empower labor or bring about industrial democracy. As I showed in chapter 3, National proposed an ESOP as the best possible choice for workers and residents; a choice that appealed to labor's class interests but also resonated with sentiments of community and local control. Unlike other communities facing plant shutdowns where corporations resisted labor-community buy-outs, such as Youngstown, South Chicago, northwest Indiana, and the greater Pittsburgh area,[3] Weirton's ESOP was supported from the beginning by capital. Likewise, despite being in a troubled industry, the Weirton mills were fairly modern, profitable, and occupied a favorable market niche with a reputation for quality. These market factors also favored a Weirton ESOP, unlike other cases such as General Motors Hyatt-Clark, Eastern Airlines, and Rath Packing Company.[4]

On the other hand, alternative choices were never seriously considered, much less debated. A proxy fight to stop National was suggested by one local resident, but quickly dismissed. An RFC member wondered about letting the mill close and then having workers and the community take it over through eminent domain—unthinkable. And as Sharon Zukin has pointed out, there was never any thought of simply moving away from steel completely, just as National was doing.

> At neither Youngstown nor Weirton was there any discussion, even in theory, of transforming the industrial landscape into a landscape of consumption. No suggestion arose of trying to compensate for the loss of manufacturing jobs by growth in the service sector. In no sense was it felt that the local community didn't *need* the jobs or the capital investment that steel provided.[5]

Even with this choice, alternative forms of worker ownership were systematically excluded from serious consideration. As the

RFC's challenge showed, democratic worker ownership was anti-thetical to the bureaucratic ESOP pursued by the JSC and fi-nancial consultants, but it was also remote from community institutions and local norms. Instead, the consumerist version of worker ownership became a "forced choice" under the forces of history and circumstance.

Zukin provides an interesting explanation of the Weirton buy-out in comparison to similar cases in Youngstown and South Chi-cago that also faced plant shutdowns and were similar to Weirton socially and culturally. Though part of a broader analysis, her core position is consistent with the general view of Weirton's ESOP. A worker buy-out succeeded here, she argues, because of two factors that were absent from Youngstown and South Chi-cago: "a docile work force and a good investment banker."[6] Zukin writes that "what made Weirton exceptional was finding a golden mean: a general strategy for revitalizing the firm based on an 'equality of sacrifice,' which,

> . . . initially derives from Felix Rohatyn's coordination of the fiscal restructuring of New York City's government in 1975. It thus reaffirms that variant of corporate restructuring as-sociated with liberal Democrats whose advocacy of "indus-trial policy" implies no desire to do away with private capital markets.[7]

Nor does industrial reform desire to do away with bureaucratic hierarchy at work. This "equality of sacrifice," Zukin adds, would require "a change of attitude from worker to investor that enabled most employees to acquiesce in the new firm's financial policy" whereby the ISU accepted an *economic* rather than *jobs* basis of decision making.[8]

This was certainly the ESOP agenda I outlined in chapter 3. But along with others, Zukin's reading of a "docile" labor force differs from my analysis in this book, and the difference is im-portant for understanding the evolution of worker ownership and class struggle in Weirton. Zukin adopts the "company town" version of paternalism (where labor was content and fully inte-grated into a company union) and thus misreads the sentiments of Weirton's rank-and-file for that of their union leaders during the negotiations. As I argued in chapter 3, Bish's election did not signal *rank-and-file* consent to an economic basis of decision making—they desired job protection and he appeared to be their best choice.

As Zukin notes, Bish "was himself replaced in 1988 when he backed management's plans to reformulate the terms of the ESOP."[9] The ISU may have accepted the ESOP agenda, but workers voted to save jobs. They were "workers by day" *and*, as I argued in chapter 6, "workers by night." Their vision of worker ownership upheld job-based decision making within the context of community norms and local control. And it was this vision that shaped worker opposition to the "investor" model that ESOP was following and to the *inequality* of sacrifice entailed in layoffs, outsourcing, and management pay raises. If worker ownership at Weirton has "degenerated," as supporters term it, into a conventionally financed and controlled company, it is not because a docile labor force failed to challenge the terms—procedural and moral—of decision-making.[10]

To a large extent, Weirton was, as Zukin puts it, "like and unlike other firms."

Although the new Weirton was among the first steelmakers to impose significant wage reductions in the 1980's, it was the first to do so by a worker buyout. Like leveraged buyouts by management in other fields, this worker buyout immediately resulted in new leadership in both management and the labor union local. But unlike many other cases of corporate restructuring, it led to a moderately happy ending.[11]

Along with everyone I met during my research, I too hoped for a moderately happy ending in Weirton, even though worker ownership there disappointed my democratic ideals. But I also found that it disappointed workers and residents who did not share my views about industrial democracy, but who felt ESOP betrayed their sense of community and their conceptions of economic justice. And it was they who were unhappy enough to act in ways that might reverse a trend that undermined what they had hoped to preserve.

Employee Participation

Despite the claims of EPG facilitators that employee participation "flattened" the organizational hierarchy and expanded decision making, structural divisions remained among labor, management, and the board of directors. Class divisions and the role of "worker by day" were reproduced through the structure of EPG, the training session, and the problem-solving orientation. Ideologically, employee participation emphasized changing "attitudes," the "culture" of the mill, but not the hierarchical structure that fostered such antagonisms between labor, management, and executives in the first place. If only people would "listen" to each other, "communicate" better, "understand" their "proper" role, then everyone could "work together."

Richard Edwards, in *Contested Terrain*, cites the "contradictions of bureaucratic control" as a source of potential challenges by workers and demands for workplace democracy.[12] The idea of the "knowledgeable worker" reversed conventional conceptions of labor and it inserted workers into a domain previously reserved for management. But the constraints of decision making on the shopfloor gradually reinforced labor-management antagonisms and revealed the contradiction inherent in running *this* worker-owned company no different from any other company. Workers could use the company bureaucracy to defend their interests and resolve their grievances by appealing to those rules and regulations, channels of influence, and the principles of meritocracy, expertise, and efficiency. Though I noted evidence of this in chapters 4 and 5, EPG members (a minority to begin with) seldom reached beyond what the structure of EPG, its ideology, facilitators, and internal communications all functioned to reproduce: "workers by day." While the rule orientation of workplace control placed new constraints on employers as well as employees, the *enforcement* of such rules favored executives and top management, not workers.

Minus any significant changes in relations of power, any efforts to recast the normative order of the company guarantee suspicion and distrust, not cooperation or any "identity of interests." During the early 1990s at the height of rank-and-file opposition to company policies, Employee Participation and Internal Communications suffered some understandable setbacks. Since then EPG has been renamed Employee Involvement Program and integrated into the human relations department. As of September 1996, it involved ten active groups and a total of sixty-five active members.[13] Likewise, the Internal Communications department has shrunk and *The Bulletin*, the company newsletter, just resumed publication after a brief respite during the early 1990s.

Even those sympathetic to employee ownership and participation, from William F. Whyte and his colleagues at Cornell's School of Industrial and Labor Relations, to Corey Rosen and his colleagues from the National Center for Employee Ownership, to Joseph Blasi of Rutgers, stress the enduring problem of labor-management conflict in worker-owned firms. As Blasi warns:

> It is not possible any more to ignore the preponderance of scholarly evidence that employee ownership loses its common sense meaning, its significance to motivation, its relevance to practical problem solving of strategic issues in firms, and its potential importance to improving economic performance and the restructuring of American industry, unless it leads to or emerges from or strengthens or works together with a pragmatic process of labor-management cooperation. . . . The absence of labor-management cooperative initiatives is not always the direct result of management entrenchment, while the presence of labor-management conflict is not always the result of unions' thirst for power. There is a more fundamental problem here: American labor and management have trouble learning to cooperate, and until this trouble is directly confronted, any new social invention which tries to subsume it will soon run into the problem all over again.[14]

Was not "learning to cooperate" the goal of employee participation at Weirton Steel? Yes, but more important was the *productivity* of EPG and controlling the labor process and workers. The reason labor and management had, as Blasi puts it, "trouble learning to cooperate" was because they were still divided within the organizational hierarchy and still at odds over their rights and responsibilities. Nor did they share a vision of how worker ownership might be organized to enhance the larger public good of the community.

Until the structural conflicts between capital and labor engendered in a growing global economy are addressed, oppositional—and at times confrontational—cultures will persist, precisely the opposite of what ESOP and EPG proponents and sympathizers are calling for. As Raymond Russell has argued, research on worker ownership suggests,

> that not much more workers' power is likely to come out of worker ownership than goes into it at the start. Occasional acts of philanthropy aside, power is not something that is very frequently just given away. It is therefore unrealistic to expect American workers to acquire any meaningful degree of power from forms of employee ownership that they receive passively as gifts from their employer or the federal government. Worker ownership in the United States is unlikely to have significant consequences for workers' control unless American workers summon up the will and the power to insist that it should.[15]

Under paternalism, and during my research in Weirton, few expected the rank-and-file to "summon up the will and the power to insist" that they have a stronger voice in their working lives and their company. But that has changed, and the question is why.

Russell further notes that examples where workers did form their own organizations resulted from the power they derived from their ties to each other and the nature of their work. I would add that workers' ties to one another extend beyond the workplace and that how their community lives are structured is equally important to working-class resistance and organization, as well as the formation of oppositional cultures. It is in this context that we might better understand how class struggle shaped the evolution of worker ownership in Weirton.

Class, Community, and Worker Ownership

By expanding my conceptual and empirical lens on class beyond the labor process and into the "community" I do not wish to blur important analytical distinctions. Rather I sought to examine class as it evolved historically and was lived by people in Weirton.

Relationships in the mill overlapped with family and community membership in ways that shaped people's experience of class and their conceptions of economic organization and justice. Following the "relational" view of class favored by E. P. Thompson, Erik Olin Wright, and Rick Fantasia, this approach yielded an ethnographic account of the process whereby people struggled to define and defend their interests under conditions that constrained and enabled their efforts.

Other research has also pointed to community-labor coalitions in worker buyouts and economic redevelopment. This work has emphasized the importance of community involvement as a stabilizing source of support as well as an important factor in the ideology and goals of economic organization.[16] I too believe that community institutions can play an important role in shaping economic development and democracy, but I found that this role is complex and often contradictory under America's economic transformation and global market forces. Though other scholars have focused on the role of religious institutions, civic associations, political alliances, and legal structures in their analysis explaining community responses to plant closings,[17] I have also looked closely at how these institutions sustained cultural forms that directed people's attention, informed their grievances, and complicated their judgments about worker ownership in particular, and economic justice in general.

In this regard, one reasonable answer to why Weirton's rank-and-file shed the label of docility to become one of the most striking examples of working-class resistance in America lies in its history and local insulation. Ironically, Weir's original efforts to create his paternalistic company town apart from urban and union influences may have established the conditions that supported rank-and-file militancy today. The localism that distrusted outsiders—be they RFC activists, New York financial consultants, National management, or the federal government—also served to incubate the challenge that gradually emerged. As people would always remind me, "We may fight a lot amongst ourselves, but when we have to, we stick together." At one level, the struggle over control is a fight among Weirtonians and they are sticking together. Local exclusiveness resisted outside influence, whether radical or conservative, but this also protected oppositional sentiments from becoming diluted, and it sustains the "family brawl" that many in town see today. If National Steel and ESOP consultants *set the stage* for worker ownership, then class struggle and Weirton's isolation as a company town *shaped the play* of the past fifteen years.

Another factor that looms large in accounting for emerging rank-and-file opposition is the demographics of Weirton's workforce. Simply put, since ESOP older workers have been retiring earlier, and along with labor force reductions through attrition, this has left younger workers who, as Sal put it, have a different "attitude," and "don't put up with what we used to." Sal's generation moved into the mill in the late 1940s and early 1950s, a period of quiescence following the bitter disputes over union organizing in Weirton. Younger workers moved into the mill during the 1960s and 1970s, a period of civil unrest in America but also the period when National began undermining the paternalistic order of mill and community life. Their oppositional outlook may have been nurtured in this environment, but it also reflects their concerns over making a living and staying in Weirton just as millworkers before them. If the quiescence of an earlier generation signaled "the best they could get," opposition today reflects an effort to keep it.

The dissension that was evident in 1987 and culminated with worker-owners blocking a major board directive in 1994 clearly demonstrated the importance of control issues to workers. Even if equity and jobs remain central to the outlook of most wage earners in the United States, the Weirton case also suggests that not far below the surface of worker consciousness lie sentiments and inclinations for greater control in the company they work for. Provided with the opportunity, and the leadership to articulate and pursue it, labor can see how the distribution and quality of both equity *and* jobs are subject to the control they can mobilize over their working lives. Such opportunities and leadership are indeed rare; seldom are the moments when structural shifts allow people with choices that are not forced from the historical start.

Even though industrial democracy was a not the explicit goal or ideology of rank-and-file opposition in Weirton, the series of challenges waged by worker-owners arose from moral grievances over the organization and policies of their company; grievances that drew upon both class interests and community norms. Collective action gradually coalesced over a series of events that betrayed the

egalitarian spirit of ESOP but also undermined traditional collectivist and localist moral codes. Rank-and-file calls for job protection and executive accountability under ESOP were class-based
but drew upon, and emphasized, the normative relationship between the mill and community. The language of protest incorporated these norms, which served to strengthen collective action in
the face of company decisions that assaulted them.

Most importantly, it was this groundswell of rank-and-file frustration that carried the more militant Glyptis into the ISU leadership. The progression of ISU presidents from Richard Arrango
to Walter Bish to Virgil Thompson to Mark Glyptis may appear to
some as a sign of a confused and fickle union membership. But as
I have argued, this pattern reflects the evolving consciousness of
Weirton's rank-and-file and their collective mobilization to defend
their class interests. The dramatic reversal in how the ISU played
its role within the company depended on this mobilization, it did
not create it.

It is also quite reasonable to assume that without the support
of independent board member Phillip Smith the ISU challenge
might have faltered. And without their legal status as voting
shareholders, workers here would not have had the opportunity to
challenge the board of directors as they did. Still, neither of these
factors would have moved workers to act *as they did* were it not
for the complex web of desire, commitment, and vision that were
deeply embedded in a local moral economy and the collective action of workers as a class. Though Weirton workers are not so
different from other industrial workers in America who look to
compensation and jobs as their main priorities, the meaning of,
and *reasons* for, these priorities embrace far more than narrow
economic self-interest.

Thus, the Weirton case reminds us that industrial reform and
worker-ownership in America are as much about how power is
structured as they are about the technology of production and
seemingly benign notions of efficiency. If the success or failure of
worker-owned companies and industrial democracy were the sole
criteria for choosing this form of economic organization, we should
be even more cautious about our choice of bureaucratic capitalist
or "investor"-oriented economic organization for two reasons:
First, corporate CEOs and executive management make bad decisions too, yet when labor makes bad decisions they are portrayed

as incapable. Hierarchical decision-making is not condemned when a conventionally organized company fails (which is far more common than not), but industrial democracy and labor are held responsible when such "experiments" fail. Second, conventional firms do not have to operate in a political-economy that opposes them, therefore the market successes of more democratically organized firms are all the more remarkable. With political and legal support for industrial democracy, and the financial backing of lending institutions, such firms could be at least, if not more, successful in meeting market demands *and* supporting democratic practices and culture.[18]

Likewise, many have asked me whether the customs and moral economy I analyze in Weirton are not also present in other companies in other cities and towns. That in fact, sleeping on the job, company theft, favoritism in hiring and promotion, dissension over compensation, and labor-management conflict are common in most companies throughout America. I hold no doubts these conditions exist throughout corporate America, largely because class relations under capitalism are lived in similar ways throughout America—*but not exactly the same way*. Class conflict, therefore, often follows similar patterns and draws on similar symbolic resources, but it can also diverge from these patterns and recombine symbolic resources in ways that "fit" the uniqueness of local context and circumstances. People may steal from their company, but not for the same reasons or with the same consequences. Americans suspect that favoritism trumps merit more often than not, but do they integrate that view within a normative order that emphasizes nepotism and localism?

In other words, the moral economy I have analyzed is unique to the confluence of history and circumstance in Weirton, but I would not be surprised to find such moral codes in different form in other cases, or throughout America for that matter. Alvin Gouldner's analysis of how the disruption of "indulgency patterns" in his gypsum plant led to a wildcat strike is one such example. Though Gouldner focused on the workplace, I have tried to show how such patterns originate and are reinforced through the intersection of work and community life. Judy Wajcman's study of a worker cooperative in England, *Women in Control*, provides a similar analysis,[19] as do some of the cases analyzed by Rick Fantasia in *Cultures of Solidarity*.[20] Future research might follow this approach and examine to what extent moral discourse over the economy links work and family, business and community. It might be fruitful to consider other cases of recent prolonged labor struggles to see how class and cultural forms of community intersected and became reconstituted over the course of time; for example, the Pittston coal strike of 1989 in Carbo, Virginia; the P-9 challenge at Hormel in Austin, Minnesota, from 1985 to 1986; and especially the United Farm Workers campaign in Watsonville, California, that began in 1985 and continues as the UFW challenges a company union that was elected in 1997 amidst charges of worker intimidation.

In my view, class and the contested culture of community will continue to shape the struggle over control at Weirton Steel in the near future. Nonmarket-oriented moral codes still frame how people evaluate worker ownership and the exercise of power in the mill. But rather than a well-articulated ideology of "community control," people expressed an ambivalence that derives from, and reflects, structural changes and the historical mixture of coercive and benevolent elements of paternalism. At the same time, class conflict has become public and could become more pronounced in the years ahead. With the potential for shareholder lawsuits curtailed by the liability amendment passed with the public stock offering, labor-management conflict through work stoppages might become the primary route of opposition, a possibility that may be even more threatening to ideals of "community" and the company's image on Wall Street than loyal opposition that is channeled through a stronger, though still local, union leadership. If Barry and Irving Bluestone are correct that a strong union presence "appears to be the virtual sine qua non" for employee participation success,[21] then it is not a question of whether unions should be more cooperative or combative. At different times, and under different circumstances, one or the other approach may be necessary in achieving labor's interests. The question is how will those interests come to be defined, and what means are available to pursue them?

I think, however, that there is less reason for concern over a stronger union voice than many in Weirton, or on Wall Street, might fear. First, the rank-and-file have not gone on strike since the 1930s and the recent work stoppages represented spontaneous opposition apart from the ISU. Protesting workers may have felt emboldened by recent union militancy (protesting "up on this hill" against the management-bonus plan) and they may engage in such actions again if long-held grievances are not addressed. But Glyptis and the ISU leadership vigorously defended workers and reinforced their solidarity with the rank-and-file, which will likely serve to constrain, rather than encourage, future acts of shopfloor resistance.

More, the ISU has shown itself willing to concede ground on once traditionally union-protected shopfloor issues "if it helps the company." Glyptis and the ISU are concerned primarily with keeping jobs in the mill for worker-owners who want to stay in their hometown among family and friends. In general, workers with whom I spoke were prepared to bend and proceed cautiously *through their union* in keeping with their sentiments and allegiances to a community they feel responsible for. Even at the height of opposition to CEO Elish and the proposed stock offering in 1993–94, the ISU maintained a steady posture and solidarity with an angry and disillusioned workforce.

Finally, now that workers hold just 49 percent of the company's voting stock, the ISU will become even more significant in advancing their concerns. To have an effective voice in company policy workers will have to vote as a bloc, and unless the ISU directors on the board can mobilize such a bloc, only splintered protest (as during the ESOP negotiations) is likely. I was told by a librarian at the local library that the Shareholders Association that was formed by Frank Slanchik in opposition to the 1993 stock offering had been disbanded and that Slanchik donated the remaining $300 operating fund to the library for the purchase a set of encyclopedias; "He said that there was no reason now for the association." With the addition of an independent board member who represents shareholders, Slanchick's association may not have been necessary, but it did play an important role in educating and mobilizing workers and retired shareholders and it, or a similar group, may form again in the future.

How workers play their role as "worker-owners" will emerge from the intersection of their interests as a class and their sentiments as members of a community. Keeping the mill alive is one thing, but keeping a normative order alive that balances the interests and desires of work and community life will be daunting, as it is in countless other small towns and urban centers across

America. But as people in Weirton often told me, "we're sur-
vivors." While this "survival of the fittest" outlook is a powerful
motivating bond between workers and townspeople, it also reinforces the exclusive localism and isolation that paternalism engendered. Inevitably, when people in town expressed this view,
they did so with a pause and disclaimer: "I wish it didn't have to
be that way, that our success meant another mill's failure." Perhaps Weirton's success need not mean the failure of others, but
can the sentiments and norms that characterize a community-ori-
ented worker owned company encompass many beyond the protective confines of local life? As ISU president Glyptis reminded
people following the bitter showdown over the 1993 stock proposal, "If we're going to have an enemy, we want it to be our competitors and not each other."[22] This would be a dramatic reversal
in a town where people have stood together but also fought
against one another. If community has become "uncivilized" and
defensive under contemporary capitalism, it may be time to seriously consider more democracy—both inside and outside the
workplace—as a means of supporting and enhancing our more
humane and civilized dreams.

Notes

Introduction

1. I have relied upon the 1970, 1980, and 1990 Census of Population and Housing, U.S. Department of Commerce, Bureau of the Census, Steubenville-Weirton SMSA.

2. This breakdown is based on detailed statistical profiles of ancestry and racial groups compiled by the staff of the Weirton public library and provided to this author.

3. According to a 1990 Census Bureau report, the Weirton-Steubenville metropolitan area ranked fourth in the country in percentage of people who have stayed in the same house for thirty years or more (reprinted in the *Pittsburgh Post-Gazette*, n.d.).

4. Barry Bluestone and Bennett Harrison, *The Deindustrialization of America: Plant Closings, Community Abandonment, and the Dismantling of Basic Industry* (New York: Basic Books, 1982); Staughton Lynd, *The Fight against Shutdowns: Youngstown's Steel Mill Closings* (San Pedro, Calif.: Singlejack Books, 1982); John Portz, *The Politics of Plant Closings* (Lawrence: University of Kansas Press, 1990); Dale A. Hathaway, *Can Workers Have a Voice? The Politics of Deindustrialization in Pittsburgh* (University Park: Pennsylvania State University Press, 1993). For a comparative analysis of the French and American experience with plant shutdowns and the relative lack of militancy among American workers, see Lawrence E. Rothstein, *Plant Closings: Power, Politics, and Workers* (Dover, Mass.: Auburn House, 1986).

5. James Davison Hunter, *Culture Wars: The Struggle to Define America* (New York: Basic Books, 1991). Also see Herbert Gans, *The War*

against the Poor: The Underclass and Antipoverty Policy (New York: Basic Books, 1995).

Chapter 1. Worker Ownership and Class in America

1. I am using a distinction made by Raymond Russell, *Sharing Ownership in the Workplace* (Albany: State University of New York Press, 1985). He identifies these components of worker ownership as "equity ownership," which is "the right to vote on certain major decisions, the right to receive a variable dividend, and the right to sell or otherwise transfer one's shares in the ownership of the corporation," and "control," which "results from the added political fact that this shareholder is able to influence the organization's decision-making process" (p. 21).

2. Louis O. Kelso and Mortimer J. Adler, *The Capitalist Manifesto* (New York: Random House, 1958). Kelso has argued that worker ownership enhances American democracy by increasing workers' economic power, redistributing concentrated wealth, and reinforcing individual property rights; see Louis O. Kelso and Patricia Hetter Kelso, *Democracy and Economic Power* (Cambridge: Ballinger Publishing Company, 1986). I consider ESOPs the "dominant" form of worker ownership in the United States, but even here there are a variety of plans.

3. Joseph Raphael Blasi, *Employee Ownership through ESOPs: Implications for the Public Corporation* (New York: Pergamon Press, 1987), pp. 4–12. Also see Corey M. Rosen, Katherine J. Klein, and Karen M. Young, *Employee Ownership in America: The Equity Solution* (Lexington, Mass.: D.C. Heath and Co., 1986), pp. 251–55.

4. Blasi, *Employee Ownership through ESOPs*, p. 13, notes that by 1986 (the period of my fieldwork) there were some 7,000 to 8,000 ESOPs nationally, with 11 to 13 million workers and between 25 to 30 billion dollars in assets, up from about 4,000 plans and 7 million workers in 1983. He speculates that this surge of ESOP formation was due to an increase from 24 percent to 52 percent of Fortune 1000 companies adopting ESOP under the 1983 tax credit legislation.

5. Ibid., p. 16. Blasi also notes that while privately held ESOP companies made up only 7 percent of ESOP participants (some 500,000 employees) and 17 percent of all ESOP assets (some $3.2 billion), 75 percent of all ESOPs by 1983 (the period Weirton's ESOP was formed) were in privately held companies that excluded 30 to 50 percent of their employees from the plan, restricted voting rights, and paid no dividends on stock.

6. *Business Week*, March 18, 1995, p. 101. Also see "The National Center for Employee Ownership" (nceo@nceo.org.), 1996, Fact Sheet, p. 1. The NCEO provides extensive information on all of these plans, and brief but useful updates through an Internet web site. For a more detailed description, see Blasi, *Employee Ownership through ESOPs*; Rosen et. al., *Employee Ownership in America;* and Russell, *Sharing Ownership in the Workplace*.

7. Corey Rosen, "Fact Sheet," op. cit., p. 1.

8. Raymond Russell, "Forms and Extent of Employee Participation in the Contemporary United States," *Work and Occupations* 15 (November 1988): 376.

9. Rosen, "Fact Sheet," pp. 1, 5.

10. Rosen, "The Employee Ownership 100" (nceo@nceo.org), 1996.

11. This view is rooted in the early Wisconsin school of labor research that emphasized the "job consciousness" of workers who were organized into "wage conscious" unions.

12. John F. Witte, *Democracy, Authority, and Alienation in Work: Worker's Participation in an American Corporation* (Chicago: University of Chicago Press, 1980); John Simmons and William Mares, *Working Together: Employee Participation in Action* (New York: New York University Press, 1985). Also see Blasi, *Employee Ownership through ESOPs*, pp. 34–36.

13. Paul Blumberg, *Industrial Democracy: The Sociology of Participation* (New York: Schocken Books, 1973); Frank Lindenfeld and Joyce Rothschild-Whitt, eds., *Workplace Democracy and Social Change* (Boston: Porter Sargent Publishers, 1982); Russell, *Sharing Ownership*.

14. Bob Stone, "Employee Stock Ownership at UAL," in *Grassroots Economic Organizing Newsletter* (New Haven, Conn.) 17 (May–June 1995): 8.

15. Ibid.

16. Corey Rosen et al., *Employee Ownership in America*, p. 38.

17. Russell, "Forms and Extent of Employee Participation," p. 387.

18. Robert N. Stern, "Participation by Representation: Workers on Boards of Directors in the United States and Abroad," p. 418, in *Work and Occupations*, 15.4 (November 1988): 396–422.

19. Blasi, *Employee Ownership through ESOPs*, p. 36.

20. John Commons, David J. Saposs, Helen L. Sumner, E. B. Mittleman, H. E. Hoagland, John B. Andrews, and Selig Perlman, eds., *History of Labor in the United States*, 4 vols. (New York: Macmillan, 1918–35); David Halle, *America's Working Man* (Chicago: University of Chicago Press, 1984).

21. Loren Baritz, *The Servants of Power: A History of the Use of Social Science in American Industry* (Middleton, Conn.: Weslyan University Press, 1960) for a critique of these programs and the cordial alliance between academe and business. Also see Richard Gillespie, *Manufacturing Knowledge: A History of the Hawthorne Experiments* (Cambridge: Cambridge University Press, 1991) for his analysis that human relations reforms served as an ideological tool for management as it tried to adapt to the demands of collective bargaining (pp. 227–39).

22. Russell, "Forms and Extent of Employee Participation," pp. 374–95.

23. Michael J. Piore and Charles P. Sabel, *The Second Industrial Divide* (New York: Basic Books, 1984); Larry Hirshhorn, *Beyond Mechanization* (Cambridge: MIT Press, 1984); Charles C. Heckscher, *The New Unionism: Employee Involvement in the Changing Corporation* (New York: Basic Books, 1988). The terms I use in distinguishing these two perspectives are borrowed from Ruth Milkman, "Labor and Management in Uncertain Times: Renegotiating the Social Contract," in Alan Wolfe (ed.), *America at Century's End* (Berkeley: University of California Press, 1991), pp. 131–51.

24. On the impact of technological innovation, see Harry Braverman, *Labor and Monopoly Capital* (New York: Monthly Review Press, 1974); David F. Noble, *Forces of Production: A Social History of Industrial Automation* (New York: Alfred A. Knopf, 1984); Harley Shaiken, *Work Transformed: Automation and Labor in the Computer Age* (New York: Holt, Rinehart and Winston, 1985); Shoshana Zuboff. *In the Age of the Smart Machine: The Future of Work and Power* (New York: Basic Books, 1988). On employee participation, see Rick Fantasia, Dan Clawson, and Gregory Graham, "A Critical View of Worker Participation in American Industry," *Work and Occupations* 15 (November 1988): 468–88; Mike Parker and Jane Slaughter, *Choosing Sides: Unions and the Team Concept* (Boston: South End Press, 1988); Guillermo J. Grenier, *Inhuman Relations: Quality Circles and Anti-Unionism in American Industry* (Philadelphia: Temple University Press, 1988); Donald M. Wells, *Empty Promises: Quality of Worklife Programs and the Labor Movement* (New York: Monthly Review Press, 1987); Steve Fraser, "Industrial Democracy in the 1980s," *Socialist Review*, no. 72 (vol. 13, n. 6) Nov.–Dec., 1983; Raymond Russell, "Forms and Extent of Employee Participation."

25. David I. Levine and Laura D'Andrea Tyson, "Participation, Productivity, and the Firm's Environment," in *Paying for Productivity: A Look at the Evidence*, Alan S. Blinder ed. (Washington, D.C.: The Brookings Institution, 1990), pp. 183–237; Edward E. Lawler III, Susan Albers Mohrman, and Gerald E. Ledford Jr., *Employee Involvement and Total Quality Management: Practices and Results in Fortune 1000 Companies* (San Francisco: Josey-Bass, 1992); also see Russell, "Forms and Extent of Employee Participation," p. 380.

26. Russell, "Forms and Extent of Employee Participation" p. 380. Also see Henry Hansmann, "When Does Worker Ownership Work? ESOPs, Law Firms, Codetermination, and Economic Democracy," *The Yale Law Journal*, 99.8 (June 1990): 1749–1816.

27. Rosen, "NCEO Library" (nceo@nceo.org.), 1996, p. 6. This web site also contains reviews of: a 1986 NCEO study, a follow-up study by economist Gorm Winther and colleagues in New York and Washington State, a 1987 U.S. General Accounting Office study, a 1990 study by the Michigan Center for Employee Ownership, and a 1993 study by the Northeast Ohio Employee Ownership Center, all of which found improvements in company performance when combining employee ownership and participation. Also see Joseph R. Blasi, *Employee Ownership: Revolution or Ripoff?* (New York: Harper Business, 1988), pp. 267–86.

28. Michael A. Conte and Jan Svejnar, "The Performance Effects of Employee Ownership Plans," in *Paying for Productivity*, pp. 143–72, but also see the adjoining "Comment by Joseph Raphael Blasi," pp. 172–81, for a discussion of the methodological problems in these studies.

29. Russell, "Forms and Extent of Employee Participation," p. 381.

30. Ibid., p. 383.

31. Ibid., p. 385. Hansmann, "When Does Worker Ownership Work?" considers many factors that affect a firm's success or failure, including cases outside the United States.

32. Barry Bluestone and Irving Bluestone, *Negotiating the Future: A Labor Perspective on American Business* (New York: Basic Books, 1992), pp. 169–86. They also cite research by Maryellen Kelly and Bennett Harrison, "Unions, Technology, and Labor-Management Cooperation," in *Unions and Economic Competitiveness*, ed. Lawrence Mishel and Paula B. Voos (Armonk, N.Y.: Sharpe, 1992), that found companies with such employee participation reforms were significantly *less* productive than companies without the reforms (also see Bluestone and Bluestone, *Negotiating the Future*, pp. 305–6 n. 23).

33. Bluestone and Bluestone, *Negotiating the Future*, pp. 184–86.

34. Blasi, *Employee Ownership through ESOPs*, p. 32.

35. Ibid., p. 33.

36. Inez Orler, "A Tribute to John C. Williams" (manuscript, n.d.), *Frontiersman ESOP* (Poisons, W.Va.: McClain Printing, 1984), and "Ernest Tener Weir: Industrialist, Founder, and Philanthropist" (manuscript, 1979), all of which are in the Weirton Public Library.

37. George Rude, *Ideology and Popular Protest* (New York: Pantheon Books, 1980); Eric Hobsbawm, *Primitive Rebels: Studies in Archaic Forms of Social Movement in the Nineteenth and Twentieth Centuries* (New York: Norton, 1959); E. P. Thompson, *The Making of the English Working Class* (New York: Vintage Books, 1966); Howard Newby, *The Deferential Worker: A Study of Farm Workers in East Anglia* (London: Allen Lane, 1977); Daniel J. Walkowitz, *Worker City, Company Town: Iron and Cotton-Worker Protest in Troy and Cohoes, New York, 1855–84* (Urbana: University of Illinois Press, 1978); Michael Burawoy, "Karl Marx and the Satanic Mills: Factory Politics under Early Capitalism in England, the United States, and Russia," *American Journal of Sociology* 90.1 (1984): 247–82.

38. Eugene Genovese, *Roll Jordan Roll: The World the Slaves Made* (New York: Vintage Press, 1976). On paternalism in southern industry, see Melton Alonza McLaurin, *Paternalism and Protest: Southern Cotton Mill Workers and Organized Labor, 1875–1905* (Westport, Conn.: Greenwood Publishing Corp., 1971).

39. Ronald Dore, *British Factory-Japanese Factory: The Origins of National Diversity in Industrial Relations* (Berkeley: University of California Press, 1973), but also see Eugene Genovese, "The Fate of Paternalism in Modern Bourgeois Society: The Case of Japan," in *Roll Jordan Roll*, pp. 662–65, and Stephen Hill, *Competition and Control at Work: The New Industrial Society* (London: Heinemann Educational Books, 1981), pp. 23, 53–60.

40. Nicholas Abercrombie and Stephen Hill, "Paternalism and Patronage," *British Journal of Sociology* 27 (1976): 413–29. Paternalism has also been viewed as characteristic of other nonindustrial/noneconomic relations where one party dominates another "for their own good" as in the case of a father and his children, men and women, or the state and its citizens. See John Kleinig, *Paternalism* (Totowa, N.J.: Rowman and Allanheld, 1984); Rolf Sartorius (ed.), *Paternalism* (Minneapolis: University of Minnesota Press, 1983).

41. Abercrombie and Hill, op. cit. p. 414. This is an important correction to Newby's definition of paternalism as based on face-to-face contact with elites in "Paternalism and Capitalism," p. 66, in *Industrial Society: Class, Cleavage and Control*, ed. Richard Scase (St. Martin's Press: New York, 1977), pp. 59–73.

42. Newby, "Paternalism and Capitalism," p. 65.

43. Richard Sennett, *Authority* (New York: Vintage Books, 1981), p. 61.

44. Newby, "Paternalism and Capitalism," looks at the impact of the size of an organization on the rise and fall of paternal structures; also see Burawoy, "Karl Marx and the Satanic Mills" (pp. 265–66), for his analysis of the Waltham system developed in northern New England textile mills.

45. Newby, "Paternalism and Capitalism," p. 70.

46. Mary R. Jackman, *The Velvet Glove: Paternalism and Conflict in Gender, Class and Race Relations* (Berkeley: University of California Press, 1994), p. 272.

47. Reinhard Bendix, *Work and Authority in Industry* (New York: Harper & Row, 1963), p. 60.

48. Jackman, *The Velvet Glove*, p. 273.

49. Newby, "Paternalism and Capitalism," p. 70.

50. Ibid., p. 71. Technological or political forces may also contradict paternalistic ideology and threaten its stability. Also see Bendix, *Work and Authority in Industry,* chapter 2.

51. Genovese, *Roll Jordan Roll*, p. 597.

52. E. P. Thompson, "The Moral Economy of the English Crowd in the Eighteenth Century," *Past and Present* 50 (February 1971) and "Patrician Society, Plebeian Culture," *Journal of Social History* 7 (Summer 1974). Also see Richard Madsen, *Morality and Power in a Chinese Village* (Berkeley: University of California Press, 1984), pp. 44–48.

53. Thompson, "The Moral Economy," p. 79.

54. Ibid.

55. Ibid.

56. Ellen Meiksins Wood, "The Politics of Theory and the Concept of Class: E.P. Thompson and His Critics," *Studies in Political Economy* 9 (1982): 45–75.

344 *Notes*

57. Madsen, *Morality and Power*, pp. 44–48. For a stinging critique of social historians who have sought evidence of a moral economy in late eighteenth century America, see Gordon S. Wood, "Inventing American Capitalism," *The New York Review of Books*, 9 June 1994, pp. 44–49.

58. Sennett, *Authority*, p. 73. Also see John Gaventa, *Power and Power-lessness; Quiescence and Rebellion in an Appalachian Valley* (Urbana: University of Illinois Press, 1980), and Walkowitz, *Worker City, Company Town*. Gaventa and Walkowitz examine local resistance to paternalism, but they too emphasize the structural and cultural limits to such opposition.

59. Erik Olin Wright, *Class Structure and Income Distribution* (New York: Academic Press, 1979), pp. 5–8.

60. Rick Fantasia, *Cultures of Solidarity: Consciousness, Action, and Contemporary American Workers* (Berkeley: University of California Press, 1988), p. 8.

61. Ibid., pp. 6–7.

62. Wright, *Class Structure*, pp. 5–8.

63. Fantasia, *Cultures of Solidarity*, p. 19.

64. Ibid., p. 17.

65. Ibid., p. 10. Also see Raymond Williams, *Marxism and Literature* (Oxford: Oxford University Press, 1977).

66. T. Lane and K. Roberts. *Strike at Pilkington's* (London: Fontana, 1971), pp. 37–38, cited in Newby, "Paternalism and Capitalism," pp. 72–73.

67. See Joseph R. Gusfield, *Community: A Critical Response* (New York: Harper Colophon Books, 1975), pp. xv–xvi, 83–87, where he distinguishes territorial, relational, and "semantic or poetic" usages of the concept community, the latter being in large part a mythic ideal that people hold as a utopia they *should* strive for and against which they judge contemporary life. It is this symbolic usage that I consider "ideological." For a review of community studies, see Larry Lyon, *The Community in Urban Society* (Lexington, Mass.; D.C. Heath and Company, 1989).

Chapter 2. Forced Choices I: Company Town

1. *Steubenville Herald-Star* (hereafter *SHS*), 11 September and 22 September 1919.

2. Ibid., 27 September 1919.

3. With cousin John K. Tener as governor of Pennsylvania from 1911 to 1915, Weir's family was no stranger to regional politics. Much of the source data for this section on Weir and the early mill and community life comes from local historian Inez Orler and the entry for Ernest Tener Weir in the *Dictionary of National Biography* (New York: Oxford University Press, 1971).

4. Weir's success is often portrayed as a "rags to riches" story, yet this friendship and his career were no doubt aided by his kinship ties to the powerful and wealthy Phillips and Oliver families in Pittsburgh. See John N. Ingham, "Ernest Tener Weir," *Biographical Dictionary of American Business Leaders* (Westport, Conn.: Greenwood Press, 1983), pp. 1584–86.

5. Thad Radzialowski, "Workers by Day, Owners by Night: The ESOP at Weirton Steel," paper delivered at the National Meeting, Labor History Society, Wayne State University, Detroit, Michigan, October 18, 1984, p. 2.

6. *SHS*, 24 October 1919.

7. Herbert Gutman, *Work, Culture, and Society in Industrializing America* (New York: Vintage Books, 1977), especially chap. 1.

8. Philip S. Foner, *Organized Labor and The Black Worker, 1619–1981* (New York: International Publishers, 1982), p. 133.

9. Kai T. Erikson, *Everything in Its Path: Destruction of Community in the Buffalo Creek Flood* (New York; Simon & Schuster, 1976), pp. 59–63.

10. *SHS*, 24 October 1919.

11. Orler, "Ernest Tener Weir" p. 14.

12. *SHS*, 23 September 1919.

13. Ibid., 29 September 1919.

14. David Brody, *Labor in Crisis: The Steel Strike of 1919* (Philadelphia: J. B. Lippincott, 1965).

15. Ibid., p. 94.

16. *SHS*, 27 September 1919.

17. Brody, *Labor in Crisis*, pp. 157–64.

18. *SHS*, 26 July and 28 July 1919.

19. Ibid., 29 July 1919.

20. Ibid., 6 October 1919, p. 1.

21. Ibid., 7 October 1919, p. 1.

22. Ibid.

23. "Ernest Tener Weir," *Dictionary of National Biography*.

24. *SHS*, 7 October 1919.

25. Ibid., 8 October 1919, p. 1.

26. Ibid.

27. Ibid.

28. *New York Times*, 8 October 1919, p. 3, reported that Emil Makinisia, leader of the Finnish Socialist Party in Weirton, had been tarred and feathered at Woodlawn, Pennsylvania, several months before he arrived in the mill. His status seemed to be a good enough reason to label all the accused "ringleaders" outsiders and this reinforced the socially constructed image that Weirton was a tranquil community that bred no resistance.

29. *SHS*, 12 November 1919.

30. Ibid., 24 November 1919.

31. Ibid., p. 16.

32. It is reasonable to assume that this "notes" section was authored by either a company official or well-to-do Anglo-American resident of the town.

33. Interviews with local historian Inez Orler, in Radzialowski, *Workers by Day*.

34. Recall Abercrombie and Hill, "Paternalism and patronage" p. 414, who emphasize that paternalism is a form of *social* organization where the paternal ideology "becomes part of the organizational rule system and the normative structure of management."

35. Bendix, *Work and Authority in Industry*, pp. 49–51.

36. Sennett, *Authority*, p. 59.

37. It is likely that Weir was familiar with the Owenite school of thought; he was an avid reader of Charles Dickens and he saw his role as something more than "merely" an entrepreneur.

38. Radzialowski, "Workers by Day," p. 3.

39. Ingham, "Ernest Tener Weir."

40. Ownership was divided among stockholders of the merging companies accordingly: Weirton Steel, 50 percent; Michigan Steel, 25 percent; M. A. Hanna, 25 percent. Weir became chairman and chief executive, Fink became president, and Humphrey was chairman of the executive committee. See Orler, "Ernest Tener Weir" p. 6.

41. Ingham, "Ernest Tener Weir," p. 1584.

42. Radzialowski, "Workers by Day," p. 2.

43. *SHS*, 27 September 1933.

44. William Serrin, personal correspondence.

45. *SHS*, 28 September 1933.

46. Ibid. This spontaneous, unorganized uprising was characteristic of labor's opposition to corporate America in the 1930s. As Frances F. Piven and Richard A. Cloward argue in *Poor People's Movements* (New York: Vintage Books, 1979), chapter 3, industrial workers at the local level, acting without union endorsement, waged the initial struggles that disrupted the political-economic status quo of the early to mid-1930s. See also Mike Davis, *Prisoners of the American Dream* (New York: Verso Press, 1988), chapter 2.

47. E. W. Miller publicly stated that efforts were underway to prevent other steelworkers from walking out at the Carnegie mills in Mingo Junction, The Follansbee Brothers plant in Follansbee, West Virginia, a few miles south of Weirton, and the Wheeling Steel Corporation plants in Steubenville. *Weirton Daily Times* (hereafter *WDT*), 29 September 1933.

48. *SHS*, 28 September 1933.

49. The AAISTW was soon integrated into SWOC, which served as a "field agent" of sorts for John L. Lewis and the CIO during the 1930s.

50. Fantasia, *Cultures of Solidarity*, pp. 17–24.

51. *New York Times*, 21 March 1934.

52. For the full text of the court decision and comments by Weir and company officials, see *New York Times*, 28 February 1935.

53. The following summary of court testimony is based upon newspaper accounts from 1933 to 1951. My main source is the *New York Times*, but I also draw upon local reports from the *Weirton Daily Times, Steubenville Herald-Star*, and *Weirton Steel Bulletin*.

54. *New York Times*, 15 April 1936.

55. *New York Times*, 13 July 1940.

56. *Life*, 6 September 1937, pp. 19–32.

57. In retrospect, the conflict between Weir's local welfare and Roosevelt's national agenda reveals an ironic meeting of perspectives. The accusation by WIU officials and company lawyers that SWOC and the CIO "were in bed" with Roosevelt and New Deal officials is not far from what many Left analysts argue today. The point is that while elites at both the national and local levels were pushing their own brand of welfare, the majority of Weirtonions were spectators who either feared for their personal and family welfare or felt that neither group of elites actually cared much about them. This mix of sentiments likely fueled both their distrust of local elites and their sense of independence from national institutions.

58. Radzialowski, "Workers by Day," p. 4.

59. Orler, "Ernest Tener Weir" p. 53.

60. *New York Times*, 26 August 1950.

61. William A. White, "Amazing Weirton," seven-part series in the *Pittsburgh Press*, 1952.

62. Ibid.

63. *Weirton Steel Bulletin* (hereafter *WSB*), November 1950, p. 34.

64. Ibid., June 1951.

65. Ibid., April 1958, p. 13.

66. Ibid., December 1951. One early contract provision allowed 1,000 employees to eat their lunch while working so they could leave after eight hours and not lose a half hour of pay. This suggests how amicable contract negotiations allowed the company to tailor minor, yet meaningful, work arrangements to the mill's separate departments. Ibid., August 1951, p. 22.

67. Ibid., January 1965, May/April, 1972.

68. Quoted in Jonathan Prude, "ESOP's Fable: How Workers Bought a Steel Mill in Weirton, West Virginia, and What Good It Did Them," *Socialist Review* 14.6 (1984): 35. A review of *Weirton Steel Bulletins* and the *Weirton Daily Times* during these years confirms this appraisal with story after story on how workers broke production records, many of which were set only a short time previously.

69. In 1980 National bought the giant United Financial Corporation of California while total corporation business devoted to steel dropped to 69 percent from 83 percent a decade earlier. See Prude, "ESOP's Fable,"

p. 34. During the 1970s National more than tripled its interest in the aluminum market and announced two weeks after Weirton's nightmare that a new plant for aluminum foil products was being planned for Europe. *SHS*, 16 March 1982.

70. Jonathon Rowe, "Weirton Steel: Buying Out the Bosses," *Washington Monthly*, January 1984, pp. 41–42.

71. Radzialowski, "Workers by Day," p. 33 n. 30.

Chapter 3. Forced Choices II: Buy It or Lose It

1. *The Great Weirton Stee(a)l* (hereafter referred to *GWS*), First Run Features, 1984, September 21, 1983. This film documentary of the ESOP negotiations was written and directed by Catherine Pozzo di Borgo, and edited and produced by Robert K. Machover, who graciously allowed me the use of a complete transcript of the film (including segments cut from the final version). I have paginated and dated the transcript for reference purposes in this book.

2. Ibid., September 24, 1983, pp. 898–99.

3. Prude, "ESOP's Fable," p. 36.

4. John Lichtenstein, "Toward Employee Ownership at Weirton Steel, Fact Sheet," unpublished report, Southeastern Ohio Legal Services, Steubenville, Ohio, August 4, 1982.

5. Ibid.

6. Figures on employee residence were hard to come by, but the *Wall Street Journal*, 6 April 1982, p. 31, estimated that 55 percent of the mill's workforce live in Weirton. According to Eli Dragisich, local businessman and member of a JSC fundraising committee, 30 percent of mill employees live in Ohio, most of these in Steubenville. *Wheeling Intelligencer* (hereafter referred to as *WI*), 30 November 1982. The remaining 15 percent reside in small towns up and down the West Virginia panhandle and in eastern Pennsylvania.

7. *Pittsburgh Post-Gazette*, 3 May 1982.

8. *WI*, 6 March 1982, p. 1.

9. See, for example, Erikson, *Everything in Its Path*; Gaventa, *Power and Powerlessness*. On a steel community, also see David Bensman and Roberta Lynch, *Rusted Dreams: Hard Times in a Steel Community* (New York: McGraw-Hill, 1987). On Aliquippa, a steel town 35 miles northwest

of Pittsburgh, see *Aliquippa: Struggle for Survival in a Pittsburgh Mill-town 1984 and Before* (Pittsburgh; School of Social Work, University of Pittsburgh, 1984). On an automobile manufacturing community, see Kathryn Marie Dudley, *The End of the Line: Lost Jobs, New Lives in Postindustrial America* (Chicago: University of Chicago Press, 1994), and also see Katherine Newman's account of the impact of a Singer Sewing machine plant closing in Elizabeth, New Jersey in, *Falling from Grace* (New York: Free Press, 1988).

10. *SHS*, 2 March 1982, p. 1.

11. Ibid.

12. The management group included William Doepken Jr., general manager of industrial relations and division counsel; Carl Valdiserri, general manager of service and maintenance; John Madigan, vice-president of industrial relations; and Eugene West, vice-president and controller. The union group included Independent Guards Union President John G. Chernenko, ISU legal counsel David Robertson, and the seven chairmen of the union's salary and hourly divisions. *WI*, 5 March 1982, p. 1.

13. *WI*, 6 March 1982, p. 1.

14. *WI*, 24 March 1982, p. 12.

15. *Pittsburgh Post-Gazette*, 8 March 1982, p. 6.

16. *Pittsburgh Press*, 14 March 1982, p. 4.

17. *WI*, 4 March 1982.

18. Ibid.

19. *SHS*, early April 1982.

20. Radzialowski, "Workers by Day," p. 13.

21. Compared to the rank-and-file, local management was significantly younger and may have had more at stake in saving the mill. According to a study done by sociologist Arnold Levine of West Virginia University during the negotiations, 32 percent of the management and professional personnel scored below 50 on the age/seniority score, compared to 21 percent of the hourly workers. Furthermore, not quite half of the hourly workers had a score of 70 as compared to 37 percent of the management and professional staff. Radzialowski, "Workers by Day," n. 36.

22. James B. Lieber, *Friendly Takeover: How an Employee Buyout Saved a Steel Town* (New York: Viking Press, 1995), p. 75. Contrary to the title, Lieber's account portrays the ESOP negotiations as anything but friendly.

23. *SHS*, 8 May 1982.

24. Lichtenstein, "Toward Employee Ownership," p. 2.

25. For the ISU's David Robertson, one reason for choosing Lazard Freres was that this firm of Wall Street bankers was "close to labor." See Rowe, "Buying Out the Bosses," p. 38.

26. Robert N. Bellah, Richard Madsen, William M. Sullivan, Ann Swidler, and Steven M. Tipton, *Habits of the Heart: Individualism and Commitment in American Life* (Berkeley: University of Berkeley Press, 1996), p. 268.

27. Lieber, *Friendly Takeover*, pp. 71–72, 76–79, 93–95. The partnership of Lowenstein and Curtis brought together two different perspectives on ESOP structure. Lowenstein held a more conventional approach to ESOP organization and workers' rights, while Curtis advocated a more democratic model, having designed what many considered the most democratically structured ESOP in the country in 1980 at Rath Meat Packing in Waterloo, Iowa.

28. Lichtenstein, "Toward Employee Ownership."

29. Radzialowski, "Workers by Day," p. 16.

30. *WI*, 21 April 1982, and *SHS*, 21 April 1982.

31. *WI*, 21 April 1982. According to ISU attorney David Robertson, "The union will lose $312,000 (in 1982) based on the current level of layoffs. The loss will amount to $124,000 to the general fund in the 12 months of 1982." The ISU also faced costs associated with the ESOP effort: $39,000 in legal fees, $10,000 for a union pension analysis, $10,000 for advice on ESOP from a union consultant, and an estimated $7,000 for lobbying trips. *SHS*, 21 April 1982.

32. Ibid., 29 April 1982.

33. Radzialowski, "Workers by Day," p. 16.

34. In the late 1970s Gilliam became involved in a much publicized legal dispute with Steubenville police after they had beaten his brother and then indicted both Gilliams under charges of inciting violence. The Gilliams declined a deal (including Tony's resignation from the Human Relations Commission) that would have dropped the charges and instead accepted a trial that eventually found them innocent and the police guilty. *Citizen Police Review Project*, Committee for Justice, Steubenville, Ohio, n.d.

35. Other core RFC members included: Willie McKenzie, a black foreman who, in 1972, had filed a class action suit against Weirton's discrim-

inatory employment practices that was still pending; John Gregory, a black worker who initiated an NLRB grievance in June 1982 against the ISU for excluding laid-off workers from voting in elections; Tom Campbell; Paul Majewski; and Ed "Skip" Mixon. Gregory collected 500 signatures on a petition calling for the ISU to change its bylaws to permit laid-off workers a vote in elections and referendums. The petition was sent to the ISU and the U.S. Secretary of Labor with a request that the Labor Department bring suit against the ISU. The RFC joined the suit as a plaintiff in July 1982. *WI*, August 1982.

36. Staughton Lynd, "Why We Opposed the Buyout at Weirton Steel," *Labor Research Review* (Chicago: Midwest Center for Labor Research, 1985), p. 44. The filmmakers Catherine Pozzo di Borgo and Robert Machover directed and produced *The Great Weirton Stee(a)l*.

37. Hutton often wrote editorials for newsletters distributed by the Committee for Justice, but it is unclear just how close his association was with this group.

38. *GWS*, 22 March 1982, p. 5.

39. Steve Paisani, interview with author, 17 November 1986.

40. *GWS*, 22 March 1982.

41. Ibid.

42. Ibid.

43. In early April an RFC leaflet listing ten demands was distributed throughout town and in the mill. A few of its main features illustrate the RFC's vision of worker ownership: complete community involvement in all ESOP negotiations and decisions; the right of all workers—including those laid off—to vote on any employee buyout before implementation; immediate voting rights over company stock whether it be directly owned or held in a trust; one person–one vote regardless of compensation or amount of stock owned; and a strong, independent, democratic union in the new company.

44. *SHS*, 25 March 1982, p. 4.

45. Ibid.

46. Lieber, *Friendly Takeover*, pp. 100–101.

47. Ibid., p. 100.

48. Perhaps this policy was a holdover from traditional company concerns over dissident workers who may have been dismissed for union mil-

itancy. ISU policy also held that only shop stewards were eligible to run for union offices, another legacy of paternalism insofar as it favored union insiders already accustomed to the "company union" way of doing things.

49. The Labor Department would not rule on this grievance over workers' voting rights until just after the ESOP vote, over a year later.

50. Lieber, *Friendly Takeover*, p. 101.

51. McKinsey and Company, Inc., *Assessing the Feasibility of an Independent Weirton Steel: Executive Summary*, n.d.; McKinsey and Company, Inc., *Assessing the Feasibility of an Independent Weirton Steel*, Washington, D.C., July 26, 1982, p. 101.

52. *GWS*, 14 July 1982, p. 105.

53. Ibid., pp. 107–8.

54. Ibid., p. 109.

55. Ibid.

56. Ibid., p. 132.

57. Also see, Nelson Lichtenstein and Howell John Harris, "Introduction: A Century of Industrial Democracy in America," pp. 1–19, and Howell John Harris, "Industrial Democracy and Liberal Capitalism, 1890–1925," pp. 43–66, in *Industrial Democracy in America: The Ambiguous Promise* (Cambridge: Cambridge University Press, 1993).

58. *SHS*, 15 July 1982, p. 2.

59. *GWS*, 28 November 1982, p. 506.

60. Ibid., 6 May 1983, p. 628.

61. Ibid., p. 637.

62. *SHS*, 15 July 1982.

63. Ibid., 5 August 1982.

64. Minutes from RFC meeting on September 21, 1982. According to a source who reported being told this by Jack Curtis, Curtis was "on the verge of resigning from his capacity as attorney handling the structure of the proposed ESOP."

65. Minutes from RFC meeting on October 5, 1982.

66. Lichtenstein, "Toward Employee Ownership," p. 12.

67. During one RFC meeting John Lichtenstein reported hearing from Dave Robertson "that there [was] a struggle between National Steel and Weirton Steel management." Ibid., July 13, 1982, p. 96.

68. *WI*, 20 August 1982.

69. Arnold Levine, *A Survey of Weirton Steel Employees on the Eve of Their Historic Vote*, Department of Sociology, West Virginia University, July 1983, cited in Radzialowski, "Workers by Day," p. 19.

70. Named as defendants were ISU president Bish and Weirton Steel vice-president and co-chairmen of the JSC Carl Valdiserri, as well as William Doepken Jr., John Madigan, and Eugene West—all management representatives on the JSC.

71. *GWS*, 13 October 1982, pp. 221–23. Lynd argued that based on Title I and V of the Landrum-Griffin Act, workers had a right to an "informed" vote and union officials had a duty to disclose all information pertinent to such a vote. He further noted that under the Securities Acts laws, in any sale of stock all "material facts concerning the financial prospects of the company" must be disclosed to the purchaser(s). A final claim, filed under ARISA statutes, held that because the JSC and union proposed a transfer of the existing pension plan sponsored by National to the new company, participants in the plan needed the appendix information to evaluate the transfer and the JSC as fiduciaries had a duty to disclose it.

72. *WI*, 13 October 1982.

73. *GWS*, 13 October 1982, p. 220.

74. John Lichtenstein, "The Darker Side of the Proposed Employee Buy-out of Weirton Steel," unpublished draft analysis presented to the RFC, 1982. These arguments and the data analysis that supported them were made available to employees through RFC leaflets.

75. Ibid.

76. *WI*, 14 October 1982, p. 1.

77. Ibid.

78. *GWS*, 25 October 1982, p. 266.

79. Ibid., 20 October 1982, p. 248.

80. Ibid., p. 249.

81. Ibid., 27 October 1982, p. 345.

82. Ibid., p. 348.

83. Ibid., pp. 348–49.

84. Ibid., p. 372.

85. Ibid., 27 October 1982, pp. 349–50.

86. Ibid., p. 369.

87. Ibid., p. 370.

88. Ibid., pp. 376–77.

89. Ibid., pp. 377–78.

90. According to John Machover, *The Great Weirton Stee(a)l*, Robertson was a key figure in the negotiations with the most influence within the ISU. Interview with the author, June 1987. Lieber, *Friendly Takeover*, p. 72, notes that he was the JSC's "key leader from the labor side."

91. *GWS*, 2 November 1982, p. 406.

92. Ibid., pp. 416–17.

93. Ibid., p. 418.

94. Ibid.

95. Ibid., p. 420.

96. Ibid., p. 421.

97. Ibid., p. 422.

98. Ibid., p. 439.

99. Ibid., p. 440.

100. Ibid., 8 December 1982, p. 606.

101. Ibid., 23 November 1982, p. 468, and RFC leaflet (n.d.).

102. Ibid. Also see *Steve Bauman v. Walter Bish et al.*, Civil Action 82–0090-W., U.S. District Court for West Virginia, Northern District (1982). As Radzialowski notes, "The only members of the JSC who had seen the full report were Carl Valdiserri, William Doepkin Jr., John Madigan, and Eugene West, all members of the management team. Much of the material in the report was, of course, provided by management to McKinsey." "Workers by Day," n. 40.

103. Ibid., and RFC leaflet (n.d.).

104. *GWS*, 28 October 1982, p. 391.

105. Prude, "ESOP's Fable," p. 47.

106. *GWS*, 28 October 1982, pp. 385–86.

107. John Litchenstein, a Yale business administration student who contributed his knowledge of steel industry production and finance, had affiliations with other activist groups and the USWA. Steve Paisani, a laid-off Wheeling-Pittsburgh millworker, was very active in the Wheeling area with the USWA and unemployed workers' committees.

108. *GWS*, 7 December 1982, p. 587.

109. Ibid., p. 590.

110. Ibid., 21 September 1983, p. 848.

111. Ibid., pp. 846–48.

112. Ibid., pp. 832–35.

113. Prude, "ESOP's Fable," p. 46.

114. *SHS*, 28 April 1983.

115. Ibid., 2 April 1983.

116. *WDT*, 8 April 1983.

117. The most telling illustration of this maze of litigation is the fact that former ISU president Arrango was co-plaintiff in a suit against National Steel as well as his own union.

118. *GWS*, 27 September 1983, p. 919.

119. Lawrence E. Rothstein, *Plant Closings*, pp. 174–75.

120. In his case studies, Fantasia, *Cultures of Solidarity*, pp. 198–218, notes how worker and community awareness of the corporate leanings of courts during strikes reinforced their oppositional sentiments and collective solidarity.

121. This was reflected during an early RFC meeting in July 1982 when one member wondered about an enthusiastic co-member; "I can't tell if you're an anarchist by personality or ideology—a bit of organization doesn't hurt." *GWS*, p. 98. Another member recalled that some in the RFC were more "politically disciplined" and sophisticated than others. Anonymous RFC member, interview with author, July 1988.

122. Prude, "ESOP's Fable," p. 44.

123. *WI*, 10 March 1982; *SHS*, 10 March 1982.

124. Prude, "ESOP's Fable," p. 45.

125. Nicholas Yenchochic, Wintersville, Ohio, letter to the editor, *SHS*, 5 May 1983.

126. Sennett, *The Fall of Public Man* (New York: Vintage Books, 1978), pp. 294–312.

127. *WI*, 4 December 1982.

128. Prude, "ESOP's Fable," p. 42.

129. *SHS*, 31 March 1983; *WI*, 2 April 1983.

130. Prude, "ESOP's Fable," p. 42.

131. Maxwell left open the possibility of later legal recourse if the plaintiffs could demonstrate that the ESOP would endanger workers' pension rights. *SHS*, 30 April 1983.

132. *WI*, 25 March 1983.

133. Don Goldstein, "Saving Jobs, But at What Price?" *Nation*, 10 December 1983, p. 597.

134. Lieber, *Friendly Takeover*, p. 184.

135. Loughhead's background in the steel industry qualified him for the top spot, and his family roots may have incidentally favored him in the minds of workers and townspeople alike. He was born and raised in Monaca, Pennsylvania, about thirty miles northeast of Weirton, and his parents were from Wellsburg, West Virginia, just a few miles south of Weirton.

136. Including hourly workers, salaried non-exempt, and the Independent Guards Union, the ESOP was approved 6,203 to 774; contract concessions 6,146 to 872; pension plan 5,943 to 1,036. Radzialowski, "Workers by Day," p. 58.

137. The path to an ESOP was not cleared until pending legal cases were dismissed in December—the RFC dropped its lawsuit—and Citicorp had managed to assemble a multibank revolving credit arrangement worth some $120 million. The company received a boost when the EPA granted Weirton Steel a "bubble" status that significantly reduced its pollution control requirements by allowing it to average emissions measurements from several spots rather than base its calculations on the worst sites. Governor Rockefeller also signed a bill that would reduce the company's annual state taxes by $450,000 as an ESOP. See Goldstein, "Saving Jobs," p. 597.

138. Prude, "ESOP's Fable," p. 45.

139. *GWS*, 21 September 1983, pp. 906–7.

140. Ibid., 24 September 1983, pp. 846–47.

141. Ibid., 24 June 1983, pp. 701–2.

142. Radzialowski, "Workers by Day," p. 21; Prude, "ESOP's Fable," p. 48.

143. Prude, "ESOP's Fable," p. 49.

144. Richard Corrigan makes this argument in "Workers at Weirton Steel," p. 1647.

145. Radzialowski, "Workers by Day," n. 58.

146. Ibid.

147. Lynd, "Why We Opposed the Buy-out," p. 47. Lynd notes that in March 1983, when the ISU and JSC stated that the 32 percent cut was "firm," the USWA agreed to concessions in their basic steel contract amounting to a 9 percent wage cut. If McKinsey's *initial* estimate that a 32 percent cut was required to "achieve parity" with industrywide labor costs was followed, then Weirton workers should have been asked for a further cut of 9 percent, or 41 percent. Instead the opposite occurred, casting more doubt on the veracity of McKinsey's analysis.

148. The estimated hourly labor cost of Weirton workers as of April 1982 was $24.91. According to the American Iron and Steel Institute's monthly reports on steel industry labor costs, other workers earned $22.63 or about 9 percent less than Weirton workers. With the wage and benefit cuts, Weirton's hourly rate of just over $20.00 was slightly lower than USWA plants. See Lynd, "Why We Opposed the Buy-out," and Radzialowski, "Workers by Day," p. 23.

149. As a "leveraged" ESOP, Weirton can pay up to 25 percent of its annual payroll to repay the principal of a loan and take a tax deduction while the tax deductible amount that can be spent on interest has no limit. See Blasi, *Employee Ownership through ESOPs*, pp. 6–8, 48–49.

150. Information pamphlet, 29 October 1982, p. 19 (in author's possession).

151. Lynd, "Why We Opposed the Buy-out," pp. 49–50.

152. Radzialowski, "Workers by Day," p. 23.

153. Prude, "ESOP's Fable," pp. 50, 48, and n. 57.

154. Ibid.

155. Lynd, "Why We Opposed the Buy-out," p. 50.

156. Prude, "ESOP's Fable," and Blasi, *Employee Ownership Through ESOPs*, p. 49.

157. Blasi, *Employee Ownership through ESOPs*. As Blasi notes, this provision provides workers some protection from more highly compensated employees dominating key decisions.

158. The independent directors were; Herbert Elish, a senior vice-president of International Paper Company, formerly vice-president of Citibank and executive director of New York City's Municipal Assistance Corporation; Gordon Hurlbert, president and CEO of GCH Management Services, Inc. of Pittsburgh, and retired president of Westinghouse Electric Company Power Systems; Lawrence Isaacs, vice chairman of Susquehanna University and former chief financial officer of Federated Department Stores, Inc. and Allis Chalmers Corporation; F. James Rechin, group vice-president and general manager of the Aircraft Components Group of TRW, Inc.; Richard F. Schubert, president of the American Red Cross and former vice-chairman and president of Bethlehem Steel Corporation; and Phillip H. Smith, formerly chairman and chief executive of Copperweld Corporation. Lynd, "Why We Opposed the Buy-out," p. 51; Radzialowski, "Workers by Day," n. 61.

159. Jonathan Rowe argues this point in "Weirton Steel," p. 44.

160. Disclosure Document, p. 81.

Chapter 4. Forced Choices III: Employee Participation

1. Corrigan, "ESOPs Are a Tax Dodge," p. 1293.

2. Kenneth Labich, "A Steel Town's Bid to Save Itself," *Fortune*, 18 April 1983, p. 107.

3. Upon a recent visit to Weirton in June 1996 I was told that EPG was now called the Employee Involvement Program.

4. Parker and Slaughter, *Choosing Sides*; Grenier, *Inhuman Relations*; Wells, *Empty Promises*; Fraser, "Industrial Democracy"; Russell, "Forms and Extent of Employee Participation"; Fantasia, Clawson, and Graham, "A Critical View of Worker Participation."

5. For what is perhaps the most extensive treatment of this issue in both an American and international context, see Bendix, *Work and Authority*. For a recent analysis on the impact of computer technology on authority relations, see Zuboff, *In the Age of the Smart Machine*.

6. *GWS*, 11 November 1983.

7. Ibid.

8. *WSB* (n.d.).

9. *GWS*, 17 October 1983.

10. Robert N. Stern, William Foote Whyte, Tove Hammer, and Christopher B. Meek, "The Union and the Transition to Employee Ownership," in *Worker Participation and Ownership: Cooperative Strategies for Strengthening Local Economies*, ed. William F. Whyte et al. (Ithaca. N.Y.: Industrial and Labor Relations Press, Cornell University, 1983), p. 116.

11. Simmons and Mares, *Working Together*, especially pp. 58–62, 259.

12. Ibid., p. 59.

13. Ibid. In 1973 as UAW vice-president, Bluestone worked with Sidney Harman of Harman Industries in Bolivar, Tennessee, to establish a union-management participation project that was quite progressive in its democratic structure. See Daniel Zwerdling, "Democratizing the Workplace: A Case Study," in *The Big Business Reader: Essays on Corporate America*, ed. Mark Green and Robert Massie Jr. (New York: The Pilgrim Press, 1980), pp. 105–19.

14. *Business Week*, 12 November 1984, p. 136.

15. *Independent Weirton*, March 1986, no. 26, p. 5. Ironically, John Kirkwood had served as vice-president of industrial relations at Jones and Laughlin Steel, a company that in 1984 merged with Republic Steel to form LTV Steel, then filed bankruptcy in 1986 and refused to pay pension and health benefits to workers.

16. At the EPG training session I attended, an AMTRAC representative was present to learn more about what he "had heard and read so much about" and how it might be applied in running trains. During an EPG meeting I was shown a letter by a Swedish firm thanking the EPG staff for allowing their representatives to learn more about the participation process at Weirton.

17. Prude, *ESOP's Fable*, p. 59 n. 60.

18. SPC instructed workers in using statistical techniques to improve and monitor the production process. Workers in this program took part in a five-day training session. OIP was more selective in its recruitment of workers and operated on larger organizational projects.

19. These were the strip steel, sheet steel, tin mill, and service/maintenance departments.

20. Senior facilitator, interview with author, July 1988.

21. *EPG Newsletter*, Fall 1986.

22. Actually, with overtime so popular, many people worked more than 41-hour weeks.

23. See Parker and Slaughter, *Choosing Sides*; Wells, *Empty Promises*; Simmons and Mares, *Working Together*; Russell, "Employee Participation."

24. These figures are extrapolated from the summer and fall 1996 EPG Newsletters.

25. *Independent Weirton*, March 1986, n. 26. As of February 23, 1986, total employment was 8,264, including 6,097 hourly; 1,247 salaried nonexempt; 867 salaried nonexempt; and 53 salaried nonexempt excluded. Laid-off individuals whose recall rights had expired totaled 713— 634 hourly, 36 SNE, and 43 exempt—while 51 individuals with recall rights were on layoff status. These figures varied during my research, but I will base my discussion on a rough 8,300 employment figure. According to the 1986 Annual Shareholders Report (pp. 6–7) there were 125 EPG groups comprised of 1,810 members. Oddly, at 15 members per group this figure exceeds the 10–12 member group size noted in the report itself, and still represents only 21 percent of the 8,429 employees listed in the report.

26. According to EPG newsletters in the summer and fall of 1986 there were 94 groups operating, which would make 26 inactive groups. The newsletters try to list as many groups as possible, but some groups may be overlooked. Still, the fall listing shows 28 groups not listed during the summer, and this suggests that more groups, if not all, were probably accounted for.

27. My description of this process is based on *Working Together Works*, an EPG pamphlet distributed to workers during the training session in July 1988.

28. Ibid.

29. Ibid.

30. See Harley Shaiken, *Mexico in the Global Economy* (La Jolla, Calif.: University of California, San Diego, Center for U.S.-Mexican Studies, 1990), pp. 78–81.

31. See Mike Parker, "Industrial Relations Myth and Shop-floor Reality: The "Team Concept" in the Auto Industry," in *Industrial Democracy in America*, ed. Lichtenstein and Harris, p. 261. Also see Mike Parker

and Jane Slaughter, "Management by Stress," *Technology Review*, October 1988, pp. 37–44.

32. Radzialowski, "Workers by Day," p. 29.

33. These were discussed during the EPG training session in July 1988.

34. See Mike Cooley, *Architect or Bee? The Human Price of Technology* (London: Hogarth, 1987).

35. In 1990 contract negotiations, controversial multicrafting and re-classification clauses were narrowly approved by workers 51 percent to 49 percent.

36. As of June 1, 1985, 927 employees had been trained representing 38 active SPC teams throughout all departments. Training was done in eight-hour sessions for five consecutive days.

37. Vicki Smith, "Employee Involvement, Involved Employees: Participative Work Arrangements in a White-Collar Service Occupation," *Social Problems* 43.2 (May 1996): 172–76, argues that in the service occupation she studied workers *do* learn new skills through participation, especially communication skills, that both enhance their self-esteem and may help them move into management. Communication skills may be developed through EPG, though I argue they are limited to technical problem-solving. The self-esteem workers gained in Smith's study emerged from their interaction with clients, but in EPG I argue that although workers' self-esteem may be raised, it also is *tested* through the program (see chapter 5).

38. Parker and Slaughter, *Choosing Sides*; Wells, *Empty Promises;* Milkman, "Labor and Management in Uncertain Times"; Smith, "Employee Involvement, Involved Employees."

39. IBM developed this aspect of "internal communications" in the late 1950s as part of an "open door" policy of labor-management relations. See Nancy Foy, *The IBM World* (London: Eyre Methuen, 1974).

40. *Bridgeport Sunday Post*, 4 October 1987, p. E-9.

41. EPG meeting, July 1988.

42. *Working Together Works*, EPG training session, July 1988.

43. Simmons and Mares, *Working Together*, pp. 234–60. Also see Thomas A. Kochan, Harry C. Katz, and Nancy R. Mower, *Worker Participation and American Unions: Threat or Opportunity?* (Kalamazoo, Mich.:

W. E. Upjohn Institute for Employment Research, 1984), pp. 133–49, 185–96.

44. Parker, "Industrial Relations Myth," p. 255.

45. Bendix, *Work and Authority*, p. 278.

46. Zuboff, *In the Age of the Smart Machine*, p. 242.

47. Quality control is credited to W. Edward Deming, a statistician, who, after being rebuffed by American industrialists, took his ideas to Japan in the 1950s where he has become an "industrial guru" of sorts. For Deming, quality control rests upon "the application of statistical principles and techniques in all states of production directed toward the economic manufacture of a product that is maximally useful and has a market." Statistical analysis would help locate "responsibility squarely where it belongs (with the local operator, the foreman, or at the door of higher management)." Simmons and Mares, *Working Together*, pp. 99–100.

48. See Bendix, *Work and Authority*, pp. 314–16.

Chapter 5. A Fragile Trust: The Normative Order of Employee Participation

1. Barbara and John Ehrenreich use the term "professional-managerial class" in place of my use of technocratic-administrative class, but the two terms are interchangeable in my view. See their "The Professional-Managerial Class," in Pat Walker (ed.), *Between Labor and Capital* (Boston: South End Press, 1979), pp. 5–45. For the Ehrenreichs this class is antagonistic to both capital and the working class in their efforts to rationalize production, they have distinct interests and cultural outlooks, and any divisions between members of this class are minor and negligible in the context of social reproduction. Daniel Bell, *The Coming of Post-Industrial Society* (New York: Basic Books, 1976), saw this rising class of knowledge workers using its privileged institutional influence in benign ways for the betterment of society through more efficient allocation of society's resources. Alvin Gouldner, *The Future of Intellectuals and the Rise of the New Class* (New York: Oxford University Press, 1979), pp. 7–8, agrees with the Ehrenreichs that this new class is "elitist and self-seeking and uses its special knowledge to advance its own interests and power, and to control its own work situation," but he insists that this class is not some "unified subject or a seamless whole" as the Ehrenreichs suggest or as benign as Bell posits.

364   *Notes*

2. For example, between 1983 and 1987 (the first years of Weirton's ESOP), 600,000 to 1.2 million middle- and upper-level executives making $40,000 a year or more lost their jobs; another 200,000 to 300,000 management employees could expect a similar fate by the early 1990s. In 1987, AT&T cut 32,000 from its payroll, of which 11,600 were management positions. GM announced a 25 percent reduction in management and salaried personnel by 1989. Ford called for a 20 percent cut in salaried employment by 1990. See George Russell, "Rebuilding to Survive," *Time*, 16 February 1987, pp. 44–45. This trend has continued throughout the 1990s.

3. Zuboff, *In the Age of the Smart Machine*, p. 397. Also see Vicki Smith, *Managing in the Corporate Interest: Control and Resistance in an American Bank* (Berkeley: University of California Press, 1990).

4. Blumberg, *Industrial Democracy*; Witte, *Democracy, Authority, and Alienation*; Lindenfeld and Rothschild-Whitt, *Workplace Democracy*; Whyte et al., *Worker Participation and Ownership*; Russell, *Sharing Ownership*; Simmons and Mares, *Working Together*; Rosen et al., *Employee Ownership in America*; Bluestone and Bluestone, *Negotiating the Future*.

5. A representative example is John F. Witte's study of a medium-sized electronics firm, *Democracy, Authority, and Alienation*, where he found "moderate participation" to be the best overall description of how much influence workers thought they should have in the workplace.

[T]he proposition that workers want more participation in those decisions that affect their own work areas is supported, but only for those decisions that tend to affect workers on an individual basis. There was little interest in participating in traditional management decisions like profit reinvestment or setting the salaries of supervisors and managers. (p. 28)

Also see Bluestone and Bluestone, *Negotiating the Future*, and Blasi, *Employee Ownership Through ESOPs*, who views this as workers' "dual culture conflict" (see chapter 1 of this book).

6. Alvin Gouldner, *Patterns of Industrial Bureaucracy* (New York: Free Press, 1954).

7. Alvin Gouldner, *Wildcat Strike* (Yellow Springs, Ohio: Antioch Press, 1954).

8. Michael Burawoy, *Manufacturing Consent: Changes in the Labor Process under Monopoly Capitalism* (Chicago: University of Chicago Press, 1982).

9. Ibid., chapter 5, Burawoy notes this as well in his analysis.

10. Sennett and Cobb, *Hidden Injuries*.

11. Zuboff, *In the Age of the Smart Machine*, p. 300.

12. This "trust gap" was not limited to Weirton or hourly wage workers. As Bluestone and Bluestone note, research in the late 1980s on the views of professionals and mid-management personnel in Fortune 500 companies showed alienation among these workers grew to levels customarily reported for blue-collar workers. *Negotiating the Future*, pp. 11–12.

13. See, for example, Elihu Katz and Paul F. Lazarsfeld, *Personal Influence* (New York: Free Press, 1955), especially pp. 82–115.

Chapter 6. Class and Worker Ownership

1. *Tribune-Review*, 4 October 1987.

2. Ibid.

3. Ibid.

4. Ibid.

5. Labich, "A Steel Town's Bid," p. 107.

6. For an elaboration of this view, see Rosen et al., *Employee Ownership in America*, and Simmons and Mares, *Working Together*. See Russell, *Sharing Ownership*, for a critical appraisal.

7. See Kelso and Adler, *The Capitalist Manifesto*.

8. Ibid. Also see Russell, "Forms of Employee Participation," and "Center for Employee Ownership" (nceo@nceo.org.), "Fact Sheet."

9. Blasi's review of the literature confirms this argument; "Employee ownership does not have an automatic effect on employees' reported attitudes about their motivation, work effort, absenteeism, or job satisfaction." Blasi, *Employee Ownership through ESOPs*, p. 34. Also see Blinder in *Paying for Productivity,* for research showing the positive impact of profit-sharing on productivity, though not necessarily on employee attitudes and satisfaction.

10. Salaried classified workers include lab and technical staff that are nonunion and hold "classified" titles. As a privately held company, Weirton Steel was not required to identify these positions, but as a publicly chartered company they would have to be announced or "declassified."

11. Alan Prosswimmer, vice-president and chief financial officer, quoted in the *Independent Weirton*, March 1986, no. 26, p. 1.

12. *Independent Weirton*, March 1986, no. 26, p. 1.

13. The following observations and quotations are from the company's third annual shareholders' meeting held on November 6, 1986, at the Millsop Community Center in Weirton. This was the first meeting to be held in Weirton; the first two shareholders' meetings were held at St. John's Arena in Steubenville, Ohio.

14. For an analysis of the "emotional logic" of community under modern capitalism, see Sennett, *The Fall of Public Man*, chapter 13, especially p. 296, where he argues that this defensiveness in the name of community signals "a bizarre kind of depoliticized withdrawal; the system remains intact, but maybe we can get it to leave our piece of turf alone." Also see Bellah, et al., *Habits of the Heart*, chap. 8.

15. As one Weirton native informed me, the term "Hoopie" is a derogatory reference to native West Virginians and Appalachian poor who worked in the state's wine industry wrapping steel hoops around wine barrels. "Backwoods people," he sighed, "are the poorest of the poor."

16. In describing class relations in Weirton this way I do not mean to impose artificially strict boundaries where more fluid class interactions actually existed, either through family relations or peer networks. However, from interviews and tagging along with friends of different social circles, it was clear to me that Weirton's class structure was more rigid than fluid.

Chapter 7. The Moral Economy of Worker Ownership

1. Until the 1982–83 ESOP negotiations over wage concessions, compensation levels had never been contested in Weirton. If such consternation ever existed during the Weir-Millsop years, it was *not* over millworker pay; even the brief 1934 strike, the reader may recall, was not about wages.

2. While this expectation was more common to men, many women also worked in the mill, at least until marriage. Several elderly women recalled to me their time in the mill and how during World War II women worked the dirtiest and most dangerous jobs.

3. Serrin, *Homestead*, pp. 300–301, documents this practice in the Homestead mills, but he also notes (as do Weirton workers) that manage-

ment often escaped the mill, taking half days to play golf with senior management being the most prominent way to "move up" in the company.

4. Serrin also notes a similar trend of "overmanning" in the Homestead mills during the postwar period, which he attributes to paternalistic nepotism there. Ibid., pp. 288, 303–4.

5. Employment figures from the company were unavailable, but my estimates are from newspaper accounts of the CIO organizing drive (1930–51) and *Weirton Steel Bulletins* (1950–80).

6. Weirton's population in 1930 was 4,480 but it grew rapidly during the Depression, reaching 15,275 in 1940. By 1950 it stood at 24,005 before peaking in 1960 at 28,201. Census data compiled by Lois Aleta Fundis, Reference Librarian, Mary H. Weir Public Library, Weirton.

7. *New York Times*, 22 August 1937.

8. *WSB*, December 1951, p. 21.

9. *New York Times*, 12 April 1938.

10. Ibid.

11. Gouldner, *Patterns of Industrial Bureaucracy*, pp. 45–56.

12. For example, it is likely that workers used the practice of sleeping to enforce informal codes of discipline and authority among one another. As noted in chapter 2, it was not uncommon for CIO agitators to be "set up" by co-workers, so it is quite possible that personal grudges were acted out and group norms enforced by not alerting a sleeper of an approaching supervisor.

13. For a recent analysis of this topic, see Derek Bok, *The Cost of Talent: How Executives and Professionals Are Paid and How It Affects America* (New York: Free Press, 1993).

14. Estimates vary, but in 1990 the average pay for chief executives in the United States was 85 times higher than for workers, while in Japan chief executives received only 17 times more money than a typical worker. And *Business Week* found that the pay of American chief executives increased four times faster between 1980 and 1990 than the pay of average workers (cited in James Coleman and Donald Cressey, *Social Problems* [New York: HarperCollins, 1993], p. 142). Kevin Phillips, *The Politics of Rich and Poor* (New York: Random House, 1990), pp. 179–80, notes that in 1979 CEO salaries were 29 times higher than the average manufacturing worker, rising to 40 times higher in 1985, then up to 93 times higher by 1988. By 1996 accounts of this disparity have reached into the mid to high 100s.

15. *Independent Weirton*, March 1987, p. 2. The paper states that the responses printed are from the first twelve people who answer the question and their responses are not edited.

16. Ibid.

17. Ibid. According to this issue (p. 12), Loughhead's salary was complemented by a bonus that in 1983 "was pro-rated on the basis of a guaranteed $100,000 and he received $41,667 for that first, partial year of his tenure. In 1984 he was guaranteed and paid a bonus of $100,000. After 1984 Loughhead's bonus is calculated on two-tenths of one percent of the corporation's after-tax income before profit-sharing and the contribution to ESOP."

18. Ibid., p. 12.

19. Local histories proudly recall how Thomas Millsop once served as town mayor for a yearly salary of one dollar. However, these histories do not reveal his income from the Weirton mill or National Steel. See Orler, *"Ernest Tener Weir"* and William A. White, "Weirton—Where Freedom Rings," part of a seven-part series in the *Pittsburgh Press*, 1952.

20. Phillips, *Politics of Rich and Poor*, p. 180, notes "there was a negligible correlation between increases in CEO compensation and shareholder gains" in American companies. Bok, *The Cost of Talent*, p. 111, also notes that "a series of studies have shown that the compensation actually paid to CEO's bears very little relation to the record of their companies."

21. For Bok, *The Cost of Talent*, p. 113, "the process of fixing executive compensation is anything but impartial" and he cites one study of large companies showing that "executive pay correlates much more closely to the salaries of members of the compensation committee than it does to the company's performance."

22. Steve Tennant, letter to the editor, *WDT*, 26 May 1987, p. 4.

23. Ibid.

24. When a new position is created or existing jobs are recombined, representatives of the company, union, and industrial relations negotiate the position and its classification (and subsequent wage rate). Although Industrial Relations was supposed to serve as a mediator between company and union, workers all agreed that it most often sided with the company.

25. The remaining critical skills raises listed went to two department supervisors, three industrial engineers, a general supervisor in human resources, a supervisor in personnel, a manager in medical/employee benefits, and a loss prevention coordinator.

26. In 1986, $20.3 million was distributed from 1985 profits, while in 1987, $15 million was awarded in profit sharing. *Independent Weirton*, March 1987, p. 1.

27. Max Weber, *The Protestant Ethic and the Spirit of Capitalism* (New York: Charles Scribner's Sons, 1976), p. 181.

28. This survey by New York psychologist David Sirota, entitled "A Report on Employee Satisfaction, Attitudes and Intentions, Based on a Survey Conducted During April 1989," is cited in James B. Lieber, *Friendly Takeover*, pp. 311–12. Lieber notes (pp. 288–89) that the ISU barely approved allowing it because of fears of how the information might be used by the company.

29. Ibid., p. 313.

30. *WDT*, 24 December 1986, p. 1.

31. Gouldner, *Patterns of Industrial Bureaucracy*, p. 51. Also see how "getting it from the mill" was condoned in the Homestead mills near Pittsburgh; Serrin, *Homestead*, pp. 299–300.

32. For an application of these concepts to urban space, see John R. Logan and Harvey L. Molotch, *Urban Fortunes: The Political Economy of Place* (Berkeley: University of California Press, 1987), especially chapter 4, "Homes: Exchange and Sentiment in the Neighborhood."

33. Serrin, *Homestead*, p. 300.

34. Lieber, *Friendly Takeover* (p. 68), notes that former president Jack Redline instituted gate checks in 1977 "to stop stealing and false invoicing, which he estimated cost $10 million annually. . . . More than fifty employees were fired."

35. *Independent Weirton*, February 1987, p. 1.

36. Ibid.

37. Ibid., March 1987, p.1.

38. Ibid., February 1987, p.1.

39. *WDT*, 8 July 1987, p. 1.

40. Ibid., 29 July 1987, p. 1. These directors were quoted anonymously. James Lieber, *Friendly Takeover*, pp. 269–70, is clear on the reasons for Loughhead's departure—he was fired. Lieber also notes, "the vote was unanimous, with the union representatives falling into line."

41. *WDT*, 29 July 1987, p. 1.

42. Local police, said many residents, often "looked the other way" especially when well-known residents went astray of the law. A social worker deplored how drunkenness was accepted in town, and how police would often just pick up intoxicated drivers and "take 'em home." For more serious offenses, I was told, a much respected local attorney could "get you off the hook" with a phone call or two. This resembles William Foote Whyte's observation in *Street Corner Society* (Chicago: University of Chicago Press, 1943, 1955), p. 138, that "the primary function of the police department [was] not the enforcement of law but the regulation of illegal activities."

43. *Miami Herald*, 11 February 1986.

44. Ibid.

45. Ibid.

46. Ibid.

47. Ibid.

48. Whyte, *Street Corner Society*, pp. 140–46.

Chapter 8. The Struggle for Control

1. Lieber, *Friendly Takeover*, p. 283.

2. Staughton Lynd anticipated this following the ESOP deal in 1984 (see chapter 3).

3. By agreeing to sell 4.5 million shares publicly, workers spared management an estimated $40 million cost of buying back the shares as the original ESOP had required. See "How Can We Be Laid Off If We Own The Company?" *Business Week*, 9 September 1991, p. 66.

4. Ibid.

5. Ibid.

6. Ibid.

7. Named as defendants were company president Elish, the current board of directors (excluding ISU president Glyptis), former board members Irving Bluestone, Virgil Thompson, David Robertson, and Willkie, Farr, and Gallagher, company general counsel. *WI*, 7 August 1992, p. 1.

8. Elish was also charged for withholding information about the contractual and bond problems from the board of directors, and Wilkie, Farr

and Gallagher, for not advising company officials to require a contract and performance bond. Ibid., p. 7.

9. Ibid., 12 November 1992, p. 1.

10. Ibid., 24 July 1992, p.1.

11. *WDT*, 9 July 1992, p. 1.

12. Ibid., 12 June 1992, p. 1; 8 August 1992, p. 1.

13. According to Robert Lenzner and Kate Bohner, "Divided Loyalty?" *Forbes*, 30 August 1993, pp. 45–46, "by 1992, Willkie Farr defended foreign companies in 34 of the antidumping suits brought by the big U.S. steel companies. Its clients include Stelco, Canada's largest steel company, Taiwan's China Steel Corp. and the Brazilian Iron & Steel Institute. On July 27 the foreigners scored big when the International Trade Commission rules that the companies Willkie Farr represented didn't have to pay any damages."

14. *SHS*, 12 May 1992, p. 1. Elish also claimed that when Willkie, Farr and Gallagher established a Washington office in 1984 to work on trade matters, Sperry alerted former Weirton Steel president Robert Loughhead, who at that time saw no conflict of interest.

15. Lenzner and Bohner, "Divided Loyalty?" p. 45. Outside director Smith hired another law firm, Grand Rapids, Michigan-based Varnum, Riddering, Schmidt & Howlett, to provide an independent assessment of Willkie Farr's compromising role. The report, which was provided to Weirton board members just before their July 1992 meeting, described Willkie Farr's defense that a "Chinese wall" exists between its Washington office and its New York office that receives about $1 million a year for Weirton Steel's legal work as "superficial and incomplete."

16. Ibid. The *Forbes* article also notes (p. 46) that "Sperry was instrumental in getting Elish in as chief executive officer in 1987, a position that paid Elish about $700,000 [in 1992]."

17. Ibid., p. 46. Company spokesperson Rick Garran denied allegations reported in the *Wall Street Journal* that Smith was dismissed because he asked tough questions, saying that Smith's replacement came because the company *reactivated* a policy for rotating committee chairmen every two years and Smith's tenure was up. *WI*, 25 November 1992, p. 7.

18. *WDT*, 18 November 1992, p. 1.

19. Ibid., 21 April 1993, p. 3.

20. Ibid.

21. Ibid.

22. Ibid.

23. Ibid.

24. *WDT*, 20 November 1992, p. 1.

25. On November 25, 1992, the *Wheeling Intelligencer*, p. 1, cited a *Wall Street Journal* report that the ISU and a few of Weirton's thirteen directors wanted to replace Elish "through a proxy battle or other means," something Elish clearly understood as a threat to his leadership.

26. *WDT*, 29 April 1993, p. 1.

27. Ibid.

28. Ibid.

29. Ibid.

30. *WI*, 27 May 1993, p. 1. The *Intelligencer* also reported that the crowd was visibly disappointed whenever the vote was read on the liability amendment, an issue that curtailed shareholders' recourse against fiduciary irresponsibility. Where other directors received about 85 percent of the vote, Elish got only 57 percent and the liability amendment only 52 percent.

31. Ibid., p. 7.

32. *WDT*, 2 September 1993, p. 1. The stock authorization would also set aside 30 million shares for worker-owners exclusively.

33. Ibid., 22 October 1993, p. 1.

34. Ibid., 23 September 1993, p. 1.

35. Ibid., 22 October 1993, p. 1.

36. Ibid., 23 September 1993, p. 1.

37. *SHS*, 3 August 1993, p. 1.

38. *WDT*, 16 October 1993, p. 1.

39. *WI*, 19 August 1993, p. 1.

40. Ibid.

41. Ibid.

42. *WI*, 23 October 1993, p. 1. The additional 30 million shares would be used for future employee programs, such as stock purchase plans.

43. Ibid.

44. *WDT*, 26 October 1993, p. 1.

45. Ibid., 28 October 1993, p. 1.

46. Ibid.

47. Ibid.

48. *WI*, 1 December 1993, p. 11.

49. *Pittsburgh Post-Gazette*, 9 April 1994, p. B-7.

50. Ibid.

51. Ibid., 7 April 1994, p. 3.

52. *WDT*, 27 May 1994, p. 1. The vote was 33,763,724 shares in favor and 4,962,776 against, with more than 75 percent of the participants in the 1984 and 1989 ESOP returning ballots.

53. *WI*, 14 April 1994, p. 9. According to the *Intelligencer*, independent directors cannot serve if they have been advisors, consultants, or have had any financial dealings with the company, its subsidiaries, affiliates, or the ISU within a two-year period prior to appointment.

54. *WDT*, 14 April 1994, p. 5a.

55. *WDT*, 12 April 1994, p. 1. Sperry had been asked to resign because his firm, Willkie, Farr and Gallagher, which had provided legal services to Weirton Steel since the ESOP negotiations in 1983, advised foreign firms directly competing with Weirton Steel.

56. *WI*, 14 April 1994, p. 9.

57. Other changes that increased worker-owners' influence on the board included distribution of all information and data on company business to board members prior to meetings; complete access of board members to senior management; more opportunity for board members to shape the agenda of board and committee meetings; and a review of the skills and characteristics of board members by the nominating committee. *WDT*, 14 April 1994, p. 5a.

58. The settlement, which awaited an August 9 hearing, found roughly $12 million in damages rather than the plaintiff's original claim of $30 million. It would award $6.25 million to be applied to the company's modernization debt. Ibid., 30 June 1994, p. 1. In April 1993, five of

the seventeen defendants were released from liability in the suit. They were Phillip Smith, Virgil Thompson, Robert D'Anniballe, David Gould, and Warren Bartel. *WI*, 14 April 1994, p. 1.

59. *Herald-Star*, 27 October 1994, p. 1.

60. *WDT*, 4 November 1994, p. 1.

61. Ibid.

62. *The Intelligencer*, 4 November 1994, p. 19.

63. *Herald-Star*, 27 October 1994, p. 1.

64. *The Intelligencer*, 17 November 1994, p. 33. The ad also named the directors who supported Elish; Harvey Sperry, Tom Sturges, Gordon Hulbert, and Dick Schubet.

65. *Herald-Star*, 18 November 1994, pp. 4-D, 5-A.

66. *The Daily Times*, 27 January 1995, p. 1 (formerly the *Weirton Daily Times*).

67. Ibid., p. 5.

68. Ibid., 17 March 1995, p. 1.

69. Ibid.

70. Ibid., 6 April 1995, p. 1.

71. *The Intelligencer*, 6 April 1995, p. 13.

72. *The Daily Times*, 6 April 1995, p. 1.

73. *Business Week*, 18 March 1996, p. 102.

74. *The Daily Times*, 20 March 1996, p. 1.

75. Ibid.

76. Ibid., n.d..

Chapter 9. Conclusion

1. Sexism was one element of control, namely, male control, that was often rejected by the women I knew and interviewed. Women constantly struggled against manifestations of sexual inequality, from excessive drinking to domestic violence, to the EPG group that sought a reevaluation of promotion policies, to a policy banning pornography in work areas,

something many male workers claimed was an "intrusion" into the (traditionally male) mill culture.

2. *The Daily Times*, 26 January 1996, p. 1, and 8 March 1996, p. 5a.

3. On northwest Indiana, see Bruce Nissen, "Shutdown of a Steel Foundry," in *Grand Designs: The Impact of Corporate Strategies on Workers, Unions, and Communities*, ed. Charles Craypo and Bruce Nissen (Ithaca, N.Y.: ILR Press, 1993), pp. 138–64; on Youngstown, see Staughton Lynd, *The Fight against Shutdowns*, Lawrence E. Rothstein, *Plant Closings*, and Gar Alperovitz and Jeff Faux, "The Youngstown Project," in *Workplace Democracy*, pp. 353–69; on the Pittsburgh region, see Dale A. Hathaway, *Can Workers Have a Voice*; for a comparison of community responses to plant closings in Louisville, Kentucky, Waterloo, Iowa, and the Monongahela Valley south of Pittsburgh, see John Portz, *The Politics of Plant Closings*; on Chicago's Southeast Side, see David Bensman and Roberta Lynch, *Rusted Dreams*; on Weirton, Youngstown, and South Chicago, see Sharon Zukin, *Landscapes of Power: From Detroit to Disney World* (Berkeley: University of California Press, 1991).

4. Labor Research Review, *Workers as Owners*; Frank Lindenfeld, "Workers' Cooperatives: Remedy for Plant Closings?" in *Workplace Democracy*, pp. 337–52.

5. Zukin, *Landscapes of Power*, p. 100.

6. Ibid., p. 82.

7. Ibid., p. 85.

8. Ibid.

9. Ibid.

10. See Russell, *Sharing Ownership*, and Hansmann, "When Does Worker Ownership Work."

11. Zukin, *Landscapes of Power*, p. 85.

12. Edwards, *Contested Terrain*, pp. 152–62. Also see Donald Wells, *Empty Promises*, chapter 6, and Fantasia, Clawson, and Graham, "A Critical View of Employee Participation."

13. Interview with local resident. Another program, Total Quality Management, involved 90 groups with 900 active employees but neither of these programs move beyond EPG boundaries.

14. Blasi, *Employee Ownership through ESOPs*, p. 45.

15. Russell, *Sharing Ownership*, p. 218.

16. See, C. George Benello, *From the Ground Up: Essays on Grassroots and Workplace Democracy* (Boston: South End Press, 1992); *Grassroots Economic Organizing Newsletter*, Ecological Democracy Institute of North America, New Haven, Connecticut; *Labor Research Review*, Midwest Center for Labor Research, Chicago, Illinois; and the Federation for Industrial Retention and Renewal Newsletter, 3411 W. Diversey Ave., #10, Chicago Illinois, 60647.

17. See note 3.

18. See Robert A. Dahl, *A Preface to Economic Democracy* (Berkeley: University of California Press, 1985). Also see Bellah et al., *Habits of the Heart*, chapter 11, and Blasi, *Employee Ownership: Revolution or Ripoff*, chapter 9.

19. Judy Wajcman, *Women in Control: Dilemmas of a Workers' Cooperative* (Milton Keynes, England: The Open University Press, 1983).

20. Fantasia, *Cultures of Solidarity*, pp. 160–66. Also see Peg Pearson and Jake Baker, "Seattle Workers' Brigade: History of a Collective," in *Workplace Democracy*, ed. Lindenfeld and Rothschild-Whitt, pp. 279–89. For a classic example, see W. Lloyd Warner, *American Life: Dream and Reality* (Chicago: University of Chicago Press, 1962), especially chapter 6.

21. Bluestone and Bluestone, *Negotiating the Future*, p. 184.

22. *WDT*, 29 December 1993, p. 18.

Bibliography

Abercrombie, Nicholas, and Stephen Hill. "Paternalism and Patronage." *British Journal of Sociology* 27, 1976: 413–29.

Aliquippa: Struggle for Survival in a Pittsburgh Milltown 1984 and Before. Pittsburgh: School of Social Work, University of Pittsburgh, 1984.

Baritz, Loren. *The Servants of Power*. Middleton, Conn.: Wesleyan University Press, 1960.

Bell, Daniel. *The Coming of Post-Industrial Society*. New York: Basic Books, 1976.

Bellah, Robert N., Richard Madsen, William M. Sullivan, Ann Swidler, and Steven M. Tipton. *Habits of the Heart: Individualism and Commitment in American Life*. Berkeley, Calif.: University of California Press, 1985.

Bendix, Reinhard. *Work and Authority in Industry*. New York: Harper & Row, 1963.

Benello, C. George. *From the Ground Up: Essays on Grassroots and Workplace Democracy*. Boston: South End Press, 1992.

Bensman, David and Roberta Lynch. *Rusted Dreams: Hard Times in a Steel Community*. New York: McGraw-Hill, 1987.

Blasi, Joseph Raphael. *Employee Ownership through ESOPs: Implications for the Public Corporation*. New York: Pergamon Press, 1987.

———. *Employee Ownership: Revolution or Ripoff?* New York: Harper Business, 1988.

Bluestone, Barry and Irving Bluestone. *Negotiating the Future: A Labor Perspective on American Business*. New York: Basic Books, 1992.

Bluestone, Barry and Bennett Harrison. *The Deindustrialization of America: Plant Closings, Community Abandonment, and the Dismantling of Basic Industry*. New York: Basic Books, 1982.

Blumberg, Paul. *Industrial Democracy: The Sociology of Participation*. New York: Schocken Books, 1973.

Bok, Derek. *The Cost of Talent: How Executives and Professionals Are Paid and How It Affects America*. New York: The Free Press, 1993.

Boyte, Harry C. *The Backyard Revolution: Understanding the New Citizen Movement*. Philadelphia: Temple University Press, 1980.

Braverman, Harry. *Labor and Monopoly Capital*. New York: Monthly Review Press, 1974.

Brody, David. *Labor in Crisis: The Steel Strike of 1919*. Philadelphia: J. B. Lippincott & Company, 1965.

Burawoy, Michael. "Karl Marx and the Satanic Mills: Factory Politics under Early Capitalism in England, the United States, and Russia." *American Journal of Sociology* 90.1, 1984: 247–82.

———. *Manufacturing Consent: Changes in the Labor Process under Monopoly Capitalism*. Chicago: University of Chicago Press, 1982.

Coleman, James and Donald Cressey. *Social Problems*. 5th ed. New York: HarperCollins, 1993.

Committee for Justice. *Citizen Police Review Project*. Steubenville, Ohio: Committee for Justice, n.d.

Commons, John, David J. Saposs, Helen L. Sumner, E. B. Mittleman, H. E. Hoagland, John B. Andrews, and Selig Perlman, eds. *History of Labor in the United States*. 4 vols. New York: Macmillan, 1918–35.

Conte, Michael A. and Jan Svejnar. "The Performance Effects of Employee Ownership Plans." *Paying for Productivity: A Look at the Evidence*, ed. Alan S. Blinder. Washington, D.C.: The Brookings Institution, 1990.

Cooley, Mike. *Architect or Bee? The Human Price of Technology*. London: Hogarth, 1987.

Corrigan, Richard. "ESOPs Are a Tax Dodge to Some and a Labor-Management Plus to Others." *National Journal*, 1 June 1985.

———. "Workers at Weirton Steel See Only One Way to Save Their Failing Plant: Buy It." *National Journal*, 13 August 1983.

Dahl, Robert A. *A Preface to Economic Democracy*. Berkeley: University of California Press, 1985.

Davis, Mike. *Prisoners of the American Dream*. New York: Verso Press, 1988.

Dore, Ronald. *British Factory-Japanese Factory: The Origins of National Diversity in Industrial Relations*. Berkeley: University of California Press, 1973.

Dudley, Kathryn Marie. *The End of the Line: Lost Jobs, New Lives in Postindustrial America*. Chicago: University of Chicago Press, 1994.

Edwards, Richard. *Contested Terrain: The Transformation of the Workplace in the Twentieth Century*. New York: Basic Books, 1979.

Ehrenreich, Barbara and John Ehrenreich. "The Professional-Managerial Class." *Between Labor and Capital*, ed. Pat Walker. Boston: South End Press, 1979.

Erikson, Kai T. *Everything in Its Path: Destruction of Community in the Buffalo Creek Flood*. New York: Simon & Schuster, 1976.

"Ernest Tener Weir." In *Dictionary of National Biography*. New York: Oxford University Press, 1971.

Fantasia, Rick. *Cultures of Solidarity: Consciousness, Action, and Contemporary American Workers*. Berkeley: University of California Press, 1988.

Fantasia, Rick, Dan Clawson, and Gregory Graham. "A Critical View of Worker Participation in American Industry." *Work and Occupations* 15, November 1988: 468–88.

Foner, Philip S. *Organized Labor and the Black Worker, 1619–1981*. New York: International Publishers, 1982.

Foy, Nancy. *The IBM World*. London: Eyre Methuen, 1974.

Fraser, Steve. "Industrial Democracy in the 1980's." *Socialist Review*, 72, November–December 1983.

Gans, Herbert. *The War against the Poor: The Underclass and Antipoverty Policy*. New York: Basic Books, 1995.

Gaventa, John. *Power and Powerlessness: Quiescence and Rebellion in an Appalachian Valley*. Urbana: University of Illinois Press, 1980.

Genovese, Eugene. *Roll Jordan Roll: The World the Slaves Made*. New York: Vintage Press, 1976.

Gillespie, Richard. *Manufacturing Knowledge: A History of the Hawthorne Experiments*. Cambridge: Cambridge University Press, 1991.

Goldstein, Don. "Saving Jobs, But at What Price?" *Nation*, 10 December 1983.

Gouldner, Alvin W. *The Future of Intellectuals and the Rise of the New Class*. New York: Oxford University Press, 1979.

———. *Patterns of Industrial Bureaucracy*. New York: The Free Press, 1954.

———. *Wildcat Strike*, Yellow Springs, Ohio: Antioch Press, 1954.

Green, Mark, and Robert Massie Jr., eds. *The Big Business Reader: Essays on Corporate America*. New York: The Pilgrim Press, 1980.

Grenier, Guillermo J. *Inhuman Relations: Quality Circles and Anti-Unionism in American Industry*. Philadelphia: Temple University Press, 1988.

Gusfield, Joseph. *Community: A Critical Response*. New York: Harper Colophon Books, 1975.

Gutman, Herbert. *Work, Culture, and Society in Industrializing America*. New York: Vintage Books, 1977.

Halle, David. *America's Working Man*. Chicago: University of Chicago Press, 1984.

Hammer, Tove Helland, Robert M. Stern, and Michael A. Gurdon. "Worker Ownership and Attitudes towards Participation." In *Workplace Democracy and Social Change*, ed. Frank Lindenfeld and Joyce Rothschild-Whitt. Boston: Porter Sargent Publishers, 1982.

Hansmann, Henry. "When Does Worker Ownership Work? ESOPs, Law Firms, Codetermination, and Economic Democracy." *The Yale Law Journal* 99.8, June 1990: 1749–1816.

Hathaway, Dale A. *Can Workers Have a Voice? The Politics of Deindustrialization in Pittsburgh*. University Park: Pennsylvania State University Press, 1993.

Heckscher, Charles C. *The New Unionism: Employee Involvement in the Changing Corporation*. New York: Basic Books, 1988.

Hill, Stephen. *Competition and Control at Work: The New Industrial Society*. London: Heinemann Educational Books, 1981.

Hirshhorn, Larry. *Beyond Mechanization*. Cambridge; MIT Press, 1984.

Hobsbawm, Eric. *Primitive Rebels: Studies in Archaic Forms of Social Movement in the Nineteenth and Twentieth Centuries*. New York: Norton, 1959.

Hunter, James Davison. *Culture Wars: The Struggle to Define America*. New York: Basic Books, 1991.

Ingham, John N. "Ernest Tener Weir." In *Bibliographical Dictionary of American Business Leaders*. Westport, Conn.: Greenwood Press, 1983.

Jackman, Mary R. *The Velvet Glove: Paternalism and Conflict in Gender, Class and Race Relations*. Berkeley: University of California Press, 1994.

Katz, Elihu and Paul F. Lazarsfeld. *Personal Influence*. New York: The Free Press, 1955.

Kelly, Maryellen and Bennett Harrison. "Unions, Technology, and Labor-Management Cooperation." In *Unions and Economic Competitiveness*, ed. Lawrence Mishel and Paula B. Voos. Armonk, N.Y.: Sharpe, 1992.

Kelso, Louis O. and Mortimer J. Adler. *The Capitalist Manifesto*. New York: Random House, 1958.

Kelso, Louis O. and Patricia Hetter Kelso. *Democracy and Economic Power*. Cambridge: Ballinger Publishing Company, 1986.

Kleinig, John. *Paternalism*. Totowa, N.J.: Rowman and Allanheld, 1984.

Kochan, Thomas A., Harry C. Katz, and Nancy R. Mower. *Worker Participation and American Unions: Threat or Opportunity?* Kalamazoo, Mich.: W. E. Upjohn Institute for Employment Research, 1984.

Labich, Kenneth. "A Steel Town's Bid To Save Itself." *Fortune,* 18 April 1983.

Lawler III, Edward E., Susan Albers Mohrman, and Gerald E. Ledford Jr. *Employee Involvement and Total Quality Management: Practices and Results in Fortune 1000 Companies.* San Francisco: Josey-Bass Publishers, 1992.

Levine, David I. and Laura D'Andrea Tyson. "Participation, Productivity, and the Firm's Environment." In *Paying for Productivity: A Look at the Evidence,* ed. Alan S. Blinder. Washington, D.C.: The Brookings Institution, 1990.

Lichtenstein, John. "The Darker Side of the Proposed Employee Buy-out of Weirton Steel." Unpublished draft analysis presented to the Weirton Steel Rank-and-File Committee.

Lichtenstein, Nelson and Howell John Harris, eds. *Industrial Democracy in America: The Ambiguous Promise.* Cambridge: Cambridge University Press, 1991.

Lieber, James B. *Friendly Takeover: How an Employee Buyout Saved a Steel Town.* New York: Viking Press, 1995.

Lindenfeld, Frank and Joyce Rothschild-Whitt, eds. *Workplace Democracy and Social Change.* Boston: Porter Sargent Publishers, 1982.

Logan, John R. and Harvey L. Molotch. *Urban Fortunes: The Political Economy of Place.* Berkeley: University of California Press, 1987.

Lynd, Staughton. *The Fight against Shutdowns: Youngstown's Steel Mill Closings.* San Pedro, Calif.: Singlejack Books, 1982.

———. "Why We Opposed the Buy-out at Weirton Steel." *Labor Research Review.* Spring, vol. 1, n.6. Chicago: Midwest Center for Labor Research, 1985.

Lyon, Larry. *The Community in Urban Society.* Lexington, Mass.: D.C. Heath & Company, 1989.

Madsen, Richard. *Morality and Power in a Chinese Village.* Berkeley: University of California Press, 1984.

McKinsey & Company, Inc. *Assessing the Feasibility of an Independent Weirton Steel.* Washington, D.C.: McKinsey & Company, Inc., July 26, 1982.

———. *Assessing the Feasibility of an Independent Weirton Steel: Executive Summary.* Washington, D.C.: McKinsey & Company, Inc., n.d.

McLaurin, Melton Alonza. *Paternalism and Protest: Southern Cotton Mill Workers and Organized Labor, 1875–1905.* Westport, Conn.: Greenwood Publishing Corp., 1971.

Milkman, Ruth. "Labor and Management in Uncertain Times: Renegotiating the Social Contract." In *America at Century's End*, ed. Alan Wolfe. Berkeley: University of California Press, 1991.

Montgomery, David. *Workers' Control in America*. Cambridge: Cambridge University Press, 1979.

Newby, Howard. *The Deferential Worker: A Study of Farm Workers in East Anglia*. London: Allen Lane, 1977.

———. "Paternalism and Capitalism." In *Industrial Society: Class, Cleavage and Control*, ed. Richard Scase. New York: St. Martin's Press, 1977.

Newman, Katherine. *Falling from Grace*. New York: Free Press, 1988.

Nissen, Bruce. "Shutdown of a Steel Foundry." In *Grand Designs: The Impact of Corporate Strategies on Workers, Unions, and Communities*, ed. Charles Craypo and Bruce Nissen. Ithaca, N.Y.: ILR Press, 1993, pp. 138–64.

Noble, David. *Forces of Production: A Social History of Industrial Automation*. New York: Alfred A. Knopf, 1984.

Orler, Inez. "Ernest Tener Weir: Industrialist, Founder, and Philanthropist." Unpublished manuscript, 1979.

———. *Frontiersman ESOP*. Poisons, W.Va.: McClain Printing, 1984.

———. "A Tribute to John C. Williams." Unpublished manuscript, n.d.

Parker, Mike and Jane Slaughter. *Choosing Sides: Unions and the Team Concept*. Boston: South End Press, 1988.

———. "Management by Stress." *Technology Review*, October 1988, pp. 37–44.

Phillips, Kevin. *The Politics of Rich and Poor*. New York: Random House, 1990.

Piore, Michael J. and Charles P. Sabel. *The Second Industrial Divide*. New York: Basic Books, 1984.

Piven, Frances Fox and Richard A. Cloward. *Poor People's Movements: Why They Succeed, How They Fail*. New York: Vintage Books, 1979.

Portz, John. *The Politics of Plant Closings*. Lawrence: University of Kansas Press, 1990.

Prude, Jonathan "ESOP's Fable: How Workers Bought a Steel Mill in Weirton, West Virginia, and What Good It Did Them," *Socialist Review* 14.6, 1984: 35.

Radzialowski, Thad. "Workers by Day, Owners by Night: The ESOP at Weirton Steel." Paper delivered at the National Meeting, Labor History Society, Wayne State University, Detroit, Mich., October 18, 1984.

Rosen, Corey M., Katherine J. Klein, and Karen M. Young. *Employee Ownership in America: The Equity Solution*. Lexington, Mass.: D.C. Heath & Co., 1986.

Rothstein, Lawrence E. *Plant Closings: Power, Politics, and Workers.* Dover, Mass.: Auburn House, 1986.

Rowe, Jonathan. "Weirton Steel: Buying Out the Bosses." *Washington Monthly*, January 1984.

Rude, George. *Ideology and Popular Protest.* New York: Pantheon Books, 1980.

Russell, George. "Rebuilding to Survive." *Time.* 16 February 1987.

Russell, Raymond. "Forms and Extent of Employee Participation in the Contemporary United States." *Work and Occupations* 15, November 1988: 374–95.

————. *Sharing Ownership in the Workplace.* Albany: State University of New York Press, 1985.

Sartorius, Rolf, ed. *Paternalism.* Minneapolis: University of Minnesota Press, 1983.

Sennett, Richard. *Authority.* New York: Vintage Books, 1981.

————. *The Fall of Public Man.* New York: Vintage Books, 1978.

Sennett, Richard and Jonathan Cobb. *The Hidden Injuries of Class.* New York: Vintage Books, 1973.

Serrin, William. *Homestead: The Glory and Tragedy of an American Steel Town.* New York: Times Books, 1992.

Shaiken, Harley. *Mexico in the Global Economy.* La Jolla, Calif.: University of California San Diego, Center for U.S.-Mexican Studies, 1990.

————. *Work Transformed: Automation and Labor in the Computer Age.* New York: Holt, Rinehart and Winston, 1985.

Simmons, John and William Mares. *Working Together: Employee Participation in Action.* New York: New York University Press, 1985.

Smith, Vicki. *Managing in the Corporate Interest: Control and Resistance in an American Bank.* Berkeley: University of California Press, 1990.

————. "Employee Involvement, Involved Employees: Participative Work Arrangements in a White-Collar Service Occupation." *Social Problems* 43.2, May 1996: 172–76.

Stern, Robert N. "Participation by Representation: Workers on Boards of Directors in the United States and Abroad." *Work and Occupations* 15.4, November 1988: 396–422.

Stone, Bob. "Employee Stock Ownership at UAL." *Grassroots Economic Organizing Newsletter*, New Haven, Conn., May–June, 1995: 8–10.

"The National Center for Employee Ownership," 1996, nceo@nceo.org.

Thompson, Edward P. "The Moral Economy of the English Crowd." *Past and Present* 50, 1971.

————. "Patrician Society, Plebeian Culture." *Journal of Social History* 7, 1974: 76–136.

Wajcman, Judy. *Women in Control: Dilemmas of a Workers' Co-operative.* Milton Keynes, England: The Open University Press, 1983.

Walkowitz, Daniel J. *Worker City, Company Town*. Urbana: University of Illinois Press, 1978.

Warner, W. Lloyd. *American Life: Dream and Reality*. Chicago: University of Chicago Press, 1962.

Weber, Max. *The Protestant Ethic and the Spirit of Capitalism*. New York: Charles Scribner's Sons, 1976.

Wells, Donald M. *Empty Promises: Quality of Worklife Programs and the Labor Movement*. New York: Monthly Review Press, 1987.

White, William A. "Amazing Weirton," seven-part series. *Pittsburgh Press* (1952).

Whyte, William Foote. *Street Corner Society*. Chicago: University of Chicago Press, 1943, 1955.

Whyte, William Foote, Tove Helland Hammer, Christopher B. Meek, Reed Nelson, and Robert N. Stern. *Worker Participation and Ownership: Cooperative Strategies for Strengthening Local Economies*. Ithaca, N.Y.: Industrial and Labor Relations Press, Cornell University, 1983.

Williams, Raymond. *Marxism and Literature*. Oxford: Oxford University Press, 1977.

Witte, John F. *Democracy, Authority, and Alienation in Work: Workers' Participation in an American Corporation*. Chicago: University of Chicago Press, 1980.

Wood, Ellen Meiksins. "The Politics of Theory and the Concept of Class: E. P. Thompson and His Critics." *Studies in Political Economy* 9, 1982: 45–75.

Wood, Gordon S. "Inventing American Capitalism." *New York Review of Books*, 9 June 1994, 44–49.

Wright, Erik Olin. *Class Structure and Income Distribution*. New York: Academic Press, 1979.

Zuboff, Shoshana. *In the Age of the Smart Machine*. New York: Basic Books, 1988.

Zukin, Sharon. *Landscapes of Power: From Detroit to Disney World*. Berkeley: University of California Press, 1991.

Film

The Great Weirton Stee(a)l. First Run Features. 1984.

Newspapers and Magazines

Bridgeport Sunday Post.
Business Week.

Fortune.
Independent Weirton.
Life.
Miami Herald.
New York Times.
Pittsburgh Post-Gazette.
Pittsburgh Press.
Steubenville Herald-Star.
Time.
Weirton Daily Times.
Weirton Intelligencer.
Weirton Steel Bulletin.

Index

Abercrombie, Nicholas, 26
Adler, Mortimer (*The Capitalist Manifesto*), 17
AFL (American Federation of Labor), 45, 50, 62
Amalgamated Association of Iron, Steel, and Tin Workers (AAISTW), 51, 57–61, 63, 65, 217, 347n. 46
Arrango, Richard: and Concerned Steelworkers of Weirton Steel, 127, 129; and ISU vote for ESOP feasibility study, 92–93; as JSC member, 85; loss of ISU presidency to Bish, 98–99, 315, 332

Bancroft, Ron, 102–103
Bauman, Steve, 94, 108, 116, 129
Bell, Thomas (*Out of This Furnace*), 79
Bellah, Robert (*Habits of the Heart*), 90
Bendix, Reinhard, 28, 53; *Work and Authority in Industry,* 172

Bish, Walter: and ESOP feasibility study, 110; and mill scandal, 265; and RFC appendix lawsuit, 121–22; as ESOP board member, 138, 278; election of, as ISU president, 98–100, 129, 325; meeting with local clergy, 117, 119; re-election loss of, 293–94, 296, 315, 326, 332; support for critical skills pay raises, 259–60, 311, 312; support for EPG, 147, 151
Blasi, Joseph, 20, 24, 328, 338nn. 4, 5
Bluestone, Barry and Irving, 23, 334
Bluestone, Irving: as ESOP board member, 138; views on employee participation, 148, 360n. 13
Brenneisen, William, 311, 314
Brody, David, 47
Brooke County, 7, 282, 285
Burawoy, Michael, 27, 208
Business Week, 315, 318

387

CIO (Congress of Industrial Organizations): organizing at Weirton, 41, 60, 62–71, 124, 251–52, 367n. 12

Clarksburg, WV, 42–43, 45, 51, 56, 58

class: and community in Weirton, 4, 13, 32, 35–36, 227, 229, 233, 237–39, 244, 258, 266, 270, 289–92, 294, 300, 306, 308–309, 314–18, 322–24; 329–35; and ESOP, 16, 20, 35–36, 128, 180–81, 229, 233, 237–39, 244, 258, 266, 270, 289–92, 294, 313, 314–18, 325, 327, 329–35; and mill theft, 266, 270, 290; and paternalism, 4, 25–26, 28, 29–30, 33, 40, 45, 54, 60–61, 87–88, 91, 93, 128, 239, 258, 270, 290–92, 316–17, 321–23, 330, 334; and social relations in Weirton, 7, 44, 87–88, 125, 128, 282, 366n. 16; as acted out through ISU, 93, 292, 294, 306, 312, 314–15, 325–26, 332, 334–35; as culture of solidarity, 32, 61, 128, 315; as revealed in Bish election, 99–100, 325–26; as revealed in Glyptis election, 296, 300, 306, 332. *See also* employee participation (at Weirton; EPG)

class: general theories of, 25–33, 363n. 1

Clinton, Bill, 15, 299

Committee for Justice, 94

Commons, John, 20

community, in Weirton: and gambling, 284–86, 291; and ISU, 274–75, 300, 314–16, 335–36; and paternalism, 4–5, 33, 40–41, 43–45, 52–55, 58, 63–68, 72–73, 76, 87–88, 91, 112, 117, 139, 240, 252, 268, 270, 272, 279–80, 282, 288, 331, 334; and property rights, 266–72, 290; and relation to democracy, 12, 80, 116–17, 124, 130, 282, 325;

as ideology, 34, 80, 124, 125, 127, 130, 234, 334, 344n. 67, 366n. 14; clergy relation to, 112, 115, 120; function of rumor in, 221; in relation to EPG, 201, 210, 213–14, 329; in relation to ESOP, 11, 20, 25, 34, 87–88, 130, 139, 223, 234, 237, 239–41, 243–46, 249, 252, 257, 263–64, 272–75, 279–81, 287–92, 294, 298, 300, 306, 314–18, 321–36; in relation to mill, 3–5, 20, 35, 68, 76, 162, 201, 210, 213, 241, 243–46, 249, 272, 275, 288–92, 294, 300, 321–23, 330–32, 333; JSC relation to, 111, 118, 122, 126; RFC relation to, 94–95, 97, 110–11, 116–17, 123–27, 306. *See also* class

community resistance to plant closings, 11, 13, 330, 324

confidential appendix. *See* McKinsey and Company: ESOP feasibility study

Contested Terrain (Richard Edwards), 327

Cronin, Charles, 284, 318

Cultures of Solidarity (Rick Fantasia), 333

Curtis, Jack, 89, 90, 103, 107, 351n. 27, 353n. 64

D'Anniballe, Robert, 306, 312, 315

Demings, Edward, 205, 363n. 47

Doepken, William, 106

Edwards, Richard (*Contested Terrain*), 327

Elish, Herbert, 222, 280, 293, 308, 317; alleged conflict of interest, 305; and labor force reductions, 295, 297; and public stock offering, 308–10; challenge to, 302–303, 305, 307, 311–12, 373nn. 25, 30; compensation of, 296, 310; resignation of, 294, 300, 312–13, 315; response to

Bricmont controversy, 297; response to management criticism, 301–302; support of Harvey Sperry, 299

employee participation: and company performance, 22–23, 328, 341n. 27; and labor-management cooperation, 22–24, 328; and productivity, 22–23; 341n. 32; and unions, 22, 23; and worker control, 23, 364n. 5; and worker satisfaction, 22, 23; combined with worker ownership, 22; ideology of, 23, 35, 104; managers belief in, 23; theories of, 21–22.

employee participation (at Weirton Steel; EPG): and class, 35, 180–81, 209–10, 327; and Internal Communications (IC), 35, 144, 180–81, 216–20, 221, 223, 317, 327–28; and industrial democracy, 103–104, 143–44, 148–49, 327; and labor-management relations, 145, 147–48, 150, 161–63, 187, 328; and mill hierarchy, 144–45, 155, 161, 180–81, 199–201, 206–16, 223, 327–29; and Operations Improvement Program (OIP), 150, 186, 190, 196, 197, 360n. 18; and Quality of Work Life (QWL), 146, 148, 182–83; and Statistical Process Control (SPC), 150, 157, 360n. 18, 362n. 36; and worker control, 35, 153–56, 158–63, 177–78, 327–29, as bureaucratic, 24, 34, 103–104, 145, 157–59, 163, 173–75, 183–84, 199, 200–201, 208, 219, 223, 327; as industrial therapy, 35, 181–98; as new form of management, 145–47, 149–51, 156–58, 171–73, 180, 182, 195–98, 360n. 16; as technical problem-solving, 34, 145, 152, 154–58, 161, 163–65, 327; by type of activity,

155–56; cost of, 152, 153, 156, 159, 186–88; definition of, 144, 182–84; employee attitudes toward, 24–25, 198–216, 217; executive support for, 146–50; facilitators, role in, 151–53, 159–64, 168–77, 180–92, 217, 221, 301, 327; facilitators, selection of, 150–51; facilitators, views of management, 160, 180, 192–98; facilitators, views of union, 166–68, 189–92; ideology of, 35, 103–104, 145, 152, 168–78, 181, 200–201, 204–209, 218–19, 223, 327; in contrast to Mayo and Taylorism, 172–73, 175–76; management resistance to, 34–35, 159–60, 173, 192–99, 205, 271, 278; management views of, 34–35, 147, 151, 192–98; newsletter for, 151, 361n. 26; number of workers in, 153–54, 361n. 25, 375n. 13; organization of groups in, 150–52, 361nn. 25, 26; organizational structure of, 150–52, 317; relation to mill normative order, 25, 145, 156–57, 160–63, 178, 180–81, 200–201, 210–16, 223; role of ISU in, 146–48, 150–51, 160, 165–68, 189–92; skills acquired from, 157–58, 198, 362n. 37; success of, based on employee involvement, 153–54, 361n. 25; success of, based on financial measures, 152–53, 186–88; training session for, 34, 144–45, 151, 152, 153, 168–77, 192, 199–200, 305, 327, 360n. 16; work speedup in, 156; worker autonomy in, 157–58, 159, 171, 173, 191, 198, 200, 210

employee representation plans, 21; at Weirton Steel, 56–57, 59–60, 65

employee stock ownership plans: and class, 20; and community,

20; and company performance, 17–18, 22–23, 328, 341n. 27; and employee attitudes, 23–24, 365n. 27; and employee participation, 22–24, 341n. 27; and legislation, 17; and pension plans, 18; and unions, 19–20; and worker control, 17–20, 329, 351n. 27; distinction from employee stock purchase plans, 18; growth of, 17, 338n. 4; history of, 16–17; number of employees involved in, 17; popularity of, 18, 338n. 4; structure of, 17–20, 338n. 5. *See also* Weirton Steel ESOP (during negotiations/after negotiations)
Environmental Protection Agency (EPA), 84, 357n. 137
Erikson, Kai, 44

Fantasia, Rick, 31–32, 61, 128, 330; *Cultures of Solidarity*, 333
field methods, 11–13
Forbes, 299
Friendly Takeover (James B. Lieber), 88

Genovese, Eugene, 29
Gilliam, Tony, 94–96, 107, 114, 116–17, 122, 124, 125, 351n. 34
Glyptis, Mark, 299, 318; and defense of work stoppage, 314–15, 335; and local media, 314–17; and worker control, 293, 297–98, 300–301, 304; criticism of executive pay raises, 311–12; election of, as ISU President, 296, 300, 315, 332; opposition to outsourcing, 296–97; position on public stock offering, 306, 308–10; response to mill fire, 308; response to Herbert Elish resignation, 313; support of Phillip Smith, 303, 310

Goldstein, Don (*Nation*), 132
Goldthorpe, John (*The Affluent Worker and the Class Structure*), 32
Gore, Al, 15, 299
Gouldner, Alvin, 201, 252, 267, 288, 333; *Patterns of Industrial Bureaucracy*, 201
Green, Eugene, 127
Gregory, John, 99, 107, 127, 131, 351n. 35

Habits of the Heart (Robert Bellah, et. al.), 90
Haden, Judge Charles II, 121, 123
Halle, David, 20
Hancock County, 7, 45, 46, 48, 49, 282
Hill, Stephen, 26
Hrabovsky, Mike, 227; loss in ISU election, 98–99
Hutton, Rev. Robert, 94, 352n.37
Hyatt-Clark, General Motors, 89, 93, 324

Independent Weirton, 254–56
Internal Communications. *See* employee participation (at Weirton Steel)
ISU. *See* Weirton Steel Independent Steelworkers Union
IWW (Industrial Workers of the World), 49–51

Jackman, Mary, 27–28
Joint Study Committee (JSC): administrative orientation of, 88–90, 93, 101–105, 325; and ESOP feasibility study, 106–108; and RFC lawsuit, 108–10, 121–23; dissension within, 90, 107; formation of, 85, 93, 129, 298, 350n. 12; meeting with local clergy, 111–13, 117–21, 127; negotiating position of, 107–108, 118, 132,

134–35; relation to community, 88, 108, 111, 120, 122, 124, 126, 128, 130; role in ESOP board selection, 132, 146. *See also* ISU
Jones, Mother, 39–40

Karber, Phillip, 306, 312
Keilin, Eugene, 138, 146, 149
Kelso, Louis (*The Capitalist Manifesto*), 17, 338n. 2
Kennedy, John and Robert, 16
Kirkwood and Associates, 149

Lazard Freres, 89, 131, 132, 136, 146, 351n. 25
Levine, Arnold, 108, 133
Lichtenstein, John, 94, 356n. 107
Lieber, James B., 88, 90, 99, 132, 263–64; *Friendly Takeover*, 88
Long, Russell, 17
Long, William, 57, 58
Loughhead, Robert, 133, 222, 240, 265, 293, 357n. 135; and compensation controversy, 150, 215, 244, 253–59, 278, 296, 368n. 17; and employee participation, 146–50, 206, 276; at shareholders meeting, 233–35; chosen as CEO, 132; retirement of, 220, 272, 275–80, 290, 369n. 40; views on industrial democracy, 143–44, 227
Love, Howard, 79–80, 102
Lowenstein, Alan V., 86, 89, 90, 107, 351n. 27
Ludwig and Curtis, 136
Lynd, Staughton, 94, 95, 97, 124, 127, 128, 129, 135, 137; argument for RFC appendix lawsuit, 108–109

Madigan, John, 107
Madonna High School, 126
Marland Heights (Civic Association), 282
Maxwell, Judge Robert, 131

Mayernick, Joe, 86, 284
McKinsey and Company, 89, 136, 277; ESOP management studies, 160, 193, 211, 235, 278
McKinsey and Company: ESOP feasibility study, 91, 98, 193; and confidential appendix, 101, 108, 118, 121–22, 128; findings of, 100–101, 107, 358n. 147; JSC support of, 101–106; RFC lawsuit over, 108–11, 121–23, 128, 131, 135, 354nn. 70, 71, 355n. 102, 357n. 131; worker response to, 100–104, 105
Mentzer, Donald, 85
Miller, Edward W., 57
Millsop Community Center, 67, 132, 232, 299, 366n. 13
Millsop, Thomas: arrival at Weirton Steel, 54–55; as CEO of National Steel, 73; as first mayor, 69; as town elite, 63, 65–66; death of, 74; legacy of, 74–77, 80, 85, 93, 95, 105, 112, 190, 213, 214, 234, 237, 239, 244, 249, 251, 255, 257, 279, 290, 302, 366n. 1, 368n. 19
Monongahela Valley, 5, 11
moral economy: theory of, 29–30, 344n. 57
moral economy (in Weirton): and critical skills pay raise, 259–63, 290, 368n. 25; and EPG, 145, 175, 181–82, 201; and ESOP, 35, 81, 237, 239–41, 243–44, 253, 255, 260–61, 263, 270, 288–92, 294, 297, 314, 321–22, 331–34; and executive compensation, 255; and gambling, 284–86; and localism, 75–77, 97, 243–44, 268, 272, 275, 285–86, 288, 322; and mayoral election, 272; and sleeping in the mill, 245–53, 271, 289, 322, 333, 367n. 12; and stealing, 244, 266–72, 322, 333, 369nn. 31, 34; and summer

work program, 273–75; and value of labor, 244–64, 289–90, 310

morality, and economy, 11, 13, 121, 334; and RFC-clergy meeting, 113–14

Murray, Charles, 68

Nation (Don Goldstein), 132

National Center for Employee Ownership (NCEO), 17, 86, 328, 339n. 6, 341n. 27. *See also* Rosen, Corey

National Industrial Recovery Act, 40, 59, 61, 99, 315

National Labor Relations Board (NLRB), 41, 59, 62, 63, 65, 66, 69, 107, 127, 251

National Steel: formation and early growth of, 55, 72–73, 251–52, 347n. 40; and ESOP negotiations, 89–91, 106, 120, 127–32; and mill shutdown liabilities, 83–84, 122–23; and terms of ESOP sale, 134–39; disinvestment in Weirton mill, 3–4, 33, 41, 74, 79–81, 83–88, 193, 324, 348n. 69; during Great Depression, 56; management, worker criticism of, 102–103, 149, 201, 205, 212, 214, 219, 236; RFC challenge to, 94–98, 106–109, 111, 115, 122–24; reorganization as National Intergroup, 135; undermining paternalism in Weirton, 41, 73–79, 81, 85, 92, 98, 102, 130, 239–40, 267, 271, 288, 316, 321, 330–31

Newby, Howard, 26, 27, 28

Out of This Furnace (Thomas Bell), 79

Paesani, Steve, 94, 356n. 107

Parker, Mike, 156, 171

Parkersburg U.S. District Court, 121

paternalism: theories of, 25–30, 32–33, 342n. 40, 343nn. 41, 44, 344n. 58, 346n. 34

paternalism (in Weirton): and Big Steel Strike of 1919, 49–52; and employee compensation, 56, 60, 67, 71–72, 134, 255, 258, 366n. 1; and ethnic-race relations, 8, 75, 128, 316; and ISU, 7, 91, 93, 148, 274–75, 316, 352n. 48; and local clergy, 111–17; and localism, 67–68, 75, 77, 87–88, 97, 112, 268, 272, 275, 278–79, 281–82, 284, 290–91, 322–23, 332, 336; and morality, 41, 52–54, 67–68, 76–77, 244, 321; and nepotism, 72, 80, 213–14, 244, 272–91, 322, 367n. 4; and New Deal, 33, 40, 59, 65; and women, 68–69, 75–76, 366n. 2, 374n. 1; as source of worker control, 81, 93, 249, 288, 290–92, 325; history of, 33–34, 40–41, 44–45, 52–77, 239–40, 251–52; 1933 strike and resistance to, 58–62, 347n. 46; relation to mill theft, 267–70, 322; relation to sleeping in the mill, 245, 246, 249–53, 322, 366n. 3. *See also* class; Weirton Steel, ESOP (after negotiations)

Pittsburgh Post-Gazette, 86

Pittsburgh Press, 86, 277

Radzialowski, Thad, 88, 355n. 102

Rath Packing Company, 324, 351n. 27

Rechin, F. James, 302

Redline, Jack, 73, 85, 87, 90, 99, 102, 107, 116, 117, 132, 144, 206, 228, 369n. 34

Riederer, Richard, 313, 317

Robertson, David: alleged conflict of interest and resignation of, 298–99, 355n. 90; and RFC lawsuit, 121, 131; as ESOP board member, 138, 150, 299, 370n.

42; meeting with local clergy, 117–20; role on JSC, 90, 101, 104–105, 109, 131, 350n. 12, 351n. 31, 355n. 90

Rockefeller, Jay, 85–86, 357n. 137

Rohatyn, Felix, 89–90, 325

Roosevelt, Franklin D.: and conflict with E. T. Weir, 40, 56–61, 65, 348n. 57

Rosen, Cory, 17–18, 19, 22, 24, 86, 328. *See also* NCEO

Rothstein, Lawrence, 128

Russell, Raymond, 18, 19, 22, 23, 24, 329, 338n. 1

Sennett, Richard, 27, 30, 54, 130, 366n. 14

Serrin, William, 268, 366n. 3, 367n. 4, 369n. 31

Simmons, John (*Working Together*), 180

Slanchick, Frank (Weirton Steel Corporation Shareholders Association), 305–306, 307, 309, 335

Slaughter, Jane, 156

Smith, Phillip: and criticism of board, 302–303; opposition to Harvey Sperry, 299, 307; opposition to public stock offering, 306–307; resignation of, 310, 371n. 17

Sperry, Harvey: alleged conflict of interest, 299, 305, 306, 371nn. 13–16; as ESOP board member, 138, 302; as ESOP consultant, 90, 103–104, 106; departure of, 310, 373n. 55

Spoon, John, 127

St. John's Arena, 92, 366n. 13

St. John's Lutheran Church, 126

Steel Workers Organizing Committee (SWOC), 60, 62, 68, 347n. 49, 348n. 57

Stern, Robert, 19

Steubenville, OH: and Big Steel Strike of 1919, 39–40, 46–48, 51, 347n. 47; and race relations,

8, 75, 351n. 34; and 1933 Weirton strike, 56, 58–59; *Herald-Star*, 43, 44, 45, 46, 52, 87, 93, 98; in relation to early Weirton, 42, 45, 249–50; RFC's relation to, 94, 124, 126

Street Corner Society (William F. Whyte), 285

The Affluent Worker and the Class Structure (John Goldthorpe), 32

The Capitalist Manifesto (Louis Kelso and Mortimer Adler), 17

The Protestant Ethic and the Spirit of Capitalism (Max Weber), 263

Thompson, Edward P., 29–30, 330

Thompson, Virgil: election as ISU president, 293–94; re-election loss of, 296, 315, 332

Towers, Perrin, Foster, and Crosby, 89

unions: and employee participation, 22–23, 334; and employee ownership, 19–20. *See also* names of individual unions

United Airlines, 18, 19, 20

United Steelworkers of America (USWA), 14, 64, 70, 71, 73, 76, 124

Urban Mission Ministries, 94

U.S. Department of Labor, 99, 131

Valdiserri, Carl, 136, 147, 276–77, 350n. 12, 354n. 70, 355n. 102

Wajcman, Judy (*Women in Control*), 333

Wang, David I. J., 302

Wall Street Journal, 108

Washington Monthly, 72, 74

Weber, Max (*The Protestant Ethic and the Spirit of Capitalism*), 263

Weir, David M., 43, 45, 51, 53, 66

Weir, Ernest T.: and Big Steel
Strike of 1919, 46, 48, 49; and
formation of National Steel,
55–56, 347n. 40; and opposition
to union organizing, 57–68, 128,
347n. 52, 348n. 57; as paternalistic elite, 25, 33, 40–41, 44–45,
49, 51, 52–55, 57–59, 61–68,
70–72, 346n. 37, 348n. 57; biography of, 41–43, 53–56, 345nn.
3, 4; conflict with Franklin Roosevelt, 40–41, 56, 348n. 57;
death of, 73; story of, in *Life*, 63;
legacy of, 73–77, 80, 85, 93, 95,
105, 112, 190, 234, 237, 239,
244, 249, 251–52, 255, 257, 267,
279, 290, 302, 330, 366n. 1
Weir, Margaret M., 282
Weirton, WV: beginning of town,
4–5, 11, 33, 43–45; Big Steel
Strike of 1919 in, 39–40, 45–51;
description of town, 4, 5–11, 34,
35, 43–45; ethnic groups and
race relations in, 8–9, 43–44, 49,
50, 52–54, 66, 75, 124–26; function of rumor in, 221; incorporation of, 69; local media in, 86,
91, 98, 126, 130, 218, 220–21,
228, 232, 235, 237, 314, 315,
316; local politics in, 280–87,
291, 370n. 42; map of, 6; population of, 7, 43, 337n. 3, 367n. 6;
position of women in, 54, 68–69,
75–76, 366n. 2
Weirton Steel (pre-ESOP): beginning of, 41–43, 54–56; Big Steel
Strike of 1919 and, 39–40,
45–51, 52, 60; distribution of
jobs in, by ethnicity, 8, 43–44;
during Depression, 55–56, 60,
249–52, 367n. 6; employment
data on, 3, 60, 249–51, 349n. 6,
350n. 21, 367n. 5; labor-management relations in, 88–89, 96,
100–102; regional impact of
shutdown, 3, 84; economic status of prior to ESOP, 83–84, 91

Weirton Steel, ESOP (during negotiations): 4–5, 34; administrative orientation of, 89–91,
101–105, 138; and democratic
alternative, 34, 80–81, 89, 97,
101, 103–105, 108, 113–15,
118–20; as way to save jobs, 99,
108, 132, 136; consultants for,
89–91, 93, 102–108, 124, 132,
134–36, 304, 330, 331; employee
compensation and wage concession controversy, 100–101,
108–10, 122, 131,134; employee
involvement in, 92–94, 104,
114–118, 127; employee vote for,
132–33, 357n. 136; selection of
board members to, 132, 138,
359n. 158; skepticism toward,
86, 102, 105–106, 130, 133; status of pensions, 89, 100–101,
105, 107, 109, 123, 127, 131,
134–35; support for, 85–88, 99,
105–106, 108, 111–12, 130, 133;
terms of ESOP transaction with
National, 134–39
Weirton Steel, ESOP (after negotiations): and Bricmont lawsuit
controversy, 296–97, 302, 310,
370nn. 7, 8, 373n. 58; and conflict over public stock offering,
293, 295, 303–10, 334, 373nn.
52, 53, 57; and critical skills pay
raise controversy, 259–64,
289–90; and democratic alternative, 143, 148–49, 231, 292,
324–27, 331, 332–33; and directors' liability amendment,
302–303, 305, 334; and employee motivation, 229–31, 238;
and employee compensation
controversy, 244–53, 264, 289;
and executive compensation
controversy, 253–59, 289, 296,
310, 311–12, 367n. 14, 368nn.
17, 19–21; and job outsourcing
controversy, 294, 296–97,
300–301, 316, 317; and legacy of

paternalism, 234, 239–41, 244–46, 252–53, 255–58, 266–70, 272–75, 278–80, 288–92, 302, 305, 310, 316–17, 321–23, 325, 330–32, 334, 336; and mill modernization, 5, 135, 234, 275–78, 293, 295–96, 303, 310, 322, 323; and pensions, 134–35, 240, 309; and profit-sharing, 144, 228–31, 277, 295–96, 311, 323, 369n. 26; and stock ownership, 136–39, 144, 228–31, 295, 309, 318, 335, 370n. 3, 372n. 32, 373n. 42; and summer work program controversy, 272–75; as way to save jobs, 296–98, 326; board of directors, actions of, 233, 276–78, 280, 296, 318–19, 335; board of directors, challenge to, 293–94, 296–309, 310–14, 331–32; board of directors support of EPG, 146–49, 188; employment level of, 295, 297, 361n. 25; financial situation of, 295–96, 308, 314, 323; ideology of, 234, 236, 300–301; management criticism of, 301, 305, 311; mill fire and consequences for, 308–309, 315; strikes and work stoppages at, 299–300, 312, 314–15, 317, 334; third annual shareholders meeting of, 227, 232–36, 238, 366n. 13; worker control in, 137–39, 227, 236, 244, 288–90, 292, 293–95, 300–307, 309–17, 323–35. *See also* Class; moral economy (in Weirton); community, in Weirton

Weirton Steel Independent Steelworkers Union (ISU): and Independent Guards Union, 66, 69; and lawsuits against company, 296–97, 314–15; and profit-sharing, 230; class struggle acted out through, 61, 92–93, 99, 294, 296, 306, 312, 314–15,

332; conflict within, 90, 92–93, 96, 119–20, 220, 259–60; elections for president of, 98–100, 131, 293–94, 296; formation of, 41, 69–71, 74, 76, 348n. 66; position on critical skills pay raise, 259–60; position on mill scandal, 265; position on public stock offering, 306–10, 335–36; position on summer work program, 273–75, 290; regulation of nepotism by, 274–75; relation to management, 88–89, 93, 96, 99, 109–10, 147–48, 294, 298, 299, 301, 306, 325–26, 332, 334–35; response to executive pay raises, 311–12; role on board of directors, 306, 312–14, 319, 332, 334–35; role on JSC, 85, 88–89, 93, 97–98, 100–105, 107, 109–10, 118, 121–22, 127, 148, 298; support for ESOP feasibility study, 91–93, 101–106. *See also* Bish, Walter; Glyptis, Mark

Weirton Steel Rank-and-File Committee (RFC), 104, 324; and legacy of paternalism, 96–98, 111–17, 305; effects of litigation by, 127–29, 131–32, 134–35, 356nn. 117, 120; factors limiting success of, 123–30, 306, 330; first public meeting of, 94–97, 112; formation of, 94, 123–25, 351n. 35, 356nn.107, 121; lawsuit over confidential appendix, 108–10, 114, 121–23, 128, 131, 354nn. 70, 71, 357nn. 131, 137; leafleting drive of, 106, 110–11, 120; list of demands by, 352n. 43; meeting with local clergy, 110–17; relation to community, 95, 97, 98, 108, 123–27, 130; relation to ISU, 96–97, 107, 110–11, 116–17; support for McKenzie discrimination consent decree, 124, 127, 351n. 35; support for voting rights griev-

ance, 99, 107, 127, 131, 351n.
35, 353n. 49
Weirton Daily Times, 58, 258, 260,
276, 277, 279, 285
Weirton Heights, 9, 282
Weirton Steel Bulletin, 63, 70, 279,
328
Williams Country Club, 66–67, 282
Williams, John C., 42–43, 48, 49,
54, 55, 66, 67
Williams, Raymond, 32
Willkie Farr and Gallagher, 89,
90, 103, 132, 136, 138, 299,
371nn. 13, 14, 15
Wilson, Frank, 40, 46
Wheeling, WV, 5, 10, 12, 13, 45,

108, 285, 356n. 107; *Intelli-
gencer*, 312; *Register*, 45; U.S.
District Court, 108
Whyte, William F., 147, 328; *Street
Corner Society*, 285
Women in Control (Judy Wajc-
man), 333
Working Together (John Sim-
mons), 180
Wright, Erik Olin, 31, 330

Youngstown, OH, 11, 84, 94, 97,
111, 112, 127, 324–25

Zuboff, Shoshana, 173, 196, 210
Zukin, Sharon, 324–26